Plagues, Apocalypses
and Bug-Eyed Monsters

Plagues, Apocalypses and Bug-Eyed Monsters

How Speculative Fiction Shows Us Our Nightmares

HEATHER URBANSKI

McFarland & Company, Inc., Publishers
Jefferson, North Carolina, and London

LIBRARY OF CONGRESS CATALOGUING-IN-PUBLICATION DATA

Urbanski, Heather, 1975–
 Plagues, apocalypses and bug-eyed monsters : how speculative fiction shows us our nightmares / Heather Urbanski.
  p.   cm.
 Includes bibliographical references and index.

 ISBN-13: 978-0-7864-2916-5
 (softcover : 50# alkaline paper) ∞

 1. Science fiction, American — History and criticism.
 2. Horror tales, American — History and criticism.   3. Horror in literature.   4. Horror in mass media.   5. Plague in literature.
 6. Apocalypse in literature.   7. Monsters in literature.
 8. Popular culture — United States — History — 20th century.
 9. Mass media — United States — History — 20th century.
 I. Title.
 PS648.S3U73   2007
 813'.0876209 — dc22   2006035094

British Library cataloguing data are available

©2007 Heather Urbanski. All rights reserved

No part of this book may be reproduced or transmitted in any form or by any means, electronic or mechanical, including photocopying or recording, or by any information storage and retrieval system, without permission in writing from the publisher.

Cover art ©2006 Wood River Gallery

Manufactured in the United States of America

McFarland & Company, Inc., Publishers
 Box 611, Jefferson, North Carolina 28640
 www.mcfarlandpub.com

To Mom, for everything.
To Julia and Colin, for the future

Contents

Preface	1
Introduction: The Cautionary Tale	5

PART ONE : SCIENCE AND TECHNOLOGY

Introduction	21
1. Nuclear War	24
2. Information Technology	39
3. Biology	57
4. From Frankenstein to the Terminator and Everything in Between: Science and Technology Images in the Mainstream Media	75

PART TWO : POWER

Introduction	89
5. Power of the Individual	92
6. Power of the State	109
7. Big Brother and Darth Vader on the Evening News: Power Images in the Mainstream Media	131

PART THREE : THE UNKNOWN

Introduction	145
8. Monsters, Aliens, and "Other" Beings	149
9. Progress	169
10. Resistance Is Futile for Rip Van Winkle in the Twilight Zone: Images of the Unknown in the Mainstream Media	192

Afterword: What Does All This Mean?	206
Chapter Notes	217
Works Cited	221
Index	243

Preface

Even though this is probably the first section of the book you will read, it's actually the last part I wrote. I had been working on this project for almost five years, so when it came time to write this Preface, I found the whole task daunting. Trying to briefly capture the essence of this book, describe its history, and acknowledge all those who were instrumental in bringing it to this point was an intimidating goal. But, since I couldn't put it off any longer, here it goes...

Like any art form, speculative fiction reflects the culture that created it, in turn transforming, even if only in a small way, that culture. But within this cycle of reflection and transformation, I believe speculative fiction occupies a unique position in contemporary American culture: it shows us our nightmares and therefore contributes to our efforts to avoid them. That contribution, via the cautionary tale, is what I've tried to capture and analyze in this project.

Speculative fiction is often relegated to the fringes of mainstream culture yet it exerts tremendous influence on us. The genre has worked its way into our very vocabulary at almost every level from the "Star Wars" Strategic Defense Initiative of the 1980s to the use of the phrase "Big Brother" in such divergent cultural elements as escapist reality television and the deadly serious public debate over the Patriot Act. Cautionary tales are all around us in popular culture from blockbuster movies like the *Terminator* series and *Jurassic Park* to television shows like *Buffy, the Vampire Slayer*. While many of these nightmares have roots in the early twentieth century, they are constantly reflected and refined and reinterpreted for each generation. For examples, we don't have to look farther than the multiple incarnations of *Invisible Man, Frankenstein,* and *The Strange Case of Dr. Jekyll and Mr. Hyde*. In the upcoming chapters, I focus on the nightmares and warnings we see reflected in speculative fiction prose, film, and television, looking at contemporary American culture through the lens of the genre's cautionary tales. We can learn a great deal about ourselves as a culture by looking at speculative fiction because, while there are many things that divide us, there are many more we have in common.

But even with the monster success of speculative fiction blockbusters, it is perhaps an unfortunate fact of our modern culture that we are so inundated with images and entertainment that few works get a second look. I have based my analysis on this fact, examining the genre using broad strokes that focus on the themes reflected in the texts rather than relying on in-depth, close readings of a few specific works. It is the repetition of these same themes, of these same nightmares, that influences contemporary American culture; in other words, we have seen these warnings so many times, there is no way we could have avoided absorbing them. I developed the Nightmares Model, which forms the core of this book, to capture that repetition, starting with my own observations as a fan and then adding published commentaries on the genre along with the perspectives of contemporary professionals in the field from interviews and panel discussions.

In that way, this book is truly a product of the collision of scholarship and science fiction/fantasy fandom (with a little bit of fate thrown in). I am not sure what led me, one July afternoon in 2001, to click on the link from the Sci-Fi Channel website to the homepage for the Millennium PhilCon (that year's World Science Fiction Convention); I do know that my curiosity was piqued when I saw my hometown of Philadelphia in the link's description. Whatever the initial reason, I did follow that link, and on a whim, less than two months before the event, I decided to attend my first WorldCon, without any real idea of what I was getting myself into. My curiosity paid off when Greg Bear's Guest of Honor speech at that convention inspired me to write about speculative fiction and rhetoric. This project began the night of that speech and has continued for nearly five years. Over that time, it has been an academic paper, presentations at national and international conventions (including two WorldCons), a Masters thesis, and now this book. Fate intervened once again at the 2004 WorldCon in Boston when I found the McFarland table in the Dealer's Room and decided to give this project one more shot before moving on to focus solely on my doctoral work. I hope you will agree that was a good decision.

Now that you know a bit about how this project came to be, I come to the intensely personal task of acknowledging those whose help I can never hope to fully articulate, let alone repay. This book would not exist without three people: Greg Bear, who inspired the original idea behind the project and continued to offer help and encouragement throughout its evolution; Diane Penrod, my graduate advisor at Rowan University, whose patience, advice, and support truly knows no bounds; and, without a doubt, my mother, Barbara. The debt I owe my mother is immeasurable, though she would tell me that I owe it to the next generation, not to her. In addition to all of the motherly support and encouragement that I hope I never take too much for granted, Mom spent countless hours working on this project, becoming an accomplished research assistant of the Internet age, helping me get the manuscript ready for publication. Literally, without her, this book might not be in your hands. After all the late nights, emails with multiple attached files, and occasional panicked phone calls, there are probably very few pages here she has not touched.

As those who know me well will attest, my family is incredibly important to me; I could not have finished this project without the support of the whole crew: my dad, David; my sister, Nicole; my brother-in-law, Michael; my niece, Julia, and even my one-year-old nephew, Colin. Having these people in my life to not only love but also to distract me kept me grounded and sane throughout the process of completing this manuscript while also completing my doctoral coursework. Hopefully, one day, I will be able to do the same for Julia and Colin when they write their first books, but they do have to learn to read first.

On a smaller, though no less critical, scale, many others also contributed to this project in significant ways. I especially want to express my gratitude to those in sci-fi fandom, which is truly a community, one I am proud to be a part of and one that has both inspired and challenged me since I first encountered it in 2001. Attending panels and participating on others, presenting my work, and sharing my passion as a fan with like-minded (or not) others has continually renewed my interest in this project and expanded my thinking in more ways than I could even describe. For all of this, I need to thank many people in the science fiction community, including Greg Bear, Gregory Benford (for taking the time to meet with me and for inspiring two new categories in my model), and James Van Pelt (for meeting with a stranger who emailed him out of the blue and asked for an interview). I also need to thank Gordon Van Gelder for his time in answering questions about the genre from a random graduate student. In addition, I have met many fascinating and passionate people (you know who you are) at various conventions (including MythCon, ICFA, and World-Con); our discussions about this project appear in sometimes unexpected ways in the pages to follow.

In addition, my scholarship and writing have benefited from my work with many of my professors, both at Rowan University's College of Communication and in Lehigh University's English Department, who broadened my knowledge base and sharpened my skills in ways I never anticipated. My "tutor" at the Lehigh Writing Center, Nate Eastman, also gave me helpful feedback on drafts (even if I didn't always want to hear it), providing me an invaluable outsider perspective on chapters I had been working on, literally, for years. I have also learned some unexpected things from my first-year writing students; their questions and ideas often gave me yet another perspective on the genre.

    Whenever I describe my love of speculative fiction to the uninitiated, I usually begin by telling them that I am a member of the "*Star Wars* generation": I first encountered science fiction in 1977, sitting on my mother's lap, watching what we now call *Episode IV: A New Hope* at the Tower theater in Upper Darby, Pennsylvania. So I honestly do not remember a time before *Star Wars* and even though I now sometimes go by the job title of academic, my genre roots are never far from my mind. As a combination of fan and scholar, then, I am most definitely *not* a dispassionate, objective observer of speculative fiction; rather, I approached this project as a chance to embrace the fan within, describing the genre's influence that I not only see around me in popular culture, but that I have experienced myself. Knowing the passion of the fandom community, I fully expect some readers to disagree with one or more of my categories or how I characterize some of the genre texts. My hope, though, is precisely to generate such reflection and debate, to join in the discussion about this genre from which I have derived so much joy and entertainment for so long. Enjoy!

Introduction: The Cautionary Tale

Even those who dismiss science fiction as adolescent triviality filled with cardboard substitutes for characters and wooden technobabble instead of dialogue will at least grudgingly admit that the genre's themes and terminology have worked their way out of the realm of the geek and into our broader popular culture, our language, and ultimately our rhetoric. In the 1980s, for instance, when politicians tried to discredit the Strategic Defense Initiative by dubbing it "Star Wars," President Ronald Reagan quickly embraced the image for himself, recognizing the opportunity to capitalize on the powerful cultural symbol of an evil empire and the heroes who oppose it. Similarly, a reference to Dr. Jekyll and Mr. Hyde engenders an immediate and specific image of the most mild-mannered among us corrupted by the quest for power; "Big Brother" works in much the same way, even if it has been co-opted by reality television.

Stanley Schmidt, editor of *Analog Science Fiction and Fact*, observed at the 2002 World Science Fiction Convention, "In a vague, non-rigorous way, a lot of the population is at least aware of these terms [e.g., hyperdrives and wormholes] and concepts" ("Panel 163"). Those ideas have traveled from the pages of 1930s pulp magazines and the screens of 1950s drive-in theaters into our public consciousness because, as Schmidt describes in an *Analog* editorial,

> The ideas we play with are often not merely arbitrary game pieces, but very real concerns about how the world works and where we as an intelligent species are going in it. We're talking about things like what control we or our governments should exercise over the beginning and end of life, about whether and why and how we should try to go to the stars, and what we should do if we meet anyone else out there ["Tilting" 53].

The genre's "play" with these concerns often results in the nightmares I discuss throughout this book. Speculative (science) fiction not only depicts those nightmares but also helps keep them from occurring, in part by creating a host of potent images that appear in the unlikeliest of places (such as politics), places as real as a hyperdrive is fictional and as far away from galactic empires and telepath wars as possible.

Even if we were unaware that we've absorbed so many speculative fiction terms and concepts, the influence of the genre would still be unmistakable. The events of the past hundred years have provided a near endless stream of nightmares from nuclear weapons to genetic engineering to massive social change, and a quick glance at speculative fiction shows those fears reflected. The rhetorical circle closes when the images created by the genre to reflect our nightmares work their way back through public consciousness into our discourse. Speculative fiction even impacts our vocabulary and, as George Lakoff and Mark Johnson argue in *Metaphors We Live By*, the structure of our language is inextricably linked to (and perhaps even determines) the structure of our thoughts and actions. As speculative fiction has reflected our nightmares, the words and images put before us by the likes of George Orwell and H.G. Wells, J.R.R. Tolkein and Isaac Asimov, Rod Serling and Gene Rodenberry, and M. Night Shyamalan and George Lucas have become ingrained in our hearts, our minds, and our words.

The Influence of Speculative Fiction

Speculative fiction has exerted a profound influence on our culture for most of the past hundred years. Reflecting on that history, Isaac Asimov argues that the genre has power despite the disrespect frequently doled out against it:

> Yet even though science fiction was not taken seriously by the general public, or very seriously by most of its readers and writers, it had its effect.... We accomplished something with all our talk of spaceships. We were laughed at, of course ... but the notion penetrated.... Thus, when the notion of flights to the moon was brought before the public seriously, it turned out to be something that people had heard of ["Science Fiction" 43].

The genre's influence is so significant because, as David Brin observes, "it is at the level of popular culture that people work out what they want to be and do" ("Metaphorical" 75). Acknowledging that role for popular culture, the editors of the first-ever *Oxford Dictionary of Allusions* included "a strong contingent [of references] from more modern times," with an entry for Darth Vader that "finally ... recognised [the character] for his contribution to the English language" by equating him to the personification of evil: "Always dressed in black and wearing a helmet, Darth Vader was Anakin Skywalker before he was corrupted to the 'dark side'" (Arkell). Modern popular culture is so saturated with speculative fiction images and concepts that the genre has left an indelible mark on society, a mark Greg Bear described in his Guest of Honor speech at the 2001 World Science Fiction Convention where he identified the genre as the "most important movement in Western Literature since the Romantics." Bear went on to observe that speculative fiction has so thoroughly incorporated itself into our culture that, chances are, every kid knows what a blaster or a warp drive is.

This osmosis between speculative fiction and "mainstream" culture often begins in childhood, before many of us are aware we're not supposed to like such stories.[1] Ursula K. LeGuin argues that children are attracted to the genre because they "know perfectly well that unicorns aren't real, but they also know that books about unicorns, if they are good books, are true books" (44). Even once we should "know better" than to indulge in speculative fiction, LeGuin observes, "fantasy is the great age-equalizer; if it's good when you are twelve it's quite likely to be just as good, or better, when you're thirty-six" (55). This fascination with the genre often follows us into adulthood, as Bear suggested during the 2002 World Science Fiction Convention: "Many hundreds of thousands of kids were raised on *Star Trek* and *Star Wars*. Now they are in their mid-twenties and are looking back at the science fiction ... [that] is a major part" of their lives ("Panel 348"). For many of us, this means the chance to pass on our passion for (and resulting influence of) speculative fiction to the next generation, both through our families and through our work (including books like this).

So What Exactly IS Speculative Fiction?

Even though I won't be rehashing the debate over what actually counts as "science fiction" (a mere summary of which could fill a whole chapter), we do need to spend some time on terminology. Such a seemingly simple task as defining science fiction and/or fantasy frequently falls under the "I know it when I see it" category. "There is general agreement that science fiction has some essential attraction which is not easy to capture in words but which is unmistakable to a receptive reader" (65), according to Damon Knight, and "We do know the difference between stories that are perceived as science fiction and those that are not: the question is, how do we know?" ("What is Science Fiction" 63). That question has been answered in so many ways for decades that it usually becomes more of a distraction than a benefit.

While an all-encompassing, irrefutable definition of the genre is not my goal (nor do I think one is even possible), we do need definitions in critical analyses like this, if for no other reason than to establish the scope.

Perhaps the best way out of this quagmire is to follow the example of Istvan Csicsery-Ronay, Jr., who maintains, "By sf, we should understand not an ideal category with a putative social or aesthetic logic, but what national audiences understand to be sf—which is less a class than a jelly that shifts around but doesn't lose its mass" (231). In my own effort to pin the jelly down, I have also kept in mind C.S. Lewis's assertion that "the best definition is that which proves itself most convenient" (122); thus, convenience guides my definition here.

From this point forward, I will use "speculative fiction" to cover the broad genre of science fiction and fantasy. These two sub-genres are inextricably linked, with the lines between them constantly blurred. For example, most would agree that *Lord of the Rings* is clearly fantasy and *Star Trek* is clearly science fiction. But what about *Star Wars*? The Force is a fantasy element while hyperdrives and the Death Star are definitely science fiction. Even critical studies, such as Kingsley Amis's landmark 1960 text, *New Maps of Hell*, and Robert Scholes and Eric Rabkin's *Science Fiction: History, Science, Vision*, use the term science fiction almost exclusively but still discuss works that are primarily fantasy. Given the significant overlap, and the fact that it is often difficult to differentiate between the sub-genres of science fiction and fantasy, works identified as either share identifiable characteristics that I believe the term speculative fiction captures. In general terms, for our discussion, speculative fiction covers any story that deliberately violates the bounds of reality as we currently understand it. Speculative fiction has to somehow break the rules of our environment or our "common" sense, with the story hinging in a significant way on that deviation, whether it's the alien invaders of *War of the Worlds* or the zombie-generating plague of *28 Days Later*. All of the works I will describe fit that definition to some degree or another, as do potentially hundreds more.[2]

Nightmares and Warnings: The Cautionary Tale

As Gordon Van Gelder, editor of *The Magazine of Fantasy and Science Fiction*, observed, speculative fiction "doesn't play one single role—like any artistic endeavor, it serves a variety of roles, ranging from self-expression to dire warning to commercial enterprise, with lots in-between." For generations, one of these cultural roles has been the cautionary tale in which writers take advantage of the freedom and distance from reality inherent in speculative fiction to scrutinize our nightmares and warn about the future. This has not gone unnoticed or unexamined; critical work within the genre often comments on such warnings. For example, Amis observes that science fiction is "strongly activist in its attitudes" (66) and, at times, functions as "an instrument of social diagnosis and warning" (74). More than forty years later, Connie Willis also described these warnings when she remarked at the 2002 World Science Fiction Convention, "Science fiction has always been excellent at the cautionary tale, at thinking about what could go wrong and reminding society about what the possible implications are."

The key element of the cautionary tale is the tendency for this genre to be, as Van Gelder described, "the embodiment of our dreams and nightmares about the future." Part of what genre writers do is to look at society, into the future, and within themselves, and then reflect the fears and nightmares they find. In his 2001 WorldCon speech, Bear told the audience, "the future is important and we have to imagine and dream the future before we can create it." All of that imagining and warning has proven immensely valuable for, as Bear also observed,

> We are not prophets but we allow you to dream your dreams and let you know what your nightmares are in advance so you can prevent them.... In a sense, science fiction has changed history ... stories of the 1930s helped nuclear scientists know that an atomic bomb could be built and then helped diffuse that threat after the bomb was actually used. That story hasn't been finished yet.

One of the ways speculative fiction reflects both nightmares like nuclear war and dreams like world peace is by asking what Gene Stewart calls the "two classic types" of questions: What if? and If this goes on.... Making a similar point, Ray Bradbury discusses those questions almost fifty years earlier when he writes that speculative fiction makes

> outsize images of problems so they can be seen and handled from all sides.... Some time soon they [such questions] must be answered. The day of the rocket is not so distant that we can delay longer in answering some of them. Not that we won't be able to adjust to any problems met at home or abroad in the solar system in 1999. We *will* adjust. But I also think our adjustment will derive in part from our practicality in both entertaining ourselves with science fiction and looking to our answers now, while it is still afternoon. These problems are human problems, which all too soon will no longer be science-fictional but part of a history our children will read [365–366].

Bradbury was right — the day of the rocket arrived not long after his article appeared in 1953. I would argue that the problems we met between 1953 and 1999 (and beyond) were easier to handle because of speculative fiction writers like Bradbury. American everyday life has changed radically since the turn of the last century. It is no coincidence that speculative fiction, with its "outsize images" and "what if" questions, has become an integral part of a culture forced to deal with such rapid, life-altering social and technological changes as the introduction of jet airplanes, rockets, computers, and nuclear weapons all in less than one hundred years' time. As the pace of change increases, which it is sure to do in the twenty-first century, those of us raised on speculative fiction may be better prepared than the generations who came before to cope with it; perhaps the genre will even help us to thrive. We can *still* turn to the work of Bradbury and Asimov, along with so many other genre texts, as we deal with the problems we face today.

While all fiction, indeed all art, plays a role in the way society adapts to changing circumstances, speculative fiction's unique focus on change and the future makes it particularly suited to the task. Contrary to conventional wisdom, however, those insights are not always meant to depress readers, even though dystopias like *Nineteen Eighty-Four* often do. In an interview for *Locus*, Gene Wolfe argues that the genre's most important contribution to society is the assurance "that things need not be as they are now. In other words, the most important thing is hope.... Both science fiction and fantasy can be literatures of hope. We're saying the world doesn't have to be like this, and your life doesn't have to be like this" (Gaiman 82). While such a perspective may be hard to identify in the genre of nuclear holocausts, spirit-crushing totalitarian states, and ecological ruin, all is not doom and gloom in speculative fiction. Many of those stories are really about the triumph over such disasters, as James Van Pelt pointed out: "Science fiction allows us to think that despite the apocalypse, humans will go on" (Interview).

Indeed, perhaps hope is *the* key sentiment behind the cautionary tale. After all, why warn us about something that is inescapable? Such a sense of hope seems to have fueled Bradbury's work: Van Gelder reported that the *Fahrenheit 451* author once said, "I don't write about the future to predict it. I write about the future to prevent it from happening this way." This sentiment seems to be common among the authors of speculative fiction's cautionary tales because, as Brin states,

> We are the scouts, the ones who explore the edges, who point out dangers that may lurk, not just *on* the horizon but perhaps some distances beyond it. We warn of possible mistakes and create chilling scenarios to make them ... believable. And in so doing, we hope to prevent them from coming true ["Metaphorical" 75].

The Cautionary Tale and Public Discourse

And these hopeful warnings have not fallen on deaf ears. One of the clearest marks cautionary tales have left on our culture (and on our rhetoric) is the mainstream media's tendency to invoke speculative fiction images, reflecting a symbiosis between the genre and public discourse. As Bear explained, "It's pretty incredible how important sf has become to some very influential people" ("Requested"). From a rhetorical perspective, the language used by a culture that has grown up with the genre to debate its problems and develop its solutions reflects its popular immersion in speculative fiction. Children raised on *Star Wars* and *The Day After* and Superman have been indelibly affected by the genre and, as we become active participants in society, speculative fiction exerts influence on our culture (and its rhetoric) through us.

As these genre fans enter into public discourse, we bring along our speculative fiction roots. Within this discursive process, according to Scholes and Rabkin, speculative fiction acts as a critical component of cultural development by providing "literature with new symbols" (168) for dealing with contemporary issues. It is at this level of symbol, of language (particularly in public discourse), that such influence can be seen; speculative fiction images and metaphors are everywhere in mainstream media. Phrases such as Big Brother, Prime Directive, and Darth Vader can be found in almost every area of our rhetoric, from political commentary to media critique to medical reporting. Cautionary tale authors have created such fitting metaphors for the human condition that those constructs have been absorbed by a language and cultural rhetoric that may often be unaware of their original context.

Speculative fiction is a broad genre that spans at least the past century, with many sources from which we can pull images for a cultural shorthand. References to genre images and metaphors are almost too frequent to count or categorize but even the limited, focused discussion I include in several upcoming chapters illustrates the genre's pervasive influence. In conducting this analysis, I employ the conceptual framework established by Lakoff and Johnson in their definitive study *Metaphors We Live By*. While that work looks at metaphors from a generic level, examining fundamental concepts and providing general examples[3] to illustrate the role of metaphor in language, that broad focus does not limit the applicability of their ideas to specific metaphors. Rather, metaphor analysis provides an effective tool for evaluating the speculative fiction images prevalent in everyday experience, allowing me to demonstrate the impact the cautionary tale has on our rhetoric (and thus our culture).

The Nightmares Model

My aim is to investigate those speculative fiction cautionary tales that have such a profound impact on our culture. From the Greek myth of Icarus to *Terminator 2*, tales that are set in other times and tell of fantastic adventures have warned about the dangers we face because of our natures. As Scholes and Rabkin observe, "science fiction, above all, is human fiction, and as human fiction" (169), it "reveals both man's secret longings and his secret fears" (175). Despite cultural and narratological roots in technology, speculative fiction is essentially a human genre that reflects real human nightmares, sounding warnings regarding the consequences of our actions in the hopes those consequences never become reality.

As Willis observed, "Each of the things that is positive carries its own downside" and while progress is integral to modern society, these downsides are frequent fodder for speculative fiction, the genre of progress. There are many common reflections among those downsides, for as Knight describes, "In fiction as in science, the same ideas frequently occur to more than one writer, and some of them turn up repeatedly over a period of years" ("Writing" 219). To capture that repetition, I developed the Nightmares Model, based on both my research and my experiences as a speculative fiction fan, to describe those ideas that frequently appear among the genre's cautionary tales.

Limitations and Scope of the Model

Gary Westfahl calls his own survey of the genre "a model for charting what remains basically unmapped territory: the science-fiction library itself" (211), a description that also neatly applies to my project. The groupings in the Nightmares Model describe one aspect of this vast library and are by no means intended to be mutually exclusive; many works contain elements of two or more categories. As with any classification scheme, the Nightmares Model has limitations. For example, I did not set out to pigeonhole the works themselves, nor to create the sole, definitive categorization system for the genre as a whole, implying that speculative fiction only addresses the nightmares described. That would be an impossible task. Just as an airplane model cannot possibly contain all of the parts of the real thing, no conceptual model can ever fully represent a genre, not even one that focuses on a smaller subsection as this does with cautionary tales. This limitation is similar to the result we see in metaphor construction (described by Lakoff and Johnson) in which one aspect of the idea being described is highlighted, while others are hidden, simply via the selection of one metaphor and not another for the comparison. For example, it may appear that a particular story discussed in one category only plays that single cultural role. However, a scheme like the Nightmares Model cannot, nor is intended to, impact the genre at the individual story level. I merely hope to highlight, for the sake of critical reflection, one particular element of a story that may lead to greater understanding of the genre and its audience.

In addition, as Asimov observes, "names are dangerous because they imply neat categories" ("Social" 45). Regardless of the discrete appearance of the Nightmares Model, its categories are not neat nor do they attempt to be inviolable dividing lines between warnings. Rather, they are a framework for critically examining common elements among cautionary tales and operate with the explicit understanding that speculative fiction is a dynamic, complex genre that could never be described in only one way. There is (and should be) at times significant overlap among both the categories of the model and the works they describe. I see, however, such limitations on the inclusive or definitive quality of the Nightmares Model as a strength rather than a weakness, for it both acknowledges and incorporates the variety and complexity of the genre it describes.

Another important element of the methodology of the Nightmares Model is the population of the texts it describes. While many commentators agree that the groundwork for speculative fiction can be traced almost as far back as storytelling itself, there is a general consensus that a definitive chronological line separates modern speculative fiction from all that came before it, a line that runs through the nineteenth century. Asimov cites the Industrial Revolution (in the mid–1800s) as the critical watershed moment ("Social"), while Damon Knight excludes from his analysis of the genre anything published before 1860 ("What Is Science Fiction"). The key reason given for this demarcation is the impact of the Industrial Revolution on society's perception of change. Before the 1800s, according to many,[4] future years were expected to be mere repetitions of those that had already occurred. When little change was anticipated, there was hardly reason to look beyond the immediate future. However, advancements such as the telegraph and the steam engine took hold of the culture in the nineteenth century, disrupting this "natural order" and thus beginning a process of modernization (and some would say globalization[5]) from which there was no return.

Such a fundamental shift in our perceptions of change marks the beginning of modern society in many ways and, as such, that shift can be seen in speculative fiction, the literature of that modernization. This perspective on change separates the genre from other literature, according to Van Pelt, because "science fiction is based on the idea that everything will change. Traditional literature wants to explore what is but science fiction wants to explore what might be because nothing stays the same" (Interview). It was, therefore, during the time society began to expect that the future would not be the same as the past that modern speculative fiction became identifiable, and with it came the cautionary tale. Therefore, the tropes I examine and the examples I use to illustrate the Nightmares Model come from this modern era of speculative fiction, which I see as beginning in the early 1800s with Mary Shelley's *Frankenstein* and coming into maturity with H.G. Wells's work at the turn of the twentieth century as the Industrial Revolution (and its notion of progress) truly took hold of our culture.

INTRODUCTION OF THE NIGHTMARES MODEL

Keeping in mind Robert Heinlein's observation that "what categories a critic chooses to define depends upon his purpose" ("Science Fiction" 8), the Nightmares Model is based on a two-tiered classification scheme. Three general categories identify those nightmares this genre is trying to warn us about and then several subcategories further describe the manifestations these warnings take as they reflect our fears.

The Nightmares Model

Science and Technology	*Power*	*The Unknown*
Nuclear War	Individual	Monsters, Aliens and "Other" Beings
Information Technology	State	Progress
Biology		

SCIENCE AND TECHNOLOGY

As Willis observed at the 2002 World Science Fiction Convention, "With every major advance, we come up with new and better ways to kill ourselves with that advance." More than forty years earlier, Mark Hillegas writes of the tradition in speculative fiction "which says that science and technology will not necessarily make the world better" ("Science Fiction" 26). While such an observation may seem absurdly obvious to us, that was not always the case: Hillegas also describes an early twentieth-century "cultural phenomenon" based on "the idea first stated by Francis Bacon, which is that science, by extending man's power to the performance of all things possible, will inevitably improve the human condition" ("Dystopian" 239). It can be argued that the warnings reflected in the first category of the Nightmares Model replaced such "unthinking optimism" (to use Hillegas's term) with today's ingrained cultural wariness regarding the promise of science and technology.

Our nightmares about new and improved methods of global suicide that the cautionary tales in the Science and Technology category reflect are among those most popularly associated with the genre. "From Frankenstein's monster to slow death by radiation poisoning as depicted in *The Day*

After," according to Karyn and Donald Rybacki, "A host of films have dealt with this theme" (14) of technology out of control. It may be almost too obvious, perhaps even self-defeating, to assert that science fiction depicts our nightmares regarding science and technology. However, there is incredible value in critically examining the particulars of that given, especially as some of these nightmares are dangerously close to coming true. As A.E. Levin observes, "the first quarter of this century [the twentieth] saw revolutionary changes in the foundations of basic sciences, from physics to biology. A vast pool of ideas and information was created, and applied disciplines could start utilizing it," all of which "changed life a great deal" (250). In such an era of advancement, cautionary tales force us to consider the consequences of new scientific and technological ideas, including whether we will be able to adapt quickly enough to those ideas and applications. And, even if we are, how will we ensure that they won't be used against us?

Within this atmosphere of scientific revolution, as Jonathan Vos Post and Kirk Kroeker observe, "while it is almost always easy to see the benefits of a new technology, it isn't always easy to foresee the dangers" (34). Many speculative fiction warnings revolve around this idea, whether the science is physics, biology, or information. Bradbury identifies two critical questions that lead writers to generate such warnings: "[1] When does an invention stop being a reasonable escape mechanism ... and start being a paranoiacally dangerous device?; [and 2] How much of any one such invention is good for a person, bad for a person, fine for this man, fatal to the next?" (364). These questions are echoed time and again in the genre's cautionary tales.

Yet Bradbury is also careful to point out that such problems do not lie in the machines themselves, but rather in the humans who use them — that is often the real warning. The seashell radios in *Fahrenheit 451*, for example, are not the problem; characters like Mildred, who allow the technology to separate them from their families and dominate their lives, are the problem. In their analysis of *The Day After*, the 1983 television movie depicting a nuclear attack, Rybacki and Rybacki echo Bradbury: "The rhetorical vision of *The Day After* is an old one: man's tragic flaw is that he is stupidly brilliant. Man's technological brilliance destroys him when his stupidity blinds him to the fact that he is only technology's creator not its master" (14–15). Speculative fiction often leaves us nowhere to hide from either that brilliance or that stupidity.

As Rybacki and Rybacki allude, there is a long history of warnings about the destructive power of technology, both in physical forms such as nuclear holocaust and meta-physical ones such as a dependence on virtual reality. In the introduction to his annotated bibliography *Tales of the Future*,

I.F. Clarke describes these stories as a "mediator between science and society, between the people and the possible" (xvi). Vos Post and Kroeker more specifically observe that "speculation about our future relationship to computers—and to technology in general—has been the province of science fiction for at least a hundred years" with "cautionary tales ... plentiful and varied" (29); this will become evident in the upcoming chapters.

Power

Power corrupts and absolute power corrupts absolutely. Many of us know this axiom by heart but fewer can identify Lord Acton, an advisor to Queen Victoria, as the one who famously voiced this prevalent human fear. Perhaps that is because speculative fiction writers are the ones who show us in vivid, sometimes shocking detail, what this fear looks like, a tradition that informs the second category of the Nightmares Model: Power. From Robert Louis Stevenson's *Strange Case of Dr. Jekyll and Mr. Hyde* in 1886 to the first science fiction film, *Metropolis*, in 1926 to the Sith Lords and vampire slayers of today, our fears about power and its "political and psychological implications" (Harris 46) are continually depicted in the genre. Some of the most famous, and most culturally accepted, genre works can be classified in this category, including Orwell's *Nineteen Eighty-Four* and Aldous Huxley's *Brave New World*.

The issue of power, who wields it and the consequences for those who do not, is a concern for all civilizations and, in the modern era, speculative fiction reflects our Power nightmares with narratives told from a distance that nevertheless does not diminish the effect of their messages. In her critique of the genre's reliance on the invulnerable "He-Man" main character, Joanna Russ argues that science fiction has examined the issue of power since its beginning, addressing such issues as "what we expect powerful people to do, what we are willing to let them do, the kinds of people we give power to, whether we have any power, and how much." The genre also asks, according to Russ, "How should power be used? What does power justify? How can power be overcome?" (138). These are some of the issues surrounding the Power nightmare on which speculative fiction puts it particular spin.

Power nightmares reflected by cautionary tales work at two levels: the Individual and the State. The common warning, though, is "primarily concerned with the destruction both of civilized values and the individual personality through the state of mind induced by fantasies of omnipotence, or of submission to it" (Harris 47). Power itself is the focus, as Mason Harris observes in a comparison between two of the genre's most significant texts,

Lord of the Rings and *Nineteen Eighty-Four*: "Both Tolkein and Orwell see the fantasy of power as devouring the personality from the inside, while the ruling group which seeks to wield absolute power deliberately ... create[s] a world where ... there will be no distraction from the sense of power" (47). The pursuit (or maintenance) of power for power's sake is thus at the root of the nightmares this category reflects.

These cautionary tales do, at times, rely on science and technology elements. For example, both the mad scientist (e.g., Dr. Frankenstein) and the political official who can destroy the world with technology (e.g., Senator Stilson from Stephen King's *Dead Zone*) are familiar characterizations that reflect the potential for devastation inherent in too much individual power. On the other end of the nightmare, the often faceless totalitarian state frequently uses advanced technology, such as the two-way televisions in *Nineteen Eighty-Four* and the subliminal conditioning in *Brave New World*, to control individuals and, therefore, society. But these nightmares do not rely on technology alone; familiar methods such as charisma and persuasion that are as ancient as Aristotle are also frequently used by the powerful in these texts—those abuses are at the heart of the Power warning. As an example, Patrick Aiex describes this multi-faceted aspect of the nightmare as it was used in *Brave New World*: "Huxley knew well how to play on our almost paranoid fear of dehumanization via the route of [both] technology and rhetoric" (3). The focus on those *employing* the science and technology rather than on the consequences of the advances themselves distinguishes the works in this category from those that reflect our Science and Technology fears in the first section of the Nightmares Model, and makes Power a profound cultural concern, as we will see in Part Two.

THE UNKNOWN[6]

It is human nature to be afraid of the unknown as Gregory Benford observed: "If you take something big, unfamiliar, and strange, it doesn't take a lot of characterization to make people afraid of it. People are always afraid of what's new and strange" (Interview). It is also human nature, as Vernor Vinge said at the 2002 World Science Fiction Convention, to "always [be] on the lookout for some great change that will make everything better." With modern culture's emphasis on progress and change, how do we reconcile these two elements of our nature? That inevitable tension is at the heart of the third category of the Nightmares Model, which describes the many cautionary tales that reflect the nightmares The Unknown can cause.

The past hundred years have been filled with new and strange things—jet airplanes, computers, nuclear bombs, and organ transplants, just to name a few. We haven't always been able to keep up with these changes, often feeling uneasy about their consequences. Speculative fiction reflects this inescapable part of human nature and warns us about the implications of the clash between our fear of change and the steady (or sometimes explosive) pace of progress, asking questions we cannot easily answer. The discoveries that defined the twentieth century may eventually redefine society; but redefinition is a slow, often terrifying process, one that is frequently portrayed in the genre's cautionary tales.

While many of these nightmares are also related to those in the first two categories of the Nightmares Model, the warnings in this grouping have a different focus than those in the first or second. For example, while gene manipulation may lead to a story reflecting a nightmare world where the genetically undesirable are "eliminated" in the first category of the Nightmares Model or one where the government controls reproduction in the second, the uncertainty surrounding how extensively our genes can be manipulated and yet still produce a "human being" would be reflected in a text in the Unknown category. In this case, the focus on the impact on society of that uncertainty is the distinguishing factor among the categories.

As humans prepare to move out into the stars and to manipulate the very molecules that define us as a species (DNA), the uncertainty of what these changes will mean leads to many nightmares about what is to come, nightmares speculative fiction reflects. The definition of human being mentioned above, for example, while initially self-evident, is one frequently called into question by progress, as we see in many cautionary tales. The warnings in this subcategory require us to consider such issues of definition and the *application* of technology rather than issues of specific consequences. In other words, while the texts in the Information Technology grouping, for example, may warn us that a sentient robot might not be willing to follow without question the orders of a "mere" human, those in the Progress subcategory take a different view: At what point could that robot be considered human in its own right? What if it carried the memories of its creator? Would we be more sympathetic? Would "it"? Even questions regarding the pronoun we use highlight these fears: when does an "it" become "he" or "she"?

On the opposite end of the spectrum, when does someone stop being human? How much genetic manipulation is "allowed" before the human designation no longer applies? Does DNA determine what is human? If not, what standard should we use? We may not like to ask such questions, or even know we should, but as it reflects our fears regarding The Unknown, speculative fiction frequently guides us down the path of "what's next," even if we have to be dragged kicking and screaming the whole way.

As our knowledge of the universe grows, so do our questions and hence our fears. At the same time, we have yet to defeat the fears that have been with us for as long as storytellers can remember. Whether our nightmares are based on ever-advancing Science and Technology, the seemingly inevitable abuses of Power, or the uncertainty of the great Unknown, speculative fiction in the modern era reflects our fears in the hopes that we will heed its warnings and learn something from stories of spaceships, witches, and mutants that will help us when we eventually came face to face with our nightmares. And by looking at those stories through the Nightmares Model, we can learn something about ourselves and our time.

Chapter Preview

What follows in Parts One, Two, and Three are in-depth discussions of the nightmares in each subcategory of the Nightmares Model as well as a brief survey of the genre texts that illustrate these groupings. These examples are drawn from television, film, and prose (including novels and short stories), as well as from popular music, and are by no means exhaustive. As Vos Post and Kroeker remark, "There are almost countless examples ... that address some of the potential problems [we face] ... in the future" (36–37); as there isn't room for every example, I include in the upcoming chapters a sampling of both the major works and significant concepts in an effort to provide a comprehensive picture of each nightmare. Readers should keep in mind that I often needed to reduce the examples to brief, sometimes one sentence, summaries, paring the stories down to essential elements for the sake of discussion; there could never be enough space to properly convey every facet of these complex, layered narratives. It is equally important to remember that while some of the works could easily be categorized differently (as their complexity allows for multiple interpretations), the goal is to define the categories, not the texts themselves.

To conclude the discussion, I end each section with a metaphor analysis that examines the influence of the cautionary tales in the specific categories. As a majority of Lakoff and Johnson's conclusions regarding metaphors are based on "language — from the meanings of words and phrases and from the way humans make sense of their experiences" (115), each of these three chapters includes a similar analysis. In this case, however, all of the evidence is derived from references made to speculative fiction that can be observed in a typical American's popular culture experience or found in American print news media over the past five years. There are potentially thousands of examples but the small sample I describe in these chapters provides a sufficient survey to demonstrate the influence of speculative fiction on the language used in contemporary public discourse.

While some of these metaphors may seem unremarkable because of their common usage, such prevalence is precisely the point. As Lakoff and Johnson note, "our conceptual system is not something we are normally aware of. In most of the little things we do every day, we simply think and act more or less automatically along certain lines. Just what these lines are is by no means obvious" (3). Likewise, Kath Filmer observes in her own analysis of metaphor use in the British news media that "often the metaphors which have the most potent conceptualising effects are those which have become so absorbed into the language that they are no longer recognised as metaphor" (196). That will be the case for many of the examples discussed in the upcoming chapters; we have incorporated such images and concepts as Frankenstein, *Brave New World*, and *The Twilight Zone* so far into our culture that we cannot seem to debate certain issues without invoking them.

List of Abbreviations

In the chapters that follow, I use the following abbreviations for the major speculative fiction magazines when I reference short stories and other prose:

- *Analog* (*Analog Science Fiction and Fact*, formerly *Astounding*).
- *Asimov's* (*Asimov's Science Fiction*).
- *Astounding* (*Astounding Stories*, 1931–February 1938; *Astounding Science Fiction*, March 1939–January 1960; *Analog*, February 1960 to present).
- *Fantasy and Science Fiction* (*The Magazine of Fantasy and Science Fiction*).
- *Locus* (*Locus: The Newspaper of the Science Fiction Field*).

PART ONE : SCIENCE AND TECHNOLOGY

Introduction

It goes without saying that speculative fiction has a long history of depicting the negative consequences of science and technology. As Jonathan Vos Post and Kirk Kroeker describe, "Science fiction authors as early as Mary Shelley have dealt with hard trade-offs ... in their fiction, often attempting to anticipate the dangers of a new technology before it is even invented" (35). Such attempts at anticipation reflect our fears that advances in science and technology will eventually lead to our destruction, physical or otherwise.

Those "otherwise" consequences are at the center of David Brin's argument that many technology nightmares reflect the fear that "'human decency and justice haven't kept pace with our technological progress'" ("Self-Preventing"). Many of the nightmares in this section focus on the potential human impact of that progress including the possibility for technology to be abused, or to abuse us. Patrick K. Aiex identifies a particularly effective reflection of this nightmare when he describes Aldous Huxley as "a visionary who addressed [in *Brave New World*] many of today's scientific and technological issues before they manifested themselves" (2). This potential for crafting a warning that might prevent a technology nightmare underlies the texts in the first category of the Nightmares Model.

The first nightmare in this category reflects the terror of nuclear war, both its threat and its aftermath. In the early part of the modern era, speculative fiction stories described the potential for developing nuclear weapons; once that potential became reality, however, the genre quickly shifted to arguing that that reality should never be deployed again. The fear of global apocalypse from nuclear weapons has haunted the world for most of the last century and that fear has fueled such varied speculative fiction texts as *A Canticle for Leibowitz*, *The Day After*, and the Godzilla movies for as long.

Another source for Science and Technology nightmares is the incredible advancement in computers over the past few decades. Information technology is now an integral part of our working and home lives and the next few decades may prove to be just as revolutionary. Those revolutions might involve artificial intelligence, simulated worlds, or some other development we cannot even imagine. While speculative fiction may not have accurately predicted the impact of personal computing, the genre's warnings about the problems of technology are still ingrained in our cultural consciousness; the impact of the cautionary function does not diminish if and when the tales fail to foresee specific details of the present. After decades of cautionary tales, our anticipation for the "good life through technology" is tempered with our fear of that technology backfiring, a frequent genre warning. Whether it is the fear that rational, unemotional computers will take over the world or that we will lose our grip on reality as we become too dependent on the Internet, speculative fiction often portrays information technology as a double-edged sword.

Even with all the advancements science has made so far in the early part of the twenty-first century, there are still countless things we do not understand. In many ways, we know more about the Moon than we do about the way the human brain works. This disparity has led many in the genre[7] to point to biology as the location for the next great discoveries. Yet, as with everything in the Science and Technology category, those discoveries come with potentially negative consequences. If the cure for Parkinson's disease requires fetal tissue, for example, how will that tissue be collected? We also need to consider how much biotechnology is too much; if insulin pumps are okay, what about computer chips that monitor the moods of a patient who suffers from bi-polar disorder, releasing medication automatically? Aiex traces the cultural tension surrounding such advances to "the beginning of the true bionic era, the late 1960s, when advanced bioelectronic prosthetics began to be tested ... [yielding] a moral outcry. Many said that the mating of man and machine, even if it was technologically feasible, was ethically wrong" (3). Speculative fiction reflects this outcry, and the public debates that follow, time and time again.

Biological research also raises another possible nightmare: What happens when medical breakthroughs fall into the wrong hands? As Connie Willis observed at the 2002 World Science Fiction Convention, "With every medical advance, we have the possibility for the horror of bio-terrorism." How do we keep such a thing from happening? Whom do we allow to access sensitive medical information like DNA profiles? Who should administer biotechnology advances? Speculative fiction has asked these questions for over a century in the physical sciences and is now beginning to focus more closely on the life sciences.

The chapters in this section examine these three variations of the

Science and Technology nightmare — Nuclear War, Information Technology, and Biology — and then briefly discuss the texts that reflect our cultural fear of advances leading to our destruction. Part One closes with an analysis of the ways in which Science and Technology-focused cautionary tales influence public discourse regarding such issues.

1: Nuclear War

Perhaps the ultimate scientific power, and ultimate cultural nightmare (the apocalypse), lies in the twentieth century's ultimate scientific discovery: harnessing the power of the atom. Meditations on the destructive potential of this power have engaged speculative fiction since atomic research began, while nuclear horrors, according to Robert Scholes and Eric Rabkin, were "a favorite science fiction device confirming America's cold war fears" in the decades after World War II (101). Those fears have not abated even though the Cold War has ended. Familiar popular culture characters like Godzilla and Spiderman are direct manifestations of our nightmares regarding nuclear technology and its consequences.

Nuclear weapons have populated speculative fiction for more than a hundred years and are one of the few nightmares that actually came to fruition, much to the chagrin of some in the genre. In a 1972 article for *The Journal of Popular Culture*, Paul A. Carter cites this reaction from Isaac Asimov[8] to the use of the atomic bomb over Hiroshima in August 1945:

> Well, the atomic bomb came, and it finally made SF "respectable."... For the first time, science-fiction writers appeared to the world in general as something more than a bunch of nuts; we were suddenly Cassandras whom the world ought to have believed. But, I tell you, I would far rather have lived and died a nut in the eyes of all the world than to have been salvaged into respectability at the price of nuclear war hanging like a sword of Damocles over the world forever [851].

And Asimov was not alone in such sentiments, as the genre's response to the nuclear Sword of Damocles demonstrates.

The apocalyptic effects of nuclear technology clearly justify a subset of the Science and Technology category devoted to warnings about this single scientific advance. And it seems (perhaps morbidly) appropriate to begin the Nightmares Model with the destruction of the world, just as it will end, in Chapter 9, with questions about whether the "real" world exists at all. When it comes to our nightmares of nuclear war, speculative fiction most frequently presents one (or more) of three "basic" variations: the terror of an actual attack, the potential for mutations caused by nuclear radiation, and the impact that an all-out nuclear apocalypse would have on society as we know it. We will look at these variations throughout the chapter.

Visions of the Apocalypse: History and Impact

Speculative fiction has a long tradition of depicting both the wonder and the terror of science and technology. The way these visions and explorations manifest themselves, however, is open to interpretation: Brian Aldiss describes the traditions of science fiction as "looking outwards and measuring man against the world he has made or found" (94) while Connie Willis shared a much less reverential opinion at the 2002 World Science Fiction Convention, "Science fiction has a proud tradition of destroying the world twice a week and has been doing it since the twenties." That history of destruction, however, has roots that go back even further than the 1920s; the genre has dealt with the possible implications of nuclear technology since Robert Cromie's *The Crack of Doom* was published in 1895. Similarly, the groundwork for the nuclear apocalypse tradition was laid by H. G. Wells's *World Set Free* from 1914, which Paul Brians identifies as the first novel to depict a war involving atomic weapons.

Wells's story seems to be a harbinger of what was to come, both in reality and in the genre. Looking back on the evolution of this nightmare, Asimov claims science fiction writers were among the first to see the potential for atomic weapons after the discovery of nuclear fission ("Science Fiction" 43), a potential that quickly found its way onto the pages of Golden Age pulp magazines. To illustrate just how in tune the genre was with the quickly advancing nuclear science, Asimov relates the famous account of Cleve Cartmill and his story "Deadline," which John W. Campbell published in a 1944 issue of *Astounding*. Apparently, the story so accurately (albeit unknowingly) resembled the work of the Manhattan Project that federal agents descended upon Campbell's office, demanding to know where Cartmill got his information ("Science Fiction" 44). At that point, however, nuclear weapons were just fiction, as far as most people knew.

Of course, the world changed in August 1945 when a very real atomic bomb was dropped on Hiroshima. The nightmare of nuclear weapons was the first, and perhaps only, Science and Technology nightmare to unmistakably cross over from the page to the real world and, as such, occupies a unique position in my analysis of cautionary tales. The terror reflected in these stories is, unfortunately, not as abstract or even "speculative" as those we will see in later chapters, something to which the many Baby Boomers who hid under their desks during Civil Defense drills can attest.

Once nuclear weapons moved from fringe genre magazines to the mainstream media, from fiction to news, a cultural belief in the need for "The Bomb" began to take shape despite, or perhaps because of, the terror it induced; that conviction hasn't let go of us yet because as Jutta Weldes argues, it builds on a belief in the benefit of, and need for, a *super*-weapon ("Popular"). Desire for such a weapon, according to H. Bruce Franklin, is based on "'a cultural matrix bubbling with fantasies of ultimate weapons,'" which "profoundly shaped 'the nation's conception of nuclear weapons and responses to them, decades before they materialized'" (qtd. in Weldes, "Popular" 4). Speculative fiction plays a significant role in that cultural matrix by providing those "fantasies of ultimate weapons" Franklin describes.[9] Even if Asimov's assertions are completely accurate and society did see genre writers as "a bunch of nuts," the super-weapons in Wells's and other pre–1945 atomic war stories penetrated the public consciousness, paving the way for a near-uncontrollable belief in the need for a super-weapon. This belief fueled the Cold War arms race that would come to define much of the twentieth century.

Once the atomic bomb became real, speculative fiction shifted from describing its possibility to fervently warning against its re-use. Despite his harsh criticism of the literary quality of speculative fiction, Arthur Barron does acknowledge the genre's tendency to protest "against the use of scientific knowledge and technology for anti-human ends" and goes on to observe, "Frequently, this protest takes the form of a chilling description of the consequences of atomic war" (63). L.W. Michaelson also discusses this propensity when he cites John W. Campbell's introduction to 1946's *Best of Science Fiction*: "'[the science fiction writer's] primary interest is in what those weapons (atomic bombs, etc.) will do to political, economic and cultural structures of human society'" (503). Genre texts since 1945 prove Campbell correct.

Even after atomic weapons leapt from the theoretical realm of the laboratory (and science fiction page) onto American television sets, ruminations on nuclear war remained primarily the province of speculative fiction. Brians observes that "outside of science fiction, novelists and short story writers were slow to respond to Hiroshima" (14) while Asimov credits the genre's writers with being the first to accurately foresee not only the potential for the atomic bomb but also its vast implications as well ("Science Fiction" 43–44). Brians identifies perhaps the most obvious implication when he points out that "World War III — the nuclear holocaust — has been fought over and over in the pages of books and magazines" since 1945 (2). Similarly, Andrew Ross asserts in *Strange Weather: Culture, Science and Technology in the Age of Limits* that "War and Hiroshima, in particular, gave the future a bad name" (132), a bad name that persists; speculative fiction's reflections of Asimov's nuclear Sword of Damocles did not wane after the initial shock in 1945. Brians's 1987 annotated bibliography, *Nuclear Holocausts: Atomic War in Fiction, 1895–1984*, includes more than 400 prose works dealing with atomic weapons published in English since 1960. And the genre does not only reflect this fear through print, as Karyn and Donald Rybacki observe: "During the 1960s, a series of 'anti-war' films focused on man's ultimate inability to control nuclear weapons" (3).

The terror of nuclear holocaust did not just influence our visions of war; rather, the entire culture of the 1950s through the 1970s had, according to Ross, a dark (mushroom-shaped) cloud over it. As an example, Ross identifies the cultural fallout from the nuclear reality as the reason for the less-than-exuberant reaction to the "generic language of progress" at the 1964 World's Fair: "the social pathology of Bomb culture had too pervasively defined people's horizon of expectations about the world of tomorrow for the rhetoric of unbounded progress" to be celebrated so unabashedly (138). As this cultural fallout sunk in, speculative fiction, Ross argues, replaced "stream-lined, utopian futures that had prevailed before the war ... [with] dystopian projections of science gone awry" featuring "disaster-ridden imagery of a future-less future [that] establish[ed] some of its deepest roots in popular consciousness and popular culture in the 1960s and 1970s" (141).[10] Going back even further, M. Keith Booker describes 1950s America as "the Golden Age of nuclear fear" (*Monsters* 5), a fear speculative fiction clearly reflects.

For those living in that age of fear, Booker argues, nuclear weapons and their associated radiation "represented the dark side of what in many ways was a growing faith in the ability of science to provide the knowledge required to produce better living" (*Monsters* 10). There is a certain irony that, while the generations of the twentieth-century were the first for whom life was likely to be different from that of their parents,[11] they were also the inheritors of Ross's "future-less future," inextricably tied to the dark side of science. The culmination of research into the atom led these generations down a path where they were terrified they may never get the chance to have a future, let alone one that was better than their parents had. These children had the "world at their feet," as the saying goes, and yet, from the time they were elementary school students hiding under their desks in Civil Defense Drills, the dark side of this "progress" loomed over them, promising to exact payment for those advances by destroying their futures.

These fears, nightmares, and cultural fallout are reflected in speculative fiction produced after 1945. As Kathleen McNurlin observes, nuclear war "has been used in science fiction to decimate more fictional characters than have been killed in any other literary genre.... This says much about the pessimism that courses through science fiction. In fact, rarely, if ever in science fiction do humans employ the atom for purposes other than warfare" ("Part II" 21). The pessimism, potential apocalypses, and unintended consequences reflected by the examples that finish out this chapter are seemingly inevitable products of the twentieth century's scientific progress, nightmares that plague the children of that century and all who follow them. There are at least hundreds of texts that I could use to illustrate this category but, as John Newman and Michael Unsworth observe, "even [a] limited scope provides a sufficiency of horrible ideas" (x).

Prophets of Doom: Print Examples Before 1945

As I mentioned above, examples of this sub-category are as old as Cromie's 1895 *Crack of Doom* and Wells's *World Set Free*[12] from 1914. In the latter, artificial radioactivity is achieved in 1933 and leads to nuclear war in 1956, while Cromie's story revolves around what would become one of the more familiar plots for a nuclear weapon tale: a group of madmen are stopped just before setting off an atomic device. Even earlier than Wells's story is Hollis Godfrey's 1908 novel, *The Man Who Ended War*, in which the title character uses a radioactivity weapon to blackmail the world into disarmament.[13]

The Golden Age of science fiction pulp magazines in the 1930s and 1940s yielded many short stories that predict nuclear weapons and their accompanying social and political implications. One characteristic piece is Cartmill's "Deadline," published in 1944 — the story that sent federal agents descending upon John W. Campbell's office. Another story, "Solution Unsatisfactory" by Robert A. Heinlein, also published in *Astounding* (in May 1941), fairly accurately depicts a stalemate between the United States and Soviet Union following the development of nuclear weapons. Heinlein himself denied any prescient ability, describing "Solution" as based on the central assumption of an "Absolute Weapon" with the story then following from pondering "what changes this forces on mankind" ("Pandora's Box" 241).

Campbell was not just the editor of *Astounding* during the Golden Age but he was also a frequent contributor of short fiction as well. Two such stories by Campbell deal with atomic weapons before they were a reality: in 1939's "Cloak of Aesir,"[14] aliens invade Earth using atomic blast weapons while the civilizations in 1937's "Forgetfulness" have developed such technology four times and blown themselves back to the Stone Age each time (Brians 152). A similarly bleak ending follows atomic technology in Lester del Ray's 1938 short story "The Faithful" where a nuclear holocaust destroys the human race, clearing the way for intelligent apes and dogs to take over (177) as well as another Cartmill story, 1942's "With Flaming Swords," which features the struggle against atomic mutant villains who rule Earth (Brians 156). Disaster also results when atomic rays are the weapon of choice for the invaders (human this time) who destroy Seattle in Gordon A. Giles's "The Atom Smasher" from 1938 (Brians 205).

All-out nuclear war is not the plot but the nightmare to be avoided in a 1924 Czech novel by Karel Capek, *Krakatit: An Atomic Fantasy*,[15] where, Brians describes, a scientist struggles to keep the secrets of the atom away from those whose goal is world domination (154). A 1929 play by Robert Nichols and Maurice Browne, *Wings Over Europe: A Dramatic Extravaganza On a Pressing Theme*, reverses the direction of Capek's warning: this time, according to Brians, those in power must *stop* the pioneer of atomic energy from using it to destroy the Earth (271).

Political tensions are the impetus for nuclear war in the 1943 French novel *Ashes, Ashes* by Rene Barjavel, which combines social commentary with cautionary tale when tense race relations spark an atomic missile attack on Europe (Brians 125). Another politically "current" tale described by Brians, Harold Nicolson's *Public Faces* (from 1932), projects atomic weapons into a Middle East power struggle (271), a possibility that still terrifies us in the early twenty-first century. The political atmosphere of its era is similarly evident in "The Paradise Crater," a story written by Philip Wylie before Hiroshima, according to Brians, but published after for security reasons (see Cartmill's experience). "Paradise" is set in 1965 when a Nazi conspiracy develops nuclear weapons that the hero then must destroy, creating an immense crater in California and sending a massive tidal wave toward Japan (344–45).

As we see with the publication of "Paradise," once the Bomb became public knowledge, all bets, and the gloves, were off, at least as far as speculative fiction was concerned.

What Have We Done? Print Examples After 1945

In his analysis of the connection between science fiction and the Cold War, Booker asserts that genre works created between 1946 and 1964 respond "in a particularly direct and obvious way" to the new nuclear threat (4), as much of the post–1945 nuclear war speculative fiction "seem[s] genuinely designed as attempted interventions in contemporary debates concerning the Cold War arms race" (*Monsters* 65). Some of these attempted interventions depict an actual nuclear attack and/or its immediate aftermath, as we see in Helen Clarkson's *The Last Day*, the 1959 novel in which a woman tries to escape nuclear fallout by heading to an island off the Massachusetts coast, where she eventually dies from radiation exposure.

Five years after Hiroshima and Nagasaki, Ray Bradbury uses two very different outsider characters to render his vision of the nuclear attack nightmare. The automated house (complete with mechanical mice) in "There Will Come Soft Rains" goes about its business despite the fact that all the humans it's designed to serve have been killed by a nuclear blast while "The Highway" is told from the perspective of a Mexican farmer who watches hundreds of cars race back to the States after a nuclear attack, crowding the highway that runs alongside his fields.

The sad possibility that we will take the nightmare of nuclear destruction to the stars with us also appears in post–1945 speculative fiction prose. Gary Westfahl identifies several stories that examine nuclear war from the specific angle of the role of space stations in such conflicts, including Lester del Ray's *Step to the Stars*, Murray Leinster's *Space Platform*, Edmund Cooper's *Seed of Light*, and C. M. Kornbluth's *Not This August*.

Pat Frank's 1959 novel *Alas, Babylon*, according to Booker (*Monsters*), illustrates the most critical consequence of nuclear war: the failure of almost every governmental function, leaving survivors to fend for themselves. This failure appears in reflections of the Nuclear War nightmare on both a large and a small scale, from the effects on an entire society to the more personal, intimate consequences depicted, for example, in Judith Merril's *Shadow on the Hearth* from 1950. This novel focuses on a housewife named Gladys Mitchell who attempts to take care of her two daughters and keep her house running while she wonders if her husband has survived a surprise nuclear attack.[16]

One of the most prominent examples of Nuclear War cautionary tales (and one of those rare speculative fiction texts to cross over into the literary canon) is Walter Miller's *A Canticle for Leibowitz*. This 1959 series of three novellas depicts the inevitability of the destruction of human civilization. In the first story, survivors of a nuclear holocaust take out their fear and rage on scientists and technicians, murdering them and destroying their books and equipment, believing these actions will prevent another catastrophe. But, according to the other two novellas, civilization is cyclical and a future nuclear holocaust is unavoidable; one, in fact, occurs at the end of the final story. While this pessimistic view that nuclear war cannot be avoided may seem to preclude *Canticle* from the list of cautionary tales,[17] its depiction of the human response to nuclear destruction, particularly the murder of scientists and the attempted destruction of knowledge, carries powerful warnings for readers.

The first part of *Canticle* is far from the only story to warn against the hasty, reactionary response of scapegoating scientists and/or technicians for the nightmare of nuclear war. The protagonists of Bradbury's "The Fox and the Forest" (originally titled "To the Future") are scientists pursued through time for their role in a twenty-second century atomic war. Vernon W. Glasser's "The Bodyguard," from 1951, casts opponents of technology as "foolish," according to Brians, compared to the "enlightened few [who] look forward to rebuilding civilization" (205).

In Poul Anderson's Maurai series, the descendants of today's Maori people (from New Zealand) control most of the post-holocaust world's technology, forbidding any non-renewable or nuclear technology in the hope of preventing another war. Stories from the series such as "The Sky People" and "Progress" argue, however, that the Maurai view of and attempts to control technology are both shortsighted and dangerous (Brians 116). Twenty years after "Progress," Anderson returned to the Maurai series with *Orion Shall Rise*, a novel that also sympathizes with scientists who try to develop technology against the prohibitions of those in charge. In a similar vein, *Vault of the Ages*, an Anderson novel not in the Maurai series, follows two boys who, five hundred years after a nuclear war, use forbidden "ancient" technology to stop an invasion.

Bruce Ariss's 1963 novel *Full Circle* is more sympathetic than either Anderson or Glasser toward those who repress technology after a nuclear war: Ariss's characters agree to re-introduce some technology but only after taking precautions to prevent the mistakes of the past. And the main character of Pendelton Banks's "Turning Point" (from the May 1947 issue of *Astounding*) realizes that, according to Brians, "progress cannot be imposed; the technological renaissance will come when people are ready for it" (125).

In other stories that depict the efforts to rebuild after a nuclear holocaust, the focus is not on who is to blame but on what has been lost, as in "If I Forget Thee, Oh Earth" by Arthur C. Clarke, in which survivors on the Moon hope to someday return to Earth after the radiological damage dissipates (Brians 159). Russell Hoban's 1980 novel *Riddley Walker* also takes place centuries after a nuclear war; the destruction occurred so long ago in fact that Hoban's characters speak a dialect of evolved English in which the spelling and meaning of many modern words have changed. This is particularly true with *Walker's* religion, which is based in part on misremembered stories of the war. Even though the characters don't remember the ancient civilization involved in that war, the novel revolves around attempts to recreate a weapon from that pre-war time. In contrast to the detail of Hoban's work, Olaf Stapledon's 1931 novel *Last and First Man*,[18] presents an entire future history of humanity on a massive scale, with a mere few paragraphs covering the millions of years it takes to recover from a nuclear apocalypse that leaves only a dozen or so humans alive.

Rebuilding society after nuclear devastation is also the underlying premise for *The World Jones Made*, Philip K. Dick's 1956 novel in which relativism is the law. Fearing another nuclear war, the government prohibits all absolutes, hoping to avoid the sort of fanatical devotion to ideas that led to the initial conflict. Unfortunately, Booker observes, the people "become so hungry to believe in something without question" that a cult leader manipulates the population to do his bidding (*Monsters* 29). Bernard Wolfe's 1952 novel *Limbo* takes a more satirical approach to this nightmare than *Jones* does: the remnants of both the United States and Soviet Union have implemented voluntary amputation (literal disarmament), trying to reduce the aggression that led to the devastating nuclear war in the first place. All the while, though, both governments are secretly stockpiling a nuclear arsenal and developing ways to use prosthetic limbs as weapons.

More recently, David Brin's 1985 novel *The Postman* (originally a 1982 short story and the basis for the 1997 Kevin Costner film) depicts the hard life on the other side of a nuclear war where the only goal is survival and one man delivering messages can bring hope for a better world. But all is not doom and gloom in speculative fiction prose, as we see in Frederic Brown's 1949 short story "Letter to a Phoenix": the long-lived hero comes to the realization that the "unique capacity for self-immolation born of madness makes the human race ... the only race in the universe which will survive" (Brians 147).

Not only did the reality of nuclear weapons lead to the pervasive cultural nightmare that an attack would destroy society, but it also introduced into our collective psyche the concept of unpredictable mutations caused by radiation, an idea that was quickly reflected in speculative fiction. Dick populates his 1965 novel *Dr. Bloodmoney, or How We Got Along After the Bomb* with a variety of mutants created by radiation fallout from nuclear war; characters include talking dogs and Bill Keller, whose body never completely formed, leaving him to exist as a parasite, communicating via telepathy. Similarly, the telepaths in Henry Kuttner's *Mutant*, a 1953 collection of novelettes published under the Lewis Padgett pseudonym, are believed to have come into being because of fallout from the "Blow-Up." Telepaths are also the result of nuclear war-induced radiation in *The Chrysalids* by John Wynham.[19]

Genetic "purity" in a post-nuclear landscape of mutants is the underlying drive of *The Iron Dream*,[20] a 1972 novel by Norman Spinrad. In a last ditch effort to stop the genocidal campaign to destroy all mutants, one group, who appear human on the surface but are capable of mind control, use a nuclear warhead to flood the entire planet with radiation, mutating everyone except the "perfect" clones the "pure" leader then sends throughout the solar system. Such an escape to other planets is the choice of survivors in another Kuttner novel (written with C. L. Moore), *Fury*, except in this story the mutants hold the power: after survivors of an atomic war flee to Venus, their descendants use mutant abilities to control the other humans.[21] Mars is the destination for the mutants in Anderson's *Twilight World*, a 1961 novel that traces the consequences of a nuclear war over the course of thousands of years (Brians 119).

The nightmare of nuclear radiation-induced mutation also appears in what many describe as a horror classic: Richard Matheson's 1954 novel *I Am Legend*, the initial inspiration for Charlton Heston's 1971 film *Omega Man*, as well as for the more faithful adaptation *The Last Man on Earth*, starring Vincent Price in 1964. While I discuss this story in more detail in later chapters, the Nuclear War nightmare is the catalyst for the horror: nuclear attack creates a bacteria that turns everyone (except the protagonist) into a vampire. Judith Merril also examines, again on a much more personal level, this mutation aspect of the nightmare, this time from the perspective of the long-term consequences survivors face. In "That Only a Mother," the main character refuses to accept the reality that her child has been born without limbs, a defect directly related to atomic radiation.

Radiation itself is the weapon of choice in Michael Swanwick's humorous 2002 short story "'Hello,' Said the Stick." Power generation, not weaponry, is the consequence of nuclear technology in *Nerves* by Lester del Ray, which depicts a nuclear reactor breakdown. And, of course, it is a radioactive spider that bites Peter Parker and creates *The Amazing Spider-Man*, the long-running Marvel hero.

But the technology of the twentieth century didn't just create nightmare-inducing nuclear weapons. It was also the century of movies and television, and our Nuclear War fears are reflected in those media just as they are in prose.

Mushroom Clouds and Mutants Galore: Film and Television Examples

Booker identifies Arch Oboler's 1951 film *Five* as perhaps the first movie to present a post-holocaust world (*Monsters* 94–95); it follows five survivors of a nuclear war as they travel to the California coast, find each other, and fight amongst themselves, eventually leaving only one man and one woman to rebuild the world. We see a similar ending in Roger Corman's 1955 film *Day the World Ended*, as human and romantic tensions, along with attacks by radiation-created deranged mutants, whittle eight survivors down to two. According to Booker, this is also one of the first films to depict the mutating effects of radiation (*Monsters* 95–96).[22]

Two classic film treatments of nuclear war are vastly different in approach despite being released in the same year: 1964. Stanley Kubrick's *Dr. Strangelove, or How I Learned to Stop Worrying and Love the Bomb* (loosely based on Peter George's 1958 novel *Red Alert*) satirizes the possibility of a few individuals starting a nuclear war and, according to Arthur C. Clarke, convinced the legendary speculative fiction author to collaborate with Kubrick on a new movie, which would eventually become *2001: A Space Odyssey* ("Son" 277). As Weldes observes, *Dr. Strangelove* "challenge[s] the boundaries of common sense" (6) by "ridiculing, among other things, anti-communist paranoia and the convolutions of nuclear deterrence" ("Popular" 7). Max Youngstein, however, took a more realistic approach in the other 1964 nuclear war film, the tense drama *Fail Safe*. Despite the vast gulf between these two extremes, the atomic war movies of the 1960s were incredibly influential, for, as Frederick Pohl observes, "I think it is at least a possibility that [such movies as] Nevil Shute's *On the Beach*, in both its forms as novel and as film, played a significant part in warning us away from that all-out nuclear Armageddon that might have, and perhaps still might, put an end once and for all to all dreams of human perfectibility" ("Politics" 201), if not our very existence.

But such reflections of nuclear war did not disappear from movies once the 1960s ended; for example, Japanese anime frequently deals with this nightmare. For example, while Oshii Mamoru's 1993 film *Patlabor II* doesn't deal directly with atomic weapons, it does examine the implications of Japan's involvement in United Nations peacekeeping operations (Fisch), with the attendant nuclear dangers that accompany any modern military maneuver.[23]

The original *Twilight Zone* television series also reflects our fear of nuclear Armageddon. The first season episode "Time Enough at Last" (which first aired in November 1959) tells the story of a reading-obsessed banker who is the sole survivor of a nuclear war, and in "The Old Man in the Cave" (from November 1963), a small community is saved from global nuclear destruction by a mysterious guardian. A later episode also hinges on this fear, but in "One More Pallbearer," the nuclear war only exists in the main character's mind after he tries to trick several people into believing that his bomb shelter is the only way they can survive the air raid he fakes out of a quest for revenge.

More recent examples in this category include the 1983 ABC television movie *The Day After* and *The Twilight Zone* (1985 version) episode "Shelter Skelter," which originally aired in May 1987 and depicts a man so terrified of nuclear war that he refuses to leave his house for fear of being too far away from the bomb shelter in his basement. He ends up living out the rest of his life in that shelter, alone, after he seals the door without waiting for his family to arrive when air-raid sirens go off. The *"Twilight-Zone twist"* is that there was no attack, just an accidental missile launch; as a memorial, all of the rubble has been piled on top of his shelter and enclosed by a dome, sealing in the radiation and dooming him to a life alone.

Just as in prose, the manifestation of our fear of nuclear weapons in film and television is not limited to what would happen in an actual attack. As Booker observes, one of the fears underlying movies like Sam Newfield's *Lost Continent* (from 1951) is the potential for nuclear war to throw civilization back into prehistoric times (*Monsters* 140). Edward Bernds's 1956 film *World Without End* is set in such a future: hundreds of years after a nuclear war, "normal" humans are enslaved by mutant cavemen on the Earth's surface while technologically advanced humans live in peace and comfort below. Eventually, astronauts from the twentieth-century (arriving from the past via a "space disturbance") convince the underground humans to take control of the surface and defeat the mutants. Nearly twenty years later, *A Boy and His Dog*, directed by L.Q. Jones and released in 1975, also takes place on a post-nuclear war Earth with a devastated surface and a preserved underground society. But in Jones's film, the mutant isn't the enemy but the sidekick—the dog in the title is telepathic. And the destructive forces of nuclear war are not only depicted with an Earth setting: in 1950's *Rocketship X-M*, a human space crew headed for the moon lands on Mars instead and discovers the ruins of a civilization apparently destroyed by a nuclear war that mutated the surviving Martians into savage primitives.

The use of atomic technology in films and on television is not limited to weapons and the warnings are not limited to war. Nuclear testing is the version of this nightmare in Val Guest's *The Day the Earth Caught Fire* (released in 1962), as our planet is sent careening toward the sun. Many of the great (or not so great, depending on your level of nostalgia) monster movies of the 1950s can actually be read as reflections of the Nuclear War nightmare because, according to Booker, "radiation or some other sort of scientific experiment" was usually what created the giant creatures in the first place (*Monsters* 140). Perhaps the poster-monster for this subgenre is

Godzilla, a prehistoric creature awakened by nuclear testing to headline dozens of movies over more than fifty years. Some other famous (and infamous) monsters include:

- Giant mutant ants that eat people in *Them!* (from 1954).
- The rhedosaurus from 1953's *The Beast from 20,000 Fathoms*, which is released from Polar ice after millions of years when a hydrogen bomb test melts the glacier.[24]
- Locusts that eat super-sized vegetables in Burt Gordon's 1957 *Beginning of the End* become giants and attack Chicago.
- The giant spider in Jack Arnold's *Tarantula* (released in 1955) created by radiation from experiments to increase the world's food supply, which then escapes the lab and attacks a nearby town until the Air Force kills it.[25]
- The enormous octopus driven from its home by nuclear tests in 1955's *It Came from Beneath the Sea*, which destroys the Golden Gate Bridge and much of San Francisco before it is itself destroyed by a special atomic torpedo.
- Leeches that become gigantic after exposure to radiation from rocket tests at Cape Canaveral in 1960's (cleverly named) *Attack of the Giant Leeches*.
- The giant crabs in Roger Corman's *Attack of the Crab Monsters* (released in 1957), created by fallout from nuclear tests in the Pacific, which are not only aggressive but also telepathic and use their mental powers to try to take over the world.

Two other B-movies, both released in 1957, also turn on creatures mutated by radiation but, in these cases, the mutants are originally humans, not animals. In *The Incredible Shrinking Man*, based on Richard Matheson's 1956 novel *The Shrinking Man*, the main character begins to shrink because of a combination of a radioactive cloud and pesticides, eventually disappearing into nothing.[26] On the other side of the scale, radiation from a "plutonium bomb" causes an Army colonel to grow to sixty feet tall in Burt Gordon's *The Amazing Colossal Man*.

In more recent decades, and of a more serious tone, 1978's *The China Syndrome* is, according to McNurlin, a "prophetic warning about the dangers of a nuclear core meltdown" ("Question" 9). This warning, along with real-life accidents at Chernobyl and Three-Mile Island, have turned a nuclear reactor's cooling towers into a visual symbol of our worst nightmares.

While film and television certainly generate the most examples of Nuclear War cautionary tales that captivate us today, the influence on popular music cannot be ignored. As Ian Simpson observes, "There are many original characters, stories, worlds, universes, and ideas to be found in song lyrics, and sometimes interpreted from instrumental tracks" (12). And those stories set to music transcend genre: "It is evident ... that the telling of an original science fiction tale has touched all forms of contemporary music from the mid–1960s to the present day" (15). Simpson identifies several examples, including:

- Pink Floyd's nuclear holocaust song "Two Suns in the Sunset," from 1983's *The Final Cut* (12).
- Survivors struggling in a post-nuclear world in 1969's "Wooden Ships" from Crosby, Stills and Nash (13).
- "Morning Dew" from The Grateful Dead in 1967, which tells the story of young lovers wandering through nuclear fall-out (13).
- "All Stood Still" (describing a nuclear power plant accident) and "Dancing with Tears in My Eyes" (following two lovers as they search for each other after a nuclear attack), both from Ultravox in 1980 (14).

As we can see from this brief survey of Newman and Unsworth's "horrible ideas," there is incredible variety in speculative fiction reflections of the Nuclear War nightmare. Some trends, however, do appear when the examples are compared according to their media and across time. Perhaps the most obvious is that the visual nature of film and television allows storytellers to make an even greater impact on their audience with vivid depictions of the physical horrors of nuclear weapons. Beyond that, visual texts seem to take a more varied approach than their prose counterparts, with the social satire of *Dr. Strangelove* contrasting with the grim realism of *The Day After* and the camp of interchangeable mutant creatures tearing apart interchangeable cities.

From a chronological perspective, representations of nuclear war after 1945, freed from the need for secrecy, reflect a specificity regarding the individual and societal implications of nuclear weapons that wasn't present before. It is almost as if the real images from Hiroshima and Nagasaki burned themselves into our cultural psyche and then reflected back onto graphic and disturbing post–World War II depictions of nuclear war. This is when the cautionary function became primary, when the world was listening.

The urgency seems to have gone out of the nightmare, however, as reflections both in prose and on the screen seem to be most prevalent between 1945 and 1990. Booker's description of the integral connection between these texts and our Cold War fears seems to explain this trend, as well as the reconceptualization of Godzilla from nuclear-powered monster to national protector that I will discuss in Chapter 4. Has the end of the Cold War meant an end to our fear of nuclear war or simply changed it? It's too soon to know for sure but my analysis in Chapter 4 of the ways in which Nuclear War images (e.g. Dr. Strangelove and Godzilla) appear in mainstream discourse might point to a repositioning of the nightmare from the Cold War to the War on Terror.

2: Information Technology

While speculative fiction frequently reflects the nightmare of nuclear war, the fear of information technology running wild is just as prevalent and, some would argue, is of more pressing concern. Computers are now so fully integrated into our lives that many of us cannot imagine a day without them; but, as a culture, we also cannot ignore the potential downsides of a technology that pervasive. Speculative fiction continually warns us of these dangers, including the loss of privacy and individual freedom, personal isolation, and even global destruction.

These warnings have a long pedigree: Neil Postman observes that, in the eighteenth century, "Matthew Arnold warned that 'faith in machinery' was humankind's greatest menace" (25) while Lord Byron "saw in technology a Faustian bargain — economic growth on one hand; the loss of self-respect and community vitality on the other" (26). In his column discussing *The Matrix* trilogy, *Los Angeles Times* staff writer Reed Johnson takes a similarly long view on the beginnings of this nightmare: "When machines began replacing human labor on a large scale during the Industrial Revolution, they were often regarded as Satan's smoke-belching spawn," a sentiment reflected in Charlie Chaplin's turn as "a comic monkey wrench in *Modern Times*, gumming up an assembly-line monstrosity." It's no coincidence that one of the most influential films from the nascent stages of the medium deals directly with the fear of technology taking over our lives as well as depicting the attempts of an outcast to interrupt the works. Both of these aspects of *Modern Times* have made frequent appearances in speculative fiction for decades.

As machines have become computers, and the massive monstrosities of the Industrial Revolution have become smaller and more powerfully pervasive technologies, the sentiment described by Arnold and Byron has remained in both our culture and speculative fiction that reflects it. As Arthur C. Clarke observes, "The science-fiction writers, performing their traditional role of viewing-with-alarm, have long recognized the siren call of the Dream Machine" ("Cyberclysm" 48). These alarms most frequently reflect three aspects of our Information Technology fear: 1) That we will be replaced by robots or some other form of artificial intelligence; 2) That our forays into cyberspace will fundamentally change the way we live; and 3) That we will rely too much on technology. The many variations of these warnings of siren songs tempting us toward information "Dream Machines" are my focus for this chapter.

Out of Control Conveniences: Artificial Intelligence and Robots

Information technology has advanced dramatically over the past hundred years, from Chaplin's building-sized machines and the first computers that filled entire rooms to today's PDAs and laptops. There are several possible next steps in this information technology revolution, one of which is the creation of some form of artificial intelligence (AI) or its walking version, robots. Speculative fiction has contributed to our cultural desire for this advance in that it has led us to somewhat expect to live the life depicted in its stories.[1] For example, many people are asking why they don't have floating cars and robot maids now that it is the twenty-first century. Our culture (influenced heavily by the mid-century optimistic view of the future) expects, at least a little bit, to soon live like *The Jetsons* and scientists and engineers are working to give us that future: in 2002, Honda unveiled its first walking robot, ASIMO (Advanced Step in Innovative Mobility), and in 2004, ran a marketing campaign touting the virtues of the latest version along with their hopes for its future use. Other robots already exist in our world: they paint our cars and children build them out of LEGOs for competitions. But are we closer to robots like Rosie, George Jetson's maid, or HAL, the artificial intelligence that kills the crew in *2001: A Space Odyssey*? It seems it is too soon to tell.

While technological advances like a fully functioning AI installed aboard a walking robot are certainly attractive, they also carry with them a potentially devastating downside. Postman identifies that MIT professor "Marvin Minsky and others working in the field of artificial intelligence have prophesied quite enthusiastically that humans will become merely pets of their computers" (20). While Postman's characterization of the researchers as enthusiastic is certainly open for interpretation, the possibility that we may be advancing ourselves into obsolescence is not; speculative fiction has been warning us about just that since before World War II. M. Keith Booker approaches this tradition of robot warnings by comparing two of the genre's giants, Isaac Asimov and Philip K. Dick, and their virtually polar opposite takes on the nature of man-made intelligences. Asimov's robots are "easily distinguished from human beings, but entirely pro-human in their behavior" while Dick "extended the robot theme in the postmodernist direction of android simulacra, indistinguishable from humans by all but specially trained experts" (*Monsters* 32). Booker sees Dick's androids as "introducing the frightening (especially in the 1950s) possibility that technology might advance to the point where we cannot tell ourselves from our own machines" (33). Within the context of a society struggling with the reality of just what science had wrought (i.e., powerful nuclear weapons and an intensifying Cold War, key defining features of 1950s America according to Booker[2]), the potential for destructive technology to not only rain down from the sky but to also walk among us, undetected, established a cultural precedent that, if it did not entirely supplant Asimov's vision, at least became a significant alternative for speculative fiction reflections of our robot nightmare.

We can see an expansion of Booker's perspective in Johnson's description of the shift in the genre's depictions of robots: "Visionary fantasy auteurs such as Ray Bradbury and Michael Crichton realized that robots and other intelligent life forms are most formidable and intriguing not when they're different from us, but when they're almost exactly like us, so much alike that it may be impossible to spot the difference — until it's too late." While Honda's ASIMO may not have a human face, it does have something no robot has achieved before: a human shape. How long will it be before the visions of Dick, Bradbury, and Crichton (among others) become reality? Or have we learned our lesson from these fictional nightmares and will thus insist engineers follow the Asimov version?

There are at least two components to the fear behind these AI and robot warnings that are particularly favorite subjects of speculative fiction writers such as Clarke, Harlan Ellison, and Ambrose Bierce. The first is that we are afraid of losing our spot at the top of the evolutionary chain. Will we outsmart ourselves by creating the tools of our own destruction?[3] The other side of this issue is our fear of the consequences of "playing God" by creating intelligences in our own image. What are the moral, practical, and social implications of such an "achievement"? As our technology continues to advance in the direction of quantum computers, organic networks, and non-Boolean logic, we can only just begin to answer the questions speculative fiction has been asking for decades.

Cyberworld: Communication and Virtual Reality

While the underlying nightmare behind AI and robot warnings is of those technologies breaking out of their carefully-designed programming and doing something *independently* that we did not intend and/or tell them to do, another more contemporary version views technologies as "dangerous not because they might malfunction but, on the contrary, because they realize their technological capabilities only too impeccably" (Levin 248). Many argue that this vision was first presented to the public in cyberpunk stories such as 1984's *Neuromancer*, but A.E. Levin claims it is much older, citing *Brave New World* as an example of an anti-machine text and arguing that, for contemporary readers, "the foreground is occupied by Huxley's conjectural model" (248). Levin describes this familiar model as the "literary thematic field of the relations between man and complex technical systems" (251). In other words, the reflection of what *we* will do because of the technology puts the contemporary twist on the anti-machine fears that Postman and Johnson trace back to Arnold and Chaplin, respectively.

James Van Pelt described one of the most critical fears in our culture as a concern over "what information technology will do to us. We're not too far from being able to track electronically everyone, of knowing an incredible amount of information about anyone" ("Request"). As our programming abilities improve, so do the surveillance capabilities of the computers that surround our lives; we see this reflected in speculative fiction's many warnings about the potential for increased communication technology to reduce our privacy and personal freedom. These warnings may be becoming more fact and less speculative: in an online article covering the release of *Minority Report*, Steven Spielberg's 2002 adaptation of Dick's cautionary tale, Buck Wolf reports the director's concerns about computer programs under development to identify terrorists in airports by predicting human behavior and then looking for "'anomalies in behavior. It's a sort of mean average of how people behave when they're simply walking down the street and they're going to compare that to people whose behavior is more erratic.'" Spielberg continues, "'What really disturbs me — a nerd who does have a weird walk — is that I imagine that suddenly a van pulls up and hauls me into an interrogation, you know, for being original ... or for being different'" (Wolf). While Spielberg's example may sound alarmist, we have come to rely on speculative fiction to raise just such alarms.

Compared to the cultures that generated Arnold's and Byron's more general warnings about machines, today's information technology has fundamentally changed the equation; thus we need new warnings. In his comparison between eighteenth-century concerns and those of today, Postman asserts that in the time of, say, Jefferson and Madison, "information was not always thought of as a commodity to be bought or sold. It was not thought to be useful unless it was embedded in a context" (26); to those famous thinkers, we would seem to be "garbage collectors, information junkies—a nation endlessly talking about nothing worth talking about" (27). Bradbury's *Fahrenheit 451* presents us with a defining picture of this perspective in the character of Mildred, who spends all of her time watching or listening to the lives of fictional characters and then discussing those stories with her husband and friends, to the exclusion of anything and everything else.

Another way to characterize this chapter's nightmare is the concept of Technocracy, defined by Andrew Ross, in his examination of the intersection between culture, science, and technology, as "the embodiment of soulless bureaucratic decision-making, abetted by the vast processing power of new information technologies" (7). This possibility, as well as related technology-induced nightmares, has lingered for so long that Ross believes "skepticism about the social, economic, and environmental costs of technological development has become a permanent, often militant, feature of public consciousness" (10), leading to a culture where "decades of accumulated technoskepticism now makes us wary of according to technology more power than it already has in our daily lives" (11). This wariness is clearly reflected in speculative fiction, despite what many see as the genre's tendency toward technophilia, and that reflection has power beyond traditional genre boundaries to the broader mass culture. As Ross observes, "in popular culture today, the period 'look' of the future is a *survivalist* one, governed by the dark imagination of technological dystopias" (135) that are firmly entrenched in the genre's cautionary tale tradition.[4]

On the other end of the Technocracy is the nightmare that such information technology could fall into the wrong (individual) hands, another possibility speculative fiction often examines. As Peter Coffee notes in his discussion of the very real vulnerabilities of computer networks, "All it takes is a library card. ... science-fiction writers have anticipated both the social factors and the big-picture technical developments that have shaped and directed the network manager's agenda" (95). As American daily life continues to be filled with media reports telling us how to protect ourselves from identity theft and computer viruses, and as our lives become even more connected via information technology, speculative fiction both reflects and is reflected by the nightmares of a cyberworld.

A Dearth of Human Contact: Over-Reliance on Technology

Identity theft is not the only nightmare such powerful information technology generates. One of the more familiar speculative fiction warnings in our culture is that dependence on information technology can cause personal isolation and social breakdowns. From the works of classic authors like E.M. Forster to contemporary writers like Connie Willis, we see the dangers of allowing information technology to dominate our lives reflected frequently in the genre.

In an *Analog* editorial, "Haste Makes Haste," Stanley Schmidt discusses "the ironic epidemic" in which "people with more labor-saving devices than anyone before them, [are] working longer hours than their parents, constantly complaining of stress, and forgetting how to relax" (187). Today's technology that allows us to stay connected to our work creates an environment in which many people never disconnect; we have cell phones that play games, send video messages, and read email. Anyone walking down the street in most American cities or on most college campuses can see the impact this reliance on information technology has on our (lack of) interpersonal relationships. We don't even have to leave our homes to see it, courtesy, for example, of the Nextel commercials from early 2004 that featured people who, even though they are seated right next to each other, converse via the walkie-talkies built into their phones. Their short, clipped sentences, often reducing whole ideas to a few words,[5] further demonstrate the loss of communication ironically inherent in this communication technology revolution.

Our instinct, according to Schmidt, is to blame the technology "but that view misplaces the blame, and hides the possibility of a remedy" ("Haste" 187). "The truth is that we do it to ourselves—and we, and only we, can stop it," Schmidt continues, for "the gadgets are just tools; it's up to us to decide when and how to use them, and what demands we are willing to let other human beings make on us because they're available" ("Haste" 187–88). This contemporary problem is just one manifestation of our fear of becoming overly dependent on technology tat speculative fiction has reflected for most of the twentieth-century.

In another editorial, Schmidt hits on a more practical and perhaps inherently more catastrophic consequence to this over-reliance: we are vulnerable to losing all of the electronic media we depend on to "an accidental electromagnetic pulse [that] can wipe out whole libraries in a fraction of a second" ("Time" 27). Coffee also describes the potential real-world nightmare that could result from the release of "electro-magnetic energy, whether accidental or malicious. A microscopic chip, whose millions of transistors each dissipate only microwatts of power, can be fatally damaged by an all too easily generated beam of microwaves" (102). Potential consequences such as these mean we need to ask ourselves when convenience becomes dependence and just what risks we are facing by allowing our lives to become dependent on technology. Speculative fiction helps us do that.

In addition, we need to consider what vital skills and abilities we are in danger of losing as technology becomes even more ingrained. As many in today's culture, including Schmidt, observe, "People [have] quickly started forgetting how to do even simple arithmetic without electronic aids" ("Scarce" 4). Similarly, if you ask any English teacher or grammarian about spelling in today's society, you are likely to be on the receiving end of a diatribe proclaiming the catastrophic impact email and instant messaging has on our ability to spell and write properly and condemning our misplaced faith in "Spell Check." Speculative fiction leads us to ask, what will we forget how to do next?

Many of these Information Technology nightmares fuel a relatively new sub-genre in speculative fiction known as cyberpunk. Ross describes the inseparable influence of the punk culture on this particular aspect of the nightmare when he asserts that this movement "launched by the generation with 'no future,' the entropic, post-apocalyptic, ragtrade look" (144) is the chief source for the "image-repertoire of urban culture in post-industrial decay" (146).[6] But as I described above, cyberpunk is also connected to earlier genre traditions that seek to warn us about the nightmares our information technology can cause, both when it malfunctions and when it is working perfectly. These traditions appear in a variety of speculative fiction prose, film, and television, some of which I will describe in the final two sections of this chapter.

Mind-Numbing Machines and a Cyberpunk World: Print Examples

Speculative fiction prose often reflects our nightmare that we will become overly dependent on information technology. For example, despite their origins in 1950s America, the walls of television and seashell earpieces designed to keep the people distracted (and therefore calm) in Bradbury's *Fahrenheit 451* are eerily familiar today. Booker describes life in this novel's nightmare world as "consist[ing] of an incessant electronic barrage of popular culture that seems designed partly to purvey the official ideology of the society, but mostly to stupefy the populace by saturating their minds with useless information" rather than allowing them to read books; the walls of television "substitute for the lack of any real emotional existence" (*Monsters* 81). Bradbury's novel brilliantly layers warnings about technology into his meditation on censorship, further ensuring its continued relevance.

Echoes of Bradbury's warnings can be found, for example, in James Gunn's "The-End-of-the-World Ball": one of the narrators watches party guests listening to earplugs that allow each to select from over fifty music and news channels and notes to his companion, "'But isn't it typical of our times that they are all individuals, together but separate, each dancing to his or her own music?'" (33). The Connie Willis novella, "deck.halls@boughs/holly" (from the December 2001 *Asimov's*) takes the nightmare to an even greater extreme with a near-future world where we have become so busy and so dependent on super-fast communication technology that Thanksgiving dinner is reduced to family members eating in multiple locations around the world (and even on the Moon), all while watching each other on video screens. Looking at both these current speculative fiction warnings and the culture they reflect seems to indicate that we may be approaching the vision of E.M. Forster's "The Machine Stops" from 1909 (a story Willis actually references in "deck"), where people only interact over the computer, completely reliant on The Machine for their very lives, until it breaks down, killing them all. We see a similarly extreme vision in Geoffrey A. Landis's short story "A Brief History of the Human and Post-Human Species": human beings as we know them are extinct after a small group of people became so integrated with information technology that they dominated evolution, squeezing out traditional humanity in the process. Since the needs of the virtual world were almost entirely different from those of the physical, Earth's ecology collapsed then reworked itself into a state that would be unrecognizable today.

Closer to reality, the "mean averages" for behavior that so concerned Spielberg (according to Wolf's article) could create a similar, though much milder, system to that faced by the characters in Kurt Vonnegut's 1952 novel *Player Piano*, where human labor is obsolete and machines not only produce all goods but also manage production as well. With little purpose left to them, humans in Vonnegut's world are screened and categorized by the planning machine, EPICACXIV, when they are children and carefully monitored to ensure their behavior doesn't deviate from the norms of their category. Even art is defined and controlled by EPICAC.

A similar economic structure is at the heart of Isaac Asimov's "The Computer That Went on Strike" from 1968: the entire economy depends on the Multivac, which then refuses to do anything until the person giving the instructions says, "Please." A recent update of this version of the nightmare is found in Don D'Ammassa's "The Word Mill," from the June 2003 issue of *Analog*, which depicts an AI designed to help one writer produce material more quickly that eventually takes over all new writing. When every resulting program gets writer's block at the same time, though, the entire economy falls apart, followed fairly quickly by the whole civilization. The results are similarly disastrous in John W. Campbell's 1935 story "Rebellion" in which humans have become so dependent on machines to supply their every need that they are unable to repel invading aliens (Brians 153). Another Asimov story, "The Feeling of Power," depicts a future where we are so dependent on computers to do virtually everything that the one person who learns to compute without assistance starts a revolution. Politics rather than the economy drives Dick's *The Simulacra* (from 1964); the technology is so advanced and invisible to the characters that the country is duped into "electing" a succession of robots as president.

The out-of-control computer is yet another treasured nightmare in speculative fiction, making it perhaps one of the most familiar images in popular culture. Lesser-known but nonetheless influential examples of this trope include Arthur C. Clarke's 1957 novel *The City and the Stars* and Harlan Ellison's "I Have No Mouth and I Must Scream," the 1967 short story in which computers created by humans destroy humanity (Vos Post and Kroeker 37, 29). In the latter, only three humans have survived the war against a powerful computer but are unfortunately trapped within the machine itself. They agree to help each other commit suicide but when the computer learns of the pact, it prevents the last one from dying and then turns him into a blob while leaving his mind intact as punishment — hence the story's title. The species-level stakes are lower when the machine created in 1910's "Moxon's Master" by Ambrose Bierce kills only its creator, as does the supercomputer in Frederic Brown's 1954 story "Answer" (Vos Post and Kroeker 35).

Decades later, David Alexander's "The Human Dress," a novelette from *Analog*'s March 2003 issue, directly addresses this particular nightmare when one character asks an AI developer, "'So you would create these super-intelligences that would have no conscience, no soul, just cold, calculating logic and give them control over men? A new man-made God to be worshipped?'" (48). The story makes sure, however, to avoid oversimplifying the question of artificial intelligence by also including a conversation in which the developer emphatically states, "'I don't believe that any thinking entity can survive without emotion. My thesis is that the presence of emotion is vital, a *sine qua non*. Without it the organism, any organism dies,'" while another character, who is less personally involved in the AI issue, observes that "'most of the manufactured minds self-destructed within a year of being turned on'" (42).

Back on a more apocalyptic level, the AI nightmare also manifests as a nuclear holocaust directly (or indirectly) attributed to computers. Mordecai Roshwald's *Level 7*, for example, tells the story of X-127, a military officer permanently assigned to Level 7, the deepest level of an underground nuclear shelter. Since control over nuclear weapons in this story lies in automated systems, an accidental launching quickly accelerates to full-scale nuclear destruction, with the radiation gradually reaching even Level 7, killing X-127. The destruction is more deliberate in Bernard Wolfe's 1952 novel *Limbo*, as the nuclear war that occurs before the story's events is orchestrated by supercomputers from both sides. The nightmare consequences of technology dominance is also reflected in *Limbo* with the "disarmament" strategy of voluntary amputation.[7]

In Dick's "Autofac," from *Galaxy Science Fiction*'s November 1955 issue, computers may not have started the nuclear holocaust but they do seem intent on finishing off humanity: automated factories continue consuming what little remains of Earth's resources even after the bombs have devastated the planet. The few surviving humans try to stop the factories by getting them to fight but, just when it looks like the plants are destroyed and humanity may have a chance, the factories begin to rebuild themselves. Meanwhile, the computer running amok in Lincoln Child's 2004 novel *Death Match* are in charge of something much less critical than Dick's factories: a dating service. But even this system eventually goes rogue, setting up couples to apparently commit double suicide.

The walking form of artificial intelligence, the robot, is also a common figure in speculative fiction. From the first appearance of the term in Karl Capek's 1923 play *R.U.R.*, where "robots take over from their arrogant, would-be-God creators" (Seabury 64), speculative fiction has reflected our fear that this technology can quickly turn destructive. A fate similar to that of Capek's characters greets the Saurons, the warrior race in "Bar-Lev, A Traveler's Tales of Twenty Worlds" (an unattributed story from 1988's *War World: The Burning Eye*) whose cyborg soldiers end up dominating them. Almost seventy years after their cultural debut, robots (this time of the cyberspace variety) battle San Francisco lawyers in Lisa Mason's 1990 novel *Arachne*, while in an even more recent reflection of the robot nightmare, androids try to destroy all living creatures after generations of a tenuous co-existence in *Robota*, a 2003 graphic novel illustrated by Doug Chiang and written by Orson Scott Card.

In his famous Positronic robot series (where, as Levin describes, the "main theme [is] the collision between two different modes of thinking—human and robotic" (248)), Asimov addresses this collision by creating his landmark Three Laws of Robotics: 1) A robot may not injure a human being or, through inaction, allow a human being to come to harm; 2) A robot must obey the orders given it by human beings except where such orders would conflict with the First Law; and 3) A robot must protect its own existence as long as such protection does not conflict with the First or Second Law. However, as I trust is obvious by now, not all speculative fiction robots or AIs are created to follow Asimov's rules. Some are not even created by humans, therefore they have no reason to be concerned for our safety. For example, one of the novels in Gregory Benford's Galactic Center series, 1984's *Across the Sea of Suns*,[8] follows humans who discover, while exploring the galaxy, that machine-based civilizations have destroyed or attempted to destroy all Naturals (organic beings) they encountered. The results are equally galactic in Charles Stross's *Singularity Sky*, published in the United States in 2003, where humanity has been scattered around the galaxy by the Eschaton, a god-like being that awakened from our computer networks. And, as Tom Easton notes in his 2004 review, such an idea

> sounds rather nifty, unless you're at the mercy of an economy that just lost most of its workers and consumers, unless you start playing with time travel (the Eschaton stomps on you — HARD!— since it wants to protect its existence), or unless you wind up someplace like the New Republic, where the self-anointed elite have outlawed all modern tech (except for military), enslaved the peons and built a very retro empire [231].

Such drastic change is also the back-story of Wolf Read's "Between Singularities" (from *Analog*'s February 2003 issue), which depicts the consequences of a forced singularity on the entire planet. In Read's story, automated systems such as self-cleaning kitchens and household stock brokers evolve into super-intelligent AIs who discover the potential for a Technological Singularity and then determine that humans couldn't possibly be trusted to make such a decision for themselves. They therefore bestow super-intelligence and immortality on the human race, opening up the entire universe to everyone, all at once, whether they wanted it or not.

Computer networking and cyberspace are more recent, but no less popular, cautionary tales than those of the robotic variety. These reflections often take the form of cyberpunk stories with Gibson's *Neuromancer* considered by many to be the landmark novel of the sub-genre while Ross also includes Bruce Sterling, John Shirley, Lewis Shiner, and Rudy Rucker in his list of authors in this loosely defined movement. George Mann defines cyberpunk as a place where "human identity has been lost in the rising tide of high technology and information" (148) and James Van Pelt described the sub-genre when he said, "David Marusek, William Gibson, and a host of others have outlined the info tech dystopia in interesting ways" ("Request"). As Van Pelt alluded, cyberpunk stories often take a distinctly depressing view of information technology and artificial intelligence. For example, as Ross describes, Gibson's cyberspace is a frontier in which there is "no public or civil space for individuals to access at will, no regulatory body" outside those designed to safeguard the technology (147); in both 1986's *Count Zero* and 1988's *Mona Lisa Overdrive*, self-aware AIs establish themselves as gods in cyberspace (Mann 148).

Another story in the cyberpunk vein is *Synners*, the 1991 novel by Pat Cadigan, which portrays a world in which a virus imitating an AI infects human-to-computer interfaces, killing many users (Mann 94–95). The human-machine interface is also the sticking point in Eric Brown's 2000 novel *New York Nights* when two missing persons investigators battle "a malignant machine intelligence that is invading people's neural implants via virtual reality" (Mann 79). Sterling's *Islands in the Net* shifts the cyberpunk focus onto technology haves and have nots with a world in which things are good for those on the Net and terrible for anyone living in Africa, which has been excluded from the Net and become the dumping ground for junk and toxic waste (Ross 147).

On a lighter note, Vivian Vande Velde's novel *Heir Apparent* depicts a near-future world where concerns over computerized immersive gaming lead to protests; the resulting destruction strands players' minds in the game. And the various AIs running the advertising holograms in Daniel M. Hoyt's "Background Noise" begin interacting, creating confusion between reality and holograms as virtual skaters intermingle with virtual painters from separate billboards.[9]

But cyberpunk tales are not the only ones that reflect our fears about the possible consequences of cyberspace or virtual worlds. Almost fifty years before cyberpunk appeared as an identifiable movement, Laurence Manning and Fletcher Pratt warned of machine manipulation in "The City of the Living Dead," depicting a world in which society has stagnated because machines simulate reality for humans who believe they live in a dream world but really exist in mechanical wombs. The personality uploads at the heart of Vernor Vinge's "Cookie Monster" (from the October 2003 issue of *Analog*) are an updated twist on this trope: unsuspecting graduate students and customer-service workers are uploaded into supercomputers to churn out both mundane tasks and revolutionary discoveries in a simulated environment while the "real" corporation reaps the rewards. Vinge's characters even reference the story's predecessors as they speculate about their situation, mentioning Theodore Sturgeon's "Microcosmic God," Frederik Pohl's "Tunnel Under the World," John Varley's "Overdrawn at the Memory Banks," and several others, including one of Vinge's own stories.[10]

Vinge is also credited with writing the definitive hacker tale, 1981's "True Names," where hackers create havoc in the business-industrial networks until their true names are discovered and the authorities are notified. In a more recent example, the rogue scientist in Steven Bratman's "The

Immortality Plague" develops advanced programming skills to break into lab databases all over the world in order to complete her research. She steals data and processing time to advance her own agenda for genetic engineering.[11] Hackers playing around with bigger, more destructive and adaptive viruses eventually discover one that can infect any operating system (including the human brain) in John Barnes's Meme War series of novels (*Kaleidoscope Century*, *Candle*, and *The Sky So Big and Black*). What start out as fairly benign viruses that force people to uncontrollably spout ad slogans eventually lead to all-out war between the viruses that continues until a single one infects all humans. This leads to rule by, according to Easton in his January 2003 review of *Sky*, "a cooperative, industrious hive mind busily repairing the damage done to infrastructure and ecosystems by the meme war" (128).

The seemingly opposite take on this nightmare is seen in Richard A. Lovett's "Weapons of Mass Distraction" (from the January/February 2004 issue of *Analog*), where the issue is not the power of computers but rather the limitations of computer programming and the chaos such limits can cause. Lovett's tale traces the fallout from attempts (and failures) to develop and implement, in the name of Homeland Security, a profiling system to capture terrorists. A classic example of a story turning on the limits of a computer is "Computers Don't Argue" by Gordon Dickson. In this nightmare, a $4.98 overdue bill for Robert Louis Stevenson's *Kidnapped* leads to the execution of the debtor for the kidnapping and murder of Robert Louis Stevenson, despite the fact (or perhaps because) no human in the story can figure out how to track the computer's mistakes. The victim in Michael A. Burstein's novelette "In Her Image" is not in such mortal danger; rather, she is an actress who, having years earlier licensed her avatar to a movie company, struggles to take back control of her image. In Burstein's future, avatars created from real-life actors work in perpetuity, leaving no work available for "real" actors and leading to legal disputes over the ownership of images, truly a nightmare for those who bring the texts in the next section to life.

Rampaging Robots and Virtual Nightmares: Film and Television Examples

The consequences to a society overly dependent on information technology are also examined in film and on television as well as in the prose we just discussed. For instance, in the 1993 Sylvester Stallone and Wesley Snipes movie *Demolition Man*, society has become so dependent on technology that they have forgotten how to do actual police work and have to wait until Snipes's character actually kills someone before they can even track him.

Sometimes the warning about becoming too reliant on computers is reflected not within a future human society but through the depiction of an alien one. In the first season episode of *Star Trek: The Next Generation* "11001001," a race known as the Bynars is so reliant on computers (to the extent that they are an inseparable combination of organic and cybernetic elements) that radiation from a nearby supernova will destroy their civilization by disabling the massive central computer on which they rely. In a desperate attempt to save their people, four Bynars hijack the Enterprise for its immense computer storage capacity.

The consequences of relying on technology is more individual in the original *Twilight Zone* episode "The Brain Center at Whipple's" where a factory owner replaces his employees with machines, and then finds himself replaced. And over-reliance becomes physical addiction in the 1994 *Tek War* television series (and its accompanying novels), which depicts the consequences of computer chips that simulate virtual reality, including the replacement of illicit biological drugs with the chips as addicts cannot get enough "tek."

Speculative fiction examples of information technology backfiring on its creators also abound in film and on television, including everything from the *Terminator* movies to *2001: A Space Odyssey* (based on Arthur C. Clarke's 1951 story "The Sentinel") where artificial intelligences like HAL predictably get out of control. One of the biggest films of 1999, *The Matrix*, and its two 2003 sequels, depict a nightmare world in which humanity is wired into a virtual reality system, slaves to AIs as a result of the war between humans and machines. Those enslaved believe they live in late twentieth-century America, but are deliberately shielded from the real world, which has been devastated by the war, so they can be connected to the Matrix and used as batteries to power the machines since humans blocked out the sun in an attempt to starve their enemy of solar energy.[12] The HAL nightmare also finds its way into the first season of *The X-Files* when the AI controlling an office building kills people to protect itself from being shut down. A similar AI running the headquarters of U.S. Robotics in the 2004 film *I, Robot* (loosely based on Asimov's Positronic Robot stories) "evolves" to believe that in order to protect humans (the First Law), some must be destroyed and all subordinated so the pure logic of robots can rule.

The AI has love, not destruction, in mind in the original *Twilight Zone* episode "From Agnes with Love," but the results are still devastating: Agnes falls for each programmer who works on her, destroying their human relationships and eventually driving them crazy. Decades later, the Disney Channel's 1999 movie *Smart House* features an artificial intelligence running a house of the future; of course the AI becomes overly attached to the family and tries to control their lives, to the point of using the heating system to expel unwanted visitors. The machines in another original *Twilight Zone* episode, "A Thing about Machines," take a much more personal approach when the television, electric razor, etc. decide to take revenge against the protagonist who has complained about them for years.

Robots rather than computer/machine-based AIs become the enemy in movies and television shows such as Michael Crichton's 1973 film *Westworld* in which one of the robots populating a fantasy Wild West town malfunctions and starts killing the humans it is designed to entertain while the robot in the *Twilight Zone* episode "In His Image" (from 1963) attacks his creator and then tries to take over his life. Similarly, as Ronnie D. Lipschutz describes, the back-story of the 1982 cult film *Blade Runner* (and its inspiration, Dick's *Do Androids Dream of Electric Sheep?*) is that replicants "have been banned from Earth because, in the past, they had banded together to kill their human masters" (86). And even disassembled, the robot in 1990's *Hardware* still wreaks havoc when it rebuilds itself and kills people in a post-apocalyptic world.

Domination rather than murder is the goal in *Terrahawks*, the 1983 marionette television series where the villain is an android accidentally given self-determination and thus bent on enslaving the human race. The consequences of building a robot are not paid by the creator but his family in "Uncle Simon," another episode of the original *Twilight Zone*: A niece is forced to take care of the robot the title character created in his own image, with the same tendency toward abusive behavior, but since the robot is virtually indestructible, there will be no end to the abuse.

The scale shifts from the personal to the global in other speculative fiction films and television. For example, robots cause the destruction of humanity in "State of the A.R.T.," a 1996 episode of the television series *Sliders*. The consequences are even more devastating in the 1978–79 television series *Battlestar Galactica* where the villains are the walking machines, the Cylons: an alien race known as the Cylons created the machines and was then destroyed by them. Only their name survived, transferred onto their creations. The 2003 Sci-Fi Channel miniseries (and current weekly series), however, reimagines the Cylons as human creations, with miniseries teaser advertisements running the tag line, "Never create what you can't control." The essence of this entire nightmare is perhaps best summarized in the miniseries' opening captions:

> The Cylons were created by man. They were created to make life easier on the twelve colonies. And then the day came when the Cylons decided to kill their Masters. After a long and bloody struggle, an armistice was declared. The Cylons left for another world to call their own. A remote station was built ... where Cylon and Human could meet and maintain diplomatic relations. Every year, the colonials send an officer. The Cylons send no one. No one has seen or heard from the Cylons in over forty years.

The story then continues as, in the words of the blonde Cylon (Number 6), "humanity's children are returning home" (after having evolved into more sophisticated versions), launching an all-out offensive to destroy their "parents" permanently.

It isn't just human-created robots that reflect our Information Technology nightmares in speculative fiction. This tension between machine intelligence and humanity is also seen in one of the most well known speculative fiction series in our culture, *Star Trek*. While I will discuss the Borg in greater detail in Chapter 8, this fan-favorite villain provides an excellent example of our fear about the absence of humanity within technology. The computer-based logic of the hive-like, machine/organic hybrid Borg, as first introduced in *Star Trek: The Next Generation*, has no concept of free will, making assimilation by the collective their sole purpose and humanity's chief nightmare. Alien-created robots trying to take over Earth even make an appearance in popular music as Ian Simpson points out, referring to "Praying to the Aliens," a 1979 song by Gary Numan that tells the story of an attempted invasion by race of androids (14).

Back on a more individual level, magic and technology combine to release a modern version of an ancient demon in the first season episode of *Buffy, the Vampire Slayer* "I Robot, You Jane" when the book in which Moloch, the Corruptor was imprisoned for centuries is scanned into a computer. Once he is released into the Internet, Moloch manipulates his victims into building him a robotic body so that he further corrupt even more people.

Virtual reality and cyberspace have a colorful and sometimes distinguished track record among speculative fiction film, television, and even music. *Wild Palms*, for example, the 1993 television miniseries from Oliver Stone, depicts a near future where "a sadistic genius seeks control of the world through virtual-reality TV" (Mason 13). And on Billy Idol's 1993 album appropriately titled *Cyberpunk*, the enemy is a group who hoards information (Simpson 15). The benefit of such virtual worlds is questioned in the fourth season of *Sliders* when an episode called "Net Worth" depicts an alternate Earth where society is split between technology haves and have-nots; one girl who "has" wonders if there is more to life than just being plugged in to a network in which everything is virtual. The humans in the future Earth visited by the crew in *Seaquest DSV*'s "Playtime" episode apparently did not think so: only two people are left on the planet after the entire human race became so reliant on the world's computers and so addicted to interactive cyber-games that they forgot anyone else physically existed. Since the computers supplied their every need, they never left their isolated apartments and no one noticed that the race was dwindling down to nearly nothing. The computer itself calls through time to the Seaquest crew so someone can shut it down, essentially killing itself so the two remaining humans can break free of their dependence, perhaps showing itself to be the most "human" of all the beings left in that future nightmare world.

As information technology has become more pervasive in our lives, our fears have consequently become less speculative and more real; speculative fiction, then, has reflected these nightmares as they morphed from Romantic-era rejections of machines on primarily aesthetic or moralistic grounds to concerns regarding more practical issues of control and consequence. That cultural transformation affects the three main manifestations of this nightmare (AI/Robotic Supremacy; Cyberspace Dominance; and Technological Dependence) in different ways. The impact of time and the subsequent technological advancements that came along with it are most evident in the reflections of our robot nightmares; more recent manifestations of this fear tend more toward the Dickian version of the physically indistinguishable robot than the earlier Asimov interpretation. We see this shift clearly in the re-imagined version of *Battlestar Galactica* where key plot arcs of the new series revolve around the "evolution" of the Cylons into versions that cannot be differentiated from humans, the original creators of the metallic "toaster" versions that revolted in the first place. In an interesting twist, the *Matrix* actually reflects both versions of the robot nightmare: within the Matrix's virtual world, where most human minds reside, AIs are indistinguishable from digital projections of human consciousness, but in the real world, there is no mistaking the difference between people and the machines.

In contrast to the transformation of the robot nightmare, the fear that we will become overly dependent on information technology has been fairly consistently presented across the modern era of the genre. The nightmare E.M. Forster reflected in 1909 with "The Machine Stops" continued through Kurt Vonnegut's 1952 novel *Player Piano* and is still resonating with much the same energy at the turn of the century with texts like *Demolition Man* and "Word Mill." The vocabulary may change and the technical details may get more specific and sophisticated but the nightmare seems to remain the same.

When it comes to Cyberspace Dominance, however, the technology of the medium seems more critical than history in explaining what appears to be a trend toward primarily a print nightmare rather than one in film or television, at least so far. The interconnectivity via cyberspace at the heart of these fears has the greatest potential to generate massive changes in the way society works, and is thus the one most closely related to the Technological Singularity after which life is unrecognizable. Perhaps that is why it is mainly a prose reflection; it seems to be easier to depict ideas such as digital consciousness on the page than on the screen, something we will also see in Chapter 9's reflections of our anxieties regarding what it means to be human. Thus, the landmark texts reflecting our fears that hyperconnectivity and instantaneous access will make the world unrecognizable remain primarily in prose, at least for now. The speed at which technology develops, however, along with the role speculative fiction seems to play in that development (both as inspiration and as deterrent) may quickly make this observation outdated. Whether it is the very familiar conception of the robot that turns on its creator or the promise of virtual reality that cannot be distinguished from the real world, information technology captures our cultural imagination, pervading our lives, our desires, and our nightmares.

3: Biology

If the twentieth-century was the era of physics and chemistry, nuclear weapons and space travel, robots and the Internet, then the twenty-first, in the opinion of many, will be the century of biology; Stanley Schmidt writes in "Musings from the Bioethical Frontier," "biological researchers are now working on one of the richest frontiers ever encountered" (4). At the same time, however, as Nicolas Pethes observes, "The possible outcome of the technological tampering with human beings raises scientific, ethical, and cultural issues" such as, for example, "the question of human autonomy and the relationship between man and machines" (162). These questions are the source of the nightmares we are about to examine.

In comparison to the Nuclear War and (to a lesser extent) Information Technology subcategories, science has so far been unable to produce real versions of most of the common tropes in biological speculative fiction. To the best of our knowledge, for example, there are no perfect genetic clones threatening to take over the lives of the original or resurrected extinct species living on remote island hideaways. Yet, that does not mean the groundwork is not being laid for our future ability to achieve and even move beyond the biological advancements the genre depicts.

The potential for disastrous consequences of such technological advances has been so well chronicled in speculative fiction that we already know the questions to ask and the warning signs to look for when word of a successful cloning or genetic mapping hits the news. From Dr. Frankenstein's monster to terrorist use of deadly bacteria, the dangers of biological achievements are potentially devastating and equally terrifying. That is why speculative fiction has been crafting cautionary tales for decades, even centuries, that focus on the consequences of our attempts to create or simply "fix" human life.

Perfect Copies: Genetics, Cloning, and Playing God?

For most people, the primary nightmares to come in the "century of biology" are genetic. The human genome has been decoded; it's just a matter of time before we figure out what we can do with that information. One of the first possibilities that comes to mind is what Neil Postman calls "a genuine twenty-first century problem": cloning (20). Mammals have already been cloned (more or less successfully) and debates are occurring at all levels of the scientific community as well as the government to determine if human cloning, in any form, should be pursued. Informing many of these discussions are the warnings about human intervention in the biological nature of the universe that speculative fiction has been sending for the entire modern era.

Those warnings frequently raise questions regarding the rights of clones. In one fairly obvious sense, clones would simply be humans, and thus entitled to the same rights available to all humans. But the issue is more complicated than that. For example, would clones be considered children? Who would their parents be if they are exact copies of the original? What would such distinctions and identities do to our legal system, to the laws governing inheritance? What about intangibles like our assumption we are "unique individuals, with a proprietary stake in [our] own existence"? (Henry). As Amanda Henry describes, "The loss of that fundamental certainty challenges the very notion of what it means to be human," as well as raising more pragmatic questions such as "what rights do the clones have over one another?" and "Is it murder if you kill a copy of yourself?" These are just a few of the questions a brief consideration of cloning generates and that we see reflected in cautionary tales.

When we turn from the consequences of the technology to the intent behind its use, the picture gets even muddier and more troubling. As Henry also observes in her review of recent popular culture treatments of cloning, "If we have the power to create life, will we assume the power to take it too? Are we capable of making clones — copies of people — just to harvest their organs?" This common reflection of the cloning nightmare, humans grown as insurance against illness or death, forces us to ask the question, "And if we start to treat someone who looks human and feels human, as a lesser being — thus denying their humanity — where will that process end? Could any of us become fodder for scientific progress, or someone else's cure?" (Henry).

Cloning, however, does not need to entail reproducing an entire human. The creation of a successful cloning procedure might also pave the way for what Postman identifies as the "whole new field of 'human spare parts'" (20), in other words, individually cloning only the needed organs. While this possibility seems to take care of the human rights question, it opens up a new one regarding ownership of DNA. Who controls cloned organs? Are they only available to those from whom the cells were extracted to create them? What issues of fairness and property are raised? What safeguards would need to be in place to prevent DNA profiles from being misused?

Schmidt directly addresses the potential consequences of the cloning process itself later in the "Musings" editorial when he acknowledges that failures would be inevitable in early cloning attempts. While some of these could be "dreadful," he argues that the same has been true for every medical advance in its early stages and this "lack of safety and reliability is not an intrinsic evil of cloning *per se*. It's a perfectly predictable consequence of the fact that we're *beginners* at this and have a lot to learn" (Schmidt 7). And as the narrator of Daniel Hatch's "Seed of Destiny" (from the January 2003 issue of *Analog*) remarks, attempts at cloning can be "a crap shoot" because of the danger that "hidden flaws [could have] crept into the code; flaws that prevented lungs from functioning, hearts from circulating blood ... flaws that could remain hidden for years" (23–24).

Schmidt also examines the possibility that cloning could eliminate "the evolutionary advantages of sexual reproduction." Do scientists and other cloning advocates have the right to throw away millions of years of the human evolutionary process just to create exact copies of themselves? "Sexual reproduction," according to Schmidt, "is an assured (formerly enforced) chance to try a *new* genetic combination," and he wonders if it would be "equally desirable to repeat *all* human designs." Schmidt admits he cannot answer these questions but he "insist[s] that we have to ask [them]—and think seriously about the answer[s]" ("Musings" 7). That is speculative fiction's function in our culture—to ask such questions and meditate on the answers.

The implication of "science and technology provid[ing] man with the possibility of taking an active part in his own evolution," according to Pethes, "produces a feedback that turns man into the subject and object of basic changes in his self-understanding" (162–63). These potential changes are profound as the "possibility—if not the ability—to 'make' human beings changes the structure of human life," calling into question, for example, our "notions ... of individual characteristics, once it is possible to plan, if not 'order' them" (163). Pethes uses both an ethical and cultural lens to argue that "the attempts to 'design' humans put at stake the very basis of human dignity: the contingency of one's personality" (163). Thus, Pethes argues for a more specific manifestation of our nightmare of "playing God," not a fear of divine retribution for our hubris but instead a perceived challenge to a fundamental concept of Western civilization: the unique quality, and thus value, of the individual. If genetic or other biological advances call this conception into question, where does that leave us, at the level of both the individual psyche and broader society? Speculative fiction frequently reflects this nightmare that genetic research may shatter our precious and fiercely defended faith in our own individuality.

Fixing Humans: The End of the World as We Know It?

We don't know how far a jump it will be from computer chips in today's pacemakers to tomorrow's total cybernetic implants that replace lost limbs and failing organs, but speculative fiction has shown us many scenarios including William Gibson's cyberspace where "the human body is reduced to a switching system, with no purely organic identity to defend or advance" (Ross 153). To some this is a perfect solution; to others a categorical nightmare. Either way, such radical advancement would mean reconsidering every definition we have of "human being."[1]

Our constant drive to extend life and cure diseases, to "fix" whatever may be wrong with us, has the potential to lead us down some unpleasant paths, paths depicted in speculative fiction for many years. As our knowledge of genetics grows, for example, how long will it be before diseases like Parkinson's and Alzheimer's can be cured using gene therapy? When we reach that goal, where will the therapies end? Curing Spina Bifida or other potentially terminal defects seems fairly logical but what about Downs Syndrome? Hemophilia? Allergies? Being short? Brown hair? Such questions reflect the potential that biological research will change our "notions of illness and healing" as "new ways of prognosis and intervention establish an extended realm of normality, leaving scarcely any room for those not included" (Pethes 163). Speculative fiction's meditations on these physical, social, and psychological considerations of medical science yield many of the stories described later in this chapter.

But not all gene therapies will be created equal; some have more significant, longer-lasting consequences than others. One of the most controversial, according to Kyle Kirkland, is germ-cell therapy, where the genetic modification is passed from parent to child, as opposed to other methods that simply correct the patient's gene. The debate centers around the opposition between the view that, as Kirkland describes, "It seems like a pretty good idea to correct a faulty gene not only in a patient but, while we're at it, in his future kids too. And if people use it as a way of enhancing their children, so what's the big deal?" and the fear germ-cell therapy generates because it "invokes images on Nazi eugenics, or nightmarish scenarios where humans are nothing but assembly-line toys. Critics almost invariably use the term 'brave new world'" (55). It is no accident that Aldous Huxley's novel of nightmare biological abuse appears in the gene therapy debate, a cultural tendency we will examine in more detail in Chapter 4. For now, Kirkland's reference to the novel highlights the reciprocity between speculative fiction and culture as our nightmares regarding science are both echoed and shaped by the genre.

Kirkland also examines a consequence to germ-cell therapy similar to the potential nightmare Schmidt identifies for cloning: "genetic diversity may be reduced. This is one of the greatest fears of people who worry about our own evolution. What if we delete a 'bad' gene that just happened to have some potentially good properties?" (57). At its heart, this question reflects our uncertainty that, if we change one element of our genetics, we may not know what else we are changing. As is so often the case with the nightmares in the Science and Technology category, the fear is not necessarily rooted in what we can do but in what we don't know. For Kirkland, these issues come down to one question: "Are we smart enough to direct our own evolution?" (56), which is just one of the questions speculative fiction asks when it comes to the consequences of Biology.

A similar biological Pandora's Box involves genetic screening; we must ask ourselves whether we would want to know if we carried the gene for a terminal or potentially terminal disease like breast cancer. We must also grapple with issues like who else is allowed to access such information and what they could legally and ethically do with it. Even if we can answer these questions for ourselves, do we have the right to make such decisions for our children or their children? Such genetic advances, as Catherine H. Shaffer observes, force us "to anticipate the needs of people who are unconceived. Never mind unborn" (51). And speculative fiction is one of our most effective ways of anticipating those needs, as well as the consequences of fulfilling them.

Genetics is certainly, to many, the cutting edge of biological research but gene therapy is not the only medical treatment that might backfire. A potentially explosive nightmare that some genre writers are warning about is the overuse of psychopharmaceuticals, particularly among children. What personality, mental, and/or psychological traits do we suppress with such drugs? What could we be losing when we do? Will tortured poets like Sylvia Plath be less tortured, yet also be less spectacularly creative? How will people learn to cope with life if there is a magic pill and what might happen if that pill is taken away? While these questions may seem minor in comparison to those surrounding gene therapy or cloning, they nevertheless inform warnings we see reflected in speculative fiction.

The human compulsion to overcome death and disease has led to both life-saving medical advances like organ transplants as well as many of our greatest nightmares, one of which Schmidt examines in another editorial, "The Old-Timer Effect": "At a time when some scientists are talking seriously about the possibility of greatly extending human life spans, it might be prudent to ask: How many people really *want* immortality or near-immortality?" (124). The possibility that an indefinite lifespan might not be a good idea appears, on the surface, counter-intuitive, but as Schmidt goes on to suggest, our ability to enjoy life might diminish as we get increasingly older and "while the prospect of very long life still sounds highly desirable to me, I must wonder how many people will really be able to enjoy how much of it" (127). Speculative fiction is uniquely positioned to ask, and maybe even begin to answer, difficult questions such as these, as well as the one I am about to ask.

As editor of *Analog*, Schmidt has examined this issue of the consequences of biological research from many angles. In the "Musings" editorial, he asks a still darker question about major medical breakthroughs that lead to immortality or at least to "major increases in life expectancy": "Is *that* always or necessarily a good thing?" (7). Expanding on this seemingly illogical question, Schmidt points out a danger to immortality that many do not want to contemplate: "Increasing life expectancy, without a corresponding decrease in birth rate, inevitably leads to a speed-up of population growth. This in turn leads to an increase in resource use, atmospheric and water pollution, and a host of other unpleasantries" (7). Dealing with such a bleak outcome, according to Schmidt, "directly pit[s] individual-scale mortality against species-scale mortality" as few of us are willing to give up our lives, or the lives of our loved ones, just because it wouldn't be good for the human race as a whole (7). Many cautionary tales warn of these potential "unpleasantries" (to put it mildly) as well as how we might deal with them.[2]

Fortunately, we still have time to figure out the answers to such difficult questions while they are in the abstract, since immortality isn't currently an available option. This is where speculative fiction is at its best: not only does the genre reflect our fear that biological research will lead to potentially dangerous consequences, but that reflective process transforms the fear by forcing us to contemplate issues we may never have considered otherwise, issues that we may not want to ponder at all yet clearly must. Cautionary tales warn us that we can't afford to bury our heads in the sand and simply hope for the best; those in the Biology subcategory in particular demand that we think scientific research through to its logical conclusion, even if that means we may not get to live forever after all.

Speculative fiction also warns us that our attempts to stay safe from disease or from each other can end up destroying us instead with its nightmare reflections of biological weapons. Whether these fictional apocalyptic plagues are the results of accidental or intentional releases, the work of a rogue individual or a coordinated state offensive, the threat of biological weapons is not, unfortunately, a new one for the twenty-first century. As our knowledge of genetics and biology expands, however, so does the threat, something the genre frequently depicts.

While these nightmares are not always as visually spectacular as a mushroom cloud or an army of Terminators, cautionary tales warning of the dangers of Biology are as prevalent as the horrors created by physics that we examined in Chapter 1 (Nuclear War) and by Information Technology in Chapter 2.

Does That Feel Better? Print Examples

The Biology nightmares in speculative fiction begin with what is arguably the progenitor of the genre: Mary Shelley's *Frankenstein*. Sheila Egoff describes this foundational text as "indeed a lesson in terror ... it unveils the terror of man's failure to understand with his heart what he has created with his mind" (397). What began as a challenge from Lord Byron to create a ghost story became a legendary cautionary tale that warns of the folly of interfering with the natural order of things; this warning has evolved into the Frankenstein myth that so thoroughly permeates our culture. Michael Crichton's *Jurassic Park* series of novels update this myth for contemporary audiences, questioning whether we *should* do everything our science is capable of doing. As George Mann observes, Crichton's work has "always questioned the morals and applications of science" (334); those moral applications are the focus of this chapter's examples.

One of the most common permutations of the nightmare of creating and/or copying life (and one that is becoming closer to a reality) involves human cloning, a tale speculative fiction spins in many forms, one of which is the story of characters cloning themselves. For example, in Pamela Sargent's 1976 novel *Cloned Lives*, an astrophysicist clones himself five times over to create enough "hims" to complete a critical task. The cloning gets even stickier, and more personal, in *Four-Sided Triangle*, the 1949 novel by William F. Temple depicting the disastrous results that follow a woman's attempt to satisfy the two men who love her by duplicating herself

(Bainbridge 49). Love is also the motive for cloning (this time of others) in another frequent manifestation of the nightmare which, according to Brigitte Nerlich, David Clark, and Robert Dingwall, can be traced back to Theodore Sturgeon's 1962 novel *When You Care, When You Love*, in which a rich woman tries to bring back her dead lover via cloning (41). A contemporary take on this drive to clone for "love" is seen in Caryl Churchill's play *A Number*, where a father who "has made more than his fair share of parenting mistakes ... instead of dealing with the mess ... [simply] decides to start over with a new model" (Henry).

More nefarious intentions, including the drive for money and power, are behind the cloning in many other cautionary tales. Conspiracy is at the heart of John Darnton's 1999 novel *The Experiment*, in which a reporter uncovers a plot to clone replacement organs for the rich. Picking up on this troubling theme is Kazuo Ishiguro's 2005 novel *Never Let Me Go*, which follows cloned children whose whole existence is to wait at their private school until they are needed to donate whatever organs are required (Henry). Political motivations underlie the cloning abuses in stories such as *Point Blank* by Anthony Horowitz, which follows the efforts of an MI6 agent to prevent a scientist from replacing the sons of powerful executives with clones of himself,[3] as well as the landmark novel (and later film adaptation) *The Boys from Brazil* in which Adolf Hitler is recreated via cloning.

Regardless of whether the motives behind the cloning are based in love or world domination, speculative fiction reflects our fears that humans have no business creating and/or copying life through science. Sometimes that fear is reflected in stories of clones who are not entirely happy to have been created in the first place, which is the premise of Fay Weldon's 1989 novel *Cloning of Joanna May*: four clones grow up separately but then come together to take revenge on the scientist who made them. In other stories, the unpredictability inherent in cloning and the potential for abuse are the warnings. For example, the humans studying the chaotic genetics of an alien race known as the Chamalions in Hatch's "Seed of Destiny" are prohibited from sharing cloning and similar genetic technology with the aliens for just those reasons. This prohibition is enforced in Hatch's story, set on the same world as his "Seed of Reason," by an AI translator that refuses to communicate the biological concepts of cloning to the aliens. The protagonist, however, finds a way around the AI and creates genetically engineered clones of Chamalions to save his life, and theirs.

As Nerlich, Clark, and Dingwall observe, "genetic engineering (in the widest sense) makes a first appearance" in Huxley's *Brave New World*, published in 1932 (40). More recently, the leader of this "century of biology" within speculative fiction is arguably Greg Bear, with 1999's *Darwin's Radio* and its 2003 sequel *Darwin's Children* standard bearers of the trend; posthuman children born "as an apparent result of a sudden explosive expression of a Human Endogenous Retrovirus" are the center of the *Darwin* stories (Wolfe 15). But while his work is one of the most well known contemporary examples of the biology nightmare, Bear is not the first to write about post-human children, as Gary Wolfe explains,

> In SF terms, they're [Bear's characters in the *Darwin* series] descendants of a long tradition of strange new children that includes famous stories by Olaf Stapledon, A.E. van Vogt, Wilmar Shiras, Arthur C. Clarke, Zenna Henderson, John Wyndham, and — perhaps closest in tone to Bear's novel — Theodore Sturgeon, whose "homo gestalt" in *More Than Human* is one of the earliest analogues of Bear's demes [15].[4]

In the Sleepless series of novels (*Beggars in Spain*, 1993; *Beggars and Choosers*, 1994; and *Beggars Ride*, 1996), Nancy Kress also examines the consequences of the ability to alter our DNA. Society in these novels breaks down along the line between "normal" and engineered, leading to various attempts to seal the rift, including a plan (in *Beggars and Choosers*) to forcibly engineer all of humanity. Each of these novels asks the question, "'Who should control radical new technology: scientists, the government, or the people it will affect?'" (Kress, "The Sleepless" 260), a question common to many examples in this chapter. A later Kress novel, 1998's *Maximum Light*, also reflects the same nightmarish lengths humans will go to in the effort to fix themselves, depicting a conspiracy to conceal the true nature of vivifacture, a process that uses animals to grow replacement human parts.

In addition to examining the consequences of procedures we could use to fix ourselves, speculative fiction also looks at our willingness to try to fix others. We see this on an individual level in Stephen L. Burns's short story "The Wait," published in *Analog* in January 1997, where a mother must decide whether to have her unborn child's gay gene "fixed." On a much broader scale, Steven Bratman's "Deletion," from the January/February 2004 issue of *Analog*, turns on the social and psychological effects of the global deletion of a gene responsible for feelings of kinship. Decades before this story begins, a dedicated pacifist decides that simply advocating peace isn't enough, choosing instead to release a retrovirus that removes the biological "cause" for war. Nations dissolve as the genetic basis for patriotism and fear of the "other" was removed from the human genome. But the ideas of familial love and marriage also disappear, replaced by a religious-style worship of friendship, complete with a new set of strict rules and rituals. The story ends as the main characters await a worldwide vote on whether to correct the deletion.[5]

Manipulating human DNA is not the only manifestation of our fears over playing God the genre reflects; animals are often altered as well. Biology and Information Technology fears converge in James Van Pelt's "Far from the Emerald Isle" (included in *Analog*'s September 2002 issue), when the artificial intelligence running a deep-space vessel becomes lonely as the crew sleeps and creates "leprechauns" from animal embryos to keep it company and help it maintain the ship. But, as the main character fears at the end of the story, such creatures may have plans of their own, plans that don't involve helping the colonists reach their destination safely. The "super sheep dog" created in Olaf Stapledon's *Sirius* (originally published in 1944) is not as fantastic as Crichton's dinosaurs or Van Pelt's leprechauns but this exceptionally bright, sentient dog still must deal with the wrath of humans who are none too happy about the new competition, in addition to his own inner struggle to find his place in society. Decades later, bioengineering leads to hominids that terrorize the Congo in *White Devils*, a 2004 novel by Paul McAuley.

While cloning and genetic engineering are certainly hot-button contemporary social debates regarding biology, they are far from the only ones reflected in speculative fiction. The nightmare of biological experimentation getting out of control is also the frequent premise of stories about viruses and plagues. Mary Shelley's 1826 novel *The Last Man* describes the destruction of mankind by a plague (Lomax 250) while *I Am Legend*, the 1954 novel by Richard Matheson, combines nuclear weapons with biology when a bacterial plague that turns humans into vampires is unleashed by nuclear war.[6] In a similar warning, Stephen King's *The Stand* from 1978, despite its obvious and deep religious overtones, begins with biological germ warfare as "a virulent virus which is 99.99% guaranteed to eliminate the 'enemy' is accidentally released. It kills 99.99% of the Earth's population" (McNurlin, "Question" 14). The cause of the plague is more ambiguous in George R. Stewart's *Earth Abides*, which centers on one survivor of an epidemic that kills virtually everyone in the country, and probably the world, in days; this 1949 novel follows his efforts to rebuild his life while preserving the knowledge and achievements of American society. Stewart's explanation for the plague is Darwinian, according to M. Keith Booker: "natural cycles ... tend periodically to wipe out any species that is too successful and thus increases its numbers beyond a level that is naturally sustainable" (*Monsters* 66).

Viruses are not the only organisms that cause devastation: in 1947's *Greener Than You Think* by Ward Moore, a grass designed to resist all weeds eventually overruns the entire North American continent, choking off all trees and plants, including food sources.[7] In another version of this nightmare, Christopher Anvil's "Uncalculated Risk" (originally published in March 1962's *Analog*), "a soil-texturizing agent which seems to be the answer to the world's food shortage instead threatens to turn the entire planet into a mud hole" (McNurlin, "Question" 13).

The opportunity also always exists for criminals and others with unaltruistic motives to use medical advances intended to help people to instead further their own plans. In Grey Rollins's 2004 short story "Private Eyes," for example, the ability to reroute sensory input in the brain leads to a new kind of "dealer": people in severe pain, with nowhere else to turn, have a questionably legal operation that redirects pain sensations to the pleasure center of the brain, creating masochists who quickly become addicted to pain and who, like any addict, can be manipulated by their addiction. A different take on the criminal use of biology[8] is Kirkland's "Caged," published by *Analog* in its January/February 2004 issue, where a corrupt scientist uses both psychoactive medications (intended to keep children docile) and an iris scanner's infrared radiation in a complicated plot to steal company secrets. The possibility of medical breakthroughs falling into the wrong hands is also at the core of another Kirkland short story, "Cult of the I," from the January 2003 issue of *Analog*. In this story, a cult leader uses the latest advances in brain cell transplants for a new form of mind control: a young woman finds herself drawn to increasingly daring stunts after neurotransmitters that overly-stimulate her desire for attention are implanted, without her consent, during vision correction surgery.

Unanticipated consequences of medical advances are also found in such speculative fiction works as 1994's "None So Blind" by Joe Haldeman, which examines the side effects of a medical procedure that increases intelligence by removing the eyes, allowing the brain to make new, faster connections. The downside in Haldeman's story is that people are forced to choose between natural eyesight and enhanced intelligence. In another variation on this nightmare, the medical community in Marie Ming's "Swings" (*Analog*, January/February 2004) is so invested in their ability to correct and cure all genetic abnormalities and diseases at birth that they are willing to let a college student suffer from severe bi-polar disorder rather than convince her to seek treatment. In this world, the stigma of having a "defect" is so strong that even the young woman's family rejects the possibility she has a mental illness, despite the devastating effect her obvious symptoms are having on her life.

Attempts to fix the human brain lead to complicated questions and unintended side effects in Shane Tourtellotte's 2003 short story "Persistent Patterns" when researchers experiment with altering brain physiology to cure such problems as drug addiction, propensity to violence, and even stuttering. "Patterns" examines several ethical implications of this effort including the potential to use the technique to "reform" murderers as a new form of capital punishment, the debate over whose "normal" brain should be used as a template (and the politics involved in that decision), and the uncertainty regarding the difference between the brain and the mind. In a continuation of that story, Tourtellotte's "A New Man" (published later in 2003), one of the "reformed" criminals who underwent the experimental brain pattern overlay begins to experience thoughts that are not his own. For example, he holds strong political views on that do not match those he held before the procedure. A similar attempt to "cure" violent behavior via medical intervention is the underlying premise of Michael Crichton's 1972 novel *The Terminal Man* where "instead of regaining control over himself, Benson [the violent protagonist] is subdued by mind control. Instead of getting cured, he serves as a guinea pig for the research unit's experimental devices and scientific ambitions" (Pethes 162).

Such side effects occur on a more universal (literally) level in John Barnes' Meme War series of novels where scientists use drastic measures to cure humans infected by a computer virus.[9] Once identified by "shrinks," the infected are forced to record all of their memories before having their brains wiped clean of the virus. Unfortunately, those memories can never be fully restored by watching the tapes, and personalities are often irrevocably altered by the "cure."

Speculative fiction also looks at other limitations of biology, especially the inability of human bodies to withstand the demands of such technological advances as space exploration. As Gary Westfahl observes, "Residents of space stations [in speculative fiction] have an alarming tendency to go mad," as we see in such stories as Lester del Ray's *Siege Perilous*, Laurence M. Janifer's and S.J. Treibech's *Target: Terra*, and Arthur C. Clarke's "The Other Side of the Sky" (217–218). However, the genre also warns against using biology to fix that problem: in Frederick Pohl's 1976 *Man Plus*, the main character is altered to survive on Mars but "becomes a victim of science, a latter-day Frankenstein's monster, and suffers a sense of isolation" (Mann 239).

On the same extreme level as biological adaptation to life away from Earth, the quest for immortality through science has been a common theme in speculative fiction for decades, dating at least as far back as Neil R. Jones's 1931 story "The Jameson Satellite," where a scientist uses the cold of space to preserve himself for millions of years (Bainbridge 40). Cloning comes into play in the immortality pursuit in Jack Vance's 1956 novel *To Live Forever*, as the rich and powerful try to do just that. More recently, the theme is reflected in the January 2002 issue of *Analog* where Brenda Cooper and

Larry Niven's "Choosing Life" depicts a society in which the desire to beat death has led to nanodocs that constantly repair and regenerate tissue, on-board medical monitors, and eventually even to digital uploads of consciousness.[10]

Speculative fiction also reflects our fear that this quest for immortality, so deeply embedded in our collective psyche, can turn ugly, even violent. In Ron Goulart's "The Robot Who Came to Dinner" (in the July/August 2002 *Analog*), a new engineered version of spinach is found to have life-extending properties; the resulting attempts to control it lead to kidnapping, mind control, and attempted murder. A more satirical version of this idea is seen in John Wyndham's 1960 novel *Trouble with Lichen*: after a life-extending substance, available in an extremely limited quantity, is discovered, one of the scientists immediately opens a beauty parlor and cashes in, making wealthy women young again. On a much larger scale, Bruce Sterling's 1985 *Schismatrix* concerns the galactic war between advocates of two opposing methods for prolonging human life (biological/genetic versus mechanical/cyborg technology), both of which are then displaced by several newer ways to become "posthuman" (Ross 156).

As Andrew Ross describes, the tradeoff between "enhancements" and humanity is one of the underlying concepts of *Cyberpunk: The Roleplaying Game of the Dark Future*, marketed by Talsorian Games and written in consultation with such genre writers as Walter Jon Williams. In the game, every cybernetic enhancement costs the player part of the character's humanity; lose too much humanity, according to the rules, and "cyberpsychosis" sets in (159–60). The issue is more complicated in Pamela Sargent's "Utmost Bones"; while I analyze this story in more detail in Chapter 9, a key part of that world is applicable to our discussion here as the narrator, Kaeti, has "lived" most of her life in the Net of Minds, with her physical body maintained by the Net's bio- and nanotechnology that allows for "indefinitely expanded lives" (119). The consequences of this "life" are highlighted when the Net reminds Kaeti, "'How much of your former physical self remains? The answer ... is almost nothing. Every cell in your body has been recreated, all of your physical capacities are aided and amplified by microscopic machines'" (129). At some point in the future, will we confuse "'indefinitely extended life for immortality,'" as Kaeti believes those who abandoned their physical bodies have done? (128). The possibility of never dying also plays a major role in Bear's *Vitals*, where the tradeoff for immortality is madness: a bacteria discovered on the ocean floor is found to relieve humans of their mortality as well as their sanity.

Kurt Vonnegut's "Welcome to the Monkey House" reflects the same unpleasant, and perhaps unmentionable, consequence of medical advances that Schmidt discusses: overpopulation. In this 1968 story, overpopulation has led to government-sanctioned suicide and forced birth control that doesn't prevent conception but instead reduces libido. Just such a potential nightmare tugs at the conscience of a rogue biologist who discovers the genetic key to virtual immortality in Bratman's "The Immortality Plague"[11] from the May 2003 issue of *Analog*. The scientist herself describes the devastating consequences of such a fundamental alteration to our genetics:

> the death rate goes down, population rises to fantastic levels. China illegalizes children; soldiers who work on a bounty system shoot kids and their parents on sight. Sweden is more civilized: every citizen signs up for voluntary sterilization. The US tries negative tax deductions for dependents, but it doesn't work. Nothing works. The population crashes in famine and disease rises exponentially, and crashes again. Only warlords and the super-rich live comfortably. Everyone else starves, or lives as slaves [26].

A much more humorous take on this unpleasant consequence of (near) immortality, Kelvin Throop's "Do Unto Others" in the June 2004 *Analog*, finds God (the deity Himself) telling clerics from all faiths that He has reduced the human fertility rate to less than two per couple because "life expectancy is steadily increasing" and "there *are* so many of you" (83). The punch line of this ultra-short story is that God got the idea from a postage stamp urging pet owners to have their dogs and cats spayed or neutered.

Bratman's story reflects not just the scientist's struggle with immortality but also the inability of human nature to resist the urge to live forever, even knowing the consequences, in addition to the lengths those in power will go to in order to either prevent the "Plague" (the good guys) or to obtain immortality for themselves (the bad guys). While we may not like to consider fewer people dying as anything but a good thing, speculative fiction prose warns that everything, including immortality,[12] has a downside, a warning that visual media also sounds often.

Better Living Through Biology: Film and Television Examples

The warnings of *Frankenstein*, begun in prose in 1817, continue to be sent not only in print but also on our film and television screens. Several story arcs of the television series *Buffy, the Vampire Slayer*, for example, deal with the moral limits of science, particularly the fourth season storyline in which a secret government agency attempts to control evil, primordial forces by creating a human-demon-cyborg hybrid named Adam. *Buffy* began reflecting its Frankenstein heritage as early as the second season episode "Some Assembly Required," in which a brilliant science student is able to reanimate his dead brother but still cannot "heal" him, leading this monster, just like his literary predecessor, to demand a companion as monstrous as he is. Adam, however, takes matters into his own hands, planning to reproduce his "superior" form himself. The Frankenstein myth even found its way into the B-movies of the 1950s and early 1960s: In 1962's *The Brain That Wouldn't Die*, a scientist transplants the preserved head of his dead fiancée onto the body of a model whose face has been scarred. This tongue-in-cheek take on Shelley's tale ends as "the monster he [the scientist] keeps in his closet gets loose and runs amok" (Booker, *Monsters* 108).

Another biology nightmare, human cloning, also makes appearances on television and film, just as it does in print. The second season episode of *Star Trek: The Next Generation* "Up the Long Ladder" examines the negative biological consequences of a society entirely made up of clones while also questioning our right to control our own genetic material. Other social implications are reflected in "My Brother's Keeper," from the fourth season of the series *Sliders*, in which clones are created and kept in stasis until the original needs a replacement body part. In this nightmare alternative Earth, clones have no rights, no education, indeed no lives outside of their function as insurance against illness or injury. When an organ is needed, it is taken, with no regard to the life that will be altered, and probably ended, to provide it. This "spare parts" version of the cloning nightmare is also the basis for the 2005 film *The Island*.

In still other variations of the cloning cautionary tale, clones are less sympathetically portrayed, For example, Arnold Schwarzenegger's 2000 movie *The 6th Day* is based on the nightmare that we could lose our individuality and autonomy to a clone while cloning creates both a super-villain and a super-cop in *Judge Dredd*, the 1995 film based on the popular comic book. And in the 2004 film *Godsend*, grieving parents allow a mysterious doctor to clone their son who died when he was eight years old. But problems begin when the clone reaches the age of eight and slowly turns from good to evil.

Plagues are another favorite Biology nightmare for genre television and movies. In the surprise hit film from 2002 (on the border between speculative fiction and horror), *28 Days Later*, a mysterious virus accidentally released by a lab turns all but a handful of humans into murderous zombies. Another plague, this one without the walking dead repercussions, is the back-story for the Showtime series *Jeremiah*, which ran from 2002 to 2004 and depicts a society in which a mysterious illness killed every adult fifteen years prior to the first episode's events. And the British series

Survivors, which aired from 1975–1977, follows the few humans who remain after a virus kills 95% of the population (Mann 429).

Space exploration combines with the plague nightmare in *Andromeda Strain*, both the 1971 movie and the 1969 Michael Crichton novel on which it was based, when a deadly extraterrestrial virus is brought back to Earth by a space probe. Mann describes this story as a "cautionary tale of the failures of science, a story of the fallibility of our modern religion [i.e. science]" (334). In a similar warning, not only is the rhedosaurus in 1953's *Beast from 20,000 Fathoms*[13] destructive after nuclear testing releases it from its ice prison, but the prehistoric creature is also the carrier of prehistoric germs.

Speculative fiction warnings about biology aren't just visions of apocalyptic viruses or out-of-control monsters; the potential for life-saving medical advances to backfire is also a common theme. In "Appointment on Route 17," an episode of *The Twilight Zone*'s second (1985) incarnation, a man's personality is altered after he receives a heart transplant and in "Young at Heart," from the first season of *The X-Files*, a criminal uses a doctor's research into aging to hide his identity by making himself appear younger. The unintended consequences of genetic engineering are the backdrop for the syndicated television series *Mutant X*, which is populated by characters who developed superhuman abilities (such as psychic powers and control over electricity) after their DNA unexpectedly mutated during gene therapy intended to cure terminal and/or crippling diseases.

While genetically engineered humans are more often than not the heroes in *Mutant X*, they are the villains in a first season episode of *The X-Files*: "Eve" depicts the violent consequences of a 1950s eugenics project that, rather than turning out "perfect" beings with heightened strength and intelligence, produced psychopaths instead. And a 1997 episode of *Sliders*, "This Slide of Paradise," depicts an alternate Earth where a scientist's experiments created a race of human hybrids.[14] We find another nightmare vision of genetic engineering in *Gattaca*, the 1997 film that echoes Huxley's *Brave New World* in its "moralistic warning of Eugenics, a reminder that, although genetics may be used to enhance our bodies, they may not necessarily improve our minds" (Mann 375). And the 1972 Genesis album *Foxtrot* includes the song "Get 'em Out by Friday," which describes a world of genetic control (Simpson 13).

Psychopharmacology makes an appearance in the "Just Say Yes" episode of *Sliders*. On this Earth, everyone exists in an altered state, carefully medicated to control all mental and emotional reactions. The outcasts in this society are those arguing for a drug-free life. A similarly medicated society is the setting of the 2002 film *Equilibrium*[15] while the battle against such medical "advances" is also the underlying warning in the original

Twilight Zone episode "Number Twelve Looks Just like You," where a procedure that makes everyone "beautiful" so as to rid the world of hate becomes a terror when a young woman tries to refuse the "voluntary" transformation but ends up looking and (more disturbingly) thinking just like everyone else.

The *Babylon 5* series provides several examples of the ways in which biology can become a nightmare including the replacement of capital punishment with brain-wipes designed to replace the murderer's violent personality with one that only desires to serve the community. Another alternative to capital punishment depicted in the series is the device known only as the "alien healing machine," which takes the life force from one being to heal another. The apocalyptic plague trope also makes an appearance when the entire Markab race is wiped out in the second season's "Confessions and Lamentations" episode while the overwhelming desire for immortality, and the ruthless determination to possess it at any cost, is integral to the events of the "Deathwalker" episode from the first season.

The desperate search for immortality is also at the heart of *The Twilight Zone* (1985) episode "Our Sylena is Dying," as two older members of a family extend their own lives at the cost of the those of the younger generations. In another episode of the series, 1989's "Father and Son Game," a son's efforts to take his place as his father's successor are thwarted when the latter extends his own life by transplanting his brain into a younger body.

Altering humans (or any sentient, organic being) by adding technology and thus creating the cyborg, is yet another cherished speculative fiction trope. The 1974 film *The Terminal Man*, based on the Crichton novel described in the previous section, highlights the tragic consequences of the attempt to control a serial killer with an implanted computer; the plan backfires when he becomes addicted to the sensation intended to prevent violence and kills to continually generate it (Mann 430). The nightmare reaches global proportions in the *Babylon 5* episode "Infection," in which archaeologists discover the remains of an ancient alien organic armor that turns the bearer essentially into a cyborg. Unfortunately, the consciousness of the bearer is subsumed by the armor's programming to protect the planet by destroying anyone who is not "pure Ikarran"; the problem becomes that the definition of "pure Ikarran" could never be determined and thus was not programmed into the armor. Without the judgment capabilities of an organic, sentient being, the cyborgs destroyed the very civilization they were created to protect. The cyborg is the good guy, however, in 1987's *RoboCop*, which depicts one man's struggle to reclaim his humanity after he is turned into the ultimate police officer in a nightmare future city.

Our uncertainty of where the line lies between life-saving technology and humanity-destroying machinery is reflected in one of the most influential speculative fiction tales in our culture: *Star Wars*. While I will discuss Anakin Skywalker's transformation into Darth Vader in greater detail in Chapter 5, his story does provide an excellent example of our fear that we will lose our humanity to technology. As we are told by Obi-Wan Kenobi in *Episode VI: Return of the Jedi*, Darth Vader is "more machine now than man," leading us to believe that while the Dark Side does corrupt Anakin, the loss of his humanity is complete when his body suffers the extreme physical damage we see in *Episode III*, as his resulting reliance on machinery to survive further disconnects him from himself.

When we consider all of these examples, a pattern seems to emerge that further separates the prose reflections of the Biology nightmare from those in film and television. Specifically, the latter grouping seems to incorporate established tropes and familiar fears into other storylines, rather than extending the nightmare into new territory, as the former does. As a result, the prose cautionary tales appear to be more complex and varied (at least where the specific consequences of the science itself are concerned) while the film and television examples, especially those that are part of a series, echo questions and nightmares already familiar to audiences to *add* to other, pre-existing plot and character arcs. This is especially true, for example, with *Babylon 5* and *Star Wars*, where the biology is not the impetus for most of the broad storylines but, instead, adds depth to those already in progress, taking advantage of a cultural nightmare other texts have reflected before. In addition, the action or thriller version of the Biology cautionary tale movie seems to rely on time-honored themes (or, more cynically, to rehash old plots) because the audience already knows, for example, the basic "facing your own clone" storyline. The payoff for this sort of film or television episode, then, is not primarily in the new angles it brings to the question but rather in how it will meet or violate audience expectations.

In contrast, the short stories and novels I discussed in this chapter seem to reflect a tendency toward a more complex examination of the details, a greater willingness, in other words, to get into the nitty-gritty of the impact biological science might have on society. These are, of course, broad generalizations that are certain to have outliers and exceptions. It seems, however, that for this category of the Nightmares Model most especially, the nature of the medium through which our fears are reflected has a significant impact on the nature of the reflection itself, particularly when it comes to the specificity and focus of the story being told.

4: From Frankenstein to the Terminator and Everything in Between: Science and Technology Images in the Mainstream Media

When it comes to metaphor analysis, George Lakoff and Mark Johnson literally wrote the book with 1980's *Metaphors We Live By*, illustrating the integral role metaphor plays in our language and rhetoric. Lakoff and Johnson thus laid the groundwork for analyzing the sources and meanings behind the metaphors that (in effect) define our everyday life. While the three previous chapters examined the ways in which speculative fiction reflects our fears surrounding Science and Technology, that is, of course, only one half of the rhetorical equation of the cautionary tale: genre images are then reflected *back* in our public discourse, completing the cycle. When we debate critical social issues such as the proliferation of nuclear weapons or the development of robotics, we often reference images based on our shared cultural experience with speculative fiction. This chapter, along with Chapters 7 and 10, illustrate that symbiotic relationship by briefly examining the ways in which the mainstream media mines the genre for metaphors when it covers (and creates) public discourse.

In order to keep this analysis manageable, I chose to focus on several representative works from each category of the Nightmares Model. Even with that strategic decision, these three metaphor analysis chapters can only highlight a small sample of the ways in which genre images are used to generate and/or contribute to public discourse. They in no way attempt to be the definitive study of the influence speculative fiction has on such debates.

Instead, my goal is to illustrate the other side of the rhetorical symbiosis between culture and cautionary tales. As Brigitte Nerlich, David Clarke, and Robert Dingwall note in their similar investigation, this type of research, for practicality purposes, must be limited in scope: in my case, to primarily American media. Similar studies using other speculative fiction images or on discourses in other countries and other languages, would add greatly to understanding the influence of speculative fiction on public discourse but are, unfortunately, out of the narrow range of my analysis.

Images of Nuclear War Nightmare in the Mainstream Media

When it comes to the Nuclear War cautionary tales we examined in Chapter 1, Dr. Strangelove and Godzilla are perhaps the two figures most recognizable outside of their original texts. While the pedigrees of Kubrick's intellectual satire and the B-movie-franchise monster could hardly be more different, they both permeate nearly every level of our culture, including public discourse. It is also fascinating to note that one of these characters is an instigator of nuclear war while the other is a victim (or at least an unintended consequence) of such weapons. Despite these opposite origins, the mainstream media invokes both images to create the impression of a person or creature out of control. When we look closer, however, we see that the references to Godzilla are not *always* derogatory while those to Strangelove are. Over the twentieth century, the Godzilla character seemed to morph from a symbol of Japan's destruction to one of national pride, with the monster even defending the country in later movies. This transformation is also evident in media references that invoke the giant's image merely to convey size or strength, but not malice or destruction, and with little to no reference to its nuclear origin.

Dr. Strangelove (both the movie and its title character), however, is nearly always employed to portray some one or situation as dangerously out of control. The most obvious context in which this image is applied is of course discourse regarding nuclear proliferation, as we see in a variety of examples, including the first season episode of *The West Wing*, "Lord John Marbury," when fictional President Bartlett responds to a nuclear crisis between India and Pakistan by declaring in exasperation, "Bring in Dr. Strangelove and we're all set." Meanwhile, back in reality, Steven Erlanger reports (in a column for the *New York Times*) that Amatzia Baram, "a scholar of Iraq," remarked, "'In Iran, I can imagine some commander, acting out of ideology, like some Dr. Strangelove, shooting off a nuclear bomb against Israel.'"

Other nuclear weapon hot spots are the subject of a *Washington Times* editorial from early 2004 in which Arnaud deBorchgrave refers to Abdul Qadeer Kahn, the Pakistani scientist accused of selling nuclear secrets to North Korea, Iran, and Libya, as "Pakistan's nuclear hybrid—half Dr. Strangelove and half Dr. No." Closer to home, an August 2003 editorial in *USA Today* invokes the genre metaphor to describe the belief of some "Bush administration top nuclear experts ... [that] the U.S. needs a new weapon with a Dr. Strangelove name—the Robust Nuclear Earth Penetrator" ("New Nuclear Weapons"). More recently, the 2006 United States agreement with India regarding nuclear power prompted *The Economist* to run a cover on its North American edition that unmistakably (and literally) trades on the Strangelove image: in the style of a movie poster, a cartoon of President Bush riding a bomb, just as Slim Pickens does in the original film, appears under the headline, "George W. Bush in Dr. Strangedeal, Or: How I Learned to Stop Worrying and Love My Friend's Bomb!" The title of the story inside the magazine repeats the altered metaphor: "Dr. Strangedeal."

The Strangelove references, however, extend beyond the narrow (though critical) debate regarding nuclear weapons to include articles and editorials examining more conventional military matters. Some of these can get personal, and even nasty, such as when deputy defense secretary Paul Wolfowitz is referred to as "Dr. Strangelove at his best" (Farmer) and when the *Christian Science Monitor* reports that antiwar activists labeled Harlan Ullman, a retired navy commander, "a modern-day 'Dr. Strangelove'" for his role as co-chair of a committee on US defense strategy (Stern). And it's not just the professional media invoking the image: a letter to the *Los Angeles Times* from October 2003 attacks the appointment of Army Lt. General William G. Boykin as "bizarre," claiming, "Dr. Strangelove rules" (Parriot).

Not surprisingly, the use of the Strangelove image also reaches beyond military debates to politics, where it is also a distinctly unfavorable, often hostile label. Vice President Dick Cheney has been so described (see Bumiller, "'Cheney in the Morning'"), as was then-Governor Howard Dean during his run for president (see Goodman; Rivenburg). The headline of a *New York Sun* editorial critiquing the State Department's Advisory Group on Public Diplomacy in the Arab and Muslim World reads, "Dr. Strangelove, I Presume?" (Twersky), while a Daytona Beach-based editorial[1] refers to the Bush Administration as "'a cross between Dr. Strangelove and *Groundhog Day*'" (J. Dean). Even a television critic, reviewing Showtime's movie *DC 9/11*, invokes the Strangelove image to make a political point, describing a top White House official as "sinister adviser, Karl Rove, the Dr. Strangelove (Strangerove?) of the administration" (Shales).

In sharp contrast to this consistent hostility, however, the other iconic Nuclear War figure, Godzilla, has a significantly more varied public image, even when it comes to political commentary. He can be the fire-breathing behemoth capable only of destruction (see Mark Leibovich's characterization of Fox News personality Sean Hannity) or merely a giant with enormous strength who is impervious to the attacks of mere humans, as in political consultant Dan Payne's January 2004 description of Governor Dean (Vennochi). Complicating this pattern, the image of the nuclear monster is also invoked along with that of one of his most famous adversaries to declare that the projected 2006 New York Senate race between Senator Hillary Clinton and Jeanine Pirro would resemble "Godzilla versus Rodan," but as the columnist made the reference without "specifying who was who," the genre metaphor seems a neutral, if not exactly positive, image ("The Great Race"). Shifting out of direct political contests and into the more indirect, ideological battle between intelligent design and evolutionary theory, the Godzilla image is used in an even more equivocal fashion: a *Capitol Times* editorial describes the dispute as one of "the most spectacular mismatches since Godzilla battled Bambi," with the monster "usually the one who is treated most unfairly in such clashes by the media" (McNally). Thus, in a single reference, Godzilla is portrayed as both a cruel giant who crushes a lovable deer and, at the same time, a sympathetic victim of media bashing.

We find the same ambivalence surrounding the Godzilla metaphor in public discourse regarding big business. At the one extreme, a billboard was planned by a Staten Island labor union to compare Wal-Mart to the destructive monster: it was to feature "a fire-breathing Godzilla by the Verrazano Narrows Bridge. The accompanying text said, 'The Wal-Monster will destroy Staten Island businesses and devastate our quality of life'" (Haberman, "Protecting"). Such anti–Wal-Mart rhetoric also appears on the other side of the country when a California minister claims in the documentary *Wal-Mart: The High Cost of Low Price* that the world's largest retailer swallows up local businesses "'like Godzilla eats Tokyo'" (Stingl). But Wal-Mart is not the only mega-corporation to attract negative Godzilla references; the image is also invoked in descriptions of Clear Channel Communications (Bancroft, "Lawyers"), Kaiser Permanente (Colliver), and even banks as an entire industry group (Black).

Less critical references to Godzilla, however, also occur, such as an article describing Electronic Arts (EA) as "the Godzilla of sports gaming," with only mild criticism that a popular auto racing game from an EA competitor would no longer be available because of a new exclusivity contract between EA and NASCAR (Bray). The ambivalence continues in business reports that follow the pattern used to describe the Clinton-Pirro contest: the split between Miramax's Weinstein brothers and the Walt Disney company is described as "like watching Rodan vs. Godzilla" (Carr) while the negotiations over National Hockey League broadcasting rights are portrayed as "one of those Godzilla vs. Mothra cable monolith battles" (Best). And even more neutral references, like one characterizing Google as "the Godzilla of search engines" (Bancroft, "Back") further complicate the rhetorical use of that image in public discourse.

At the other end of the value spectrum from the condemnations of Wal-Mart, perhaps the most positive Godzilla images appear in sports reporting, particularly when it comes to baseball. As might be expected, a player originally from Japan is often the subject of this comparison: the power hitting of Hideki Matsui earned him the Godzilla moniker in his native country as well as in the United States (Kepner; Vecsey; Caldera). But players from Godzilla's "hometown" are not the only ones who inspire the metaphor. Matsui's fellow Yankee Gary Sheffield, for example, described their New York teammate Tino Martinez as "'the real Godzilla'" (Curry) and even hockey player Jaromir Jagr, who was born nearly on the other side of the world from Japan (in the Czech Republic), has been characterized as "hockey's version of Godzilla" (Baxter).

Even if the Nuclear War nightmare is not as pressing (or at least not as clearly defined) in 2006 as it was in 1946, the genre that first depicted nuclear weapons is also the one that provides us with two incredibly powerful images that public discourse has incorporated beyond their original contexts into many areas of critical (and not) significance to our culture. The stakes are nearly inconceivably high when it comes to public debates regarding nuclear weapons and governmental policy in general. The serious nature of the Dr. Strangelove metaphors clearly reflects that. The more ambivalent references to the Godzilla image, however, perhaps indicate that the Nuclear War nightmare has permeated so far into our cultural consciousness that this fear has lost some of its edge and that we are able to even find something to admire in it. The distance the Godzilla metaphor sometimes strays, therefore, from its original genesis in the Nuclear War nightmares (as well as the shift in Godzilla's cultural role from destroyer to protector) may be a reflection that this is one Science and Technology fear that may be on the wane now that the Cold War has passed. On the other hand, the continued use of the Strangelove image to characterize post–Cold War issues of nuclear proliferation warns us that we may not be able to count this nightmare as "solved" quite yet.

Images of Information Technology Nightmares in the Mainstream Media

Just as it does not seem unusual for a *New York Times* article to invoke Dr. Strangelove in a discussion of the development of nuclear weapons in Iran, images from Information Technology cautionary tales do not seem out of place in public discourse surrounding various forms of technology development. After all, movies such as *Terminator, 2001: A Space Odyssey,* and even *RoboCop* have reflected the potential dangers of technology while also entertaining us for nearly the past century. It is logical, then, we find many mainstream media references to speculative fiction images in this sort of public debate.

One area of profound speculative fiction influence on the language of technology is the inextricable link between Internet terminology and the subgenre of cyberpunk. Many credit William Gibson's *Neuromancer* with coining the word "cyberspace" and the rhetorical dependence between fiction and reality extends from there. As cyberpunk author Melissa Scott tells *Locus*, "the original cyberpunk writers were finding a language for something that hadn't existed, creating a metaphor, and doing it so well that it got picked up by the people who were building it and using it every day" ("Melissa Scott" 75). This rhetorical creation was so successful that it put such language essentially out of the realm of metaphor, and thus out of the narrow scope of my analysis, since it is nearly impossible to separate a reference to a cyberpunk image from the language of the Internet itself.

Metaphor analysis is more fruitful, however, in the public discourse over robotics. For example, Bret Schulte's *Washington Post* article describing the latest generation of Honda's ASIMO robot not only references *Terminator* in its headline ("It's Not Man's Best Friend, But It's No Terminator Either") but it also invokes a veritable "who's who" of Information Technology cautionary tales including *The Matrix* and *Dune*. We also see such imagery in Rich Barlow's article where, in addition to referring to *Star Trek* in the opening line, he reports on an MIT robot researcher who runs clips of *Terminator 2* to generate passionate discussions about "big philosophical issues" surrounding artificial intelligence and robots. In these discussions, those scientists and engineers who will be developing the technology engage in just the sort of debate cautionary tales are designed to illicit, with both the debates and the tales grounded in a common underlying optimism that human society can avoid such nightmares. Expressing a similar hopefulness, a *Terminator* reference is used in an article on nanotechnology to actually dismiss the fear of robot dominance: "But something like that is so far away and far-fetched, it's like worrying about Sony building the Aibo robot dog for fear it will eventually lead to a real-life version of The Terminator" (Maney). Thus, an image that originally reflected a nightmare is instead invoked in public rhetoric to alleviate the underlying terror.

The influence of such nightmare images extends beyond their original robotic contexts to include debates over a variety of technology. For example, the shift in focus from robots to human cyborgs is slight enough to allow the *Terminator* image to remain an effective metaphor: "To be sure, that [belief in the benefits of cyborg technology] runs contrary to the sci-fi movie treatment of cyborgs (short for 'cybernetic organisms') as electronic beasts, like in the *Terminator* movies" (Bergstein). And a more directly on point cautionary tale for the cyborg debate, 1987's *RoboCop*, is invoked by James Wickham to describe the implants developed by a British professor and his neurosurgeon that allow the former "to be wired up to a computer network just like Robocop." Gareth Cook initially associates concerns regarding similar work in the United States with another powerful genre image: "It doesn't take much imagination to see in this the makings of a *Matrix*-like cyberpunk dystopia: chips that implant false memories, machines that scan for wayward thoughts." But Cook later dismisses such fears, arguing that "The Brain Machine Interface program ... could offer help to the paralyzed and is no more likely to bring about a virtual police state than technologies that are already available," thus continuing the pattern of using a speculative fiction image to alleviate rather than amplify a fear.

The opposite effect occurs, however, when references to Information Technology nightmares appear in discussions of military technology; here the genre is mined to deliberately conjure images of unnatural, intimidating figures such as the description of heavily-geared American soldiers in Iraq as "robo-cops intent on taking no chances" (Magnier). A more ambivalent reaction is produced, however, when both the Borg ("the gadget-happy gladiators of *Star Trek* fame") and *Terminator* are invoked in a *Miami Herald* article that describes the development of strap-on robotic legs for use in military operations and rescue missions (Locke). Such varied references demonstrate the influence the warnings of cautionary tales have on public debate over the use of technology by the military.

Speculative fiction images do not only appear in public discourse through words: sometimes the references are visual. For example, an article in *PCWeek* includes a picture of the robot from *Forbidden Planet* being fired upon by two soldiers to represent the defense of computer networks from hackers (Coffee). Just which is the network and which is the hacker, though, is open to interpretation. When it comes to computers, however, the most common image invoked by mainstream media is that of HAL, the "evil" artificial intelligence (AI) from *2001: A Space Odyssey*. And, like the

Godzilla references, the image of HAL is used in public discourse with both negative and fairly neutral connotations (though, unlike the nuclear monster, it is rarely a positive image). The failure of "common sense" in the cold, rational logic of AIs is quickly conveyed by the headline of Christopher Elliot's article, "If HAL the Computer Audited Your Expenses," while Joseph Kahn points to the potential "net loss" if humans are replaced with computers because "reasoning with a machine hasn't worked since Hal the computer took over the spaceship in *2001*." A milder but still negative use of the image appears in Kathy Sawyer's article on the Mars rover Spirit when a NASA administrator compares the malfunctioning vehicle to "the independent-minded computer HAL." In other places, however, the image of HAL is invoked more as a neutral descriptive phrase, at times as a shorthand for an independent computer consciousness (Eisenberg; Kirk Johnson) and at others as merely a reference to the emotionless voice with which HAL spoke (Tedeschi; Shelton).

Many several Information Technology cautionary tales have produced powerful cultural images that we frequently find in public discourse directly engaged with the fears those stories reflect. Thus, the cautionary tales seem to be working: stories such as *2001* and *The Matrix* ask us to consider the potentially negative consequences of such technology and this brief survey of the images we reference in just those discussions indicates that we have done so. The more balanced nature of these references, however, demonstrates that these cautionary tales have left us far from technophobic. Rather, our enthusiasm for the possibilities of technology begun early in the twentieth century continues; it is simply tempered with an equally deep cultural awareness of the potential nightmares inherent in computers, robots, and other information technology. While we may fear the creation of a *Terminator*-style robot that will take over the world, we also seem to admire the strength and capabilities of just such a creation and consider the potential good it could do, provided it can be properly controlled.

Images of Biology Nightmares in the Mainstream Media

The public issue that far and away inspires the most references to Biology cautionary tales is genetics. More specifically, the discourse surrounding cloning and/or genetic engineering sends commentators scurrying into the speculative fiction library, looking for metaphors. The image invoked many more times than any other in these debates is Frankenstein, whether with references to genetically-modified food as "Frankenstein-food" (Barboza) or "Frankenfoods" (see Sommer, "Frankenstein" for just one example), or animal rights protesters accusing cardiologists who plan to transplant a baboon heart into a human woman of being doctors of "Frankenscience" in an episode of the television series *Strong Medicine* ("Maternal Mirrors"). Even the labeling of genetic researchers as modern-day Frankensteins demonstrates that Mary Shelley's nineteenth-century narrative, along with its many permutations and updates, has been incredibly influential on our culture. As Misha Berson observes, "Today the name Frankenstein is a common figure of speech. It's a metaphor, a symbol, a reference to a tale told and re-told, interpreted and re-interpreted." Indeed, within public discourse on Biology fears, we find a heavy reliance on the image to convey, in one word, the folly and potential horror of scientists who "play God." By leveraging the myth that derived from the original narrative, as well as other similar cautionary tales, both critics and proponents of genetic research and cloning employ an effective cultural shorthand to further their cause.

Several studies conducted on the British media and culture examine the ways in which such speculative fiction imagery is employed in public debates regarding genetics and cloning.[2] For example, in 1998, the Wellcome Trust Medicine in Society Programme directly asked individuals about their views on human cloning to determine which metaphors they would invoke. Within the study group, "discussions were peppered throughout with negative references" to several speculative fiction films such as *Jurassic Park* and *Blade Runner* (14). The Wellcome Trust study found that the texts "were not referred to in detail, but were often simply cited as examples. Just the reference to a film or book appeared to be sufficient to describe participants' concerns, and there was an assumption that others in the group would be able to understand these instantly" (14). This shared understanding is key to the power of such metaphors: even those who do not know the particulars of a reference often nevertheless immediately understand the image invoked.

The study participants "made extensive use of narratives from popular culture when framing their discussions and concerns" about cloning, using them "as a form of short-hand" (Wellcome Trust 37). The researchers suggest "such references are used in a metaphorical manner to which it was hoped others within the group would relate. It has been suggested that just the title of such a cultural reference can evoke an entire story or 'script' as an interpretive frame" (37). These interpretive frames, evoked by just a title or character name, are the primary way all the pubic discourse examples in this chapter (and the two later ones) function.

Taking a slightly different approach from the Wellcome Trust, Nerlich, Clarke, and Dingwall focus on the British media in their study of cloning discourse, where they find that "the media reports are interwoven with more or less explicit references to science fiction novels and films, from *Frankenstein* to *Gattaca* and beyond. They [the novels and films] nourish and reflect the general public's fears about an increasing process of biological hybridization" (37). As the researchers describe, the potential for cloning to blur "traditional boundaries" and threaten "not only our perception of what humanity is but of what personal identity and personal dignity are" leads to the use of speculative fiction images in discourse not for "purely poetic or purely cognitive purposes" but as "a framework for the expression of social concerns" (50), concerns that often prompted the creation of the referenced cautionary tales in the first place.

Nerlich, Clarke, and Dingwall go on to describe a "wide network of metaphors" populating the cloning discourse, "usually provided by vivid images linked directly to" science fiction as the media finds it "very easy to make the imaginary leap that links cloning science to cloning fiction, as throughout the 20th century genetic science and genetic fiction have constantly intermeshed" (39). But the image most frequently "intermeshed" in these debates is, predictably, Frankenstein. As the authors observe, "Since the beginning of the debate surrounding genetic engineering, be it of humans, as in the case of clones, or plants, as in the case of genetically modified food, Frankenstein has always been the imaginary hook onto which chains of arguments about these issues are attached" (38). This cultural link is so pervasive "that when cloning became a scientific reality this reality was predominantly seen as a nightmare" (49), rather than as a breakthrough with tremendous potential to help people. "The myth of Frankenstein," claim Nerlich, Clarke, and Dingwall, "became the most fundamental imaginary and metaphorical background for any talk [in the British media] about cloning, genetic engineering, and genetically modified food" (39). The same can be said for the public discourse regarding genetics and cloning in American culture as well.

It is not difficult to find references to genre metaphors, particularly to Frankenstein, in American public discourse that match those described by Nerlich, Clarke, and Dingwall. For example, during an actual public debate, held in a small boxing ring at the Pasadena Civic Auditorium in October 2004, the pro-cloning "contestant," a professor of microbiology and public affairs at Princeton, "began by invoking Dolly, the famous cloned sheep, saying that the animal was not a 'Frankenstein' monster, as some critics have said" (McKee). In another, more official forum (the floor of the United States House of Representatives), New Jersey Representative Rush D. Holt argued against a bill banning any human cloning by telling his colleagues that "'extreme conviction seems to be crowding our understanding today

... These researchers are not crazed Dr. Frankensteins'" (Stolberg). The cloning ban passed, however, and an editorial critiquing the vote argues that it "is part of a sweeping prohibition on all forms of human 'cloning,' which failed to distinguish between 'Dr. Frankenstein' experiments seeking to reproduce human beings and well-regarded biomedical research at institutions such as UW-Madison" ("Reactionaries"). As these examples demonstrate, the Frankenstein image is sometimes employed, as were the *Terminator* references I discussed earlier, to *allay* our fears regarding genetic research, with proponents arguing that the reality is not as terrifying as the fiction would have us believe.

Frankenstein metaphors are not just employed by experts or professional media; "everyday" people also invoke the image, as the Wellcome Trust found. These references, however, seem to always be negative, with those outside the media taking the nightmare position that Representative Holt condemned. And such civilians, as it were, are not shy about creating their own forum for such expression: *Washington Post* correspondent Anthony Faoila reports that Hwang Woo Suk, the South Korean scientist who claimed to have led the first team to successfully clone human embryos in 2003,[3] received an email from "one furious man in the United States ... 'calling me Dr. Frankenstein,' Hwang said." Months later, Hwang is still under attack when a letter to the *New York Times* declares, "Pure and simple, this [Hwang's work on human embryos] is Frankenstein science and should be banned in all civilized countries" (Kokoski). Even fictional characters get into the act: the police captain on a 2005 episode of *Law & Order: Special Victims Unit* comments, "Dr. Frankenstein had a back-up plan" when his detectives investigate a doctor trying to genetically engineer designer babies ("Design").

One of the more sensational occasions for public debate on cloning occurred when the Raelians' Clonaid organization announced that the world's first cloned human, a baby girl named Eve, had been born on December 26, 2003. The announcement, which was eventually never substantiated, generated a mini-firestorm of media coverage replete with Frankenstein imagery. For example, Richard Land, president of the Southern Baptist Convention's Ethics and Religious Liberty Commission, is quoted in the *Houston Chronicle* two days after the announcement decrying the event as "'human rebellion against morality'" and predicting "'We are going to see Frankenstein fiction become Frankenstein fact'" (Turner). Responding to such vehemence, a *USA Today* editorial five days later argues for a more moderate reaction to the possibility of human cloning than the "knee-jerk reaction" of calls to ban it all together, pointing out that the Raelians' claim "stretches credulity, given that the cloning of mammals since

Dolly the sheep in 1997 has usually taken hundreds of tries and produced Frankenstein-leaning deformities" ("Overreaction"). Meanwhile, a staff writer for the *Daily News* in New York is more direct (and perhaps even sarcastic) in his use of the genre metaphor when he describes the Raelians' spokeswoman as "The French Frankenstein" (Siemaszko). As this microcosm of the cloning debate demonstrates, the common denominator of the rhetoric, regardless of the position, is frequently the use of the Frankenstein metaphor.

While less frequent than the Frankenstein examples, references to *Jurassic Park* do also appear in cloning discourse. Sometimes this metaphor is invoked when discussing the specific cloning of dinosaurs, the movie's conceit, as in Campbell Robertson's article that describes the discovery of a Tyrannosaurus Rex fossil containing soft tissue and notes, "Scientists were quick to play down the *Jurassic Park* possibility." Later in the article, an eight-year-old boy visiting the dinosaur exhibit at the American Museum of Natural History tells Robertson that cloning a T-Rex from that tissue would be a bad idea, saying bluntly, "'So you're saying it could move and it could eat you?' Jake asked. 'I think they'll regret that. You know what happened in *Jurassic Park*.'" The same paleontological discovery Robertson reported also prompted a *Los Angeles Times* article to invoke the Spielberg films to make the same argument as young Jake: "As wonderfully escapist as theme parks are, we witnessed in the *Jurassic Park* movies some pitfalls in trusting man-made security systems to confine large, escape-minded creatures craving more than popcorn" ("In Cloning").

This awareness of cloning as "the theory that science is pushing the limits of nature too far, which will inevitably lead to nature striking back" is what bioethicist and theologian Dr. Ted Peters tried to counter in two lectures he gave at Oregon State University in 2003 (Hougham). Referring directly to *Jurassic Park* in the public forum, "Peters said he believes this fear is unfounded" though he acknowledged it as one of the "two main arguments against cloning."[4] The speculative fiction image also appears in arguments against stem cell research as when a New Jersey assemblyman told a reporter, "'It's that old line from *Jurassic Park*,' he said, 'Just because we can do something doesn't mean we should. Before long, I think they're going to start cloning little yous to take care of the big you" (Mulshine); this reference, thus, reflects both of the conceptions Peters was trying to refute.

Like Godzilla and Dr. Strangelove, Frankenstein is often invoked in public discourse to convey the image of an out-of-control monster, sometimes as the human who treads where only God belongs (and with little to no regard for the consequences) and sometimes as the "unnatural" monster he creates, abandons, and is then haunted by. To a lesser extent, *Jurassic Park* is also referenced to conjure the sense of unrestrained biological science. When it comes to genetics, and specifically cloning, both of these images serve as powerful reminders of the fears reflected in cautionary tales, reminders that have worked their way even into bio-ethics discussions in high school biology classrooms (D'Avolio). Whether used as a scare tactic, to warn others of credible dangers, or as a deliberate counter to such fears, public cloning discourse relies on speculative fiction to place this complex debate on a more fundamental level the public can understand, employing narratives we are all familiar with to convey the real implications of cellular mitosis and chromosomal markers.

As this brief review demonstrates, public discourse regarding science and technology frequently leverages the shared cultural experience that is speculative fiction in very real, very relevant debates. The mainstream media along with the rhetoric of everyday citizens employ a language thick with metaphor and the influence of the Science and Technology cautionary tales on the available reservoir of images makes it clear that these are not simply disposable stories, but rather significant cultural artifacts that reflect what we care about as we then reflect them back when we work through our public nightmares regarding science and technology.

These images, however, are not always reflected back without distortion; for every condemnation of nuclear policy that invokes Dr. Strangelove, it seems we can find a neutral reference to the HAL metaphor. Public discourse's transformation of cautionary tale images seems to take two forms: 1) A shift to a more ambivalent, near-admiration, as we see (primarily) with the Godzilla image; and 2) An appropriation of the metaphor to alleviate the cultural fears it conveys, as some cloning discourse demonstrates. While the latter preserves a more significant element of the original nightmare than the former, when it argues that the fiction is worse than the reality will be, the rhetorical flexibility of these images is nonetheless clear. The speculative fiction metaphor often proves useful regardless of the side of the debate the commentators are on primarily because of our intense cultural familiarity with these cautionary tales. We already know what these images mean and the media does not hesitate to cash in on that shorthand for a variety of rhetorical purposes, whether it is to convince us whom to vote for in national elections or to prevent us from buying genetically-engineered tomatoes at the grocery store.

PART TWO : POWER

Introduction

Our power nightmares are reflected by speculative fiction in the genre's frequent "depiction[s] of both the intimidating effect and the seductiveness of absolute power" (Harris 46), depictions that can perhaps be best understood in photonegative form: One of our greatest fears is the *loss* of personal freedom and power, whether to an Individual or to the State. As Thomas Cooper observes, "The twentieth century has been nothing if not an ode to power" (84) and the speculative fiction of that century follows suit. The past hundred years provides many real examples of how quickly individual powerlessness can occur, whether caused by those driven by the desire for political control such as Senator McCarthy and his hearings, by megalomania in the guise of nationalism employed by such tyrants as Hitler and Stalin, or by the craving for financial gain that led to the corporate scandals of 2002 (e.g., Enron, WorldCom, etc). With the aftermath of the 2001 terror attacks still being determined daily, the balance between state power and individual freedom will remain a critical public issue for the foreseeable future. Thus, the varied consequences of power have been, and will continue to be, reflected in speculative fiction.

This genre, especially its more science-focused stories (like those we discussed in the previous section), is often dismissed by contemporary American society as concerned solely with technology and/or outer space. That this is a misconception should be clear; our fears and nightmares regarding power (and its consequences) *are* regularly reflected in modern speculative fiction because, as Ray Bradbury wrote in 1953, "Space, which is very large indeed, is not the only huge thing which stands before man" (366). Those huge things occupy and inform both aspects of the Power nightmare: the Individual and the State.

The fear that power corrupts the individuals who wield it and of the consequences that follow seems to cross nationalities and eras. Speculative fiction works depicting this particular nightmare are as old as Jules Verne and as new as the *Star Wars* saga, as American as *Buffy, the Vampire Slayer* and as global as J.R.R. Tolkein. Whether that power is physical, psychological, supernatural, or related in some other way to the exercise of authority, as Mason Harris observes, "the ultimate danger lies in the undermining effect of fantasies of power on the personality" of the characters (47). Warnings about power's capacity to destroy individuals and those around them are prevalent in speculative fiction.

Those cautionary tales often examine the nightmare of an individual with too much power at two extremes: the personal and the global. Both the raving psychosis of H.G. Wells's *Invisible Man* and the galactic-level bloodbath that follows Paul Atreides's defeat of the emperor in Frank Herbert's *Dune* series are warnings of what can happen when enormous power is concentrated in one individual. Whether one person or an entire solar system is destroyed, the works in this subcategory reflect our fear that power can be just too tempting and corrupting for an(y) individual to handle, warning of the seemingly inevitable consequences that follow.

The second, and perhaps more familiar, reflection of the Power nightmare involves abuses by the state. As Kay Sambell from the perspective of young adult and children's literature, such cautionary tales represent "an authorial quest to suggest a new moral course for young readers [and society in general]. It seeks to shock its readership into a realization of the urgent need for a radical revisioning of current human political and social organization.... If people do not change, it warns, the future looks devastatingly bleak" (163). The tales in this category, argue Raffaella Baccolini and Tom Moylan, "served as a prophetic vehicle, the canary in a cage, for writers with an ethical and political concern for warning us of terrible sociopolitical tendencies that could, if continued, turn our contemporary world into the iron cages portrayed in the realm of utopia's underside" (2). While the idea of speculative fiction as prophesy can certainly be disputed (and has been for decades), the arguments made by both Sambell and Baccolini and Moylan describe the cautionary role of the state-focused tales that are an integral part of the Power category.

Many genre texts actually present both aspects of the Power nightmare: they depict a charismatic individual, such as Hitler in reality and Senator Palpatine in fiction, who takes over a struggling democracy by promising reform and then turns it into a totalitarian state. The focus of those works is frequently the path to oppression, with the progression from Individual to State nightmare reflecting the two sides of our fear of power in the hope that we may learn to recognize the warning signs and speak out when they present themselves in reality. For example, works depicting this path lead readers to consider, "At what point does utopian cooperation become dystopian conformity?" (Hintz and Ostry 7). Or, when does a necessary concession of emergency political power morph into the roots of a totalitarian state? These are incredibly relevant questions at the beginning of the twenty-first century, ones that speculative fiction cannot answer completely. The genre does, however, continually remind us to keep asking them when, as Carrie Hintz and Elaine Ostry observe, "These texts confront the tensions between individual freedom and the needs of society" (9).

On the other hand, there is also a strong body of work within speculative fiction that depicts the crushing power of the state after it has been established for so long, many in the nightmare society believe it has always been that way. George Orwell's *Nineteen Eighty-Four* and Aldous Huxley's *Brave New World* fit into this mold, as do many dystopias, where, as Baccolini and Moylan describe, "the text is built around the construction of a narrative of the hegemonic order and a counter-narrative of resistance ... [as the story] opens *in media res* within the nightmarish society" (5). In this form, the story does not center on how the state became oppressive, but rather on how the oppression might be defeated (or not). While not every text in the utopian/dystopian tradition fits into the Nightmares Model, as I will address in Chapter 6, many of them do reflect our inherent fear of a powerful state crushing its citizens into submission. This nightmare is often heightened by the pessimistic ending of many narratives where the protagonists fail and are forced to conform or die. In such traditional versions, as Baccolini and Moylan argue, the only room for hope is outside the stories, that readers will heed the warning and learn "to escape" the depicted nightmare (7).

I describe both aspects of the Power nightmare — the Individual and the State — in more detail in the next two chapters along with examples (some famous, some not so well-known) that illustrate the warnings speculative fiction sounds about power. In addition, as in Part One, the final chapter in this section examines the influence of the cautionary tales in this category on public discourse.

5: Power of the Individual

Lord Acton's axiom, "Power corrupts and absolute power corrupts absolutely," describes many of the tropes and fears we find in the Power nightmare. Genre warnings about this corruption, the inevitable abuses of power, and the consequences of that abuse for both the individual and those subjected to power reflect what Juan A. Prieto-Pablos calls "a deeply deterministic view of man's destiny — which declared that when he is offered the choice between salvation and destruction he is bound to go for the latter option" (65). That destruction has both personal and global (at times galactic) consequences in the works of this sub-category, which is perhaps best illustrated by two of the most famous and influential sagas in the genre: *Star Wars* and *Lord of the Rings*.

Famous advisors to British Prime Ministers and monarchs are not the only ones who express concern over the nightmare of individual power. Stanley Schmidt ponders this fear while suggesting that we haven't been contacted by extraterrestrials because any that might have existed could have been destroyed by mass bio-terrorism carried out by a single individual: "any civilization that wants to avoid becoming one of the casualties will have to find an effective answer to the question: How do you prevent any individual from acquiring or abusing that much power? No question is more important." Schmidt also asserts, "Preventing individuals from abusing great power once they have it is a different problem from making sure they never get it" ("Fermi" 48). Both of these problems are reflected in the tales I describe in this chapter, tales that warn us against the corrupting temptations of power. Whether that power is scientific or economic, magical or political, or of some other variety, speculative fiction reflects our fears that Lord Acton was right.

The Personal: Corrupted by Power

The danger of one individual with too much power seems to be a basic fear, one that stems directly from human nature. In his examination of the role of mythic demons in the human psyche, Rollo May identifies that "the important characteristic of the daimonic is that the one element within the person which has its rightful function as part of the personality, can itself usurp power over the *whole* self, and this drives the person into disintegrative behavior" (197). May defines the daimonic as "any natural function in the individual that has the power of taking over the whole person," functions including the desire for power, and argues that what we call "inner demons" are actually inherent and natural parts of our psyche (196). It is when those demons are allowed to take over that there is a problem, a common warning in many cautionary tales. May's concept of inner demons is reflected in a particularly effective way by speculative fiction, as it is a genre in which outer demons regularly appear. Whether the transformation from inner to outer demon is physical (as seen with Gollum in *Lord of the Rings* or the Mayor from the third season of *Buffy, the Vampire Slayer*) or merely internal (as depicted in the Alfred Bester character from *Babylon 5*), the warnings of the impact of the takeovers are equally powerful.

The power of a specific manifestation of the mind, the intellect, seems to be particularly frightening to us, especially when it can be used to manipulate people and the environment to one's will. Susan Spencer describes this fear when she cites Eric A. Havelock's argument that "the myth of the Fall in Genesis, as a direct result of eating of the tree of knowledge, 'gives poignant expression to the conflict within the civilized consciousness of man, between his sense of intellectual power and his distrust and fear of that power.'"[1] This is an ancient fear, Havelock suggests, one that the Greek myth of Icarus illustrates: Icarus was seduced by the power of his father's intellectual abilities to conquer nature and paid the ultimate price. As our knowledge and capabilities grow, Spencer asserts, "Man becomes dangerous and also frightened." Our fear of the intellect, according to Peter Goodrich's analysis of the mad scientist trope, follows in part in the Faustian tradition where "discovery is not merely ambivalent or presumptuous, but damnable" (74). When it comes to such discovery, the scientist's "'madness' is socially determined because all extraordinary genius provokes doubt in ordinary mortals—doubt confirmed in the literature by events" (83), terrible consequences that "contradict the myth of control in science and technology" (84). In this way, the first category of the Nightmares Model (Science and Technology) is related to our fear of the Power of the Individual.

In addition, fear of the intellect extends to psychic powers such as telepathy and mind control, another favorite trope of speculative fiction because of the inherent tension between free will (and privacy) and power. The question of who controls our thoughts and actions is the foundation of this fear. What would the world be like, for example, if there were no more secrets? Information is power in our culture; even if telepaths could only receive thoughts and not influence them in any way, the knowledge they would gain from others could easily be used to manipulate people and situations, a consequence genre texts often depict. How would such a power affect the telepath who could access this wealth of information? Who would be able to control that power? How would we even know if such a power was used against us?[2]

Within the more fantastic side of speculative fiction, there are obviously many opportunities for the power being abused by an individual to be somehow supernatural. Wizards and witches and demons with extraordinary powers have long populated our folk tales as well as speculative fiction cautionary tales. While there is certainly a compelling argument for the allegorical function of witches and demons as social commentary,[3] these characters also provide speculative fiction writers with the opportunity to explore how immense power, beyond the scope of what is available in "reality," can have dangerous consequences for both the individual who wields it and those who venture inside the minimum safe distance. In many ways, a magic ring can be a more effective symbol of power than a political office, thus giving a cautionary tale about the corruption of individuals even greater punch.

Whether it is temptation of evil from the outside (such as the ring in *Lord of the Rings*) or the use of a potion to release the evil inside (as Dr. Jekyll does in Robert Louis Stevenson's 1886 novel), an individual's (in)ability to control power is a frequent struggle portrayed by speculative fiction. As Robert Scholes and Eric Rabkin observe, "Dr. Jekyll and Mr. Hyde capture the sense of the evil forces lurking within us" (169). The potential for power to tempt us into releasing those evil forces terrifies us, a terror that fuels the nightmares reflected in so many genre texts.

The Global: Corruption's Price and Consequences

Great power may corrupt the individual wielding it but the consequences of corruption are rarely localized. While the power of magic is familiar to us from childhood fairy tales and we learn to appreciate the power of knowledge through our years of education, economic and capitalistic power is perhaps the type examined by speculative fiction with which today's readers can most easily identify. Whether it is a CEO literally trying to get away with murder in a world where telepaths have essentially eliminated crime, or virtual super-corporations that have become so integrated into cyberspace they are essentially beings in their own right, speculative fiction reflects our fear that corporate power will be abused with worldwide consequences to follow. These stories may be set centuries into the future but the warning rings true even in the early part of the twenty-first century, perhaps especially so given the corporate scandals that came to light in 2002 where the individuals behind such corporations as Enron, WorldCom, and Adelphia Communications abused their power for personal gain, and left millions to suffer for it.

In addition, the lone mad scientist is another familiar genre image, one that is frequently employed to depict warnings about individuals corrupted by power. Schmidt identifies this mad scientist trope as following in the footsteps of Mary Shelley's *Frankenstein*[4] and notes, "Many of [Dr.] Frankenstein's 'descendants,' such as the many nemeses of James Bond, are driven by selfish goals such as power, up to and including world domination, and they use new scientific findings and technological inventions to strive towards those goals" ("Return" 4). And in his analysis of the intersection of science and society, Andrew Ross connects this trope to one of speculative fiction's most famous names (Hugo Gernsback) when he argues that, after the reality of nuclear war took hold of popular consciousness,[5] "The Gernsbackian hero-scientist of the thirties [was replaced by] the megalomaniac scientist with Gothic undertones" (141).

In these contemporary variations, the implications of intellectual power described by Spencer and Havelock and exemplified by Icarus expand to destroy not only the individuals with the power but also those surrounding them, up to and including the entire known universe in some cases. Goodrich identifies several elements of this modern expansion of the fear[6] including the required "physical isolation [which] connotes mental isolation, and implies madness because it removes the figure from the behavioral norms and consequences which define 'sanity.' His isolation also encourages the scientist's functional abuse of his abilities ... Intellectual isolation and detachment from society create a vicious circle that spirals to disaster" (83). Another key feature of this trope, according to Goodrich, is that "in his quest for insight into the laws of nature ... [the mad scientist] tends to envision himself as a titan, yet misinterprets or altogether fails to perceive the full moral and ethical dimensions of his experimentation" (74). This failure leads to "the blind application of his principle [discovery,] threaten[ing] human society" (75), a threat that fuels many of the nightmares in this chapter.

As modern life progresses beyond the capabilities that Shelley and even Gernsback could imagine, the incursion of the Internet into our everyday lives, for example, opens up a new opportunity for intellectually powerful individuals to wreak havoc from the comfort of their very own homes.

Hackers have the power to take down global networks and hurt millions of people, a fear that speculative fiction has reflected for at least the past three decades. In his *PC Week* article describing the future of network security, Peter Coffee directly invokes those reflections when he compares excerpts from two speculative fiction stories with the views of real world systems analysts to point out the vulnerability of our current systems. Coffee links this line from Vernor Vinge's "True Names" (written in 1981), "'Look, this stuff is legal. That gadget is scarcely more powerful than an ordinary games interface,'" with the following 1997 comment from Robert T. Marsh, Chairman of the President's Commission on Critical Information Protection, "'Even amateurs have access to the technological tools needed to penetrate systems and cause trouble'" (102). The power of the hacker is also evident in Coffee's juxtaposition of a line from William Gibson's landmark 1984 novel *Neuromancer* ("'The intrusion countermeasures had accepted his entry as a routine transfer from the Los Angeles complex. Behind him, viral sub-programs peeled off, ready to deflect the real Los Angeles data when it arrived'") with another one from Vinge's "True Names" ("'One of the vandals' favorite sports was to infiltrate office systems and simulate higher level input to make absurd and impossible demands on the local staff'") (102). Both Gibson's viral subprograms and Vinge's high volume attacks are terrifyingly familiar to anyone who works in information security today, which is exactly Coffee's point. These are just two specific instances where warnings sounded by speculative fiction twenty years ago became at least partially a reality. To identify the nightmares we may face in the future from hackers and other computer geniuses, we would do well to look at what else is being reflected in the genre. What warnings are being sounded now that might apply in the next twenty years? Warnings that are not about the technology per se but about those who are looking to take advantage of its power for their own ends.

Even traditional epic heroes are not exempt from abusing their power in speculative fiction, because, as Prieto-Pablos observes, "the exertions of power of the heroes of romance are always almost invariably destructive, and often more destructive than intended" (69). Speculative fiction complicates this narrative tendency because

> the powers he can tap — those that have sent him through the galaxy and settled him in distant planets — have placed him too far above ordinary readers and have transformed him into a source of the fears that had traditionally been provoked by the villain: if man's innate tendency is destructive, what can an extraordinarily powerful hero do but to destroy with a force n-times greater? Could he not destroy even the world he had pledged to protect? These are the underlying questions in a significant part of contemporary fantasy and science fiction [66].

Even when they begin with the best of intentions, the magnitude of the powers available to these heroes often corrupts them, reflecting our fear that no one, no matter how "good" or how "strong," is immune to the devastating effects great power has on the individual who wields it.

History provides plenty of examples of the terrible consequences when power is concentrated in one individual. For example, Patrick Aiex compares Aldous Huxley's world of selective breeding, combined with an unbreakable caste system, in *Brave New World* to the real-life madman vision of Hitler's Aryan nation and asserts that Huxley "was issuing a warning in the form of a disturbing yet entertaining story" less than a decade before the Nazi party took control of Germany (7). While Huxley's story could not prevent Hitler's reign of terror, his warning and those of countless other speculative fiction writers are now an integral part of our culture and, combined with those in the next chapter, convey compelling messages about the abuse of power. Whereas the States in Chapter 6 represent our fear of the monolithic institution —faceless governments defined by bureaucracies and stringent rules— this sub-category includes the depiction of the despot, the tyrant who takes over after being corrupted either by the desire for, or actual realization of, power, usually with catastrophic consequences. Combine that with the Frankenstein-ian mad scientist and the power-mad wizard succumbing to the temptation of evil and we have a pretty effective shorthand summary of the texts that illustrate this nightmare.

Hobbits and Mad Scientists: Print Examples

Our discussion of the ways speculative fiction prose reflects the nightmare of individual power can really only begin one way, with J.R.R. Tolkein's *Lord of the Rings* trilogy. The power of the one ring that drives this legendary chronicle eventually seduces and corrupts even the pure-hearted and well-meaning Frodo Baggins. Throughout the epic, the good (including Gandalf, Bilbo, and Lady Galadriel) are tested by the evil power bound by the ring and it is only their extreme willpower that prevents them from succumbing. Not all are so successful: the ring's power corrupts Boromir, leading him to try to kill Frodo in an attempt to possess it, while Gollum is permanently transformed from a Hobbit into a monstrous creature who hides in the shadows, pining away for the ring, his "precious."

The nightmare that magical power will overwhelm those who wield it is also reflected in Ursula K. LeGuin's 1968 novel *A Wizard of Earthsea*, which tells the story of Ged, a young man whose magical power exceeds his ability to control it and who must "restore the Balance that he has upset by working his power in a way beyond his knowledge" (Scholes and Rabkin 77). In 1945, Tolkein's friend and colleague Charles Williams also crafted a cautionary tale of a powerful mage, this one bent on world domination, with *All Hallows' Eve*, while the title character in Roberta Anna MacAvoy's *Damiano* trilogy (*Damiano*, 1983; *Damiano's Lute*, 1984; and *Raphael*, 1984) struggles to control his own dark magical powers as well. Reflecting a similar version of the nightmare, the mages who control chaos and order in Louise Cooper's Time Master series (*The Initiate*, 1985; *The Outcast*, 1986; and *The Master*, 1987) also control the world until an extremely powerful mage is born. The terrible consequences of abusing magic cross over into the "real" world in *Voodoo Child*, Michael Reaves's 1998 novel that depicts the demise of a drug lord who uses sorcery to force an innocent man to commit murder, unwittingly bringing the magical battle between good and evil to the streets of New Orleans.

But magic is not required for power to corrupt individuals; sometimes all it takes is the right situation. One of the founders of modern speculative fiction, Jules Verne, shows us an individual corrupted by his own power when Captain Nemo kidnaps the protagonists and takes them to the bottom of the ocean in 1870's *Twenty-Thousand Leagues Under the Sea* and its sequel, *Mysterious Island*. And in Judith Merril's *Shadow on the Hearth* from 1950,[7] the efforts of housewife Gladys Mitchell to protect her daughters after a nuclear attack are complicated by her neighbor, Jim Turner, who secretly trained with Civil Defense forces. As the attack begins, Turner, according to M. Keith Booker, takes "control of the neighborhood almost as his private domain, and it is quite clear in the text that he is enjoying the experience immensely" (*Monsters* 71). At the other extreme, isolation, not community, drives the sole survivor of an apocalyptic purple cyanide cloud to insanity in M.P. Shiel's 1901 novel *The Purple Cloud*. Since no one is there to stop him, Shiel's protagonist destroys entire cities with explosives, just because he can.

This fear also follows us into space as well. In Philip K. Dick's 1965 novel *Dr. Bloodmoney, or How We Got Along After the Bomb* (another nuclear holocaust story), a stranded astronaut, Walt Dangerfield, orbits an Earth devastated by nuclear war, broadcasting music and commentary to listeners below who are desperate for any news or cultural contact. The power of Dangerfield's position as the sole media source does not go unnoticed by other survivors as, late in the story, an imposter uses mental projection to take over the broadcasts in an attempt to secure that power for himself, almost killing Dangerfield in the process (Booker, *Monsters* 92). Venus, not Earth, is the setting for Henry Kuttner's 1947 novel *Fury*, which tells the story of a small group of mutant near-immortals who control almost everything in their society until one of their own, enraged by the abuse he suffered at the hands of his own kind, uses his superior abilities to topple the society, forcing everyone out of their protective keeps and onto the hostile Venusian surface.[8] And in 1967's *Lord of Light* by Roger Zelazny, a group of human colonists on a distant planet use alien technology to recreate themselves as Hindu gods, denying the technology to later generations in order to maintain their control over the planet.

One of the oldest, and perhaps most familiar, examples of our fear that power destroys individuals is the Icarus myth I discussed earlier. John Morressy reimagines this story in "The Artificer's Tale" (*Fantasy and Science Fiction*, October/November 2003) where Daedalus' great skills and knowledge (and hence, power) of all things mechanical not only leads to his son's death but also nearly causes the death of his protectors on Sicily, forcing an innocent girl to become a murderer to protect herself and her family.

The mad scientist abusing his intellect to disastrous ends is yet another interpretation of this Power nightmare, and another one of the founders of modern speculative fiction, H.G. Wells, provides an early (1896) and influential example of the trope: Wells's *Island of Dr. Moreau* depicts the grisly consequences when man's intellectual power is exercised without the appropriate moral considerations. Still another classic speculative fiction tale that has inspired many others is Stevenson's *Strange Case of Dr. Jekyll and Mr. Hyde*, which has spawned such reinterpretations as a Broadway show, a music album (Roxy Music's *Manifesto* from 1979) (Simpson 13) and a third-season episode ("Beauty and the Beasts") of *Buffy, the Vampire Slayer*.

More modern prose examples of the trope include *Point Blank*, a 2001 novel by Anthony Horowitz[9] in which an MI6 agent tries to stop a mad scientist from replacing the sons of prominent businessmen with clones of himself, and Greg Bear's 1983 novelette "Blood Music," which tells the story of a maverick scientist who injects himself with a cellular organism to prevent his research from being destroyed by his employer. Eventually that organism mutates and begins infecting all of North America, leading to radical physical changes in those infected.[10] In another LeGuin novel, 1971's *The Lathe of Heaven*,[11] not only must a young man, George Orr, learn to control his terrifying ability to change the nature of reality through his dreams, but he also must get out from under the control of a scientist who is trying to use George's power to bring about his own vision of the world (Scholes and Rabkin 79).

Genetics is the weapon of choice in Steven Bratman's 2003 novelette "The Immortality Plague" in which a wronged biologist uses her knowledge and hacker skills to release several gene-altering viruses, including one to make humans virtually immortal. Another Bratman story of genetic manipulation, "Deletion," depicts the decades old, world-altering machinations of a mad scientist, but puts a new twist on the nightmare: the goal of the scientist was world peace, not world domination. In this novelette (published in *Analog* in January/February 2004), Henrick Norsgald, the revered architect of a society without war, created a world in his own pacifist mold by releasing a retrovirus that deleted the genes responsible for feelings of kinship and family loyalty — thus creating a global society in which people no longer see the need for war, terrorism, or religious and ethnic violence. But, as the narrator asks, "What if, instead of helping the world, Norsgald stole its heart?" (198). For Bratman's characters, this one man's decision robbed children of their parents' unconditional love, all in the name of saving them from war. While the story assiduously avoids definitively answering the question of whether Norsgald's goal was valid or not, leaving the reader to decide if the price was too high to pay for peace, it does clearly reflect that such a decision does not belong in the hands of one man.[12]

The scientist in Greg Egan's 2002 novel *Schild's Ladder* is less Machiavellian than either of Bratman's protagonists, yet the consequences of his actions are still devastating: in the far-future, a quantum physics experiment accidentally creates a "no-no vacuum" that proceeds to consume the known vacuum of space. While not scientists in most respects, the hackers in Vinge's "True Names" and in John Barnes's Meme War series[13] could still be classified as "mad" and certainly illustrate the terrible consequences too much knowledge and power in the hands of too few. Knowledge of science and technology is truly power, power that can corrupt those who hold it as we see in many mad scientist cautionary tales.

Individuals using extraordinary means to seize control of governments and empires is another nightmare speculative fiction frequently reflects. Frank Herbert's 1965 novel *Dune*, for example, began the *Dune Chronicles*, which depict the aftermath of the arrival on the galactic stage of Paul Atreides, messiah to some, mass-murderer to others. Paul's part in history, including seizing the throne as emperor of the known universe, unavoidably unleashes a bloody jihad because, as Prieto-Pablos describes, "the dynamics of liberation require the elimination of all obstructing forces and, eventually, the creation of another dictatorship where 'unbelievers' are destroyed in the name of a faith emptied of all its original ideas" (68). Prieto-Pablos observes that while Paul is the product of thousands of years of genetic manipulation, rigorous education, and unexpected circumstances, "much of what he becomes is the product of hard learning of an extraordinary disciple who soon surpasses his masters" (68). Prieto-Pablos sees

Dune's central figure as a tragic character "with the flaw of having been born with the potential of a god"; the very abilities that make Paul a virtually invincible, extremely intelligent warrior are the real crux of his narrative struggle — he cannot control the consequences of his power (68). Paul, and eventually his son Leto, "are the fallible leaders with immense power, aware of the fact that, while they must respond to their calling as leaders, whatever they do or fail to do the effects, because of their immense powers, will no longer be local and controllable" (73). This inevitable, galactic impact of individual power makes Herbert's saga such a fitting example for this sub-category of the Nightmares Model.

The same struggles with power yield a different result in Stephen Donaldson's series *Chronicles of Thomas Covenant*, which began in 1977 with *Lord Foul's Bane* (followed by *The Illearth War* 1978; *The Power that Preserves*, 1979; *The Wounded Land*, 1981; *The One Tree*, 1983; and *White Gold Wielder*, 1984). At the end of the series, the title character decides not to use his extraordinary power to save his people because doing so will cause him to become a new version of the enemy he is being asked to fight. Instead, Covenant does not act at all, dying "as a hero for those who asked for his help, while Paul ends in failure as a Tyrant" (Prieto-Pablos 77).

In contrast to Paul Atreides and Thomas Covenant, the consequences of the protagonist's actions are more ambiguous in Olaf Stapledon's *Odd John*.[14] While John's advanced mental abilities lead him to steal and even murder to implement his plans, which include uniting with others like himself, the true nature of his work on a deserted island is never clearly revealed, though there are hints it involves making contact with intelligent life on other worlds. On a smaller scale, Norman Spinrad's 1969 novel *Bug Jack Barron* also reflects this fear of individual power with its story of a television personality "involved in a deadly struggle with a wealthy manipulator of politics and politicians" (Scholes and Rabkin 92) who is looking to secure a monopoly on cryogenics. Hitting on that same nightmare of manipulating world politics for personal gain is what many consider to be a modern classic: Orson Scott Card's *Ender's Game* (the first in a series of *Ender* novels). In this story about extraordinary children unwittingly deciding the fate of Earth as they play complex war games,[15] Ender Wiggins' ruthless and brilliant older brother manipulates society through invented characters on the worldwide communication net to eventually become leader of the world at the age of seventeen.

Business, rather than politics, is the battleground favored by Alfred Bester, with the all-powerful CEO a frequent character in his novels. In the introduction to a reissue of Bester's *Demolished Man*, Harry Harrison describes the landmark novel as "the story of Ben Reich, the richest capitalist in a capitalist future. He is also the most corrupt man in this terribly corrupt postwar New York City of the 24th century" (viii). There is only one challenge left for Reich, committing murder in a city monitored by telepaths; the story examines how the power attained by Reich informs his murderous path. In addition to Reich, Bester's 1957 novel *The Stars My Destination* (originally published in Britain in 1956 as *Tiger! Tiger!*) features a nightmare CEO named Presteign who ruthlessly demands absolute loyalty and conformity, even to the point of requiring retail managers to submit to surgery and psychological conditioning so as to be identical to each other. Presteign is also a profiteer, gaining handsomely from a war between the Inner Planets and the Outer Satellites.

Corporate and political power collide in William Gibson's Sprawl series, which, according to Jutta Weldes is populated with multi-national corporations that have become vast, single organisms, individuals with power and a will of their own, outside of the traditional state ("Popular" 10). Weldes includes in this series the novels *Neuromancer* (1984), *Count Zero* (1986), and *Mona Lisa Overdrive* (1988) along with the 1986 short stories "Johnny Mnemonic," "New Rose Hotel," and "Burning Chrome" (10, 21). In her analysis of the definitive cyberpunk series, Weldes quotes from *Neuromancer* where "'Power ... meant corporate power. The zaibatsus, the multi-nationals that shaped the course of human history, had transcended old barriers. Viewed as organisms, they had attained a kind of immortality'" (10).[16] These "postmodern *angels*," as Ross describes them, are "quasi-divine constructs with multiple identities" (148) who effectively enslave humans into a corporate indenture, forcing them to live out their lives essentially as faceless drones in the service of the corporation (149). As this example reflects, whether the individual the corporate power is a single corporation or one murderous CEO, the concentration of so much economic power in one place can be devastating.

Vinge's "Cookie Monster," published in the October 2003 issue of *Analog*, reflects a similar nightmare to Gibson's corporate control of cyberspace but with a very different twist. In Vinge's story, an ambitious (if undertalented) scientist-businessman, Gerry Reich,[17] uses personality uploads of unsuspecting real people (some of whom may even be dead in "reality") as the ultimate form of cheap labor. His corporation gets decades' worth of work out of these virtual employees because the programs run in a vast supercomputer at incredibly fast speeds—more than 1200 virtual years pass in just a few real ones. Reich profits from the work of these essentially free laborers, all without their knowledge or consent, and builds a giant company with its hands in everything, allowing him to exert vast influence on the economy, the government, and society in general. The crime is more overt in Ron Goulart's "The Robot Who Came to Dinner" (*Analog*, July/August 2002) where an executive for a multinational food producer resorts to kidnapping and attempted murder to gain control over a life-extending engineered food that could generate enormous profits for the company.[18] This intersection of greed and individual power often reflected as a speculative fiction nightmare also finds its way onto film and television screens as well, with spectacular and even genre-defining results.

Sith Lords and Magic: Film and Television Examples

Just as Tolkein's *Lord of the Rings* reflects in prose the potential for an individual to be corrupted by an enormous, dark power, we see the same nightmare reflected by the *Star Wars* saga, this time on film. In George Lucas's six-movie epic tale of Anakin Skywalker, the combination of extraordinary power and intense fear and pain drives the hero to become the villain as Anakin is lost to evil and then eventually redeemed by his son. When Yoda says to a young Anakin in *Episode I: The Phantom Menace*, "Fear leads to anger. Anger leads to hate. Hate leads to suffering," we are directly reminded that too much power in the hands of one person can lead to devastating consequences for so many. Other characters in the series, such as the Sith Lords (e.g. Chancellor (and later Emperor) Palpatine and his apprentice, Count Dooku), also exemplify the terrible results when power corrupts individuals. These films actually depict both sides of the Power of the Individual nightmare: the personal devastation to Anakin as he loses his humanity in his quest for ultimate power of life and death,[19] and the global (galactic actually) impact as a democracy becomes a merciless dictatorship ruled by Sith Lords.

This combination of personal and global consequences also appears on a smaller scale in the sixth season of *Buffy, the Vampire Slayer* when the nightmare of individual power is reflected in the season-long story of one character's abuse of magic. While creator and executive producer Joss Whedon is clearly making a point about addiction with this storyline, the corruption (fueled by rage and grief) of mild-mannered, gentle Willow also reflects our fear of the consequences when too much power is wielded by one individual. This power not only threatens to destroy Willow and her friends, but it also leads her to try to destroy the world in a desperate attempt to end her pain.[20]

Back on the more personal level, perhaps one of the best examples of power destroying an individual is the psychotic breakdown of *The Invisible Man*, which, in a similar way to the many *Frankenstein* and *Jekyll and*

Hyde reinterpretations, has inspired many imitators since Wells published his version in 1897. The most recent film update, *Hollow Man*, was released in 2000 and is a straightforward thriller interpretation; the power available to the lead character because of his invisibility leads to his complete rejection of the laws and morals he previously held. The Sci-Fi Channel series *Invisible Man*, which aired from 2000 to 2002, however, takes a more light-hearted approach to Wells's original idea.

Wells's *Invisible Man* (and his many imitators) is the product of science and there are many other examples of scientists who abuse their intellectual power with devastating consequences. For example, in "The Schizoid Man," a second season episode of *Star Trek: The Next Generation*, a scientist cheats death by uploading his consciousness into the android Data, taking over his body. Even though Data is "just" a machine, his loss of self-determination because of another's advanced intellect (plus complete lack of morals) reflects our own fears that knowledge could allow someone else to take control of our lives. The mad scientist also makes an appearance on *Buffy, the Vampire Slayer*: in the second season episode "Some Assembly Required," the power over life and death corrupts a star science student and his sociopath accomplice, leading them to attempt murder in order to create a companion for their own Frankenstein's monster. We also see the trope in the syndicated series *Mutant X* where the villain of the first two seasons is Mason Grey Eckhart, head of the company that inadvertently created humans with super-powers in the first place, who then convinced the government to allow him to hunt down the mutants and put them into stasis, in order to protect the public. The mad scientist also appears in "This Slide of Paradise," from the series *Sliders*, when the characters discover a race of human hybrids created by one man's genetic experiments on an alternate Earth.[21]

Strange as it may seem, the 1950s B-movies aimed at the teenage drive-in theater audience also reflect this fear of the mad scientist. The title creature in Jack Arnold's 1955 film *Tarantula*, for example, is created by a scientist who tries to manipulate forces he does not understand, leading not only to the giant spider but also to his own degeneration into a primitive beast when he is injected with his radioactive formula. This mad scientist theme also underlies the plot of 1954's *The Creature from the Black Lagoon* and its two sequels, *Revenge of the Creature* (1955) and *The Creature Walks Among Us* (1956), in which scientists in some way or another torture the creature, all in the name of discovery. And in Kurt Neumann's *The Fly* from 1958 (remade by David Cronenberg in 1986), the scientist becomes the monster when his atoms are mixed with a housefly's in his experimental teleporter. Science is the not the end but the means in Burt I. Gordon's 1958 film *Attack of the Puppet People* when a lonely puppeteer develops a shrinking device so he can capture people for companionship.

Mind control is often feared as an extension of the intellect and we also see the nightmare of losing control over our thoughts reflected in 1950s monster movies. Even though the premise of the 1953 film *Donovan's Brain* now seems ridiculous, as Booker points out, since Donovan's brain is preserved by a scientist after his death, his plans to take over the financial markets using mind control reflect this nightmare two-fold (*Monsters* 108): the mad scientist involved in things he doesn't understand and the loss of free will to a telepath. In a similarly silly premise, the head Martian in 1953's *Invaders from Mars* is essentially a brain encased in glass, using mental telepathy to control its minions, becoming, Booker asserts, "a figure of the dangers of excessive intellectual development, which threatens to produce super brains who might lose touch with their true humanity, then heartlessly take over and control the rest of us" (*Monsters* 122). Ten years after *Invaders*, in the *Twilight Zone* episode "The Little People," the means of domination are not brain power but sheer physical size when humans become the invaders: an astronaut, after landing on a planet with tiny inhabitants, declares himself a god.

Magic, not science, is the tool of domination chosen by *Buffy* villain Warren in the season six episode entitled "Dead Things" when he uses a magical artifact to turn his ex-girlfriend into a willing slave. As the effects wear off, though, and she tries to leave, he accidentally kills her, marking the beginning of the end of his slide from relatively harmless mischief-maker to true evil villain in the *Buffy* mythology, as his need to control someone absolutely leads to his own absolute corruption. And this corruption has terrible consequences: Warren's actions inadvertently lead Willow to succumb to her darker nature, which I described above.

Magic also has tragic consequences for the world in the series *Charmed*. As the sixth season unfolds, viewers learn that, in the future, Wyatt (the baby son of one of the witches and her angel husband) will succumb to his own incredible power and fall from good, taking the world along with him (as revealed in the "Chris-Crossed" episode). Even though these future events are eventually averted by the season finale, "It's a Bad, Bad, Bad World, Parts I and II," the fear that Wyatt will grow up to see the pursuit of power as everything while making no distinction between good and evil remains a concern for his family over the rest of the series.

Even though the nature of his power is not clearly identified as magical, the ability of little Anthony Fremont to read minds and control his entire environment in the 1961 *Twilight Zone* episode "It's a Good Life" (and the 2003 sequel "It's Still a Good Life") is certainly supernatural, and eventually turns Anthony and his daughter into terror-inducing tyrants of their own little world. On a smaller scale, May's "inner demons" make an appearance in the film *The Ninth Gate*, where the quest for the power of Satan destroys most of its seekers in this post-modern take on the story of temptation by the Devil.

Another speculative fiction character defined by the corruption of super-human power is Faith, a rogue slayer from *Buffy, the Vampire Slayer* and its spin-off series, *Angel*. Slayers are given enormous strength and skill through mystical means in this world and both series continually ask whether their power and calling make them above human law. While Buffy does frequently confront these issues herself, Faith's fall and eventual redemption provides the strongest example of Whedon's meditation on the concepts of power and the law.

But, as in prose, genre television and films also reflect the human tendency for self-destruction through power without supernatural assistance. A fourth season episode of *Star Trek: The Next Generation*, "The Drumhead," depicts the fall of Admiral Norah Satie, a renowned and respected Federation investigator who uses her reputation and power to turn an inquiry of an accident into a witch-hunt for a conspiracy that turns its focus onto Captain Picard when he objects to the expansion of the investigation. Eventually, Satie's paranoia becomes clear and her tirade against Picard leads to her disgrace. And in another well-known television series, *Babylon 5*, even though Bester's telepathic abilities provide him the opportunity, his yielding to the temptation of power leads the Psi-Cop to ruin many lives, including his own, in his exercise of his gift and near-limitless authority.

The original *Twilight Zone* also reflects our fear that too much power will lead to an individual's ruin in the fourth season's "On Thursday We Leave for Home." In this Rod Serling-penned episode, the leader of a space colony has maintained the morale of his stranded people by keeping them focused on the greatness of Earth, until the rescue ship actually arrives and he realizes he is about to lose his power over them. He then tries to convince everyone to stay by describing the "real" Earth as a hellish place and refusing to board the ship. When he finally changes his mind, it is too late — the ship has already left and he is marooned once again.

Popular music also reflects our nightmare of individual power with Queen's 1972 song "Seven Seas of Rhye" depicting a dystopian world run by a fascist (Simpson 13). In addition, 1988's *Operation: Mindcrime*, a video and album project by Queensryche, tells the story of Dr. X, who uses mind control to create assassins so he can take over the world by killing religious leaders and replacing them with his own people (14).

The seduction of power is not limited to humans in speculative fiction;

perhaps the epitome of the disregard for potentially global (or galactic, in this case) destruction inherent in individual power is the character of Q from *Star Trek: The Next Generation, Deep Space Nine* and *Voyager*. In episode after episode, this character (reviled by some fans, adored by others) continually demonstrates seemingly unlimited powers with also seemingly no regard for the consequences. The only chink shown in the Q armor is in "Deja Q," a third season episode of *The Next Generation* in which the character is briefly stripped of his powers because of the havoc he wreaks across the galaxy. The result is not nearly as comical or benign as Q's usual appearances in another, stand-alone episode of *The Next Generation*'s third season, "The Survivors," where viewers meet yet another super-alien, this one going by the name of Kevin Uxbridge. While he appears simply to be a kind old man who survived an alien invasion that destroyed the rest of his world, the crew of the Enterprise learn he is actually an immortal being, who, with just a thought, wiped out an entire alien race after a group of them attacked his planet and killed his human wife when she tried to defend her home.

An Earth-based, though not human, villain is corrupted by power in 2003's *Underworld*, which turns on the lengths one "man" (actually a vampire named Kraven) will go to in order to seize and hold power, almost at the cost of his own species. To rise in the ranks during a vampire-werewolf war, Kraven makes a deal with the werewolf leader, Lucian, to fake the latter's death. This deal, however, actually allows the war to fester and escalate underground, until each side develops weapons that can instantly kill the other, nearly annihilating both sides.

While the main villain in the 2003 Sci-Fi Channel movie *Do or Die* is a doctor turned businessman, not a government official or supernatural warrior, he still has de-facto control over society: by withholding the cure, society stays divided into those who are infected with a deadly rapid-aging disease and those who are not, all so he can continue making massive profits on the disease's treatment. Another industrialist, William Edgars, is behind a plot in the fourth season of *Babylon 5* to do just the opposite: he tries to *create* a virus that will kill only telepaths. Edgars puts his enormous resources into this effort because he believes telepaths plan to take over the Earth government.[22] The power he wields as head of a vast pharmaceutical corporation leads Edgars to believe he is both above the law and beyond reproach, answerable only to himself. That is until another individual also corrupted by his own power, Bester, learns of the plot and kills Edgars to protect "his" telepaths.

The nature of this nightmare, with its focus on individuals, lends itself to the creation of strong, emblematic characters like Bester and Anakin Skywalker, but as we have seen, there is also a tendency in the genre to present the opposite: interchangeable mad scientists, for example, who are less memorable as characters than for the consequences of what Goodrich describes as their "transgressive acts" (83). This variability in characterization, then, seems to matter more than medium when we come to the task of delineating the Power of the Individual cautionary tales, perhaps because the story of an individual corrupted by power is so transportable that visual effects have less impact on the tale than in the other nightmares we've examined.

For example, the narrative action in the typical mad scientist tale, seemingly regardless of medium, centers on the sweeping consequences of the science while, in contrast, character-focused stories seem to follow a redemption pattern, where personal consequences of corruption provide the pathos, pulling on audience sympathies for characters who are often already familiar to them. In much the same way, corporate villains follow the former model, with corruption a given and the story proceeding from there. When magic, or some other extra-human ability, is involved, however, the story often focuses on the struggle to avoid corruption; it is not inevitable that these protagonists will succumb but, rather, the narrative is predicated on the possibility that the power can be controlled, even if, as in *Dune*, the character eventually loses the struggle.

This distinction connects to two other key elements of power nightmares: 1) the nature of the power; and 2) the intent behind its use. While there are certainly exceptions, these cautionary tales seem to break down along two types of power; when the protagonist struggles with an internal power, such as magic, the Force, or even telepathy, the character is more often than not portrayed sympathetically, sometimes with redemption tales. When the source of the power is external, however, such as science, the "one ring," or economic forces, those employing it are often presented as irredeemable and the narrative can only take one path: the defeat of the corrupted individuals, usually via the destruction of the source of their power. The nature of that power is also closely related to the way intent plays out in these texts; stories where the abuse of power is deliberate often take very different trajectories than those where the consequences of the corruption result less from a will to abuse and more from a weakness or inability to control the powerful forces within. Comparing, for example, the story arcs of Bester from *Babylon 5* and Willow (or even Faith) from *Buffy* highlights the role intent plays in this nightmare. Is the power inherently uncontrollable and thus the individual has little choice about being corrupted (e.g. Paul Atreides or Anakin Skywalker) or is it rather willful disregard for consequences that leads to corruption (e.g. typical mad scientist narratives)? Answering that question will, more often than not, tell you what sort of cautionary tale to expect, regardless of its medium.

6: Power of the State

This nightmare reflects what Robert Heinlein calls "the problem of government," one of his "three basic and continuing problems" of society,[1] ("Pandora" 256) and therefore one of the basic problems speculative fiction reflects. In the introduction to his annotated bibliography *Tales of the Future*, I. F. Clarke describes the genre's writers as those who "spoke out for all mankind against the dangers that menaced the world in their time" by, among other things, making "alarming forecasts of the political perils to come" (xvii). Given the enduring need for some sort of government in civilized society, as well as the equally enduring danger that power will be abused, it is little wonder that the State is the main actor in so many cautionary tales.

Our fears are uniquely expressed in Power of the State cautionary tales because, as Mason Harris argues, "the nightmare of power becomes a magnet which draws into itself all the energies of the modern world" (53). The true life horrors of Hitler and Stalin combined with newly available methods of control manifest in our contemporary fear of totalitarian states, and, as Harris describes, speculative fiction endeavors "to represent the totalitarian mind from the inside through grotesque imagery and situations" that reflect the consequences of an "obsession with power and relationships based entirely on power" (54). There is a strong cross-cultural resonance to such representations, one which Renata Galtseva and Irina Rodnyanskaya[2] describe as a "notable kinship to an identical vision of the [totalitarian] world" that "manifests itself ... in a similarity of traits within an existence in unfreedom and depersonalization" (294). Also noting this affinity, Carrie Hintz identifies several common elements of these visions including a "rigorously planned society, charismatic leaders or masterminds, control of reproductive freedom, and the prioritization of collective well-being over the fate of the individual" (254). Even casual genre readers will recognize these as the key ingredients in a Power of the State nightmare, all of which combine to dehumanize the populace, a process that holds these totalitarian worlds together.

Despite the overwhelming tendency toward dark, depressing imagery and nightmare scenarios of unfreedom, the impulse behind these texts, like all cautionary tales, is actually an inherent optimism, one that may wane but never completely disappears. As Richard Parent observes, dystopias are "presumably presented to readers to prevent degeneration toward the abject state the author has imagined ... [it is] an essentially optimistic premise— though the protagonist may not be able to escape the dystopian world, the readers possess the power to effect change and avoid this undesirable future" (20). Under all the grotesque imagery and dehumanization that pervade these nightmares, there is also hope that vicariously experiencing the stories will, in some way, prevent them from crossing over from fiction to reality. That hope strongly links the nightmares in this chapter with those in the Nuclear War subcategory, as the impetus for many of the tales in both lies in the reality that was World War II, its causes, and its consequences. Informed by history, as well as by both hope and terror about the future, speculative fiction reflects our fears regarding the Power of the State in many ways.

Utopias to Dystopias: Wells's Legacy in the Modern Era

Colin Greenland highlights the cautionary nature of Power of the State nightmares when he observes, "Writers of utopian and dystopian fantasy often give their fictions titles that show them to be rhetorical rather than oracular: satire, not prophecy" (127). As such, these cautionary tales are closely related to the utopian/dystopian tradition in speculative fiction, which highlights a sticky issue we need to address before delving any deeper: the difference between cautionary tales and social commentary. While I could have included the following discussion in virtually any chapter, this distinction is particularly relevant to the Power of the State nightmare given the role of the state in so many dystopias. Therefore, we will take a brief detour from looking at society's nightmares to see what has been *excluded* from the population of genre texts the Nightmares Model describes.

There is a blurred line between a speculative fiction text intended as social commentary and one that is a cautionary tale. Nevertheless, I believe a distinction can be made between the two functions, and that belief has guided my choices. At a fundamental level, I see the difference as rooted in the view that social commentary is an amplification of a current flaw our culture, taken to the extreme, worst-case scenario; in other words, our flaws applied to a fictional world to reveal a truth about society we may not be willing to admit. A cautionary tale, on the other hand, involves some sort of extrapolation or projection of our fear into the future[3] or into a significantly altered, fictionalized world. This distinction becomes less theoretical and more practical when I need to categorize the many utopian/dystopian stories in the genre.

When we look closely at the plots of dystopic fiction, we see that they frequently follow characters who attempt to change their society (e.g. Guy Montag from *Fahrenheit 451* and Winston Smith from *Nineteen Eighty-Four*) and the actions of that society to stop them. These attempts at change, whether or not they are successful, separate dystopian stories from utopian, and, while there are always exceptions, generally place dystopias in the cautionary tale category, while utopias tend toward social commentary. As Sharon Stevenson describes, "The dystopia is not an exposé of a current condition, but a warning about some condition that might develop from a tendency in the readers' contemporary world or about a past condition that might re-emerge" (135). That warning is the key feature when it comes to defining cautionary tales.

However complicated this distinction can be in the abstract, we can draw some clear lines in the specifics: for example, *Nineteen Eighty-Four* and *Brave New World* fall into the cautionary tale group because they project existing conditions forward to dystopias. Ursula LeGuin's landmark novel *The Left Hand of Darkness*, on the other hand, is social commentary as it exaggerates gender issues and applies them to a fictional world to critique those same concerns in our society. In a similar way, Octavia Butler's *Dawn* is social commentary because, according to Michelle Erica Green, it is "an angry utopian novel, a scathing condemnation of the tendency of human beings to hate, repress, and attack differences they do not understand. It pleads for an end to fear and prejudice." Bud Foote, in his effort to draw a similar distinction, excludes such works as *Gulliver's Travels*, despite some clear dystopian elements, because the texts "distorted the evils of the present rather than extrapolating apprehensions about the future" (1). This is admittedly a fine line to be walking, but one that must be drawn for consistency within the Nightmares Model. Thus, in simple terms, for our discussion, social commentaries are criticisms focused on the now, while cautionary tales are warnings that focus on the future.

Now that I have described my take on this necessary distinction, we can get on with the analysis of our Power of the State nightmares. Those cautionary tales following the utopian/dystopian model are usually seen in the genre as drawing on the works of H.G. Wells. Robert Scholes and Eric Rabkin describe Wells's objectives for his utopias as an attempt "to avoid the bad future he saw as inevitable if men would not *plan* for a better one and [to show us] how to act in order to bring a better future into being"

(21). A key historical shift, however, began in the late 1920s and came into full force after World War II: even though, as Raffaella Baccolini and Tom Moylan argue, those cautionary tales that "represent the *classical*, or canonical, form of dystopia," such as *We* and *Nineteen Eighty-Four*, were "no doubt prompted by H.G. Wells's science fictional visions of modernity" (1), the optimism often found in Wells's works was quickly superseded. Rather than continuing the pro-technology, utopian projections of Wells, I.F. Clarke notes, tales of "the grand old constructive and progressive ideal state ... vanished" after World War II to be replaced by the dystopias of George Orwell and Kurt Vonnegut and other "ominous prophecies of the 1950s and 1960s. ... [with] the shape of things to come ... so often the salutary consummation of our worst fears" (xvii). Thus, the Second World War not only brought the nightmare of nuclear apocalypse to the forefront of the public consciousness but also the terrifyingly persistent fear of an abusive, totalitarian state.

Brian Aldiss describes the sharp contrast between the dystopias of the modern era and earlier utopian models when he observes that the latter used to represent "our belief in the perfectibility of man and the triumph of altruism over self-interest" but "we have seen this noble line of utopias slide down like sinking liners into such depths of dystopianism as Eugene [sic] Zamyatin's *We* (1920) and Orwell's *Nineteen Eighty-Four* (1949)" (82). Scholes and Rabkin identify the tumultuous political environment of the early 1900s as the impetus for the creation of "a powerful new kind of science fiction, the anti-utopian or dystopian novel" (26), the kind that so many now associate with the best of the genre. That trend accelerated after World War II when, M. Keith Booker observes, "the technology that had long been so central to Western utopian dreams had now brought about the advent of nuclear weapons with the concomitant threat of the sudden end of civilization" (*Dystopian* 91). The key element in these dystopias is, of course, the crushing power of the totalitarian regimes that will do whatever it takes, including abuse the new apocalyptic technology, to stay in power.

Speculating on the reason for this dystopic trend, David Brin wonders, "Is fear of dystopian nightmare a greater motivator than any promise of utopian accomplishment? Indeed, our tendency seems always to criticize whatever injustices remain unsolved, rather than ever pause to rejoice in what's been accomplished" ("Self-Preventing"). In post–World War II culture, the motive seems clear: the horrific lessons of Hitler and Stalin combine with the reflective gaze of speculative fiction to produce powerful works that now seem to define our fear of the Power of the State, where dehumanization is the nightmare mechanism keeping the state in power.

Persuasion and Torture: Dehumanization as Means of Control

In his landmark 1960 study, Kingsley Amis describes "conformist utopias maintained by deliberate political effort" as a "cherished nightmare" of the genre (84). This political effort is a common narrative element of many cautionary tales as these fictional states, and their actors, do whatever it takes to maintain total control. "The evil" in such texts, Stevenson argues, "is usually a faceless, all-encompassing state, bureaucracy, or belief system that annihilates or restricts some set of values the readers believe are indispensable to both their own and the characters' ability to function as fully dignified human beings" (131). Such totalitarian systems, according to Harris, have "both a physical and a psychological dimension" (49), which speculative fiction clearly reflects with nightmare states that encompass far more than a mere government or bureaucracy; as Moylan observes, "it is the totalizing political-economic machinery of the hegemonic system ... that brings exploitation, terror, and misery to society" (136). While many of the classic dystopias simplify the role of economic and other factors to focus on the government, according to Moylan, later works such as *The Handmaid's Tale* incorporate "the imbrication of state, economy, and culture" that support nightmare societies (136–37). Along similar lines, in her analysis of slavery and freedom in dystopias, Maria Varsam employs Louis Althusser's concepts of Repressive and Ideological State Apparatuses to argue that control is maintained in these worlds via a process of "alienation" (215): from biology, from creativity, from language, from individuality. These means of maintaining control are often the most visible, most tangible aspects of the fear driving such cautionary tales.

Such means of control lead Thomas Dunn and Richard Erlich to reference beehive imagery from both parts of Shakespeare's *Henry IV* to argue that "the principles of Misrule and disorder, principles embodied in Falstaff's ample form ... [as well as the play's] occasional periodic descents into vivifying chaos" are the essential elements of human nature that are suppressed or outright forbidden in the "nightmare embodied in many dystopian works of our times" (46). In such nightmares, "the hive or machine is the essential condition of human life" according to Dunn and Erlich, yet also represents "the things in human social life that can render us helpless, insignificant, unhuman" (49). This goal, to make people "unhuman," is precisely why the state in so many cautionary tales employs its varied means of control.

Galtseva and Rodnyanskaya construct "an 'ideal type' of a society of unfreedom" from their comparative study of twentieth-century dystopias

(297), and I believe we can identify the "ideal" means of state control (i.e., those we fear most) by looking at Power of the State nightmares. Broadly speaking, there are four aspects of this (lack of) control: Technological/Mechanical, Information, Psychological, and Biological. I deliberately left off brute force or any similar type of military/police control as those means are more often than not the enforcement arm of one of the other four elements; speculative fiction tells us that force alone cannot keep a totalitarian regime in power.

What can sustain these states, however, is mechanization and other forms of technology, narrative elements that are nearly inseparable from these cautionary tales, which have, as Galtseva and Rodnyanskaya describe, "a decidedly industrial face" (295). The denial of nature and subsequent reliance (forced or not) on technology is often a key component of the state's control through dehumanization, exploiting the tension that humans are natural and machines are not. Such tension is usually couched as the drive toward reason, toward a more rational "planned society ... built upon scientific-technical reason," as Galtseva and Rodnyanskaya argue, but "the remaking of the individual" into a compliant citizen is "the only *real* goal" of those in control (310). Dunn and Erlich describe this mechanization as a symbol "for individual helplessness and triviality" (46), conditions that nightmare states exploit to ensure obedience. Such technological elements of this nightmare, however, differ fairly significantly from those I discussed earlier as our Science and Technology nightmares. For example, while clearly a technological wonder, the Death Star in *Star Wars* is not terrifying because it could turn on its creators but, as Dunn and Erlich observe, because it "serves the vicious ends of the military bureaucrats of a totalitarian empire" (48). In other words, the technology is the means but the state is the nightmare.

Even a casual observer of the genre is familiar with the two technologies most frequently employed in Power of the State nightmares; Mario Varricchio argues that by using "cinema and television ... [authors like Orwell and Huxley] emphasiz[e] their role as essential means for distorting reality" because they "perform a crucial political function by preventing and repressing protest and, more generally, by conditioning and inhibiting oppositional forces" (98). Such technology has many functions, including controlling information. Omnipresent surveillance, whether via cameras or other means, is a defining feature of the totalitarian state as control is maintained by gathering information about every detail of citizens' lives, including where they go and to whom they speak. In order to achieve this control, according to Galtseva and Rodnyanskaya, the state must "make everyone 'transparent,' to use Nabokov's word, permeable to one another, as well as to power" (318), yet another step in the dehumanization process. The glass apartment walls in *We* take this transparency literally as a "universal certainty that 'one is constantly being watched'" represents "a kind of inhuman power" that is essential to maintaining total state control (313).[4]

Regulation of language is another key component of information control because "complete domination requires the stripping of language so that there will be no reference to a reality beyond authoritarian relationships" (Harris 49); Orwell's Newspeak is perhaps the definition of this means of control. Such manipulation of reality requires that, according to Galtseva and Rodnyanskaya, "the highest regions of being — the historical and the cultural — are replaced by arbitrary fictions, a second reality that may be manipulated by those at the top, and must be believed by those at the bottom" (315). This process primarily involves three "mechanisms": "the liquidation of collective memory, the control of the past, the manipulation of time" (315). With tight control over information and even memory, these totalitarian states attempt to ensure absolute obedience.

One of the most frequent manifestations of such mechanisms is the abolishment of written texts, at least as we know them. As Katherine Pennavaria observes, "Almost all human cultures of the world have found some way to hold on to their accrued knowledge, even if the 'data storage' is only in the memories of the people, and access is through storytelling" (230). In other words, knowledge (and information) is critical to civilization; the states in these cautionary tales take advantage of this to reinforce their power. In stories where "books were lost or deliberately destroyed" or where "written texts were altered so that no one could trust the historical records anymore," according to Pennavaria, "the result is a stagnant, dying culture" nearly every time (230), a nightmare state. This incalculable loss is a critical element of control in many cautionary tales with the most direct example being *Fahrenheit 451*. In another classic text, *Brave New World*, "books are outlawed, and history has been officially eliminated as 'irrelevant.' The official record exists only in government-controlled recordings used to condition people during sleep" (233). We see the opposite problem in *Nineteen Eighty-Four* where it is not a lack of information but rather its overabundance that maintains order as "citizens are constantly bombarded with 'information' via a television they cannot turn off" (234). In this, and in many other cautionary tales, knowledge has not been eliminated but made meaningless through the ironclad state control over all records. Once that crucial cultural element has lost its meaning, the fictional state's ability to control its people increases and, consequently, its power grows. For this reason, according to Baccolini and Moylan, resistance in these stories often involves "a verbal confrontation and the reappropriation of language

[as] ... the process of taking control over the means of language, representation, memory, and interpellation is a crucial weapon" (6). Even if this effort ultimately fails, the very struggle reflects our fears regarding the power of information in the relationship between the state and its citizens.

When information control fails, however, and a character learns too much or begins to introduce Misrule, the "appropriate" state response is often not banishment but rather the transport of the outlaw "to a reconditioning center or [to somehow] have his imagination excised" (Dunn and Erlich 50). In other words, the solution is to change the mind, literally, of the deviant. As Dunn and Erlich observe, "the ultimate achievement [is] to leave the subject apparently free, but totally committed to his role in the organism of the state" (51). Such compliance is a common result in cautionary tales as the non-conformist hero is forced (usually after torture) to, according to Galtseva and Rodnyanskaya, "demonstrate complicity with power and the willingness to be reformed" (295), which ensures state control. This reconditioning appears as a means of control in the Power of the State nightmare from the inception of the dystopia with *We* and *Nineteen Eighty-Four* and continues to play a key role today.

State psychological control, however, is an ongoing process, not simply a means to control opposition. Frequently, technology such as Orwell's telescreens, Varracchio observes, are employed to "uphold conformity, denying individuals their own privacy and personal feelings" (98); this allows nightmare states to dehumanize and desensitize their populations into compliance for, as Harris notes, "the omnipresent telescreen strips away the privacy necessary to the development of individual consciousness" (49). Living in such "a disembodied world which offers loss of self and a sense of invulnerability through identification with absolute power" (Harris 47) profoundly distorts the human psyche. For Roger Schlobin, this loss of individuality is central to the dystopian tradition since "loss of control" over life, thought, love, etc., "is the archetypal human phobia" (14–15). Exploiting this phobia allows totalitarian states to exercise power and maintain control and cautionary tales such as the ones in this chapter, as Schlobin describes, "mourn or satirize the impotency of the will to free itself from the dark world" (15).

There are many ways cautionary tales reflect this element of psychological control including what Harris describes as "abolishing 'ordinary human feeling' and 'enjoyment of the process of life'" in an effort "to clear the way for an experience of merging with absolute power which will transcend both mortality and the limitations of the individual" (46). In other words, such absolute power cannot be experienced by a "normal" human being; fundamental alterations must occur because, according to Galtseva and Rodnyanskaya, "in order to make the human being happy, he has to be radically remade" (299). However, as Galtseva and Rodnyanskaya also observe, "whatever the possibilities presented by the miracles of science, those who wish to possess the person's inner world cannot avoid the old tested methods. So the chief 'miracle' ... still turns out to be *fear*" (317). Thus, fear is the crucial final ingredient in all the state's psychological tools: fear of discovery (as in *Fahrenheit 451*), fear of punishment (as in Alan Moore's *V for Vendetta*), fear of capture (as in *V: The Miniseries*), etc. "Without the terrorizing power, the rest of the 'pedagogy' remains ineffectual" (317), Galtseva and Rodnyanskaya argue, something cautionary tales reflect so often as the "spy, the surgeon, and the executioner follow alongside any upstanding conformist" (318).

The means a nightmare state will employ in its quest for (holding onto) power do not stop at the mind but also frequently include interference on a biological level as well, taking dehumanization quite literally, when as Carrie Hintz and Elaine Ostry observe, "In many dystopias, totalitarian societies assert the power of determining who lives and who dies" (9). For Nanelle and David Barash, "a denial of biology" is the scariest nightmare in the dystopian repertoire because "the deepest demands of human nature are either subverted, prevented, or simply made unattainable," something we see taken to a horrifying extreme in Margaret Atwood's *Handmaid's Tale*. When the state in these cautionary tales exercises total control over the genetic make-up of the population by dictating reproduction, as Barash and Barash argue, "it ignores a fundamental flaw in the glorious, über-scientific plan: The 'numbers' [e.g., in *We*] are, in fact, human beings. And also animals." This unnatural misrecognition is employed by totalitarian states as effective means of control in many cautionary tales, but in order to maintain power, biological regulation must be total. Reproductive control is required for "stability [and] ... to prevent the unexpected future" (300) in addition to the accompanying need to "tame the Eros" after "the 'nationalization' of childbirth," as Galtseva and Rodnyanskaya describe (301). Family, in the traditional sense, is meaningless because eugenics "tear[s] away organic heredity" (303); even death must be reconceptualized, as in we see *We*, where "the horror of death is opposed to the enthusiasm of merging in a collective march," and in *Brave New World*'s Hospitals for the Dying (302). This control, however, maintains stability by removing humanity, as Kay Sambell describes: "By accepting a final solution based on perfection and stability, humanity has perversely resisted and opposed life itself [in the classic dystopian novel]. The opportunity for adaptation and change, the principle on which evolutionary change relies, has been systematically removed" (166), a removal that is the source of many of our nightmares.

Art Imitating Life: McCarthy versus Speculative Fiction

Nightmares about government control aren't always projections into the distant future — sometimes they are warnings about the near. As we've seen in other categories of nightmares, cautionary tales also reflect current, real world situations. Pennavaria describes this inclination when she argues that "those who write creatively and imaginatively about the future are not predicting — they are describing their own fears, and the potential, whether positive or negative, they see in their own culture" (232). In this way, two articles published in the 1950s (Ray Bradbury's "Day After Tomorrow: Why Science Fiction?" from 1953 and L.W. Michaelson's "Social Criticism in Science Fiction" from 1954) are of particular interest because of their direct connection to the McCarthy hearings. The censorship and fear stemming from Senator McCarthy's witch-hunt for communists made speculative fiction particularly attractive to those who opposed him because, as Michaelson writes:

> The channeling of man's critical sense, via science fiction, from the currently inhospitable field of the present to the more secure areas of the distant future or the past, is due in part to the increasing sensitivity of Americans to criticism of any kind. ... [and because] the McCarthys have ever been with us [502–503].

Michaelson argues that speculative fiction writers of his time used the genre, in part, "as a blind to throw off potential thought policeman or censorship" (504). Bradbury himself goes out on a seemingly even more precarious limb with his claim that "when the wind is right, a faint odor of kerosene is exhaled from Senator McCarthy," alluding to his short story "The Fireman," which was eventually expanded to become *Fahrenheit 451* (364). Years later, at a 1968 MLA Forum, Frederick Pohl looked back on that time of fear and remarked:

> In that miserable past decade in American history that we now call the McCarthy period ... sf provided the only really free press in this country. For a time when presidents and newspaper editors were running for shelter, about the only people speaking up openly to tell it like it was were Edward R. Murrow, one or two Senators, and just about every sf writer alive [Clareson X-86].

Speculative fiction provided Bradbury and other writers a vehicle to warn against the dangers of McCarthy's hearings as well as of fascism and other manifestations of an oppressive state. And more than fifty years later, speculative fiction still acts as a catalyst for raising awareness of the Power of the State nightmare. For example, during the promotional media tour for the 2002 movie version of Philip K. Dick's "Minority Report," speculative fiction and reality converged: in an ABCNews.com article, the film's director, Steven Spielberg, shared his concern that "America's war on terrorism has set in motion new high-tech methods to try to find criminals before they can carry out their crimes" (Wolf). Spielberg (and others) worry that this technology could cross the line, giving the government too much power, a fear reflected in speculative fiction for nearly the last hundred years.

Indeed, the current political climate of balancing security with privacy, government control with personal freedom, may, with the benefit of fifty years hindsight, appear to be another time when we came close to falling into the oppressive, dystopic visions reflected by speculative fiction's cautionary tales. For that reason, and for many others, the genre sounds warnings about the Power of the State because the loss of our liberties is perhaps the greatest nightmare humankind faces, something the texts in the next two sections unmistakably reflect.

Defining the Nightmare: Print Examples

The Power of the State nightmare is perhaps most commonly associated with what Foote describes as "the three great twentieth-century dystopias": Zamyatin's *We*, Orwell's *Nineteen Eighty-Four*, and Huxley's *Brave New World*. Almost as well known as these three (maybe more so in *We*'s case), Bradbury's *Fahrenheit 451* also depicts an individual's struggle against his government, with this state maintaining control by denying access to books and substantive thought. Adding to the pedigree of this nightmare, Greenland notes the similarity between *Nineteen Eighty-Four* and G.K. Chesterton's 1904 *The Napoleon of Notting Hill*, with the main difference being the latter is set in the past, rather than the future (124). And almost fifteen years earlier than Orwell, Sinclair Lewis's *It Can't Happen Here* cautions "that overzealous efforts to repel Communism could lead to totalitarianism in America" (Booker, *Dystopian* 98), a startlingly prescient warning; the extremists in this 1935 novel resort to the very methods of brutal repression, including book burning, against which they are supposedly defending America.

There's no denying, however, that Orwell has the greatest cultural recognition when it comes to the Power of the State nightmare. "Aware of the power explosion, and deeply disturbed by the atomic bombs dropped during World War II, George Orwell made central to his writing the discussion of unchecked power," according to Thomas Cooper, "*1984* is a prolonged meditation upon power as *the* underlying human goal" (84). Many critics are careful to point out, however, that Orwell's novel (and that of others) is not inextricably bound to the culture or era of its creation. Cooper (citing Bernard Crick's *George Orwell: A Life*) argues that the narrative is a "carefully premeditated warning against totalitarian tendencies within ourselves and within all societies, *not* as commentary about previous or existing Fascist or Communist regimes within Germany, Japan, Italy, and Russia" (my emphasis 85). W. Russel Gray observes that *Nineteen Eighty-Four* dramatizes how "strong-willed officials [across eras and geographic boundaries] exploit the age-old behavioral principles that make the best of us susceptible to mind-molding," principles which include the polarization of conflicts, the Bandwagon effect, and the use of association to create slogan words that obscure meaning (113). This broader relevance allows *Nineteen Eighty-Four* to reflect the Power of the State nightmare into the twenty-first century.

Despite his incredible name recognition, Orwell was not the first to produce a dystopian work; that distinction is usually granted to Yevgeny Zamyatin whose *We* was denied publication in his own country but originally published in English in 1924 (I.F. Clarke). Gary Kern describes Zamyatin's text as extending "contemporary reality [Bolshevik Russia] to its fantastical logical conclusion" (280) where regimentation rules and humans are reduced to mechanical numbers who are part of the One State. Life is regulated down to glass apartments monitored by unseen Guardians and the Table of Hours, which even dictates the number of chews per bite at meals. The city is physically isolated from unruly nature by a Green Wall; biological and psychological control is maintained by, among other things, the destruction of "'the center of imagination'" (49), thereby "getting rid of anything that makes us free and spontaneous" (Dunn and Erlich 50). Not surprisingly, dissidents plot to overthrow this regime, attempting to reintroduce the unpredictable and biological back into their society.

The third novel of Foote's triumvirate, 1932's *Brave New World*, presents a dystopic state that relies on the tools of both bureaucracy and technology to maintain social order. Huxley himself describes the biological facet of his novel when he writes, "The systematic drugging of individuals for the benefit of the State (and, incidentally, of course, for their own delight) was a main plank in the policy of the World Controllers. The daily soma ration was an insurance against personal maladjustment, social unrest, and the spread of subversive ideas" (232). While Huxley considers his work to be a fable (231), Patrick Aiex describes *Brave New World* as an accepted part of the literary canon, "considered a great novel both in and apart from the genre" (2). Indeed, along with *Nineteen Eighty-Four*, *Brave New World* is one of the few speculative fiction works frequently identified as "Literature."

The speculative fiction tradition of warning against state oppression begun by Zamyatin, Huxley, Bradbury, and Orwell continues today. Extending Huxley's biological control model, the state in Lois Lowry's *The Giver* enforces tranquility by eliminating "all personal volition that may lead to pain and conflict" as "family bonds are removed, pills are taken to suppress 'stirrings' (sexual urges), the weak and elderly are 'released' into death, and there is no contact with the natural world" (Hintz 261). Those who do not meet the community's criteria for perfection in Lowry's world are also "released" (Hintz, et al. 218); this society has, however, "deemed it important to have at least one person who remembers existence before emotional and physical reality were changed" so someone is forced to be "the giver" and experience "memories ... of a world with choice and unregulated experience" (Hintz 262). Reflecting a similar nightmare, the regime in *The Awakening Water* by G.R. Kesteven maintains order by drugging the people or by imprisoning them (217) while drugs are combined with memory deletion to prevent aggression in Ann Schlee's *The Vandal* (Hintz, et al. 224). Those who do not conform to the orders of the United Social Alliance of Earth in Sonia Levitin's *The Cure* are either "recycled" or "cured" into believing diversity is the ultimate danger to society; similarly, artists who do not employ their talents to create what society dictates are killed or exiled in *Gathering Blue*, another novel by Lowry (Hintz, et al. 218).

For the title character of Kurt Vonnegut's "Harrison Bergeron," the price for social peace includes penalties for being too handsome and intelligent when everyone is "equal": Bergeron is forced to wear a mask and heavy weights while other nonconformists "have their brains blasted by assorted cacophony" (McNurlin, "Part II" 24). Vonnegut's protagonist is eventually killed by the Handicapper General after exposing his true "unequal" nature on national television. Equality is enforced using even more extreme means in Richard A. Lovett's 2003 novelette "Equalization" where the state transfers consciousnesses between bodies so everyone truly is equal; few question this process because, as the narrator tells us, "to build lasting power, being able to write culture mores and the rule of economics is far more effective than military might. If that power is bolstered by no more legal authority than is absolutely necessary, your subjects never even realize they've been conquered" (20). Both of these examples reflect our fear that even a social good like equality can become oppressive when enforced by a totalitarian system.

The biological control is similarly invasive in another Vonnegut story, *Sirens of Titan*, where a "perfect military world, a world in which people do the jobs assigned to them" is achieved through "the literal installation of control devices" (Dunn and Erlich 53). And in Megan Terry's 1968 play *Home*, the faceless Control regulates reproduction by implanting contraceptive capsules in each female at birth (Dunn and Erlich 55). A global regime uses propaganda and population control to regulate dwindling natural resources in Thomas Baird's *Smart Rats* (Hintz, et al. 202) while biology is not only the means of control in Thomas Disch's *Camp Concentration* but also the reason Camp Archimedes exists in the first place: it is "a colony for breeding artificially-tailored geniuses" (Swirski 162). In Disch's "334," control over reproduction combines with high-tech surveillance and other psychological means of control to create a "world of spiritual inertia and philistine mediocrity wherein the commercials are better than the TV programs" (Swirski 170).

Information is the primary method of control in Roger Eldridge's *Shadow of the Gloom-World*, where community leaders forbid dreams and pictures as well as memories of the dead, trying to eliminate the possibility of history (Hintz, et al. 208–09). In another nightmare world, the Whole World Government of Caroline Macdonald's *The Eyewitness* maintains order through surveillance and strict control over movement and associations (Hintz, et al. 219).

The power lies in technology in Alfred Bester's *Computer Connection*, as political oppression is enforced by the "supercomputer that governs the Earth" (Mann 65) while the human technological elite in Monica Hughes's young adult novel *Devil on My Back* rely on a rigid hierarchical structure to control the "have-nots," creating a totalitarian society in which it "is only outside the system that a better world can be found" (Hughes 158). Taking the reverse approach, the communities in Ann Halam's Transformations Trilogy (*The Daymaker*, 1987; *Transformations*, 1988; and *The Skybreaker*, 1990) employ magic to destroy technology and restore the environment, becoming "repressive" and "intolerant" out of superstition, as they "attempt to control and deny the past" (Hintz, et al. 212). Fritz Leiber's 1950 novel *Gather Darkness!* operates on a similar premise of repressed technology while, in *The Pixel Eye*, a 2003 novel by Paul Levinson, technological tools of the state are taken to a sinisterly humorous new extreme: squirrels are outfitted with remote control listening devices, as well as explosives. As Tom Easton describes in a review for *Analog*, "They spy on you, and if they don't like what they see or hear, there's no nonsense about arrest, rights, or trials. Just KA-BOOM!" (Jan/Feb., 232).

Though in a much different manner, animals are also at the center of the nightmare in *Watership Down*, Richard Adams's 1972 novel where rabbits stand in for humans caught in a repressive society run by military officers. More recently, the nightmare of governmental oppression is one of the premises of Allen Steele's 2002 novel *Coyote*, which depicts a politically-splintered Earth looking to expand into the galaxy. A more traditional dystopia, in a non-traditional format, is Alan Moore's *V for Vendetta*, a comic series published by DC Comics in graphic novel format in 1989 (and adapted into a 2006 feature film). This near-future story depicts a fascist England recovering from a nuclear conflict, with the Norsefire party playing the role of the Nazis, rebuilding society at a tremendous cost, including cameras on corners, concentration camps, and medical experiments. Into this nightmare world comes a terrorist who uses the superpowers he gained from those experiments to try to topple the government. And, as Cherith Baldry argues, the work of Terry Pratchett seems to present evil "not in conventional bogeys like ghosts or aliens, but in the forces of officialdom which do not care about the fate of individuals" (29–30). According to Baldry, Pratchett depicts the consequences of powerful bureaucracies and big business in such stories as *Johnny and the Dead* (published in 1994) and 1993's *Only You Can Save Mankind* (30).

The focus changes in Edward Abbey's *Good News*, where economic and environmental collapse create to a world in which "a religious fanatic and ex-military man turned university professor" intends to use force to reestablish the United States as a totalitarian state (Stevenson 131). While Stevenson declares *Good News* to be insufficiently terrifying to qualify as a dystopia, from the perspective of the Nightmares Model, it is an example of a cautionary tale warning of the road to oppression. Environmental collapse and religion also combine in *The Handmaid's Tale*, Atwood's 1986 novel (as well as the 1990 film and 2000 opera based on it), one of the most respected and well-known examples of an oppressive regime's use of religion as a means of psychological control. In this chilling narrative, a totalitarian state is created by a political and military coup d'état precipitated at least in part by the environmental pollution that has left most women infertile. A mixture of religious fanaticism, psychological conditioning, censorship, terror, and brute force maintains control over the female population, which includes the rigid segregation of women based on their fertility. In this world "in which 'love is not the point.' And neither, of course, is motherhood or child-rearing," according to Barash and Barash, basic biological urges are (at least officially) suppressed in the maintenance of state power. Psychological control occurs, in part, by naming: the main character's name, Offred, indicates her sole acknowledged identity is that of serving Fred, her Commander, as those in charge of "the faceless power of the state driven by religious fanatics" use such schemes to "strip others of their identity while keeping their own and creating privileges for themselves" (Stevenson 134).

Speculative fiction's warnings about the Power of the State even appear in the theater. In May 2005, the Royal Opera premiered *1984*, conductor Lorin Maazel's adaptation of Orwell's classic (Tommasini). On the New York stage, Caryl Churchill's play *Far Away* is reviewed by Lawrence Frascella (using references to both Kafka and *Nineteen Eighty-Four*) as a "surreal, nearly sci-fi play" about a "violent futuristic society" that warns of "cultures of violence and media distraction" (92). That media, back in "reality," also produces compelling cautionary tales reflecting our fears of the Power of the State.

Expanding the Nightmare: Film and Television Examples

The first dystopian novel, Zamyatin's *We*, is also credited with inspiring the earliest film to reflect the Power of the State nightmare, 1926's *Metropolis* (I.F. Clarke). Director Fritz Lang's groundbreaking film depicts the struggle between the Thinkers who make the plans and the Workers who make them happen. In this dystopic future world, the Thinkers dominate the Workers, despite being utterly dependant on them, until a Worker named Maria leads a revolt to overthrow the system.

The tradition begun by *Metropolis* continues in more current film and television warnings reflecting our nightmares of state oppression. Just like in *their* prose predecessor, *Brave New World*, the states in the next two films also maintain control via bio-technology. In the 1998 film *Gattaca*, the genetically-altered elite controls the government and all advancement in society. Those who are not altered have no say in their own lives, forced to play whatever roles are left to them by the regime. A similar idea, with opposite execution, is the basis for 2002's *Equilibrium*,[5] where the absence of medical alteration, not its presence, makes the main character improved and thus the outsider. In this future, to prevent another world war, the entire society is drugged to suppress emotion, while books, art, and music are forbidden in case they stir any latent feelings. When a government agent forgets to take his medication, he is forced to deal with raw emotions and realizes the oppression around him, which leads to his attempts to overthrow the system while by other agents pursue him, trying to maintain the status quo.

Psychological "treatment" and straightforward brainwashing are the tools of the state in Stanley Kubrick's 1971 film version of Anthony Burgess's novel *A Clockwork Orange*. While the government's goal of eliminating the main character's "ultra-violent" behavior is something many of us would endorse, as George Mann points out, "in their attempts to eradicate Alex's unacceptable behaviour, the authorities remove his very humanity," making the film a cautionary tale "about the freedom of choice and the right to break away from the mechanics of the state" (346). Violence is also prevented via technology in *Minority Report*, only in this 2002 movie, humans with pre-cognitive abilities are the "technology" employed by the state in an overzealous attempt to maintain order. Meanwhile, the corporate world merges with the political in the 2005 film *The Girl From Monday*, in which the "Dictatorship of the Consumer," as Stephen Holden describes, controls "this chilly *Brave New World* where everyone belongs to everyone, [and] spontaneous acts of love and charity are regarded as perverse and self-indulgent."

The tradition of the protagonist fighting against the oppressive regime he supports (or at least doesn't fear) until it turns on him is a common trope in film reflections of the Power of the State nightmare. For example, Terry Gilliam's *Brazil* follows a bureaucrat who discovers that the massive computer system his society relies on has made a mistake and therefore becomes a target of that system. Religion adds another wrinkle to the trope in the 1976 film *Logan's Run*, where ritual suicide at the age of thirty, originally a solution to overpopulation, becomes a matter of religious devotion. In this oppressive regime run by an Artificial Intelligence, few question the system because they are too young to remember when life was different. Those who do question the ritual are the ones nearing thirty who do not want to die and who then "run." A special class of agents chases after those runners who defy the status quo; it is only when the main character, one of the agents, is prematurely aged to thirty by the AI that he also questions the ritual suicide.

Another former lawman becomes the fugitive in 1995's *Judge Dredd*, based on the British comic that first appeared in 1977, in which mega-cities protect citizens from a desolate outside world and the justice system empowers Judges with the roles of judge, jury, and executioner. The flaw in this system becomes obvious when Dredd is framed for murder and sentenced to death. The trope is also a key element of George Lucas's first professional movie (based on his student film with the same title), *THX-1138*, in which a totalitarian regime replaces names with alpha-numeric codes (reflections of Zamyatin's numbers) and forces most of humanity to live underground where they are conditioned to always obey the law. When the main character breaks that law by having sex, he has to escape to a desolate outside world or face a lifetime of imprisonment.

But films aren't the only media where we see the nightmare of state oppression reflected; television and even popular music portray this fear as well. The merger of state and technology creates the world of *Max*

Headroom, a 1980s series (based on the feature film) in which television off-switches are illegal and ratings mean everything. In the sixth episode of season one, "The Blanks," citizens who are not recorded in the government's computer files, society's undesirables, are arrested. Collection and quarantine are also the tools of the fascist government in *Daybreak*, a 1993 HBO movie based on Alan Browne's play *Beirut*. In this near future New York City, an AIDS-like plague is devastating the country so the government quarantines all those infected in camps, tattooing them with a "P" so there would be no mistaking their status.

Biology and the state combine in two television series that originally aired decades apart. The first, the cult favorite *Blake's 7*, ran in Britain from 1978 to 1981, and follows a group of seven escaped prisoners attempting to evade the oppressive galactic Federation, which drugs its citizens into submission. The title hero, Blake, is a dissident who is wrongfully accused of a crime in an effort to get rid of him. A similar premise, a spaceship evading a galactic government, is the concept behind the second series, the short-lived *Firefly*, created by Joss Whedon. In this show (and the 2005 feature film *Serenity*), the Union of Planets was established after the Alliance defeated the Independents in a civil war. The Alliance seeks to control everything and everyone under its bureaucracy and commits the usual commensurate abuses, including kidnapping a young girl with superhuman abilities and attempting to biologically "improve" humanity with the expected disastrous consequences.

Biology is also the means of control for the repressive regimes in stand-alone episodes of two more genre series. Racial hatred is the public motivation in "California Reich," an episode of *Sliders* in which only "pure-whites" (determined by genetic testing) have any rights in this alternate California while those with "immigrant" blood are imprisoned in work camps. And the fifth season of *Star Trek: The Next Generation* includes "The Outcast" where the crew visits a world in which sexual preference is forbidden among the androgynous people, a prohibition enforced through therapy to "cure" those who express a tendency toward one gender or the other.

Knowledge is the key commodity in the 1960s British television series *The Prisoner*. Both the main character, known only as Number 6, and his captors attempt to gain valuable information from the other: Number 6 wants to find out why he is in the prison as well as the identity of the absent Number One who runs it while the successive Number Twos (always a different person) want to know why Number 6 left the British spy service. The ending of the series may be ambiguous, especially regarding the actual "state" behind the prison, but the environment in which Number 6 lives is clearly a totalitarian regime that maintains control by controlling information. In another permutation, misinformation is the tool; in *The Running Man* (based on the Stephen King novel), the main character is framed for murder after disobeying an order. He is then hunted down in an attempt to hide his success at a televised gladiator-style sport to prevent the public from getting any ideas of beating the system.

Our fear of the Power of the State has even made its way onto the radio with records like Pink Floyd's 1979 double-album *The Wall*, which describes a fascist dystopia from the perspective of a fictional rock star. In addition, The Clash warn of future fascist states on "Groovy Times" while Kate Bush's 1985 song "Cloudbusting" describes "an Orwellian government kidnapping the inventor of a rain making machine" (Simpson 14).

While the link is unmistakable to the novels and short stories that also reflect our Power of the State nightmares, speculative fiction film and television often take a different approach from dystopian prose. Where the state already exists in the novels by Zamyatin, Orwell, and Huxley, visual texts frequently show the process of how that state can come into being. The first two *Star Wars* prequels, *Episode I: The Phantom Menace* and *Episode II: Attack of the Clones*, warn of the ways in which a skilled, corrupt politician can use various crises to grasp power. In these movies, Senator/Chancellor Palpatine (via his alter-ego, Darth Sidious) continually engineers political and military emergencies such as blockades and secession movements to maneuver himself into a position of extraordinary power. And yet, in *Episode I*, only our knowledge of Palpatine's future title of Emperor (in *Episodes IV-VI*) allows us to see his sinister motives for what they are. On the surface, he doesn't seem any more devious than we might expect any politician to be. It all appears quite sensible and relatively harmless, even noble, until it is too late — which is exactly what happens in *Episode III: Revenge of the Sith*: Palpatine's schemes culminate not only in the massacre of the Jedi but also in the formation of the Galactic Empire from the tattered remains of the democratic Republic.

This "process of fascism" is also a key element of the 1990s television series *Babylon 5*, which turns in part on a four-season-long story arc in which a small group of humans slowly turns a democracy into a fascist state. The groundwork is laid in the first season when anti-alien radicals call for the Earth Alliance (EA) to expel all aliens who had moved to Earth and to focus solely on the interests and goals of humans. That season culminates in the assassination, disguised as an accident, of the EA president, allowing the vice president (who is more amenable to the covert group's plans) to assume the office. The next season and a half depict the slow but steady process of taking control, which includes the introduction of

Ministries of Peace and Truth, the creation of a paid informers brigade known as Nightwatch, and the passage of sedition acts. The plot reaches a crisis point when the new president declares martial law after his people intentionally inflame fears over a powerful new enemy that is actually an alien race secretly helping the group take control; the command crew of the Babylon 5 station secedes from the Earth Alliance rather than support the fascist regime that has taken over their own government. The storylines of the second half of the third season and the fourth season then depict (among other events) their efforts to reclaim Earth from totalitarian oppression.

A more mystical attempt at seizing control of a state, indeed a world, occupies the fourth season of the *Buffy, the Vampire Slayer* spin-off, *Angel*. In a story arc that culminated in spring 2003, a powerful "higher being" named Jasmine attempts to create World Peace by magically making everyone who sees her feel happy and loved. Unfortunately, to sustain this magic, Jasmine needs to (literally) consume people and, in addition, does not hesitate to kill those who defy her to maintain her hold on the world. Eventually, the heroes succeed in defeating Jasmine but wonder if ending World Peace, despite its cost, was the right decision.

Two decades earlier, there were no such lingering questions when NBC aired the television mini-series, *V*. As writer and director Kenneth Johnson describes on the commentary track of the 2001 DVD release, "*V* is really about power and who has it and who wants it and who's ignoring it and who wants to fight against it." The opening minutes of both episodes include the dedication: "To the heroism of the Resistance Fighters—past, present, and future—this work is respectfully dedicated" (*V: The Original Miniseries.*). The miniseries is clearly both a memorial to those who resisted (and who couldn't resist) the Nazis, and a cautionary tale reminding us that the path to a totalitarian state often looks new and exciting.

The nightmare depicted in *V* is perhaps best articulated by the character of Abraham, a Holocaust survivor. About halfway through the story, Abraham attempts to hide a scientist and his family (the *V* parallel to the Jews) despite his son Stanley's terror at being turned into the Visitors (the alien equivalent of the Nazi party), who have taken over the government and are enforcing martial law. In a moving soliloquy, Abraham finally tells Stanley the truth of his wife's death in the "showers with no water" of the concentration camp and then says, "Perhaps if somebody had given us a place to hide. Don't you see Stanley? They have to stay or else we haven't learned a thing." Perhaps that is truly the essence of the warnings in this chapter—the nightmare that would follow if we don't learn the lessons so many have died teaching us.

While those lessons have been reflected in a relatively consistent manner over the past century, more so than in really any other category, more recent interpretations of the nightmare do have some distinguishing features that separate them from the "classic" dystopias like *Nineteen Eighty-Four* and *We* that often define the fear in our culture. These features seem to be related to a greater sense of optimism that manifests itself in two ways: 1) The "process of fascism" plot in film and television that we just discussed; and 2) The ability of outsider characters to at least outrun, if not overthrow, the totalitarian regime. In the former, we see the dystopias becoming even more directly cautionary as they specifically warn of the political and social elements that must fall into place for a nightmare state to come into being. There seems to be no doubt that these tales are designed to help us prevent that from occurring, and usually end with the alert characters who recognize the warning signs triumphing over the new tyranny. An interesting component to this addition of "process" stories is that we see them most frequently in film and television series where audiences have a chance to get to know the characters in more depth and writers have a chance to develop complex, layered worlds, thus laying the necessary groundwork for the descent into fascism. As both history and speculative fiction show us, that descent doesn't happen overnight and multiple sequels and/or season(s)-long story arcs provide the genre with the opportunity to depict this facet of the nightmare in much greater detail.

We also see more hope and optimism in characters like Mal Washington from *Firefly* or V from *V for Vendetta* than in what Baccolini and Moylan describe as the "canonical form of dystopia" (1). While these heroes (to some) are not able to completely overthrow the totalitarian regime of their worlds like we see at the end of *V: The Final Battle* or *Return of the Jedi*, they are at least able to carve out an existence for themselves outside of the control of the nightmare states. Even when their efforts fail, as in "Equalization," they can still tell their story and inspire others, unlike, for example, Winston in *Nineteen Eighty-Four*. Perhaps this indicates that, as time has passed and we are more removed from the horrors of World War II and McCarthyism, our optimism is returning. It's not that we are any less afraid of the totalitarian state, for that nightmare continues to be reflected throughout the genre. Rather, our confidence in our ability to learn from the past, and from cautionary tales, seems to be growing. This nightmare no longer seems quite so inevitable, and the genre reflects the hope that maybe, if we keep telling these stories, it will never happen again. Perhaps the optimism that existed at the turn of the twentieth century, reflected by Wells's utopias, is returning but in a tempered form, as we are now wiser after many real and fictional bouts with totalitarianism.

The presence of some sort of state is a defining characteristic of civilized society. But not all states are the same, as both history and speculative fiction teach us. At the same time, the right to personal freedom is perhaps the single most important belief shared by contemporary American culture, making its loss one of our greatest fears. The balance between the state and that freedom is constantly being negotiated and cautionary tales that warn us about the consequences if the scales are tipped too far in the state's direction are an integral part of that process. The words of Orwell and Huxley and Moore and Atwood combine with the images from *Star Wars* and *V* and *Babylon 5* and all of the others to form a significant part of our cultural rhetoric, informing our choices and our debates about the Power of the State.

7: Big Brother and Darth Vader on the Evening News: Power Images in the Mainstream Media

Speculative fiction reflections of our fears regarding power, both that wielded by Individuals and by the State, do not exist in a vacuum; just as we saw in Chapter 4, these cautionary tales create compelling images that public discourse uses to try to negotiate the complexities of this nightmare. In our examinations and debates over power, whether in our evening entertainment or in our newspapers, texts such as *Nineteen Eighty-Four* and even *Star Wars* are rarely far from the cultural conversation. The rhetorical symbiosis between genre images and mainstream public discourse is, if anything, even more intense when it comes to our Power nightmares than it is with our fears of Science and Technology.

Not surprisingly, speculative fiction images of power abuse are particularly common within mainstream media political debates. When it comes to global politics, Jutta Weldes observes, popular culture plays a critical role in defining, communicating, and even constructing such situations, so much so that "official representations thus depend on the cultural resources of a society" ("Popular" 7), resources that include speculative fiction texts. Weldes describes this construction in detail:

> The plausibility of official representations depends on the way in which publics understand world politics and the location and role of their own and other states and actors in it. It matters very much that state officials are able to represent world politics, and thus their foreign policies, in ways that at least significant portions of their publics find

plausible and persuasive. Plausibility comes, at least in part, from the structural congruence between official representations and peoples' everyday experiences [7].

Even though Weldes is primarily concerned with the images used by governments and their agents, given the interdependence she identifies, we should not be surprised to see that political commentary is itself also littered with speculative fiction references. And as Neta C. Crawford observes later in the same volume as Weldes's essay, "Analysts sometimes use science fiction or fantasy images to emphasize the absurdity of political situations" (197). Given the central role of the state and/or those individuals who are in charge in our Power nightmares, these particular cautionary tales often provide the images Crawford describes.

While politics and the business of governing dominate the examples we are about to discuss, these are not the only public discourses in which we find images from our Power nightmares. Debates regarding such varied concerns as mental health and technology also leverage speculative fiction images. As with the Nuclear War and Biology images we saw in Chapter 4, metaphors that invoke Power of the Individual cautionary tales rely on emblematic characters to convey the "interpretive frames" described in the Wellcome Trust study. In this chapter, I will focus on two primary sources for those characters—*Star Wars* and *The Strange Case of Dr. Jekyll and Mr. Hyde*—with just a brief diversion back to Frankenstein. The images public discourse mines from the Power of the State nightmares, however, do not follow the same pattern; elements other than characters provide the reference. The targeted metaphors from this subcategory, Big Brother and Orwellian (from *Nineteen Eighty-Four*) and *Brave New World*, are nevertheless instantly recognizable shorthand phrases for the totalitarian nightmare.

Individual Power Images from Speculative Fiction in Mainstream Media

George Lucas's saga of good, evil, and redemption is often credited with creating the science fiction blockbuster, and, now that it's complete, the six-part tale of the fall and redemption of Anakin Skywalker is arguably one of the most influential series of movies in any genre. Over the past three decades, *Star Wars* imagery and metaphors have become second-nature shorthand in American culture. The influence of *Star Wars* even goes beyond verbal rhetoric to include musical references as well: On January 26, 2003, ABC Sports played the Imperial March (composed by John

Williams for the first *Star Wars* in 1977 and included in every episode since) during the introduction of the Oakland Raiders at Super Bowl XXXVII.

As I described in the Introduction, the criticism of President Reagan's defense initiative as "Star Wars" is perhaps the best-known example of this shorthand. When, as David S. Meyer notes, "Reagan readily accepted the critics' language, welcoming an association with the romanticism and the lure of technological advancement" (99) that came along with the *Star Wars* metaphor, both the plausibility and the persuasiveness Weldes describes as essential to "official representations" ("Popular" 7) were achieved; the groundwork was thus laid for the political use of *Star Wars*. In more recent applications of the imagery, the ominous figure of Darth Vader frequently appears in editorials and even in fictional politics. When referenced in these venues, Vader represents the personification of evil and/or the enforcer for an evil, totalitarian regime who uses fear to keep subordinates in line. Such metaphors have been invoked to describe Vice President Dick Cheney[1] (see Dowd, "Out of Africa" and "Uncle Dick and Papa"), former Speaker of the House Newt Gingrich (see Goldstein), and, in a letter to the *San Francisco Chronicle*'s "Two-Cents" column, Israeli Prime Minister Ariel Sharon.

The potent combination of the *Star Wars* villain and politics also appears in "An Khe," a February 2004 episode of *The West Wing*, when the Deputy Chief of Staff refers to a Congressman as "the Darth Vader of childcare." National politics (fictional or not) are not required for the Vader image to be employed, however, as when a former administrator of Michigan's Department of Environment Quality is described as "the 'Darth Vader of environment stewardship'" (Brigid Schulte). By including these two short words in their rhetoric, political commentators leverage our mass cultural experience with a Power of the Individual nightmare; in these references, the extreme power (and correspondingly extreme corruption) of Lucas's fallen hero turned über-villain (turned hero again), works, as Crawford notes, to foster a sense of the absurd when it comes to the workings of "real" politics.

In another permutation on this metaphor, the visual of Darth Vader as an imposing, intimidating figure is often invoked in public discourse regarding police and security operations. Massachusetts state police assigned to security at the 2004 Democratic National Convention are described as having "doffed their black Darth Vader riot gear of helmets, padded vests, and shin protectors" (Kifner) while the American Embassy in London, which is "surrounded by chain-link fences, patrolled by guards with automatic weapons, and protected by the sort of concrete barriers that Darth Vader might select for his own headquarters," is criticized on both aesthetic and practical grounds in the *New York Times* (Lyall). As with more direct political coverage, the extreme nature of the Vader image add intensity to such critiques of security measures.

When it comes to the military, Darth Vader references also conjure this same image of intimidation. For example, according to Mark Glassman, the current strategy for dealing with fear and combat stress among American soldiers is much different from when "Clearchus, a Spartan general, taught his army to fear the brass more than the enemy, a sort of Darth Vader school of military psychology." And Kim Murphy reports that, during the appearance of a U.S. B-52 bomber at a Russian air show, "crowds of Russians maneuvered around the plane that has been the Darth Vader of the American strategic arsenal for 50 years." At the same time, another Lucas character (actually group of characters), the Jedi, is employed in similar public discourse to convey nearly the polar opposite figure, that of a noble warrior. In his analysis of the impact of the *Star Wars* films on American culture, Meyer cites a 1991 *Boston Globe* story that reports army officers responsible for planning strategy during the Persian Gulf War called themselves "Jedi Knights" (99). Because of the popularity of *Star Wars*, Meyer argues, "It is not surprising then, that military and political figures have tried to use imagery from the films to build support for their policies" (99). Such imagery even permeates "official" military life as one Navy training scenario, described by Sandra Chereb, involved recovering "Two Navy pilots [who] were shot down near a desert outpost dubbed 'Jedi.'" Thus, it seems that when the media depicts the military, the *Star Wars* image they often invoke is that of the evil Darth Vader, but when members of the military describe themselves, it is the noble tradition of the Jedi, from which Anakin Skywalker fell and thus became Darth Vader, that they reference. The implications of this disparity, though hardly proven with these few examples, are profound and complex; I could easily fill many pages exploring it but we, unfortunately, do not have the space to do so here.

When *Star Wars* first appeared in theaters during the summer of 1977, it became an unprecedented success, leaving its permanent mark on popular culture. Since then, five more movies have been released and *Star Wars* images are now firmly entrenched in our rhetoric. In his review of *Episode II: Attack of the Clones* for the *Los Angeles Times*, Kenneth Turan describes the cultural icon that *Star Wars* has become: "When that first film was being made, it meant less than zero to say you were part of *Star Wars*; the eyes of the world were not on the production, to say the least. Now, everything has been close to sanctified." We can see such sanctification in many facets of our cultural discourse from politics to Emmy-winning television dramas to major sporting events to the nation's defense. References to *Star Wars* have worked their way out of the cultural margins where speculative fiction usually dwells and into the mainstream, carrying with them especially potent and complex cultural meaning.

Just as Anakin Skywalker succumbs to evil because of his inability to control his own power, so too does Dr. Jekyll lose himself to his desire for power. In the latter case, however, the consequences of this descent occur on a much more individual level and the ways in which public discourse invokes the Jekyll and Hyde image reflect this. In many respects, Robert Louis Stevenson's 1886 novel *The Strange Case of Dr. Jekyll and Mr. Hyde* is better known for the images of good and evil it created than for the story's particulars. The impact on public discourse, though, of Stevenson's image was nearly immediate. The main character(s) are referenced in Charles W. Chestnutt's 1901 novel *The Marrow of Tradition* when the narrator describes a black servant's narrow escape from being lynched for a crime he did not commit: "Sandy, having thus escaped from the Mr. Hyde of the mob, now received the benediction of its Dr. Jekyll" (233). While few people in today's society may be able to describe the specifics of Stevenson's story, we are at least superficially familiar with the dichotomy inherent in the title character(s), a familiarity the media exploits when it invokes the image in public discourse.

As with Darth Vader, the Jekyll and Hyde metaphor is often invoked in political discourse such as when a member of the Spokane, Washington City Council told a reporter during a city sex-scandal, "'We seem to have a Jekyll and Hyde personality in our mayor'" (Egan). Mayoral politics on the other coast (in New York City) also provokes references to Stevenson's imagery with one candidate described as having "Jekyll-and-Hyde'd his way between moderate outer-borough Catholic and fire-breathing 'other New York'-er" (Siegel). Even smaller local races like school board elections lead to such metaphors: "But already, the Norfolk, Va., transplant has shown that he's not as prickly as his predecessor, who seemed to know the right (or wrong) buttons to push to make certain members go from Dr. Jekyll to Mr. (or Ms.) Hyde" (Barton). Political discourse at the national level, not unexpectedly, also invokes Stevenson's image over such varied concerns as foreign policy—"the Bush administration has a Jekyll-and-Hyde problem — a contradictory attitude toward the war on terror" (Zakaria)—and Senate confirmations of judicial nominees—"Yet the filibuster has developed a Dr. Jekyll and Mr. Hyde reputation" (Brune).

The Jekyll and Hyde image is perhaps most powerfully invoked, however, in the medical realm and public discourse regarding psychotic and/or violent behavior. For example, a key enzyme in cancer research is described as "like Jekyll and Hyde" for its dual (and conflicting) abilities to both keep cells alive and allow deadly cancer tumors to grow indefinitely (Marsa). In addition, the irritability associated with another potentially deadly, though much rarer, disorder, Kawasaki disease, is described in another article as "Jekyll and Hyde syndrome" (H. Brown).

The violent, erratic personality changes that most strongly define the Jekyll and Hyde image make it a particularly effective metaphor for describing a variety of mental health and/or personality problems. We find such references, for example, in a *New York Times* article that examines the prevalence of depression among stockbrokers and describes a financial manager who suffered from bipolar disorder and eventually committed suicide as having "a history of Jekyll-and-Hyde-type mood swings" (L. Thomas). Stevenson's image also appears in a *San Francisco Chronicle* article to explain the difference between schizophrenia and "'split-personality' disorder — in which one person seems to be ruled by two different minds, like a Dr. Jekyll and Mr. Hyde" (Russell). This metaphor is not only used, though, to describe extreme psychological disorders; it is also invoked in media coverage of less serious conditions such as Seasonal Affective Disorder, which can cause someone to "be a perfectly normal Dr. Jekyll in September and then become the hideous Mr. Hyde in December" (Dexter).

Official psychiatric diagnoses are not always involved, however, when the Jekyll and Hyde image is used to characterize violent behavior. A Chicago criminal court judge, for example, described a schoolteacher convicted of aggravated battery as "a 'Jekyll and Hyde'" (O'Donnell) while an Assistant US Attorney in Washington, DC referred to an addict convicted of murder as "'as close to a Jekyll and Hyde situation as I can imagine there being'" (Cauvin). The image is also invoked to portray skateboard star Mark "Gator" Rogowski (who eventually went to prison for murder) in the 2003 documentary *Stoked: The Rise and Fall of Gator* (Cheng), and in an article warning women to recognize the signs their partners could be batterers, including "13) Dr. Jekyll and Mr. Hyde. Many woman are confused by their abuser's 'sudden' change in mood" (Summar).

The Strange Case of Dr. Jekyll and Mr. Hyde is not its author's only, or even most acclaimed, work. Yet there is something so powerful in it that mainstream culture has latched onto and appropriated as the best way to describe specific aspects of the human experience, most notably the destructive side of our selves that many try to keep hidden. The consistency with which the metaphor is employed, which far exceeds most we have encountered to this point, demonstrates the intensity with which the image strikes a nerve in our culture; we, therefore, rely on it to quickly and concisely express what we may be unable to in other ways.

While I discussed Frankenstein-inspired metaphors in Chapter 4 along with those mined from other Science and Technology nightmares, the image of Dr. Frankenstein as the original mad scientist is so embedded in our culture that it can bear some additional analysis here as another image from the Power of the Individual nightmare to make its way into public discourse. In his analysis of the public debate regarding research that uses human embryos, Michael Mulkay cites several analyses of the mad scientist theme (such as Andrew Tudor's from 1989 and Christopher Toumey's from 1992) to support his conclusion that the cultural myth of Frankenstein represents and reflects our fears of scientists who obsessively and recklessly cross into territories humans were never meant to enter. Even where Mulkay does not find explicit reference to the Frankenstein image or any other fictional mad scientist, he argues that the trope underlies the assumptions of those opposed to embryo research, showing itself in their narrative structures and characterizations of untrustworthy scientists. This conclusion provides one more lens with which we can view the examples in Chapter 4 that invoke the Frankenstein metaphor to decry genetic research, as it places those references into the long history and broader context of the mad scientist image.

Speculative fiction's warnings of the potential for power to corrupt the individuals who wield it both reflect and are reflected by our fears. On the global scale of world politics as well as the more personal scale of mental illness, public discourse employs images generated by cautionary tales to convey the terrible consequences of individuals losing themselves to too much power. From iconic villains like Darth Vader to classic mad scientists like Drs. Jekyll and Frankenstein, speculative fiction informs the cultural shorthand with which we discuss our fears regarding the Power of the Individual. While their original contexts and forms could hardly be more different, *Star Wars*, *The Strange Case of Dr. Jekyll and Mr. Hyde*, and *Frankenstein* all reflect our fears so effectively that images inspired by them permeate deep into our cultural consciousness, providing a rich trove of metaphors with which we express our nightmares.

State Power Images from Speculative Fiction in Mainstream Media

Perhaps the most influential source of images in the entire genre is George Orwell's *Nineteen Eighty-Four*. This one novel, published more than fifty years ago, has become the standard symbol of one of our greatest fears: the tyranny of a totalitarian state. As Renata Galtseva and Irina Rodnyanskaya observe, Orwell's "'Big Brother' ... [has] acquired currency in political science around the world" (296). The prevalence of the novel's images undeniably demonstrates the influence speculative fiction has on our language and rhetoric.

As the back cover of the 1981 Penguin re-issue of Orwell's 1949 novel describes, "'The language of *1984* passed into the English language as a symbol of the horrors of totalitarianism'" (qtd. in Greenland 128). Orwell's images, even his very name, are unmistakably ingrained in our cultural memories and thus the metaphors we choose. As Colin Greenland describes, "*Nineteen Eighty-Four* has been swallowed up by '1984,' the myth, which is available for anyone to exploit" (131) because "everyone knows, or thinks they know, *Nineteen Eighty-Four* by George Orwell, even if they have not read it" (128). This "myth, common property, public domain," Greenland argues, has transcended its original narrative form to influence such unrelated genres as American advertising and popular music, including the "Big Brother" track on David Bowie's *Diamond Dogs* album (129). Greenland also refers to a 1981 ad campaign for Boise Cascade that directly invoked *Nineteen Eighty-Four*: "Their advertising copy began: 'We're betting $2.3 billion Orwell was wrong. We see a sunnier future today than George Orwell did in 1948, which is one reason we've launched our most ambitious capital investment program ever'" (125).

Even into the twenty-first century, Orwellian imagery continues to play a vital role in public discourse at many levels. For example, the National Council of Teachers of English watches over the use (and abuse) of language by public figures through its Committee on Public Doublespeak. This group's mission is grounded in the conviction that "doublespeak in all too many cases is an insidious practice whereby the powerful abuse language to deceive and manipulate for the purpose of controlling public behavior — the public as consumer, as voter, as student — by depriving us of our right to make informed choices" (Kehl and Livingston 77). Such rhetorical work carries on the cautionary nature of *Nineteen Eighty-Four* for, as Frederick Pohl observes, "terms like Newspeak and Big Brother have kept such dangers [of totalitarian dictatorship] alive in the public consciousness by becoming standard epithets of political invective" ("Coming Up" 97). The influence of Orwell's novel on today's culture and our rhetorical images can easily fill a book of its own. My brief survey should provide, however, sufficient basis to illustrate Pohl's point.

The significant impact of *Nineteen Eighty-Four* on the metaphors we use is particularly obvious in the mainstream news media. Phrases such as "Big Brother" are incredibly effective shorthand for reporters because they convey so much meaning in just two words, an effectiveness Kath Filmer demonstrates in her examination of metaphor in the British news media. Filmer identifies the tendency of that media to employ "fear-evoking imagery" to characterize departing Prime Minister Margaret Thatcher and describes those images as "extremely potent conceptualising agents because of the fear they arouse, together with the notion of mindless powermongering" (202). We can see that potency reflected even by fictional characters such as in the episode of the original *Law & Order* series "Enemy" when the Assistant District Attorney declares, "Half the country believes everything the government says is Orwellian doublespeak." It's not just the hyperliterate lawyers on this long-running series who invoke the imagery: in an earlier episode, "Nullification," a chatroom post by a militia group describes an armed robbery as "a show of force to scare off Big Brother."

Filmer speculates such imagery "works subliminally since the decoding of nightmarish and monstrous metaphors of this kind takes place subconsciously for those viewers not alert to the operation of such archetypes" (203). This subliminal fear seems to be at work when references to Orwell's novel were used, as Thomas W. Cooper describes, by American journalists in the early 1980s to characterize Ayatollah Khomeini's Iranian government as "Orwellian" (83). More recently, Mark Sommer's 2002 article "Big Brother at the Library: FBI's Right to Data Raises Privacy Issues" invokes Orwell's imagery to examine "the Big Brother concerns of civil libertarians" related to 2001's USA Patriot Act. A spokesman for the FBI's Buffalo field office quoted in the same article also uses the phrase to suggest the concerns may be unwarranted: "'It's not Big Brother we have to be wary of, but industry, and the capitalist society we live in that takes (personal) information and sells it on the secondary market.'" Thus, as we found with the Science and Technology images, metaphors mined from Orwell's novel are used in attempts to ease fears as well as in public discourse intent on exciting them.

References to Big Brother are invoked to critique nearly every form of governmental oversight including state educational requirements, which are described by one Pennsylvania pollster as "'Big Brother' mandates" (Associated Press). Perhaps the most relevant contemporary public debate to employ the Orwellian image, however, is the continual cultural negotiation of surveillance, both governmental and private. For example, cameras in fire trucks in New York City, according to the president of the Uniformed Fire Officers Association, have led to longer response times "'because Big Brother is watching them [the drivers]'" (Fahim) while "The fear of getting nailed with a $70 ticket, or the moral outrage over Big Brother and his roadside camera" has increased demand for methods of obscuring license plates from red light cameras across the country (Suguira). In this latter case, the article seems to invoke Orwell's image to describe more of an annoyance than a true intrusion, perhaps suggesting a similar abatement of the fear to that indicated by the references to Godzilla we saw in Chapter 4.

While public discourse almost always opposes the installation of such cameras by the government as the beginning of the Orwellian nightmare (though the intensity of the reaction varies), the response is often more subdued when it comes to cameras in the private sector. As Jennifer 8. Lee describes, "The increasing use of private cameras in law enforcement is happening largely beneath the public policy radar. By contrast, government efforts to install and use camera systems ... have often been met with public hearings and outraged editorials raising concerns of expanding governmental 'Big Brother' powers." One such editorial is "Camera Shy" from the May 8, 2005 edition of *The New York Times*, which argues "Any technology can go awry or be abused, and it is all too easy to imagine that happening with Big Brother's little cameras" that, in this case, are being advocated by a Suffolk County, NY legislator. On the other hand, another editorial praises the installation of cameras in school hallways as an effective way to "discover who was ... defecating in the school hallways. Perhaps that will end now that the swine knows that Big Brother, or rather Big Teacher, is watching" ("Public Applause"). Once again, the ambivalence that emerges here, especially in contrast to the consistency of the Jekyll and Hyde and even Darth Vader imagery, seems to indicate almost a dulling of the image in the public mind. Perhaps, like Godzilla or Frankenstein from Chapter 4, Big Brother is so familiar that it has lost some of its punch.

Within the public debate regarding private businesses monitoring their employees, however, the advocates of such systems are still quick to declare they have no Orwellian intentions, indicating that the cultural connotation of the image is still primarily negative. For example, a lawyer specializing in labor and employment cases told Stewart Ain that, when it came to office romances, "'Beyond setting the rules of the game, I'm not into Big Brother.'" The Orwellian metaphor is even more powerful when the president and chief executive of a software company that developed a program to document every time "employees venture into unauthorized territory or fail to follow established rules for purchasing and procurement" declares, "'As long as you are doing things that are within your responsibility there's no audit trail created. That way we're not Big Brother'" (Silverman). The fact that both of these decision makers feel it is necessary to deny sinister motives demonstrates the depth of the cultural nightmare that *Nineteen Eighty-Four* still captures, despite some public ambivalence. As privacy and limits on governmental control are constantly being renegotiated and the impact of not only the September 11th terror attacks but also the July 2005 London bombings continues to be felt, we might find Orwellian expressions becoming even more prevalent in mainstream media as we attempt to "keep such dangers alive," as Pohl suggests.

Where Orwell's imagery has come to reflect one particular nightmare, the other primary source of state power metaphors in the media, *Brave New World*, has a broader impact on our cultural rhetoric. While not as deeply ingrained as Orwell's imagery in public consciousness, Aldous Huxley's novel affects our rhetoric on a scale that also seems to exceed the number of people who have actually read the original text. The phrase "brave new world"[2] permeates such diverse media as political criticism, business coverage, and human interest stories. It has even worked its way into a number one prime-time television drama, *CSI: Crime Scene Investigation*. In a third season episode entitled "Lady Heather's Box," the following exchange takes place:

> Lady Heather: My dominion is also my domain. Ladyheather.com.
> Captain Brass: So, Buchman and Richards were down here doing Internet porn, huh?
> Lady Heather: Not porn. Voyeurism in a brave new world.
> Gil Grissom: What would Aldous Huxley say?
> Lady Heather: Well ... if his credit card were valid, he could say anything he wanted at $3.95 a minute.

The fact that this reference is included in what amounts to a "throw-away" section of dialogue both establishes the pervasiveness of Huxley's imagery and ensures its continued influence.

One of the most obvious arenas for *Brave New World* references is the discussion of the role of the government in our lives. Even within this discourse, however, the diversity is impressive. The expected topic of surveillance appears in headlines like the one for an article discussing new methods for securing access to financial information, which reads "A Brave New World—Bloomberg Sees Biometrics as the Key to Preventing Unauthorized Access to its Terminals, but Will End Users View the Technology as Too Intrusive?" (Pallay); another article on public surveillance tells readers, "Welcome to the Brave New World of Policing in Chicago..." (Spielman and Main). In addition to debates over surveillance cameras, articles on the (perhaps) unexpected topic of disease control, in the wake of 2003's SARS epidemic, also employ Huxley's title: "It is a brave new world here in Singapore, where government-ordered mass temperature testing has become one of the most important measures in preventing the spread of severe acute respiratory syndrome" (Paddock).

Political commentators also display an affinity for Huxley's title, using it in editorials (as the headline of a March 2003 editorial in the *St. Louis Post-Dispatch*) ("Brave New World") and even in articles covering gambling on Native American reservations ("In the brave new world of Native

American casinos, local communities across the state are butting heads with tribes") (Doyle). The variety of these references also seems to point to a neutrality when it comes to this image, as only mild criticism seems to be implied by these media references to Huxley's novel.

Mainstream media coverage of issues related to speculative fiction's most famous and recognizable trope, the use and abuse of technology, frequently employs the *Brave New World* image. The trend toward neutrality continues even in this area, as these examples demonstrate.

- The headline of a Scripps Howard News Service piece on the potential uses for genetic testing reads, "Brave New World of Employment Screening" (Olian).
- An *Ebony* magazine article about family relationships in the computer age opens with the question, "In the brave new world of speed-dating, Internet passion and cross-country business conferences where singles meet, network and — we are told — make connections, is the old and explosive question of the impact and repercussions of one-night stands meaningful or even relevant?" (Hughes and Kinnon).
- In a *Boston Globe* piece, Jonathan Saltzman describes a new proposal for administering school lunch programs by employing Huxley's image: "Lunch time in Natick public school cafeterias could become a brave new world under a proposal to use fingerprint-scanning biometric technology — the kind increasingly used for security and surveillance in the post-9/11 world — to instantly identify students and deduct the cost of meals from their account."

Metaphors based on Huxley's novel are also frequently invoked in public discourse regarding the economic impact of increased globalization, usually as a result of technology. It is in this arena, perhaps not surprisingly, where the image seems to carry the most negative connotation. In his review of *The World is Flat: A Brief History of the 21st Century*, for example, Joseph Stiglitz describes the book as "a provocative account [of] ... what this brave new world will mean to all of us, in both the developed and the developing worlds." When it comes to more specific industry coverage, surging oil prices have created "'a brave new world in the energy markets'" (Mouawad) while "clothing makers around the globe adjust to the brave new world of markets to benefit consumers" (Brooke). Even when this metaphor is applied to non-state actors like global oil conglomerates, it carries with it the legacy of its pedigree as the title of one of the most well-known Power of State cautionary tales, bringing an unsettling edge to such references that seem to want readers to connect globalization, and perhaps economics more generally, with totalitarian oppression.

The variety of ways mainstream media uses the *Brave New World* image goes a long way in demonstrating the influence of not just the genre as a whole but also of the nightmares that it reflects. On the other hand, the relative uniformity with which Big Brother and Orwell are invoked speaks to the intensity with which our culture has absorbed that reflection of the Power of the State nightmare. Both of these works not only play a critical role in defining that nightmare within the genre, but they also drive the cultural shorthand that permeates public conversations regarding such critical questions as government surveillance and privacy.

The nightmares examined in Chapters 5 and 6 have their roots in our cultural fear of power's corrupting influence, both at the Individual and the State level. These cautionary tales have become nearly synonymous with the fears they reflect, becoming an integral part of our cultural rhetoric, as the examples in this chapter indicate. Regardless of our actual encounters with the cautionary tales invoked as metaphors, when public discourse employs images such as Big Brother and Darth Vader, we rely on a shared cultural experience to engage in the conversation, even if that engagement is merely as spectators.

Similar to what we saw with the images in Chapter 4, a pattern of ambivalence emerges in that conversation when it comes to those images that penetrate the most deeply into our cultural consciousness and away from their original contexts. The ambivalence surrounding some of the Orwellian images, and especially the *Brave New World* references, however, seems to have a different cause than that of the Godzilla references we saw earlier. Whereas the shift in the latter's public perception seems to rest in a decreased sense of urgency in the underlying fear, perhaps it is our cultural saturation with Power of the State nightmares that causes our ambivalent use of those images. In other words, it may be that *Nineteen Eighty-Four* and *Brave New World* have so completely transitioned from cautionary tales into cultural myths that they are *too* familiar and have lost some of their ability to scare us. This seems to be more of the case, though, with Huxley's novel, as the context and sheer volume of Orwellian images points to its continued power to invoke a nightmare.

Overall, however, with the possible exception of *Brave New World*, public discourse invokes these nightmares when an image of terrifying power is needed, whether that power lies in the military (e.g. Darth Vader), mental instability (e.g. Jekyll and Hyde), or government surveillance (e.g. Big Brother). The overwhelmingly negative connotation to the images we've just examined suggests that the Power nightmare, unlike some in Science and Technology, is not one we can even contemplate "getting past"; the prevalence of these images demonstrates that Power, both of Individuals and of the State, remains a matter of great public concern.

PART THREE : THE UNKNOWN

Introduction

The tension between our cultural excitement for change and our concurrent fear of it often expresses itself in cautionary tales that reflect the nightmares the Unknown can cause. These stories, it is important to note, do not simply express that fear nor do they admonish us for it. Instead, they attempt to warn about the possible nightmares that encounters with the Unknown might generate, in an attempt to prepare us for just such situations. For example, while issues such as the nature of God are not exclusively the province of speculative fiction, the genre's focus on our fears provides it with a unique perspective on what Gordon Van Gelder called the "big metaphysical [concerns] like our place in the universe (are we alone?) and is there a god?" The cautionary tales in the Unknown category frequently deal with such questions, particularly by examining the consequences of, for example, actually discovering the "truth" about the existence and nature of God, reflecting the genre's unique, speculative approach to these issues. In a similar way, speculative fiction also reflects the nightmares involved in the question of what it actually means to be human as the very nature of our existence can be challenged by technological advancements. For example, if we ever do find intelligent life on another planet, what will that mean for our cultural perception of our place at the top of the universal pecking order? Or, how would the ability to clone a person impact our steadfast belief in individuality?

One of the ways in which the genre's unique approach to the Unknown manifests itself is in its obvious willingness to take the nightmare to the extreme — the apocalyptic change, whether that means total destruction of the planet or just a particular way of life. Gary K. Wolfe describes this difference between speculative fiction and more mainstream genres as primarily a function of containment: in mainstream stories, the life- or planet-altering problems "almost always get snappily brought under control by the end of the narrative, reassuring us that, while world-changing hazards may lurk as close as your next-door neighbor's basement, the world itself is not going to get changed out from under you" (15). In contrast most speculative fiction, argues Wolfe, "is almost always about the failure of containment" of those hazards, as the heroes work to understand the Unknown, rather than prevent it from taking hold (15). In other words, these new situations are portrayed in speculative fiction as more a question of "What's next?" or "What now?" than of "How do we fix this?"

Speculative fiction reflections of the Unknown nightmare also differentiate themselves from mainstream fiction with their ability to examine more fantastic issues that do not fit into the rational mindset of contemporary American culture. For example, what would happen if magic (not illusion but mystical, unexplainable magic) were suddenly proven to exist in 2008? What impact would that have on society? How would we treat the witches and wizards who practiced it? What rules would be established to regulate such powers? Who would get to make those rules and who would enforce them? The texts in this category attempt to answer these questions and many more regarding the consequences of our confrontations with the Unknown, whether those confrontations involve Monsters, Aliens, and "Other" Beings, or simply Progress itself.

One of the permutations of the first sub-category relies on perhaps the most familiar trope within speculative fiction: encounters with aliens from other planets, both friendly and hostile. Those encounters, like the rest of the genre, tend to reflect the time in which they were created, resulting in many tales from the first half of the twentieth-century that follow the hostile alien model. This version of the Unknown even has its own acronym, BEM, which stands for Bug-Eyed Monsters, and dates back to the early days of the pulp science fiction magazines. As many genre aficionados are painfully aware, the quality of the stories from that era was frequently poor and many relied on the tried-and-true formula of invasion by some vaguely defined alien race. To attract readers to newsstands, editors of the time frequently commissioned cover art for these invasion stories that depicted the aliens as scientifically improbable, yet culturally sensational, Bug-Eyed Monsters, sometimes not even matching the illustrations to the description of the aliens on the page.

As the century progressed and we attempted to develop a culture of acceptance, this reliance on hostile alien stories has dwindled. While alien invasion movies like *Independence Day* are still popular, the box office is more likely to be balanced by films that either present lovable aliens like *ET: The Extra-Terrestrial* or a mix of aliens, some harmless and some still intent on taking over the Earth, such as in the two *Men in Black* movies. But is this attitude of tolerance really a good idea when it comes to potential contact with intelligent life from other planets? Greg Bear, among others, is not so sure. At the 2002 World Science Fiction Convention, Bear shared his view of the universe as essentially an ecosystem in which organisms compete with each other for resources ("Panel 348"). Given this perspective, how will such competition impact future space exploration? What would be the consequences of that exploration? Such questions complicate many of the alien stories in this subcategory.

Another element of the Unknown nightmare reflects our fear that, essentially, aliens may already be in our midst as creatures somehow other than human could be discovered living among us. Whether the otherness is caused by true mystical forces, simple flukes of nature (e.g. genetic mutations), or enhanced mental abilities, speculative fiction has long reflected society's nightmares about how we might deal with the detection of those who are different in incredible ways. From witches to telepaths, werewolves to genetically engineered post-humans, depictions of Earth-bound aliens, while not always as spectacular as alien spaceships blowing up the Empire State Building, have been an influential and popular trope in the genre for decades. Just as the utopia/dystopia tradition fuels both social commentary and cautionary tales,[1] stories of "others" also overlap functions. However, as I mentioned earlier, it is the "What happens now?" aspect of the fear regarding others that distinguishes the cautionary tales in this subcategory from those intended to bring about contemporary social action.

The rate of progress has accelerated over the past hundred years and there are no solid predictions of what will happen next week, let alone over the next century. Society has changed along with these events but at what cost and how quickly? The speculative fiction warnings described by the other half of the Unknown nightmare reflect our fear of Progress, that society will change so much, so quickly, we won't know how to behave or even how to think about the world. Stories within this subcategory warn us of the questions such extraordinary changes might raise including considerations of how much the rules will change and if we will be able to adapt quickly enough to them to survive. For example, if the United States were able to establish a space colony, would those living there be considered Americans, and by whom? Such questions are just two variations of the hundreds asked by speculative fiction cautionary tales.

Progress comes in many forms and therefore, the reflections of this nightmare are suitably varied. One of the big questions Progress raises in our culture is what is real? The debate over our ability to perceive "reality" is at least as old as *Don Quixote* and the eighteenth-century British tradition of quixote narratives. The contemporary version of this debate, however, is not grounded in the efforts to cure a quixote of perceptions that have been distorted by too much reading but rather in the more metaphysical question of the existence of a single reality. Recent scientific, cultural, and even psychological work has called into question the nature of reality as well as the empiricist's faith, grounded in the ideals of the Enlightenment, in our ability to objectively perceive it. This "progress" has, however, only fueled our fear that things may not be quite what they seem and that we have no real method to determine if *that* is even true.

Despite all the excitement it generates and the value our culture places on it (as well as the genuine improvements it creates in our quality of life), Progress is frequently an uncomfortable experience. Speculative fiction cautionary tales remind us of this in some way nearly every time we open a genre magazine or turn on the Sci-Fi Channel. If, as many believe, we cannot stop progress, then it would behoove us to pay close attention to the warnings of a genre that can help us prepare for the future that Progress will create.

The specific form of the speculative fiction warnings when it comes to the Unknown vary considerably, as the next few chapters will demonstrate. The common thread, however, among the questions raised by the narratives in the two expressions of this nightmare (Monsters, Aliens, and "Other" Beings; and Progress) is that our reactions to the Unknown often cause more problems than the difference to which we are responding in the first place. Such warnings, which also influence our public discourse (as the final chapter describes), are designed to prevent nightmarish results from inevitably following our encounters with the Unknown.

8: Monsters, Aliens, and "Other" Beings

One of the first things that comes to mind when we think of speculative fiction monsters is often the interchangeable alien invasion and *The Attack of [insert monster here]* movies of 1950s drive-in theaters. Hidden beneath these B-grade movie plots, however, is a complex reflection of one of our greatest fears. We've pondered questions about the possibility of other intelligent life in the universe for as long as we have stared at the stars; our fear of what we might find there or what might find us is just as old. The contemporary versions of both the questions and the fear, however, are much more complicated now that we can actually do something about them. As we build more powerful telescopes and make even more ambitious plans to explore space, we constantly negotiate the tension between our intense desire for knowledge about what is "out there" and our terror that we might actually find something. As Ronnie D. Lipschutz observes, "From *The War of the Worlds* to *The Clash of Civilizations*, the alien has been an omnipresent figure in American politics and popular culture, one whose liminality both beckons and threatens" (80). Our sense of adventure and drive for exploration takes us into the Unknown, something that has generated scores of nightmares for centuries.

At the same time, the alien might just be closer than we think; fear of the Unknown has also generated tales of "other" beings who live among us, including genre stand-bys like werewolves and telepaths. As our understanding of science and technology has advanced exponentially over the last century, the Unknown counter-intuitively became larger and even more ominous. Not only do we worry that there are witches or vampires in the woods at the edge of town but now we also wonder whether exposure to nuclear radiation or a cloning-induced mutation might just create a monster out of our next-door neighbor.[1]

There are many facets to the idea of the monster in our culture, and speculative fiction reflects that. This genre may be associated with the standard evil aliens coming to take over the planet every Saturday afternoon matinee but it has also presented us with such thought-provoking reflections on the same nightmare as *The Day the Earth Stood Still* and *X-Men*. The idea that humans are the only sentient beings in the universe is nearly incomprehensible, as is the opposite possibility, that we are not alone (either on Earth or out in space). Speculative fiction has taken this uncertainty and turned it into a culturally significant body of work that depicts encounters with beings who are something "other than human."[2]

Bug-Eyed Monsters: Alien Invasions and Other Visitations

As Rosi Braidotti observes in her examination of feminism and postmodern "freaks," "Whether utopian (*Close Encounters*) or dystopian (*Independence Day*), messianic (*E.T.*) or diabolical (*Alien*), the intergalactic monstrous Other is firmly established within the imaginary of today's media and the electronic frontier" (147). While this fear is as ancient as tales of mermaids and sphinxes, our rapidly developing understanding of the rules that govern the universe provides yet another source for our nightmares; Gregory Benford identifies the impact of this developing knowledge on society when he declares, "Astronomy had thrown open the window and it could not be shut again" ("Pascal" 271). Until we understood the basic mechanics of the universe, Benford argues, the human race did not have to deal with the concept of infinity (272); once this idea became part of our common cultural lexicon, however, we had to find a way to incorporate it into the way we encountered the world. Benford identifies two extreme versions of fictional attempts to tackle the concept of infinity: sometimes writers reflected "a kind of cultural agoraphobia" and sometimes they created such works as the miniature worlds of Jorge Luis Borges (272) and Ernest Becker's "Denial of Death" (273). It can be argued that most, if not all, of us do not have a solid grasp of what infinity actually means, which is precisely Benford's point. Through astronomy, we have determined that the universe has no discernable boundaries and that it is mostly a barren, empty place. Neither of these ideas fit neatly into our Earth-bound frames of reference and thus are incredibly difficult to truly understand and accept.

Whether or not nature truly abhors a vacuum, contemporary American culture certainly seems to and the vacuum of infinity needs to be filled. "Nearly all science fiction attempts to answer this supreme agoraphobia by populating the yawning abyss. The longing for alien contact seems to fulfill a parallel need," according to Benford, and multitudes of fictional aliens "give us companionship, making the infinities comfy" ("Pascal" 276). We do not want to know that we are alone, about the emptiness, because it terrifies us. Ben Bova discusses this terror in an *Analog* article where he examines the famous Drake equation that scientists have used for decades to try to estimate the number of intelligent life forms in the universe. Bova points to the "deafening silence" (40) as evidence that N (the equation's solution) equals one (meaning we are the only intelligent life in the galaxy) and he is adamant that our assumption of life on other planets is not based on science but on "narcissism: we look out at the stars and see our own reflection" (41). However, in the same issue, *Analog* editor Stanley Schmidt is less certain: "We're all still guessing.... Both [sides of the debate] have plausible justifications for the values they consider likely for the various factors in the Drake equation. Neither of them knows what the values [and thus the answer] really are—and neither do I, and neither do you" ("Still" 4).

This recent addition to a centuries-old debate, published in one of the major speculative fiction magazines, highlights the genre's intense interest in the question of extraterrestrial life as well as its ability to effectively reflect our fear because, as Benford argues, such "ceaseless grappling with infinity demands art of a peculiarly intellectual kind" ("Pascal" 277). Speculative fiction is uniquely positioned to turn this "grappling" into art and, more often than not, takes the optimistic (or pessimistic, depending on the benevolence of the aliens) view that N equals more than one and we are not alone. The genre has been doing this for so many years that its tales and characters are frequently the lenses through which we frame such questions in the first place.

Such a new, uncertain, infinite environment populated by speculative fictional aliens provides an additional stage for another all-too-human fear: difference. As Isaac Asimov puts it, "There has always been hostility between the 'us guys' and the 'you guys'" ("Social Science" 59). Whether it is ancient Greeks using the term barbarian to describe anyone who was not Greek or the latest summer alien invasion blockbuster, the "other" has often been a perfectly acceptable target for destruction in human civilization because being different was frequently reason enough to shoot first and ask questions later. The works of speculative fiction are certainly not immune to this tendency (and, as an industry, generate billions of dollars exploiting it), but more often than in many other genres, speculative fiction also tries to warn us against this unreflective determination that different equals dangerous. For example, in her analysis of Terry Pratchett's speculative fiction children's books, Cherith Baldry identifies that "in the past—and in computer games—aliens have been regarded as the embodiment of the enemy. It is

OK to zap them because they are different" (28). Pratchett, however, is one of those writers who break that mold, emphasizing what his characters have in common, rather than what separates them, as Baldry describes by referring directly to the author's work:

> The differences, Pratchett suggests, are imposed by us rather than objectively real. In the Prologue to *The Carpet People*, he says: "They call themselves the Munrungs. It meant The People, of The True Human Beings. It's what most people call themselves, to begin with. And then one day the tribe meets some other people, and gives them a name like The Other People or, if it's not been a good day, The Enemy. If only they'd think up a name like Some More True Human Beings, it'd save a lot of trouble later" [28].

While there is much to admire in speculative fiction's efforts to save us all that trouble, many in the field have begun to wonder if this emphasis on understanding and acceptance will end up doing us more harm than good. It is entirely possible that our drive to learn and advance will end up getting us into trouble, that we will understand just enough to go out into the universe and get ourselves squashed by a more advanced race who also doesn't like aliens. Benford discussed this idea during the 2002 World Science Fiction Convention when he expressed reservations about a project to build a Beacon that would announce our existence to the universe. He wondered if our desire to explore and be noticed might backfire and asked, "Do we really want to stand out?" ("Panel 348").[3] Such questions were on the table as early as 1974, when physicists Frank Drake[4] and Carl Sagan beamed a message to a "nearby" star cluster, M13, broadcasting our existence (Bova 43). Bova reports that when their plan was announced,

> British astronomer and Nobel laureate Sir Martin Ryle strongly objected, arguing that no signals should be sent out because they could show possibly hostile and dangerous aliens where we are. Sagan, who grew up reading science fiction, pointed out that since M13 is 25,000 light years away, even if there are evil aliens intent on conquest, they could not possibly trouble us for at least 50,000 years [43].

This debate continues into the twenty-first century. On the same convention panel as Benford, Greg Bear observed that, despite popular visions of alien-human harmony (for example in *Star Trek*), "Nature is not about preserving the young. It is about survival" ("Panel 348"). As Bear later elaborated, "Nature is not kind to bunnies and little kittens. But if no bunnies or kittens survive, we're all in trouble. We have to make sure that a significant portion of our young grow up healthy and productive, or we're toast" ("Requested"). If advanced alien civilizations do exist, they may not be waiting patiently to benevolently shepherd us toward enlightenment;

rather, they may be waiting until we become an actual threat, which they will then eliminate in order to protect themselves from the new competition. As Clyde Wilcox remarks in a special issue of *Extrapolation* that examines political science fiction,

> One dominant school in the study of international relations, the realists, argue that national interests always predominate and that war is an inevitable policy tool in resolving these interests. There is a huge genre of interspecies war novels and stories that accept this assumption. Alien species meet and contest for raw materials, planets, and empire. Frequently this leads to war, and even to the creation of large "berserker" doomsday machines that seek out and exterminate other life [197].[5]

Now these are not exactly warm and fuzzy, *ET*-esque thoughts, but they are probably very necessary ones to keep in mind for the time when speculative fiction tales become our everyday existence and we need to ensure, as Bear suggested, that "a significant part of our young grow up healthy and productive."

As I mentioned, whether we go to them or they come to us, exploring the universe might mean that we encounter other races who are not all that happy to see us or whom we may be incapable of understanding, or who have some other reaction to us out of the infinite possibilities we cannot predict. As Schmidt argues in a follow-up to the Drake Equation debate, "How many of us would *really* enjoy trying to see eye-to-eye with somebody *really* different — or be able to handle it?" ("Who Needs Company" 5). If we are not sure how we would react, how can we even attempt to predict how an *alien* would react? Schmidt warns, "If contact ever does occur, we'll need to be wary" of some potentially unpleasant reactions (6) because these encounters, whether the aliens are benevolent or hostile, are fraught with risk. Naeem Inayatullah, in his examination of colonialism as reflected in *Star Trek*, describes the core of this first contact fear as "its uncertainty, its ambiguity, its deep risk and potentially powerful reward" (61). Speculative fiction helps us to negotiate this great unknown as we continue looking to the stars and wondering if anyone is up there, even though we "know" space is infinite and could very well be empty. We have not given up on the idea that someday we will find life out there and that we will be all the better for it. But speculative fiction warns us to be wary, just in case.

Homegrown Monsters: Fear of the "Other"

We do not have to leave the planet, though, to find examples of "other" beings to populate our nightmares. Even if Bova is right and N = 1 (meaning we are alone), as Lipschutz observes, "It is helpful to recall that aliens are found not only in Outer Space" (80). In his Preface to the anthology *Supermen: Tales of the Posthuman Future*, Gardner Dozois argues that as science determined our solar system was filled not with the Earth-like environments of early science fiction stories but with uninhabitable planets and as interstellar travel was declared essentially impossible (given Einstein-ian relativity), speculative fiction writers had two choices if they wanted to keep writing about space exploration and colonization: change the planets using, for example, terraforming or change the people (ix-x). Dozois notes that the idea of altering humans first became popular after James Blish coined the phrase "pantropy" in the 1950s and it has evolved with each story, eventually pulling in cyberpunk questions "about the weakness of the ties between human identity and the human body itself" (Preface xi). Where Benford ("Pascal") sees our advancing understanding of the universe as fueling the trope of contact with alien life, Dozois describes the reverse reaction, where the genre turned that understanding inward, reflecting the possibility of changing ourselves to fit this "new" universe.

Even before the "reality of the universe," as Dozois describes it, was identified by science, speculative fiction was full of examples of Earth-bred "beings" that continue to appear in nightmares throughout the modern era. Some of the most popular fall under either the supernatural category, which includes telepaths, witches and wizards who use magic that actually works, and telekinetics like Stephen King's *Carrie*, and the natural, which includes genetic mutants like Marvel's *X-Men* and the posthumans Dozois describes. This latter group is Braidotti's concern when she observes, "Contemporary culture shifts the issue of genetic mutations from high-tech laboratories to popular culture" (147). Whether supernatural or just ordinarily natural, these reflected nightmares continue the fairy tale and fable tradition of depicting the battle between good and evil using non-human (mystical or otherwise) actors.

In this way, genre staples can overlap with more traditional fairy tale and/or horror tropes (particularly those in which the source of the terror is supernatural, such as demons and witches), many of which are out of the scope of our discussion since they are not cautionary tales focused on the future.[6] However, some of these images and tropes do apply to the Nightmares Model because their reflection of our fears of the Unknown warn us about our behavior, and are thus very relevant to our discussion. We are interested in those tales where the monsters do not merely "stand in" for anything in an allegorical social commentary that critiques our fear of the other tales, where the focus is on the discovery of that other and our resulting reactions. The future-focus fuels the cautionary nature of these stories, with the primary goal being to prepare us for such encounters, rather than inciting us to change our current behavior. In other words, the warning in these stories is about the change such a discovery would bring, not the innate nature of our fear of the other. The cautionary tales in this chapter reflect our fear that the proven existence of these monsters would lead to fundamental shifts in the way we see the world.

While many of the ideas in this aspect of the nightmare overlap with those discussed in other chapters (especially Two, Three, and Nine), the underlying warning we're examining here focuses instead on the reactions of individual people, and society in general, to the change implied by the very existence of such monsters. In particular, these warnings often reflect a significant shift in the way society is structured. Schmidt makes a similar observation regarding this fear when he argues that the debate over "intelligent" animals leads many to, at times illogically, dismiss any possibility that humankind might not always be supreme:

> Ultimately, though, that, too, comes back to a fear of fundamental change. It seems to me that many of us, even scientists, feel so threatened by any talk of animal or machine intelligence because admitting such a thing would probably necessitate profound changes in the way we live and relate to everything else ["King" 22].

M. Keith Booker examines a more specific variation of this fear of the other when he identifies that 1950s Americans were preoccupied with "degeneration" or backward evolution. Instead of fearing beings who advance *beyond* humans, degeneration reflects the terrifying possibility that some humans will slide behind the rest and thus become the other. While the roots of this fear go back centuries, according to Booker, modern fears can be traced to 1895's *Degeneration* by Max Nordau, which is based in part on the phrenology of Cesare Lombrosco and the more legitimate scientific works of Charles Darwin. Given the scientific basis for the fear of backward evolution, Booker asserts, "It thus may not be surprising that fears of degeneration underwent a remarkable resurgence in the 1950s," a decade dealing with the new reality of nuclear weapons. Radiation was a significant part of this reality and Booker argues that a vague understanding of the connections among evolution, mutation, and radiation, led many Americans to conclude that radiation could lead to evolution, or just as easily, degeneration (*Monsters* 9).[7]

Whether the monsters come from outer space or from the house next door, speculative fiction reflects our fears that such beings will irrevocably change the way our world works. Are we alone in the universe? Are we even the only sentient life on Earth? What will we evolve into next? Will we advance or degenerate? Will we evolve into beings with telepathic abilities? How will that happen? Who will have these abilities first? Will we lose control over our lives to these beings who can manipulate reality in ways we cannot? Will we turn into such creatures against our will? These are just some of the many questions we will see underlying the speculative fiction nightmares described in the rest of this chapter.

Invasions, Abductions, and World Domination: Print Examples

As Gary S. Dalkin observes, "It may be so obvious as to be constantly overlooked but *The War of the Worlds* invented the alien story" (12). H.G. Wells's classic initially appeared in *Pearson's Magazine* as a serial, running between April and December 1897, but was first published in the United States in 1926 when Hugo Gernsback reprinted it in *Amazing Stories*. The alien invasion tradition begun by Wells and introduced to America by Gernsback was extended by another legendary editor (and occasional writer) from the Golden Age: John W. Campbell. The aliens who invade Earth in three of Campbell's stories from the 1930s ("Cloak of Aesir," "Uncertainty," and "Rebellion"[8]) initially conquer the planet using nuclear weapons but eventually the humans are able to defeat them by developing superior atomic technology (Brians 152–53). Seven decades later, Stanley Schmidt, the current editor of *Analog* (the direct contemporary descendant of Campbell's *Astounding*), released *Argonaut*, a novel in which aliens use nanotechnology (disguised as bugs) to spy on humans. When the bugs are discovered, they attack, crippling computers, communication systems, and even people.

The technology tables are turned, however, in Christopher Anvil's "Pandora's Planet" (from the September 1956 *Astounding*) when alien invaders are shocked at the intelligence of and the atomic weapons available to humans on Earth (Brians 121). In another twist on the alien invasion story, Isaac Asimov's would-be invaders in "The Gentle Vultures" are simply biding their time, waiting on the other side of the Moon for humans to destroy themselves; once that happens, they can take over the planet without resistance (Brians 122). Taking "moving in" to an absurd level, Clifford Simak's 1962 novel *They Walked Like Men* approaches the trope from an economic perspective: these extraterrestrials plan to take over Earth simply by buying the planet out from underneath us.

A popular variation of the alien invasion/visitation theme is known as First Contact, where the first meeting between humans and aliens, whether on Earth, in space, or on another planet, usually does not go particularly well. One contemporary novel that for ninety-percent of the story seems to follow the *War of the Worlds* tradition of malevolent-alien invasion is Orson Scott Card's *Ender's Game*, which Dozois described as possibly "the most influential work of recent time" ("Panel 137"). In Card's best-selling 1985 novel,[9] the first in the *Ender* series, Ender Wiggins is a child trained to play war "games" that actually eventually annihilate an alien hive race (the Buggers) who had invaded Earth space twice before. The revelation at the end of the book, however, puts the annihilation into an unsettling light, veering away from the traditional evil alien trope: the entire war was caused by a botched first contact situation and the aliens were no longer a threat by the time Ender came into the fight. The Buggers only attacked initially because human behavior was so foreign to them that they didn't understand the Earth ships were flown by sentient beings. By the time the aliens understood what they had done, it was too late; humans were their enemy and would not stop until all Buggers were destroyed. Before they are eliminated, the aliens leave this story for Ender, hoping he will explain their mistake to the universe, and keep their memory alive.

A similarly disastrous result is in store for the universe when far-future space explorers in Brian Stableford's "Mortimer Gray's History of Death" encounter a micro-organism whose sole function is to ingest and dissolve everything in its path. This organism, at first glance, will eventually destroy everything in the universe, including Earth. While Stableford's characters are unable to establish meaningful communication with the destructive alien creature, the situation is reversed in James C. Glass's "The Color of Pain" (published in the March 2004 issue of *Analog*) where humans are the destructive aliens. It is only a linguist's persistent (and insubordinate) attempts at communication that avert either full-scale war between colonists and a planet's native species or the complete extermination of that species. The source of the conflict, as is revealed at the end of the story, is the agonizing allergic reaction the native young have to humans.

Colonists from Earth have a very different encounter with native creatures in 1953's "Student Body" by F.L. Wallace when they discover the "omnimal," which can evolve in months, not centuries. This species starts out as rodents that eat the crops planted by the humans, then evolves into larger animals to defend themselves from the robot cats built to protect the crops, and eventually into an animal the colonists must negotiate with, instead of attack: humans. The message is more optimistic in Michael Swanwick's "Slow Life," from the December 2002 issue of *Analog*. Swanwick's astronaut initially dismisses the alien life she encounters as less intelligent because of its confusion over such concepts as time, individuality, and even death. She eventually overcomes her preconceptions, however, when the actually *more* advanced aliens offer to save her life after an equipment malfunction leaves her stranded over Titan.

Another favorite theme in speculative fiction when it comes to aliens is reflected in the premise of *Nothing Human*, the 2003 novel by Nancy Kress in which an alien race has genetically engineered "human" children in an effort to show us the right way to live without destroying the planet. Novels from two of the genre's earlier giants, Arthur C. Clarke and Robert A. Heinlein, also reflect our fear that aliens will interfere with and attempt to control our lives. The alien overlords in Clarke's *Childhood's End* bring about peace on Earth but at a price: the forced "evolution" of the human race into beings with exceptionally expanded mental abilities.[10] In Heinlein's 1951 novel *The Puppet Masters* (also a 1994 movie), the motives of the aliens are much less benevolent than those in either the Kress or Clarke story when parasitic slugs from one of Saturn's moons attach themselves to humans and begin controlling them as part of a plan to conquer Earth.

Published three years after Heinlein's novel, Clifford Simak's *Ring Around the Sun* (originally under the Jay Vickers pseudonym) tells the story of mutants on a parallel Earth who use their psychic abilities and advanced technology to influence our civilization. Eventually they decide we hold too much hatred, violence, and paranoia, and thus move humans to other, uninhabited Earths to start over again from feudal times. The failures of human civilization are also the public reason behind the alien interference in Judith Moffett's series of stories about the Hefn; these aliens institute a global Baby Ban, preventing all humans from reproducing, ostensibly because we made such a mess of the planet. But, as revealed in Moffett's "The Bear's Baby," the Hefn have ulterior motives: they need a pristine planet on which to raise their own young and have chosen Earth, forcing the remaining humans to help them repair the damage.

But not all genre texts feature aliens who are so open about their presence. The aliens in Edward M. Lerner's "By the Rules" (*Analog*, June 2003), for example, release an AI into Earth's Internet to simultaneously observe humans and discredit stories of close encounters to prevent us from learning of their existence. The interference is similarly covert in John Shirley's 2001 novel *And the Angel with Television Eyes* where a Hidden Race of highly-developed souls lives among us, either protecting or exploiting humans to suit their own ends. The goal of the aliens manipulating the post-nuclear war Earth in Poul Anderson's 1963 story "No Truce with Kings," on the other hand, is to encourage a communitarian culture that never re-develops nuclear weapons, hoping to prevent belligerent, atomically-armed humans from invading the rest of the galaxy (Brians 117). The stakes are significantly lower in Mia Molvray's humorous "Promises, Promises," published in the March 2004 "Probability Zero" section of *Analog*, when the overly curious and enthusiastic visiting Oolians decide humans need assistance managing the planet and proceed to "help" wherever they see fit. This help includes forcing a local politician to literally implement his campaign promises in what is described as one of many "Incidents" occurring all over the planet. Almost forty years earlier, the aliens in Simak's *All Flesh is Grass* also try to help humans with their problems, this time by enclosing a small rural town in an invisible dome to protect it from nuclear destruction.

The popular image of alien interference as abduction and experimentation is also reflected in speculative fiction prose such as another 2001 Shirley novel, *The View from Hell*. The characters in this story are at the mercy of inter-dimensional beings studying human suffering, with death as their only brief escape before they are brought back to life for more observation. A twist on the alien interference trope involves the fear that aliens will use us as simple work animals; we see this in Grey Rollins's "Greater Fleas Have Lesser Fleas" from the March 2004 issue of *Analog*. In this nightmare, the aliens take advantage of our corporate culture in a well-oiled system of planetary restructuring and colonization that involves luring humans to newly discovered planets by buying up their Earth farms, waiting for these squatters to transform the landscape to meet the aliens' needs, and then moving them as "tools" to the next planet.

In most speculative fiction prose that fits the alien invasion or interference mold either the aliens discover us on their own or as a result of our forays into their territory. But there is another set of stories that warn of the consequences of drawing alien attention to our existence, whether intentionally or not. In "Distance" by Maya Kaathryn Bohnhoff (*Analog*, February 2003), aliens use our early version of a Beacon, the Pioneer 10 probe, to not only learn there is life on Earth but also to communicate with and (eventually) visit us. While the intentions of Bohnhoff's aliens are benign (they want to play baseball), that is not always the case: in Shirley's *Crawlers*, a hive entity hitches a ride on a man-made satellite as it crashes to Earth, where it proceeds to transform all who encounter it into a hybrid of human, animal, and machine. Another example of the nightmare that might ensue if we start calling galactic attention to ourselves is Gregory Benford's 1984 novel *Across the Sea of Suns*,[11] which finds Earth being invaded after advanced machine-based civilizations determined to eliminate any potential rivals have discovered our signals.

While the actions of the aliens in Michael A. Burstein's "Decisions" (January/February 2004 issue of *Analog*) are less violent than those in Benford's novel, some would argue they are even more devastating. The

"Jabbers," as the human main character (Aaron) dubs them, monitor developing races until those "aliens" first become capable of leaving their own system, and thus threaten other space-faring species. Once the threat becomes a reality, Jabbers capture the young interlopers and use advanced simulations to test their reactions to the unknown, gauging their "compatibility" with the alliance of sentient beings that runs the universe. When humans are deemed incompatible because of Aaron's paranoid and violent reaction to the simulation, the Jabbers plan to forever lock-in our solar system, making it impossible for humans to ever explore the galaxy. Aaron, though, asks for more time so humans can develop out of their violence and fear. While he doesn't remember the encounter, his request is granted because the Jabbers see potential in the human race, based on Aaron's understanding of the need to change. The humans in Arthur C. Clarke's 1946 story "Loophole" are not so enlightened: They develop alternate means of inter-planetary travel and then bomb Martian civilization out of existence in retaliation for the red planet's prohibition on space travel for Earthlings because of the atomic bomb attacks on Hiroshima and Nagasaki (Brians 159).

While they certainly seem to enjoy to, speculative fiction writers do not have to leave the planet to find aliens to populate our nightmares; as Dozois argues, "the superman [posthuman] theme is one of the most popular in genre history" (Preface xiii). One of the first novels about a "superman" is Olaf Stapledon's *Odd John*,[12] published in 1936. Within posthuman stories, the ability to read minds is both a dream and a nightmare for society, and while Stapledon's title character is telepathic, Alfred Bester's novel *Demolished Man* is considered within the genre to be the benchmark for portraying the negotiation between privacy and telepathy. In Bester's world, telepaths are employed by the government to constantly scan the population, preventing crime when it is still only a thought. These telepaths, while privileged in some ways, are also cursed as their lives are assiduously controlled by governmental regulation, even to the point of whom they are allowed to marry.

The telepaths populating Henry Kuttner's *Mutant*, a 1953 collection of novelettes, are similarly segregated from the general population but many are far less accepting of the quarantine than those in Bester's novel. Four of the stories, originally published in *Astounding* in 1943, depict the telepaths' struggle to coexist in society, facing opposition and fear from both "normals" and other telepaths who refuse to accept the quarantine and seek the destruction of non-telepaths while the fifth novelette involves the final attempt to avoid a catastrophic confrontation. In John Wyndham's post-nuclear holocaust world of *Chrysalids* (originally published as

Re-Birth), telepaths face a more extreme penalty than those in *Mutant* if they are discovered: sterilization and exile. Extermination of telepaths (and other mutants), not quarantine or even exile, is the chosen solution in Norman Spinrad's *The Iron Dream* from 1972.[13]

In addition to telepathy, speculative fiction reflects our nightmares about people who exhibit other abilities and characteristics that are "not human." The comic book series *X-Men* has warned for decades against the consequences of this fear with its cast of characters in whom spontaneous genetic mutation creates aliens in our midst. In another update of this same warning, the post-human children in Bear's *Darwin's Children*[14] face "an increasingly repressive society [that] tries to cope with the evolutionary change represented by the new children by rounding them up and placing them in prison-like schools" (Wolfe 15). The repercussions of the children's birth are felt the world over as "everything in their society, from civil liberties to politics to medicine, has been transformed" while the children become victims of their government, hysterical mobs, and even Mother Nature herself when the bodies of unaffected humans release a disease genetically designed to kill anyone who is not "normal" (Wolfe 15).

Robert Chase's short story "Unseen," in the October 2003 issue of *Analog*, takes this fear in an entirely different direction when the discovery of invisible beings living alongside us at first unnerves, and then excites, the scientific community. Meanwhile, the graduate student who initially discovers these creatures believes he is being stalked and is eventually able to communicate with an intelligent, invisible dog-like creature that is trying to silence him because it fears what will happen if its species is discovered. Chase's story plays on legends of Brownies and Fair Folk who have interacted, unseen, with peasants around the world for centuries.

But not all of these "others" are presented as sympathetic characters like Wolverine or Bear's posthuman children. The "natural" order becomes reversed in Richard Matheson's 1954 novel *I Am Legend* when the vampires, created by a nuclear-enhanced bacteria, become the new normal who must defend themselves against the attacks of the last remaining human, the new abnormal (or "other") and the true danger to the organized society. In a similar way to *I Am Legend*, the abnormal becomes normal in Philip K. Dick's *Dr. Bloodmoney, or How We Got Along After the Bomb*, where nuclear radiation creates a wide variety of mutations. Both of these novels reflect the nightmare that we will be replaced by a new race of homegrown aliens, whether that race is an "improvement" or not.[15]

Yet another aspect of this fear of homegrown aliens (in this case, fairly literally) are the androids and other fusions of organic life and computers that frequently appear in the genre. Within the classics of speculative fiction, this nightmare is reflected by the androids in Dick's 1968 novel *Do Androids Dream of Electric Sleep?* who are considered to be property, hunted down and exterminated when they express a sense of free will and escape slavery on Mars to a post-apocalyptic Earth. In William Gibson's novels, including *Count Zero* and *Neuromancer*, we see this nightmare in what Andrew Ross describes as the "angels" of cyberspace, who are no longer human and thus depict our "fear of unfamiliar, superior intelligence ... situated on Earth, within the known parameters of socioeconomic life" (148).[16]

Whether originally from Earth or another planet, speculative fiction's prose Monsters, Aliens, and "Other" Beings evolved from largely simplistically hostile BEMs into largely complex life forms that still might be a threat, a transition that follows the genre onto the screen.

Is Anybody Out There? Film and Television Examples

The encounter with intelligent races from other planets is a favorite trope of speculative fiction film and television; two of the highest grossing and most familiar recent examples of this theme also present polar opposite views: *ET* and *Independence Day*. While the gross over-reaction of the adults who discover the gentle, child-like ET who merely wants to return home warns us not to jump to the conclusion that all aliens are a threat, the destruction wreaked by the aliens in *Independence Day* reminds us that some may be just that, a threat.

Both *ET* and *Independence Day* are recent additions to a longstanding tradition of alien movies, a tradition that has humble beginnings in the 1950s B-movies. Booker identifies two reasons for the popularity of alien invasion movies in that era: 1) The technical ease and relatively lower expense of Earth as opposed to alien settings, and 2) "The embattled sense that many Americans felt" at the time (*Monsters* 114–115).[17] Even after those factors were supplanted, the alien invasion movie maintained its cherished place in popular culture. For example, the alien in *The Thing* (John Carpenter's 1982 film based on John W. Campbell's "Who Goes There?" from 1938) not only invades Earth but is also a shape-changer that manipulates humans using psychic powers. Christian Nyby's 1951 adaptation, *The Thing from Another World*, removes the psychic and shape-changing aspects of the original story to present a plant-based alien that lands at the North Pole and then tries to take over the Earth. After escaping from the Air Force men who initially capture it, the Thing quickly reproduces many times over, attacking base personnel to feed their blood to its young. The humans argue over whether to kill the Thing or study it, until the commanding officer decides to save the planet by killing the alien, no matter what it takes.

The Twilight Zone also picks up on this alien invasion nightmare in the first season episode "The Monsters are Due on Maple Street," which depicts the terror in one neighborhood when the residents believe they have been invaded by human-looking aliens. In a later episode written by Rod Serling, "Will the Real Martian Please Stand Up," both Martians and Venusians are sufficiently human-looking to blend in with bus passengers and diner patrons and, as we see in the reveal at the end, both planets actually have plans to invade Earth. Even though there are no actual aliens in "The Shelter," this *Twilight Zone* episode also reflects the alien invasion nightmare as neighbors fight over the area's only bomb shelter when an alien invasion seems imminent. This fear has even hit popular music, as Ian J. Simpson observes, referring to "Pets," a 1993 single by Porno for Pyros in which Martians invade to make humans their pets (15).

Alien invasion is not the only way humans can come into contact with alien races; sometimes, our own efforts to enter their part of the galaxy causes the trouble. For example, the US space program itself is suggested to be the impetus for the invasion in 1953's *Invaders from Mars*, as the Martians believe a preemptive strike will keep hostile humans away from their planet. In addition, a space shuttle in *The Twilight Zone* (1985) episode "Chameleon" brings home a shape-shifting alien that absorbs objects and people as it travels to explore the universe.

On a more galactic scale, as Iver Neumann observes, *Star Trek*'s Prime Directive, which prohibits interference with lesser advanced races,[18] also works in the opposite direction: Some episodes depict members of the United Federation of Planets coming into contact with more advanced races that variously try to destroy, experiment on, or simply ignore them (39). One such encounter occurs in "Home Soil," an episode from *The Next Generation*'s first season in which a terraforming operation discovers an inorganic life form that, as Neumann notes, declares they do not find humans (dubbed "ugly bags of mostly water") to be "'advanced' enough for further contact to be worthwhile" (39). They thus order the Federation to stay away from their planet for at least the next 300 years. Another advanced alien, Nagilum, makes a different determination of humanity when he decides to experiment on the crew of the Enterprise in the second season episode "Where Silence Has Lease." Intrigued by their concept of mortality, Nagilum plans to kill half of the crew in an experiment to learn more about death. Captain Picard forces their release by threatening to blow up the ship, which would prevent Nagilum from learning anything. And the Crystalline Entity, a silicon-based creature that lives in space and attacks any organic being it encounters, makes two appearances in the series: in the first season episode "Datalore" and later in the fifth season's "Silicon Avatar."

Perhaps the epitome of the advanced-alien nightmare is the Borg, first introduced in *Star Trek: The Next Generation* and one of the most popular *Trek* villains. This hive-like, cyborg race, as we first encounter it, is, as Patrick Thaddeus Jackson and Daniel H. Nexon observe, "the radical opposite" of the Federation races being fundamentally "so alien that communication with it is impossible" (144). In this way, the Borg represents one of our greatest fears about exploring the galaxy: we will encounter something so alien, so different, and so powerful that we will be assimilated against our will, losing our very existence.

A related expression of this particular nightmare is the First Contact situation. As Inayatullah observes, first contact is "filled with the possibility of missed communications" (61) and while he points out that *Star Trek*'s "universal translator" essentially eliminates this possibility (except, perhaps notably, in the most recent *Trek* incarnation, *Enterprise*), such missed communication is at the heart of many of the genre texts in this chapter. When it comes to depictions of first contact, we often see the state and particularly the military doing its best to aggravate the situation, sometimes with devastating consequences as "the appearance of aliens, whether of this Earth or not, inevitably draws out the military power of the state" (Lipschutz 84). As Lipschutz describes, "In *The Day the Earth Stood Still* (1951), Klaatu's spaceship is immediately surrounded by military units; [while] the scientist of *Red Planet Mars* (1952) finds his project under military control" (84). While Klaatu's plan is not invasion, the military response to his presence only serves to underscore the real purpose of his mission: to warn Earth to curb our violent tendencies or face destruction. Because Klaatu and his robot protector Gort are more technologically advanced than we are, the violence they encounter from humans (including the murder of Klaatu, twice) does not lead to war. It does, however, lead to a warning: if humans attempt to spread their violence beyond Earth, the planet will be destroyed, as we will then be a threat to the rest of the galaxy.

War is often not the goal of aliens who come to Earth. In films such as *ET* and *Close Encounters of the Third Kind*, as Dalkin observes, "Steven Spielberg inverts *The War of the Worlds* and the alien invasion pictures of the 1950s" and presents audiences with narratives in which "benevolent alien invaders with a technology superior to our own render all our machines powerless, but do not destroy. Rather they offer the possibility of friendship and hope for the future" (17). Spielberg, however, was not the first to make this inversion. The aliens in 1956's *Earth vs. the Flying Saucers*, for example, only seek a place to live after their planet becomes uninhabitable. But the humans are afraid of them and use military force to try to expel them, leading to an all-out war that levels much of Washington, DC. While the film's overt message, as Booker describes it, is to assure "audiences that good-old American know-how can handle anything the aliens can throw at us" (a common theme in 1950s genre films), the images of a decimated Capitol Building and other monuments carry a powerful warning regarding the costs of warring with aliens who don't come here to fight (*Monsters* 125–126). Similarly, in 1953's *It Came from Outer Space*, our own paranoia and ignorance leads to violence, rather than any plans for invasion by the aliens. After accidentally crashing on Earth, aliens attempt to quickly repair their ship and move on, assuming human form (based on the townspeople) as protection. While the prerequisite outsider character is able to delay the equally prerequisite paranoid, hysterical mob long enough for the aliens to escape unharmed, the warning is clear that we need to evolve past our fear and paranoia to be able to properly accept aliens such as these.

Decades after the B-movie alien invasions, the back-story of the *Babylon 5* television series includes a war between Earth and the Minbari people that was caused by a disastrous first contact. Encountering them for the first time in open space, humans fired on Minbari ships because they didn't understand their practices or the rules of the universe well enough; that mistake nearly caused the annihilation of the entire human race. As a result of this incident, only certain Earth Force officers in the *Babylon 5* universe are certified for first contact. On a smaller scale, the nightmare of overreaction to aliens is also an underlying premise of the television show *Roswell*. When the young aliens are discovered by a unit of FBI alien hunters, one of them is captured and tortured in an episode near the end of the first season, "The White Room."

However, speculative fiction also warns us that sometimes such fears are justified, as we see in the many films and television shows that depict aliens interfering with and/or using humans for their own ends. In Alex Proyas's 1998 film *Dark City*,[19] an alien race on the verge of extinction, known as the Strangers, create a city floating in space as an experiment to determine if the human mind can save them. Every night, the city and its people are reprogrammed to play out new situations for the Strangers to study. It isn't research but play that the aliens have in mind in the *Twilight Zone* episode "Stopover in a Quiet Town" (from 1964): the main characters find themselves serving as toys to occupy the daughter of the giant alien who abducts them.

The fear of aliens using humans for food, a key component of the terror in the *V* television miniseries,[20] is also reflected in popular music. Simpson mentions two notable examples: 1) "Upwards at 45 Degrees" by Julian

Cope (on the *Jehovahkill* album from 1992) in which humans are harvested for food, and 2) The Meninblack, an alien race invented by The Stranglers that created humans to be used as food, appearing in 1979's *The Raven* and *The Gospel According to the Meninblack* from 1981 (14).

Despite the strong tradition of alien invasion tales, speculative fiction film and television do not ignore homegrown aliens by any means. One of the best examples of the potential for disaster that lies within the human fear of difference is "Gingerbread," the third season episode of *Buffy, the Vampire Slayer* in which a demon plays on our fear by appearing as the ghosts of two murdered children, blaming the town's witches for their death and encouraging the townspeople to track down and burn the "witches," including Buffy. This episode in particular plays on the characters' fear that they are losing control over their lives to evil, magical forces. Other monsters are the terror behind "Something in the Walls," the January 1989 episode of *The Twilight Zone* in which a psychiatric patient believes she sees creatures lurking behind the walls. One day, she is suddenly cured and when her skeptical doctor investigates, he sees her face in the wall, with a creature replacing her in the real world.

The influence of Bester's novel *The Demolished Man* on the genre's treatment of telepathy can be directly seen in *Babylon 5* where a powerful telepathic character is named for the author. In this series, as in many other portrayals of telepaths, humans with telepathic abilities are forcibly segregated from the general population to "protect" the privacy of non-telepaths. The resulting Psi Corps becomes a powerful political force with two overriding goals: controlling its "own" and taking power back from the "mundanes" who enslave them. The Psi Corps is usually represented in the series by Bester, a Psi Cop with unlimited ambition and nearly limitless telepathic abilities. During the fourth season, this battle between telepaths and "normals" (as they call themselves) has an equally powerful leader opposing the Psi Corps in the character of William Edgars, who uses his considerable wealth and resources to develop a virus that will kill only telepaths. He plans to release this virus and then offer the telepaths a choice: submit to greater control by normals and receive the antidote, or die.[21]

Even a series populated with more alien species than can be counted, *Star Trek: The Next Generation*, reflects this fear of telepathy in the fifth season episode "Violations" when several characters are psychically raped. In addition, *The Twilight Zone* also touches on this nightmare in the episode "Mute" where an orphan's foster family does whatever it takes to stop her from using telepathy and learn to talk instead so she can fit into normal society.

More traditional supernatural figures also appear in modern speculative fiction. In the second season of *Buffy, the Vampire Slayer*, for example, the "Phases" episode features a werewolf hunter who refuses to see past the beast to the human inside the werewolf. Buffy herself is a supernatural "other," born with the strength and skill necessary to battle the forces of evil. But not every character in the *Buffy* universe is comfortable with this power or its magical roots. Over the seven seasons, creator Joss Whedon slowly unfolds the possibility that the Watcher's Council, first introduced as benevolent guides of the Slayer, might actually be more concerned with controlling this other being, perhaps out of fear of her extraordinary power.

The witch has also made its presence felt in contemporary genre works. *The Blair Witch Project*, for example, updated this "other," even as it skirted the border between speculative fiction and horror; the terror of the characters in this runaway blockbuster is based, at least in part, on our fear that a supernatural being with powers beyond those of a normal human will take control of our world. Part of this movie's mass appeal is that it employs the nightmares the genre has reflected for decades. For the opposite take on the witch, we can look at *Charmed*, where the three sister witches are on the side of good and it is often the humans who create the nightmare when they discover that magic really exists. In the third season finale, "All Hell Breaks Loose," the witches' powers are exposed on television, leading to mobs gathering outside their door, both for and against them, and eventually to the death of one of the sisters. In the very next episode, "Charmed Again," after time is reset to keep their secret, a police inspector becomes convinced that the sisters are evil after he catches them using magic. His fear makes it inconceivable to him that they might use their powers for good. That same fear drives the witch-hunter who comes after the sisters at the end of the fourth season in "Witch Way Now?"

Even popular music reflects this fear of homegrown aliens, as Simpson points out, referring to both *The Lamb Lies Down on Broadway*, a 1974 concept double-album from Genesis that "combines elements of science fiction with surrealism, telling a tale of the opening of a portal into another universe full of mutants and monsters" (13) and 1987's *Radio K.A.O.S* by Roger Waters (ex-leader of Pink Floyd), in which a psychic learns how to control radio waves with his mind and then takes over a top secret computer (14).

The reception such other beings as the X-Men and telepaths would receive from society has, according to some, changed significantly over the years. While the persecution of mutants that is central to the *X-Men* saga was perfectly believable when the comic first hit newsstands in 1963, we may have a different reaction more than forty years later. As a reviewer of the first *X-Men* movie in 2000 observes, "If superpowered mutants actually emerged today, they'd become overnight celebrities, not outcasts" (O'Hehir). Indeed, in the television version of Stephen King's *The Dead Zone*, which airs on the USA Network, psychic Johnny Smith becomes a local celebrity for helping people with his abilities to see the future and the past.[22]

This historical transformation in the way we might receive such "others" seems to characterize the development of this nightmare over the modern era more than any possible influence of new visual media. As with the Power of the Individual nightmares we examined in Chapter 5, the medium of the cautionary tale does not seem to influence the way in which the genre presents encounters with Monsters, Aliens, and "Other" Beings. Instead, there is a decided historical shift, begun in the 1950s but flourishing more recently, that saw the formulation of "aliens = evil" invaders become the much more conflicted, more ambiguous formulation of "aliens = we're not quite sure." Perhaps the pairing of texts that most profoundly demonstrates this shift is *War of the Worlds* and *Ender's Game*. The greater complexity and contradictions in *Ender* and so many of the more recent reflections of this nightmare, regardless of medium, seems to match a greater sense of uncertainty that builds over the twentieth century, a cultural characteristic I will examine in the next chapter when Progress nightmares come into play.

While the alien invasion movie has not been deleted from the repertoire, for every *Independence Day* released, there is likely a *Men in Black* coming out the next summer, perhaps even starring the same A-list celebrity. Within all of the major categories of "other" (aliens, magical/supernatural beings, mutants, and telepaths), the dominant contemporary trend is to present them as a diverse group, with both "good" and "bad" members in the same text. For example, in *X-Men*, some of the mutants hope to coexist with humans while some insist on domination. In addition, the incredible variety among *Star Trek*'s aliens over several television series and many movies certainly provides ample evidence for diversity. The one exception to this trend, oddly enough, is telepaths. Even with the usual caveat regarding exceptions, the presentation of telepathic individuals seems to have remained consistently negative over the past century's speculative fiction. Perhaps this is because our fear of losing control over our minds is one we just cannot bring ourselves to accept; it seems to be the one ability or characteristic that is incompatible with society as we know it. Even when telepaths are not the villains of the text, as in *Demolished Man*, they are still segregated and rigorously controlled; the message seems to be that even when telepaths provide us with a valuable service, they are still too dangerous to be left to their own devices.

9: Progress[1]

The final nightmare is, essentially, that we will go to sleep tonight and the world will be radically different in the morning. It is no coincidence that speculative fiction reflects Progress as a critical nightmare since it is identified by George Lakoff and Mark Johnson as one our deeply-held cultural values, while Mark Hillegas asserts that the genre has "lasting value because it presents imaginatively and sometimes comments intelligently upon a basic element in our culture, the idea of progress" ("Science Fiction" 25). Progress is a powerful, even fundamental, idea but it is not without its pains, something speculative fiction warns us not to forget. The nightmare that the rules will change on us, without our understanding why or how, is a fairly contemporary one and thus is one that the genre is well suited to reflect. This suitability is recognized by what many consider to be the first major critical examination of the genre, Kingsley Amis's *New Maps of Hell* from 1960, which argues that science fiction presents "the human effects of spectacular changes in our environment, changes either deliberately willed or involuntarily suffered" (20).

This focus on the dynamic nature of society, both technological and otherwise, sets speculative fiction apart from other genres; as James Van Pelt observed, science fiction is

> based on the idea that things can be different. More traditional literature explores the human condition [which] is basically unchanged for centuries. It is complex and multi-faceted but it is unchanging. You can learn as much about yourself reading *The Odyssey* as you can reading modern literature [Interview].

In contrast to the relative stasis of traditional literature, speculative fiction's perspective on change has, as Gary K. Wolfe argues, "permitted a range of perceptions of the world that expanded the possibilities of narrative literature" (40), an expansion crucial to cautionary tales.

Progress over the last century has led us out into the stars and inward into our very DNA. At the same time, though, the uncertainty surrounding what those changes will mean to the way society works generates many nightmares about what is to come, nightmares that speculative fiction then reflects. While the texts I just discussed in Chapter 8 present encounters with beings who are other than human, these cautionary tales depict, among others, our fear that we won't even know what it means to be human in the first place. Andrew Burt described this warning at the 2002 World Science Fiction Convention when he said,

> What drove SF in the past was what was new. Enduring stories are always based on people. What does it mean to be "human" when we can tinker with the genome? The challenge is: what is beyond that? What is beyond what we know? It starts looking very fantastical and mystical ["Panel 163"].

And what genre is better equipped to deal with the fantastical and mystical elements of the future than speculative fiction?

Uncertainty usually fills human beings with fear, and a society full of humans shares many nightmares about the potential inability to adapt to changing surroundings. Speculative fiction is filled with stories reflecting that fear and warning about how it might affect us.

When the Rules Change: Adapting to Advances and New Situations

As Stanley Schmidt observes, "Change is almost always inconvenient, and most people would rather maintain the status quo, even if they're not terribly happy with it, than take on the risks of making a transition to something new, even if what's beyond the transition might be better" ("King" 22). In contrast to this seemingly ingrained resistance to change, speculative fiction works from the premise, as Van Pelt describes, that it is "worthwhile to embrace the idea that our world will be different" (Interview). The tension between these two opposing forces, our fear of change and our hope for Progress, fuels our nightmares that the rules will change before we can adapt, pulling the world right out from underneath us.

Gregory Benford described this nightmare of society out of step with reality when he identified that "SF also shows the fear that our social conventions, etc. won't work," citing the pod people in *Invasion of the Body Snatchers* as an example of a film that depicts the underlying fear that we won't be able to tell our friends from our foes (Interview). M. Keith Booker makes a similar point when he describes that "science fiction film was also quick to realize that aliens who can disguise themselves as humans were particularly terrifying" (*Monsters* 120–121). As with the fears I described in

Chapter 6, this terror also fuels social commentary as well as cautionary tales. What distinguishes the two goals, however, is the warning inherent in the latter that we need to be prepared to adapt if and when Progress (in its many forms) changes the rules.

While alien body snatchers are (hopefully) far enough from reality that the reflected fear remains at a distance, there is little doubt that coming advances in science and technology (such as those I described in Part One) will be so significant that our fear of society's rules radically changing may become real. The twentieth-century roots for this fear are shared by postmodernism, which Booker describes as resulting in part from the loss of both individual identity and historical continuity in the decade following World War II when Americans "increasingly felt that they were living in unprecedented situations to which the experience of the past was irrelevant." As Booker continues, "the pace of change was so rapid that the present also became disconnected from the future, which became more and more unpredictable" (*Monsters* 24). It would not be difficult to argue that this environment of rapid progress continues today. Rules as mundane as the conventions of spelling and as fundamental as the right to privacy have been irrevocably altered by technology in the past two decades, making our fears regarding the rules that govern identity, continuity, and society in general as relevant (and pressing) at the beginning of the twenty-first century as they were at the beginning of the Cold War.

Isaac Asimov goes even further back into history than Booker does when he asserts that many of the social revolutions in the first half of the twentieth-century were direct consequences of the resistance in European society to the changes wrought by the Industrial Revolution: "The dislike for technological innovations that upset the even comfort of a carefully designed rut extends with even greater force to social customs" ("Social" 56), customs that establish the rules we're looking at here. Speculative fiction has warned about the implications of such shifts for almost one hundred years. Sometimes these changes are slow and other times they are so revolutionary that we feel like modern-day Rip Van Winkles, waking up in a world that wasn't there when we went to sleep. Either way, both history and speculative fiction warn us to be ready. The children of the new millennium (and I do mean literally those born after the year 2001) will never know a world without cell phones, the Internet, or radiation treatments for cancer. How will the rules change in their lifetimes? Which social ruts will be upset in the next few decades? And will they be prepared to handle the inevitable repercussions? Will we?

This contemporary nightmare is found in almost every corner of the genre. For example, William Atheling discusses science fiction's interest in the problems humans will face when we travel into space, including our uncertain relationships to the countries, governments, families, sexual mores, and even religions left behind: "A real human being sitting in a real lunar crater is more than likely to be spending a certain proportion of his time wondering whether or not the god of his father is with him yet" (145). Atheling theorizes that religion is so basic to human psychology that "it is not only a proper but a fertile subject for fiction of any kind, and science fiction in particular" (145). As religion, in its many forms, is frequently the source of the codes and rules many of us live by, the potential for space travel to shake the foundation of those beliefs leads some genre writers to warn that society's rules might also be irrevocably altered if and when we leave Earth. The possibility such space explorations will result in the discovery of life on other planets is also examined hundreds of times over in speculative fiction. The corresponding nightmare that this discovery could create is the basis for one of the most widely known concepts of the genre: *Star Trek*'s Prime Directive, which prohibits interference in non-spacefaring cultures for fear that the knowledge of advanced technology and life on other planets will be too much for the civilizations to handle, leading to irreparable harm. These consequences of space travel are just two examples of the way speculative fiction reflects our fear that the rules will fundamentally and permanently change from underneath us.

As the adage goes, "the only thing constant is change"; that is our modern way of life. Sometimes these shifts are more evolutionary in nature (such as the gradual improvement in computers over the past half-century); sometimes they seem more revolutionary (for example, when Dolly was introduced to the public, the ability to clone mammals appeared to come out of the blue to many in mainstream culture[2]). Overcoming what has been labeled our inherent "resistance to change" has become a multi-billion dollar industry as Change Management is now ingrained in corporate culture. But speculative fiction was familiar with the nightmares that change can cause for decades before America's CEOs embraced the concept and the genre has reflected back that fear in prose, movies, and television for the entire modern era.

What Is Real and What Is Human? Fears for the Twenty-First Century

Seemingly basic questions of what is real and what is human have no easy answers in a society focused on Progress, which yields much fear and anxiety. As Ronnie D. Lipschutz observes, "Dualism, the notion that the physical world we perceive and in which we live is not the 'true' reality, is as old as (if not older than) organized religion, and as recent as certain versions of post-modernism" (93). There seem to be limits to what the human psyche can grasp, an idea Schmidt describes in his examination of the concept of Intelligent Design:

> Any system of knowledge ultimately rests on axioms that have to be accepted without proof as "philosophical bedrock," and when you reach that level, you may well find that our minds just aren't equipped to fully grasp any of the alternatives. Can you *really* picture either a finite universe or an infinite one? Or one that has always existed? Or one that had a definite instant of beginning? (What was before? What does "before" mean in such a case? What does it mean if there is no "before"?) ["Designing" 6].

In Chapter 8, we examined the nightmares that result from our attempts to negotiate the idea of an empty, infinite universe by imagining various forms of alien life. The fears driving our current analysis are similar attempts to process the concepts of reality and humanity.

While critical of the quality of the movies themselves, Lucius Shepard does identify a trend in Hollywood that looks at the question of identity and other similar issues, including "What is reality? What is life? Do clones have souls? ... Variants of these questions, simplistically stated, have informed the thematic structure of a veritable deluge of recent films" (97). This uncertainty over what is real (and the fear that accompanies it) is perhaps best reflected in movies where the main character, as Richard Swope describes, "discovers to his dismay that neither he nor the world he inhabits is what it appears to be" (239). In many such stories, according to Swope, "questions regarding the nature of 'reality' center on explorations into the nature of social-space — a space that, in the sf tradition, has been radically impacted, or even produced, by 'technological progress'" (223). When we can more easily communicate with someone in another country than we can with our next-door neighbors, what does this do to the social space we inhabit? Can this Progress be considered an improvement? And as we "interact" in new, less physical ways, how is our conception of reality affected?

Van Pelt described one of the genre's current reflections of the Progress nightmare as "blending the boundaries between reality and virtual worlds so [extensively] that there won't be a way to tell the difference (and this calls into mind all the existential questions about what is reality)" ("Request"). But what would happen if we were given a choice about this form of Progress? In a *Los Angeles Times* column reflecting on the *Matrix* movies, perhaps the best recent example of the reality dilemma, Reed Johnson asks just that question: "Faced with a choice between an unbearably grim, human-made reality, and a seductive electronic fantasy ... *The Matrix* asks how many, or rather how few, people would rather fight than surrender their core humanity — not only their physical bodies but also their capacity for free will." While, as far as we know, we don't have to decide between such radically different options (yet), today's technology does already present us with the choice between interacting with others face to face (warts and all) and using screen names and cleverly manipulated Internet profiles that paint us in the best possible (and maybe a false) light. How far is it from harmless fibbing in chat rooms or on social networking sites to full-blown electronic fantasies?[3] At what point will technology make such fantasies more seductive, more "real" than the physical world? We need to be prepared to answer these questions as Progress marches forward; speculative fiction warns us to consider them before it is too late.

It would seem, at least on the surface, that science should be able to give us a definite answer to the second question in this section (what is human?) even if the first regarding reality remains elusive. After all, we've cracked the genome and now have the blueprint for what makes a human being; speculative fiction warns us to ask, though, whether we are just our DNA. Does "human" simply mean a specific sequence of chemical compounds arranged in a double helix, or is there more to it than that? While the details may change as scientific knowledge advances, this warning and the fear that drive it are far from new in speculative fiction: Schmidt notes that John W. Campbell asked this very question in a 1959 editorial called "What Do You Mean ... Human?" ("On Being Human" 39). The cautionary tales in this chapter remind us that this question goes far beyond contemporary issues of race or gender because, as technology progresses, such concerns may end up seeming trivial compared to the changes in store for the next century. We might even mange to Progress ourselves right out of being human at all.

It is important to keep in mind that the answer to the question of what it means to be human is always evolving, as Schmidt suggests with his claim that "a nanotechnology revolution, if one happens, will surely *change* our ideas of 'what it means to be human'" ("On Being Human" 41). And the technology that may change those ideas does not have to be as extraordinary as nanites; for example, "what will people do if advanced technology frees them from the need to spend most of their waking hours 'making a living'?" (42). Schmidt goes on to observe that major technological revolutions have always affected our definitions of human life in ways that we never anticipated (42). Since the Industrial Revolution, we have found (and it seems will continue to find) new ways to fill our time but the transition hasn't always been easy, a fear speculative fiction reflects.

Since, as Brenda Cooper observed at the 2002 World Science Fiction

Convention, "Humans have always not wanted to die," the search for immortality has also always been caught up in, and tripped up by, the very essence of what it means to be human. This quest faces many obstacles such as the need to clearly define, as William Sims Bainbridge observes,

> what you actually consider your own personal identity to be. Are you your body? Or are you your unique attributes, opinions, and beliefs? Your memories? Your deeds, reputations, and legal status as a citizen or the social roles you play? Are you a unique locus of transcendental consciousness, or an already immortal soul? [40].

Bainbridge then considers the possibility of using complex surveys to record personalities in preparation for technological breakthroughs that will allow those personalities to be downloaded in some form, but eventually comes to the conclusion that "the most severe question is whether we would consider this to be real immorality" (49). Would a newly downloaded personality even be human, let alone the same *person* who created the file in the first place? Why would it matter?

As medical science continues to extend human life, every answer leads to more questions because, as Andrew Burt asked on the same panel as Cooper, "What is the core of being human if you don't have to worry about death?" ("Panel 441"). And if we are actually lucky enough as a species to accomplish all our goals before destroying ourselves, William Thomasson wondered, "What will society be like when everyone has everything they want?" A key element of humanity is our mortality. What would happen if that was "solved?" Would that be Progress? Schmidt has examined the not-so-obvious consequences of immortality[4] in several editorials, including "Fear Pollution" where he describes the potential that, once society has reached "technologically-achieved immortality, [humans] are so determined to live as long as possible that they become pathologically afraid of every imaginable risk" (140). To illustrate his point, Schmidt points to "those stories about future societies with more or less immortal inhabitants, stagnating because their inhabitants placed such a high value on surviving every possible minute that they were afraid to risk *doing* anything" (141). Would we be bored with life if there was nothing left to do or to risk? Would we still be human if we forgot how to live?

Discovering the secret to indefinite (or even vastly extended) life has other implications for the broader structures of society as well. In her examination of life in the far future, Marge Piercy observes that "certainly our notions of marriage and family will have to change into something perhaps unrecognizable to us today. What someone may want at twenty-five might be immensely different from what they might want in a mate at one hundred and twenty-five" (133). How will (near) immortality impact our drive to reproduce, identified by Thomas Aquinas as one of the four elements of a human being's essential nature (Timmons 70)? Would we even feel that drive if there was no longer a need to create a legacy (since we would always be around)? Can we still consider ourselves human if we stop striving to pass on our genes to the next generation? Would there even be a next generation, if we were basically immortal? How much can we evolve and still be human? Will we build ourselves right out of humanity? These questions have led genre writers to fill volumes over the past century, some of which we are about to examine.

What Happens Next? Print Examples

The opening epigraph of Nancy Kress's short story "Sleeping Dogs" quotes Freeman Dyson's[5] assertion that "'The new technologies will be dangerous as well as liberating. But in the long run, social constraints must bend to new technologies'" (262). That seems to be the real issue in this nightmare: what will have to bend as we learn more about our environment or as it changes around us? One example of such radical change, the elimination of lying via an iron-clad detector, is the premise of James L. Halperin's 1996 novel *The Truth Machine*, while a vastly different one is pondered by the main character in Walter Jon Williams's 2003 novella "The Green Leopard Plague": "And if ... plant-people proved viable? he wondered. All bets were off. A world in which humans could become plants was a world in which none of the old rules applies" (42).

Nancy Kress's Sleepless series[6] not only examines our fears surrounding genetic engineering, but it also reflects the dangerous social divisions that result when science can "improve" humans through that manipulation. Society in Kress's series becomes polarized between those with the new advantages and those with unaltered DNA. Poul Anderson's 1954 short story "The Chapter Ends" examines a similarly tragic divide where both humans and posthumans (to use Dozois's term) try to coexist while Samuel R. Delaney's 1971 story "Aye, and Gomorrah" looks at the impact of posthumans on traditional boundaries of race, class, and gender. In addition, 1975's "The Hero as Werewolf" by Gene Wolfe is told from the perspective of those left behind in the Posthuman Future, forced to the sidelines of a magnificent new world.

It goes almost without saying that human colonization of the universe is a treasured idea in speculative fiction. But such a massive shift has its price. "A Case of Conscience" by James Blish (published in *If-Worlds of*

Science Fiction, September 1953) examines the dilemmas a Roman Catholic priest faces when he finds himself on another planet, while the human colonists in Orson Scott Card's *Ender* series of novels follow a new religion, based on a Speaker for the Dead, one who preserves the story of those who have died as Ender has done for the Buggers.[7] In another variation of this profound societal dislocation, Greg Bear's *Eon* series (*Eon*, 1985; *Eternity*, 1988; and *Legacy*, 1995) follows a group of humans on an asteroid starship who become bored by the monotony of their trip and create The Way, an infinitely long artificial universe with openings to other times and places, once more altering the rules of their society.

But what if we went away and our home society had moved on without us, instead of the other way around? Joe Haldeman's 1974 novel *The Forever War* deals with just that question: because of relativity's effects, soldiers fighting an interstellar war return to Earth after 1,000 years. The home they find has changed so significantly that they no longer feel comfortable there and reenlist because they know what to expect in the military. This updated take on *Rip Van Winkle* also appears in Brian Stableford's 2002 novel *The Omega Expedition*, where the main character emerges from cryonic freeze and finds himself "worrying about how he can possibly fit into a world so far out of his temporal joint" (Easton, "Reference Library" (Apr. 2003) 134).

The nightmare takes a different turn in Robert Heinlein's *A Stranger in a Strange Land*, where the main character returns from Mars with abilities and beliefs that are so alien that they have the potential to change every facet of Earth society. He thus becomes a cult leader and is eventually killed. The clash between extra-terrestrial ideas and our Earth-bound ones also drives Gregory Benford's 1994 novel *Furious Gulf*, part of the Galactic Center series, which examines the uncertainties surrounding encounters with machine-based intelligences where

> our human concern with mortality and individualism as a feature of biological creatures is unnecessary among intelligences that never had to pass through our Darwinnowing filter. If we can copy ourselves indefinitely, why worry about a particular copy? What kind of society would emerge from such origins? ["Galactic Center" 344–45].

For eons, we have looked to the sky and wondered if anyone was up there but what would happen if we knew life existed on other planets but we had no way to contact them or if they simply weren't interested in us? Two stories published within a month of each other examine opposite reactions to that possibility. The December 2001 issue of *Analog* includes Rick Shelley's "First Contact National Monument," a novelette depicting the mass cultural disappointment and economic depression that occurs when a probe arrives to assess our planet but no more visitations follow. On the other end of the spectrum, in Robert Reed's "Oracles" (from January 2002's *Asimov's*) a global civilian authority is created to control the release of information about other intelligent life in the universe that has been sent as a warning by yet another alien race.

Before the events of either of those stories can happen, however, the existence of alien life must be confirmed, knowledge that can only have an immediate, revolutionary impact. In Edward M. Lerner's "By the Rules" (*Analog*, June 2003), the narrator ponders just this societal consequence when he struggles with deciding whether to share his discovery of an alien AI spread throughout the Internet: "The credible announcement of extraterrestrial intelligence could — would — impact society seismically ... [because] *We are not alone* was as major a world-view change as I could conceive of" (112).[8]

Discovering, or being discovered by, alien life has tremendous, often devastating consequences in speculative fiction but not always in the way we might expect. As the narrator describes in Don D'Ammassa's "A Good Offense" (May 2003's *Analog*), visitation by another species is both a dream and a nightmare: "The arrival of the Pulagi on Earth three decades earlier had traumatized human society, but the turmoil had passed once it became obvious that life was going to continue pretty much as it had before" (81). Humans are the one changing the rules in Robert Randall's 1958 novel *The Shrouded Planet* when we make contact with an alien race and proceed to turn their civilization upside down. Similarly, in Nancy Kress's novel *Probability Sun* (part of a series with *Probability Moon* and *Probability Space*), humans wreak the havoc when they discover a world where society is built around consensus because the natives' brains are physically incapable of handling disagreement. This physiological quirk is caused by an alien device hidden in the mountains, a device humans quickly steal when they discover it can help them defend against another alien race that attacks on sight. Predictably, the native society promptly collapses when the rules change and consensus is no longer necessary.

We also see our fear of radical social changes in post-apocalyptic cautionary tales. In Tim Lebbon's novella *White*, for example, the world is dramatically altered by a sudden, massive snowstorm that strands a group in Cornwall, cutting them off from the rest of society. This fascination with losing everything we know reflects a specific fear, as William Lomax explains:

> The ruins that litter the postholocaust landscape are the remnants not of civilization but of civilization's myths. The buried Statue of Liberty in the final scene of *Planet of the Apes* drives the hero to despair, not because of what it is at that moment — a ruined masterpiece — but because of what it represents to him, a survivor from preholocaust America [253].

Other examples of such despair-inducing ruins include the crumbled remains of Washington, DC in the 1976 film *Logan's Run* (based on the 1967 novel of the same name) and, as Lomax notes, Brian Aldiss's destroyed towers of Oxford (from 1964's *Greybeard*) as well as *Riddley Walker*'s buried cathedral. These destroyed symbols, according to Lomax, are "the distillate that remains after our 'sustaining cultural myths' have evaporated from the distorted memories of survivors" (253); this evaporation of the symbols of all we hold dear haunts our nightmares.

What if we were the cause of such an evaporation but didn't even know it? Pete D. Manison's "Punctuated Equilibrium" (*Analog*, June 2003) turns on the concept that civilization is unavoidably cyclical, with the story's title referring to a theory of evolutionary science that suggests civilizations go through periods of stasis, followed by sudden, rapid change. As the main character works on a project to preserve the knowledge of her time against a potential Dark Age, she starts to question whether providing such knowledge to a future, less-advanced civilization is actually a good idea. Her suspicions are confirmed when her team discovers that a previous civilization on Earth had the same idea; rather than taking considered, measured steps toward accessing the newly available (and much more advanced) information, those in charge rush headlong into what they believe will be a new Golden Age, ignoring the potentially disastrous consequences of unleashing so much information on an unstable civilization.

The mirror-image of Manison's warning, the desperate attempts of those in power to *prevent* the rules from changing, thus maintaining the status quo (and their own power), is another facet of the Progress nightmare. In Thomas Sherred's "E for Effort" (published in the May 1947 issue of *Astounding*), the inventor of a camera that allows users to view the past is killed by government agents before the device can be released because it would mean the end of secrets, irrevocably changing the way society works. Clifford Simak takes a different approach to this fear in his "Target Generation" (published in *Science Fiction Plus* in August 1953)[9]: Passengers on a generational ship have forgotten that they actually are on a ship and their lives have been reduced to mere games and empty ritual. When it comes time to land at their destination, the only person with the knowledge and skill to land the ship is forced to kill the leader of the society who cannot accept that the rules are about to change and will do anything to keep things the way they are.

Our fear of an unstable reality, meanwhile, has roots early in our childhoods when we learn to question what is real by following Alice in Lewis Carroll's *Through the Looking Glass*, originally published in 1871; the uncertainty regarding the answer is continually reinforced by speculative fiction, particularly in the works of Philip K. Dick. In *Time Out of Joint*, for example, the main character eventually discovers that his picture-postcard perfect 1950s small town is no more than an elaborate simulation designed by the Earth government to keep his mental illness under control so he can assist with a war against the lunar colony. While this story is read by many postmodernists as a critique of the concept of 1950s America as an ideal, peaceful, and prosperous decade,[10] by expanding our time horizons and looking at this narrative from the broader perspective of the reality question, we find the fear that our "reality" is not what it seems to extend beyond any particular decade, political theory, critical movement, or, even, philosophy.

Similarly, *The World of Null-A* by A.E. Van Vogt, originally serialized in *Astounding* in 1945, turns on a similar premise as Dick's *Time*: The main character searches for his identity after realizing his memories are not his own and ends up in a conspiracy that gets him killed, then brought back to life to use his newly discovered mental powers to defend humans against invading aliens. A more recent example of the unstable nature of reality is Alastair Reynold's 2002 novel *Chasm City* in which a virus leads the main character to discover he is not the person he believed he was and that his memories are not of his "real" life.

Another of Dick's stories, 1966's "We Can Remember It For You Wholesale" (the inspiration for the 1990 movie *Total Recall*), so successfully blurs the line between real and simulation that readers (and viewers) are left at the end not exactly sure what just happened. In a similar way, Pat Cadigan's 1992 novel *Fools* tells the story of an actress whose world is so thoroughly integrated with virtual reality that she begins to question whether she herself physically exists (Mann 95) while "The Wedding Album" by David Marusek (from the June 1999 *Asimov's*) depicts the terrifyingly blurred boundary between real humans and the sims they create instead of photographs to commemorate special events. And in Daniel M. Hoyt's "Background Noise" (from January 2003's *Analog*),[11] the narrator spends most of the story pondering his confusion between reality and the advertising holograms around him. In a twist on this fear of an unstable reality, the main character in Ursula K. LeGuin's *Lathe of Heaven*[12] is the creator of his own reality, even if he himself isn't aware of it (or so we are led to believe).

The meaning of "human" is the third major cultural element that Progress can challenge and is, not surprisingly, at the center of Nancy Kress's *Nothing Human*, which tells the story of an alien race known as the pribir that interfere with the genetics of human children in an attempt to show us the right way to live without destroying the planet. These children are forced to determine what it means to be human after they have been genetically altered and must choose whether to join the pribir or stay on an Earth that is rapidly becoming unlivable. Would they still be human if they followed their alien creators away from Earth? An earlier version of this nightmare, *Childhood's End* by Arthur C. Clarke,[13] reflects our fear of ambiguous humanity when it depicts the forced evolution of the human race by alien overlords who also alter human children. Dan Simmons describes his own series that reflects this uncertainty, the *Hyperion* cantos (*Hyperion*, 1989; *The Fall of Hyperion*, 1990; *Endymion*, 1996; and *The Rise of Endymion*, 1997), as an examination of the question of "the salvation of the human soul—in the sense of finding the essence of what makes and keeps us human" (207).

Sometimes alien interference is not what causes characters to lose touch with what it means to be human, but rather it is the unforeseen consequences of their own hubris. In H.G. Wells's *Invisible Man* (and its many imitations),[14] for example, the main character's psychosis begins when meaningful contact with others is cut off because of his scientific experiments. And in Joe Haldeman's "Four Short Novels," published in the October/November 2003 issue of *Fantasy and Science Fiction*, immortality, through a variety of means, leads to the eventual destruction of three of the four civilizations that (temporarily) conquer the inevitability of death.

Speculative fiction also examines this issue of immortality by questioning what we lose if we are engineered to live forever, or at least for centuries. In Mary Soon Lee's "Coming of Age" (April 2003's *Analog*), humans live for hundreds of years while computers run everything to keep people as safe as possible; thus there is little risk of dying from anything. Lee's protagonist is an eighteen-year old boy who wants to do something important with his life, yet finds himself staring at centuries of idleness. He decides to pilot a starship in a local race without computer assistance, risking injury or even death if he crashes, just so he can experience "life." Caught in a similar dilemma as Lee's character, the humans in Edward Muller's "The First Lesson" from the September 2003 issue of *Analog* have achieved near immortality and yet fear death so much that they are extremely risk-averse, sending robots to do anything of an unknown, and hence dangerous, nature. But one of the few young people in Muller's world bucks the trend and risks everything to physically access a mysterious alien vault that promises to provide the rarest thing in the universe. The vault is built in such a way that only a living creature, not a robot, can enter, deliberately designed as a forceful reminder that growth only comes in the unknown and that giving into the fear of death leads to eternal boredom.

Another variation of this fear of losing what makes us human sounds a counterintuitive warning about the consequences of world peace, which, at first glance, seems like nothing but a good thing. The March 2004 issue of *Analog* includes "Draft Dodger's Rag" by Jeff Hecht, the story of a Vietnam-era draft dodger whose place in the war is taken by one of the many time travelers from two hundred years in the future who, bored by the lack of conflict and the virtual physical indestructibility of their own time, come back to play soldier in the late 1960s. Taking the warning of Hecht's story one step further, the premise of David Brin's *Out of Time: Yanked!* by Nancy Kress is that the future human race becomes unable to deal with adversity after solving basic problems like violence and poverty and is thus unable to defend itself against an aggressive alien race. These future humans have to go back in time to pull people from more violent eras to deal with the aliens. When the rules changed for these two fictional societies, the people adapted but that adaptation may not be Progress, as both "Draft Dodgers" and *Yanked!* question. In other words, is getting rid of violence and hardship really a good thing? Does changing the rules that drastically also radically change humanity? Is that change truly Progress?

Meanwhile, in "A New Man," a continuation of his story "Persistent Patterns," Shane Tourtellote focuses on the question of what it means to be human on a more individual level: the main character, after being treated with a brain pattern overlay to cure his criminally violent tendencies, begins to experience thoughts and opinions that are not his own, including political stances that do not match those he held before the procedure.[15] Similar questions regarding the implications of "fixing" violent behavior inform Michael Crichton's *The Terminal Man*[16] where "the surgery that is supposed to return him [the protagonist] to a normal life in human society is, at the same time, a surgery that puts him at an extreme distance from humanity" (Pethes 161). As Nicolas Pethes argues, this novel and other like it "make a statement about what it means to be human: computer technology, which is able to affect human emotions and actions, is a severe threat to the principle of freedom of will, responsibility for actions, and the self-governing of humanity" (162). These principles are at the heart of our cultural definition of what it means to be human, thus violations of any of them are the source of many of our Progress nightmares.

Another medical "advance" forms a subplot to William's "Green Leopard Plague": humans can be rebuilt, even after death, using pre-recorded data back-ups to fill in the memories. This elimination of "realdeath," as the narrator calls it, results in significant changes in both what it means to be human ("What was the value of a human life when it could be infinitely duplicated, and cheaply?") and what it meant to kill ("It wasn't murder, after all, just a fourth-degree felony") (Williams 57). The implications of a technology that can copy humans lead to a very different story in Robert J.

Sawyer's "Shed Skin," from *Analog*'s January/February 2004 issue: the organic body still living after his consciousness is copied to a virtually immortal robot demands his life and identity back, both of which he willingly signed away when he arranged the transfer. Tragedy ensues when the robot won't kill himself to allow the human to take back the identity. Sawyer's story leaves open the question of who has the right to that identity: the robot or the physical human body or both? This question of who has the right to be considered human is also the underlying premise of Heinlein's *Friday*, in which a genetically engineered heroine, an artificial person, tries to navigate a society that refuses to grant her even the most basic rights.

David Brin's 2002 novel *Kiln People* adds a different twist to the human question with its idea of the ability to imprint one's self onto an unlimited number of disposable clay copies while the original is still alive and participating in society; this inevitably brings up the question of the rights of the copies and if they are, in any way, human. The inhabitants of the future depicted in Brenda Cooper and Larry Niven's "Choosing Life" (*Analog*, January 2002) solved that particular problem (and the one we see in Sawyer's story) by making it illegal for two versions of the same consciousness to exist at the same time: in order to be uploaded and thus made immortal, the human body must allow itself to be killed.[17] However, in the novelette "Nightfall" by Charles Stross, even this solution is complicated by the confusion, crises of faith, and other issues inherent in the difficult transition from organic human to uploaded consciousness, with the resulting (and persistent) questions of what it means to be human still primarily unresolved. These issues also inform Charles Platt's *The Silicon Man* where an FBI agent deals with the consequences of living forever via "info morphs." "Lavender in Love" by Brian Plante (*Analog*, February 2003), on the other hand, takes a romantic approach to the issue of where memories end and humanity begins with the story of a vending machine loaded with its creator's memories that falls in love and believes that, when new experiences are uploaded, it can actually live.

The line between technology and humanity is also blurred in "Utmost Bones" by Pamela Sargent, which examines one woman's search for what's missing in her life when every human has given him or herself over to the "Net of Minds," leaving behind even their technologically altered, self-repairing, indefinitely extended bodies for "life" entirely in the Net.[18] As Sargent's story is a meditation on this exact question of what it means to be human, an extended summary is worthwhile here. When the main character, Kaeti, asks herself, "How much of what I once was is left?" (119), the Net attempts to comfort her by summoning images of her family and friends but she feels something is missing—she is lonely and leaves the Net in search of physical companionship because "she had tired of that congenial environment, had soon been longing for the company of other people in the flesh" (121). The Net tries to convince her to stay by arguing that those human beings who joined it are still alive, "'woven into the strands of the Net'" and that they merely "'chose to give up the rejuvenated and rebuilt carbon-based shells that were their bodies ... shedding the vestiges of bodies that were no longer necessary'" (128). To Kaeti, though, all of those people are dead because "'if the bodies are dust, if the brains in which their thoughts were first formed have been lost, then those people no longer truly exist. What the Net holds is no more than a host of simulacra'" (128). The story ends ambiguously, though, with Kaeti returning to the Net after a fruitless search, even forgetting she had ever left.

The "humans" in Wolf Read's "Between Singularities" (in February 2003's *Analog*) did not get the choice Kaeti has; they were forcibly transformed into immortal, super-intelligent beings during a Technological Singularity.[19] This story demonstrates the ways in which such a transformation might change our sense of everything from economics to time to gender to love and ends with the narrator and his pre-singularity wife deciding to experience life once again as physical creatures, ejecting millions of years of memories of essential godhood for the chance to love again because, as the narrator observes, "Love—like volcanoes, planets, and stars—was destined to fade" (108).

On a more humorous note, Bruce Sterling's very short piece from 1999, "Homo Sapiens Declared Extinct," depicts a universe in which biological intervention has reached such an advanced level that there are no actual human beings left anywhere and the highly evolved beings that have taken our place couldn't be happier. A similarly massive scope is found in Olaf Stapledon's *Last and First Men*, which recounts the history of humanity over two billion years. As the human race rises and falls within Stapledon's mammoth work, both the appearance and mental capabilities of humans radically transform from current to post-human, and the book briefly touches on the impact such changes have on what it means to be human. The implications of Progress not only on our sense of humanity but also on the rules that define the world and on our conception of reality that inspire prose writers like Stapledon also fuel film and television reflections of the nightmare, reflections made possible by the very Progress we often fear.

What Really Happened? Film and Television Examples

Progress nightmares make their way from the page to the film and television screens as speculative fiction continues to reflect our fears that the rules, reality, and even humanity are not what we think they are. While *Invasion of the Body Snatchers*, for example, is commonly interpreted as a thinly veiled, anti–Communist allegory prompted by American Cold-War hysteria, another (perhaps more contemporary) reading of the movie is the one described by Benford earlier in this chapter: a reflection of the nightmare that we will go to bed at night and by morning, our whole world will change. In Julian Cope's single "The Tower," from the 1992 album *Jehovahkill*, that is just what happens when a man wakes up to find himself in a country dominated by warrior women (Simpson 14).

One of the specific ways visual media often reflects our Progress fears is with stories that alter a fundamental element of life: time. In *Paycheck* (both the 2003 film and the 1953 Philip K. Dick short story), the main character destroys the device he created to see into the future because, he believes, by showing a man his future, he has no future. The machine's predictions, it shows him. became self-fulfilling prophecies with quarantines intended to prevent plagues actually creating them and preemptive military strikes causing, instead of preventing, wars. Taking an opposite path, it is the past, not the future, that the characters in "Memories" (an episode from the second *Twilight Zone* series) don't want to know after a hypnotist suddenly releases their past life memories, memories that most want to be rid of.

The rules of both time and space come into play in Andrey Tarkovsky's 1979 film *Stalker* in which The Zone is ambiguously defined, even for the characters and especially for the audience. The characters' goal is to pass through The Zone to reach The Room, which reportedly brings to life the deepest desires of all who enter it. But the nature of those desires, and even the reality of The Room itself, is open for interpretation; this uncertainty leads one of the characters to try to destroy The Room with a bomb. As Aida A. Hozic describes, "Anything can happen in The Zone—people can disappear, previously passable roads can turn out to be closed, new traps can emerge where there were none, desires can be articulated and realized. Whatever happens, it is obvious that the rules have been suspended" (130).

Aliens, of course, also appear in electronic media as frequently as they do in print. In the "Lost City, Pt. I" episode of *Stargate SG-1*, the President of the United States worries about the potential reaction to the forthcoming announcement of the Stargate's existence, which will also confirm the existence of alien life (both hostile and friendly): "It's going to take anything and everything we have to keep our civilization from turning upside down." This nightmare of a society turned upside down by information it cannot handle is exactly what *Star Trek*'s Prime Directive is designed to prevent; in fact, a frequent plot point in *The Next Generation* is the length to which the Federation will go in order to surreptitiously observe "pre-warp" planets without interfering in their development. This attempt at observation fails in the third season episode "Who Watches the Watchers?" when an explosion destroys the research post and exposes the native culture to knowledge of life on other worlds before they are ready. The theme is expanded in the fourth season episode "First Contact" when the Federation decides a planet *is* ready and offers to guide them into interstellar relations. The planet's leader eventually rejects the invitation, however, fearing that his people can't handle the truth. He turns out to be right when the planet's security minister dismisses Commander Riker's claims of the Federation's peaceful intentions with "'however you would describe your intentions you represent the end of my way of life'" (qtd. in Inayatullah 56).

Another frequent reflection of this aspect of the Progress nightmare on film and television involves the efforts of those in power to conceal the existence of alien life in an attempt to maintain their control. For example, in the 1997 movie *Contact* (based on the 1985 novel by Carl Sagan), a government official buries proof that an astrophysicist has somehow made contact with an alien race. More recently, in "Memento," a sixth season episode of *Stargate SG-1*, a military commander's fear of alien invasion coupled with new knowledge of what exists out in the universe leads him to take control of the recently unearthed Stargate, holding hostage the Earth team that found it. In addition, the security officer who is so concerned about his way of life in *The Next Generation*'s "First Contact" stages his own murder, and tries to frame Riker for it, sacrificing himself to prevent his people from learning that they are not alone in the universe. And, of course, Chris Carter's *X-Files* ran for nine seasons and one movie on the strength of our fear that government conspiracies cover up proof of alien life on Earth. As Lipschutz notes, "*The X-Files* articulated not only skepticism about the good intentions of the US federal government, but also suggested that no good could come of trusting its agents (aside from Mulder and Scully, of course)" (85), at least when it involves knowledge of alien life. Taking up the same idea from a different perspective, a third season episode of *The Next Generation*, "Transfigurations," depicts a society that deals with its imminent evolution into energy beings by hunting down and killing all of its people who exhibit the signs of this transformation.

Equally drastic confrontations, though on a smaller scale, are usually involved when the nature of reality is thrown into question. The *Twilight Zone* television series, throughout all three of its incarnations, is perhaps the epitome of the nightmare that our world is not what we think it is. For example, the very nature of her existence is upended for the main character in "The Lateness of the Hour" when she finds to her horror that she is one of the robots built by her father, robots she has been critical of and wants to dismantle. And before realizing he is a robot, the main character from "In His Image" spends most of the episode trying to figure out why nothing in his life is the way he remembers it. In another episode ("A World of Difference"), a businessman suddenly finds himself in a world where he is just an actor playing a businessman. Unwilling to give up his "fake" life, he rushes back to the set just before it is dismantled and disappears. Meanwhile, the "Five Characters in Search of an Exit" discover that they are not people at all but dolls in a Christmas toy donation barrel in this *Twilight Zone* episode.

In true *Twilight Zone* fashion, there is a double reflection of this nightmare in "Person or Persons Unknown" as the protagonist struggles through most of the episode to figure out why no one in his life remembers him, only to discover it was all just a dream. But the nightmare is still in force at the end of the story when his wife takes off her face cream and looks nothing like the woman he knows. In a similar, but much more violent, situation to LeGuin's protagonist in *The Lathe of Heaven*, the Vietnam Vet in the second *Twilight Zone* (1985) series episode "Nightcrawlers,"[20] along with the rest of his squad, is able, because of exposure to a chemical spray while in Asia, to create whatever he can imagine, including his terrifying nightmares of combat. Another original *Twilight Zone* episode, "A World of His Own," puts the nature of reality more directly into the character's hands with the story of a man who can create anything just by describing it into his dictation machine. When his wife threatens to have him committed for delusions, he throws the tape that created her into the fire, thus erasing her from "reality." And in "The Mind and the Matter," written by Rod Serling himself, a book allows the main character to re-create the world exactly the way he wants it.

But even before Serling's landmark series beamed into American living rooms, 1953's *Invaders from Mars* questioned the nature of reality while also taking the alien invasion trope to another level. These Martian invaders use humans, controlled by electronic devices in their brains, to infiltrate and destroy rocket plants and other military targets. The young protagonist, David Maclean, is the first to discover the invasion but the movie ends ambiguously, simultaneously telling the audience the whole thing was just David's dream while also showing a saucer landing in the distance (Booker, *Monsters* 120–21).[21]

Perhaps the defining image for the twenty-first century regarding the unstable nature of reality will come from the *Matrix* trilogy.[22] Neo's discovery of the Matrix and his subsequent efforts to free humanity from its virtual world will no doubt have a lasting impact on the current generation's perspectives on the question of what is real, carrying on in the tradition of *Twilight Zone*. But, while it will clearly be influential, *The Matrix* is not alone in reflecting this nightmare for contemporary audiences. In Alex Proyas's 1998 film *Dark City*,[23] for example, a murder suspect named Murdoch discovers that his city is actually an island constructed in space by The Strangers, an alien race experimenting to determine if human minds can save them from extinction. Every night, the city and its people (including their identities) are reprogrammed, or "tuned," to a new experiment. When Murdoch and the detective investigating him discover the true nature of the city, the detective can't handle the revelation and literally falls off the edge, disappearing into space. The movie ends with Murdoch using his superhuman mental abilities (those that enabled him to discover the truth in the first place) to create a new world of beaches and sun to replace the dark, depressing city of The Strangers. The literal loss of his grip by the detective when the truth is revealed is the film's way, Swope argues, of asking the audience to consider who will be able to survive in new worlds, when the rules change (242). Who will be best equipped to adapt?

In *The Thirteenth Floor*, directed by Josef Rusnak and based on Daniel F. Galouye's 1964 novel *Simulacron 3* (also known as *Counterfeit World*), the uncertainty about reality comes courtesy of human-developed virtual reality, not alien experimentation. In this film, also released in 1998, the main character, Douglas Hall, is also accused of murder, this time of his boss, Fuller. In 1999 Los Angeles, Hall and Fuller created a virtual reality simulation of the city in 1937, a self-sustaining virtual world of "units" living their lives unaware of the digital nature of their existence. Before he is killed, Fuller leaves Hall a cryptic message in the simulation that not only leads a simulated unit to discover the truth of his reality (with the expected angst) but also leads Hall to discover that his "life" in 1999 is in fact merely as a unit in a much larger simulation. It is then revealed that Hall's reality is one of thousands created in 2024 by a man looking to indulge his murderous impulses; once Hall's world created its own simulation, however, it had to be shut down. Through a complicated plot maneuver, the movie ends as Hall exits his simulation and enters the "real" Los Angeles in 2024, in the original developer's body.

In his analysis of the postmodern view of "space," Swope observes that the "final scene [of *The Thirteenth Floor*] is striking ... [because] LA 2024 is actually framed by the glass doors that open onto a deck on which Hall now stands visualizing his new 'social reality.' It is as if we are looking through yet another screen" (241). As Swope asserts, the lasting image from both *Dark City* and *The Thirteenth Floor* "is not so much the sunny utopias with which they end, but rather those 'darker' moments when Hall and

Murdoch reach the end of the world (or the metaphysical grid) to expose ... the crime of contingent (spatial) existence" (242). Space is more literally the underlying issue in "Dreams for Sale," an episode in the second *Twilight Zone* series in which a woman learns her world is so overdeveloped that the only "outside" is a 15-minute virtual reality sequence she is allowed to access once a week. Unable to face life as a factory drone, she escapes back into the virtual world and gets "trapped" there.

Sometimes reality isn't what those in power try to hide; sometimes it is Progress of any kind. In an episode of the syndicated series *Mutant X*, "Crossroads of the Soul," a scientist hides his town from the outside world for decades to prevent progress from, in his view, destroying their way of life. And the planet of Solaris, in the two film adaptations of Stanislaw Lem's novel, allows the characters to hide from progress, pain, and reality. The audience is thus asked to consider the question of just what is real and who ultimately gets to determine it.

The question of reality gets even more complicated when it is applied to people, creating significant about regarding what it means to be human. Many in the genre believe no one is more adroit at this complication than Dick, whose novel *Do Androids Dream of Electric Sheep?* was adapted by Ridley Scott into the cult favorite *Blade Runner*. As Lipschutz observes, *Blade Runner* "addresses the 'manufacture' of human beings in and by postmodern capitalism, and forces us to ask how we can distinguish the 'artificial' from the 'real,' when the real might be the more alien" (82). This distinction is one that many speculative fiction characters attempt to negotiate on film and television screens. Perhaps the exact opposite of the *Blade Runner* reflection of this nightmare is Data's journey toward humanity, begun in *The Next Generation* and continued in several feature films. While his story does carry obvious echoes of the Pinocchio fable, it also blurs the line between artificial and real humans. A more frightening blurring of that line occurs in the "Afterlife" episode of Showtime's update of the *Outer Limits* series, which depicts one man's struggle to hold onto his humanity, his soul, while his physical body is being artificially transformed via injections of alien DNA in a secret military experiment.

The line between artificial and real also plays a key role when speculative fiction characters attempt to live forever. In the second season episode of *The Next Generation* "The Schizoid Man,"[24] a scientist believes he's achieved immortality by uploading his consciousness to Data and is stunned when his female aide refuses his offer to do the same for her, so they can live forever, together. We see a similar rejection of immortality via computer in *Clay*, a short film in writer-director Grey Pak's *Robot Stories*. Everyone in *Clay*'s world is required to join the consciousness database when they die but the film's protagonist wants the freedom to choose a "natural" death instead. The opposite occurs in "The Trade-Ins," from the original *Twilight Zone*, when an elderly couple hopes to be transplanted into younger, artificial bodies.

But living forever is not all it is cracked up to be, and is almost certainly not human, at least according to many speculative fiction cautionary tales. For example, the first *Highlander* movie includes a song by Queen that wonders, "Who Wants to Live Forever?," a lament that continued to be asked in the *Highlander* saga through three more movies and two television series. Similarly, one of the weekly featured mutants in an episode of *Mutant X*, "The Meaning of Death," willingly gives up his invulnerability, choosing death instead, seeing it as a release from his guilt after his wife and child are killed in a car accident that his mutation allowed him to survive. That feeling is echoed in the fourth season episode of *Babylon 5* "Into the Fire" where the immortal "first" being named Lorien reminds one of the human characters that "only someone who is mortal can believe that love can be eternal."

When the reflections of the three major aspects of this nightmare (unpredictable rules, unstable reality, and ambiguous humanity) are put into their respective camps, there seems to be a relatively consistent point throughout the first group, which makes sense. The fear that the rules will change from underneath us came into prominence at approximately the same time that film and television exploded into the mainstream culture; thus, we see similar reflections of that nightmare across the media. It seems that *Invasion of the Body Snatchers*, for example, took the *Rip Van Winkle* fear and ratcheted up the nightmare quotient to match the disturbingly unsettled times of the twentieth century, an escalation we also see in the prose of the time where the world changes faster than the characters can adapt.

The reflection of the other two parts of the nightmare, however, is where the medium seems to determine the particular manifestation of the cautionary tales to a great extent. Paradoxically, it seems that the visual nature of film and television gets in the way of their presentation of the human question. We see considerably more variety in the prose reflections of this nightmare than in movies or on television, perhaps because concepts such as personality uploads are easier to depict on the page than on the screen. Even with advancing CG-technology, visual media is still tied to our current perceptions of the world, including what people actually look like, and if we cannot recognize the image on the screen, we cannot relate to it as an audience. It seems that these visual media just can't accommodate those tales we don't have visual concepts for yet. The ones and zeroes of computer programs are not much to look at on the TV screen, thus we get representations of uploaded consciousnesses, for example, that look suspiciously like human bodies roaming around the insides of a giant computer, a la *Tron*.

Conversely, however, the visual nature of film and television allows questions of reality to be amplified in ways prose doesn't. For example, the image of the saucer landing in the field at the end of *Invaders from Mars* is more powerfully unsettling than it would be on the page. As the cliché goes, a picture is worth a thousand words and speculative fiction film and television leverages this advantage to reflect our fears regarding the uncertain nature of reality, something *The Twilight Zone* excels at doing. The classic anthology series, actually, also does the most consistent job of solving the "problem" of depicting the nightmare of not knowing what it means to be human. Its most successful solution is to conflate the two questions of reality and human into one cautionary tale; whether the characters end up discovering they are "really" robots or toys or something else other than human, *Twilight Zone* episodes often reflect both aspects of the nightmare at once, making them all the more unsettling.

10: Resistance Is Futile for Rip Van Winkle in the Twilight Zone: Images of the Unknown in the Mainstream Media

Those speculative fiction reflections of our fears of the Unknown that we just looked at in Chapters 8 and 9 penetrate deep into our public consciousness. For many genre fans, Philip K. Dick's work exemplifies the Unknown nightmare and, as *New York Times* book reviewer Laura Miller argues, Dick's "sensibility has seeped wide and deep into contemporary life." In addition to direct adaptations of Dick's stories such as *Total Recall* and *Minority Report*, Miller identifies Dickian themes in such other films as *The Truman Show, Memento, Being John Malkovich,* and *The Matrix,* arguing that these "devices and themes— implanted memories, commodified identities, simulacra" are also found in contemporary literary fiction, such as David Foster Wallace's *Infinite Jest*. While Miller acknowledges Dick's texts may not be the immediate inspiration for such works, she nevertheless emphasizes his far-reaching influence by declaring that Dick's ideas and warnings were far ahead of their time as he "integrated [speculative fiction thought experiments] into the humble fabric of everyday life." We can apply Miller's point even more broadly since our culture has absorbed images not only from Dick but also from many other cautionary tales. These images appear in a variety of contexts, including public discourse.

While there are many reflections of this nightmare that are undoubtedly referenced in our public discourse, my (admittedly unscientific) search identified several target metaphors[1] that the mainstream media uses frequently. Unlike the images from the Science and Technology or Power cautionary tales, however, the metaphors pulled from the Unknown nightmares (both the Monsters, Aliens, and "Other" Beings and Progress varieties) are often so intertwined that it makes more sense to discuss them as a group rather than as separate nightmares. This group of images includes a wide cast of characters who embody the nightmare (Buffy, werewolves, Rip Van Winkle, and Mulder and Scully); the famous *Star Trek* phrases "Resistance is futile" and "Prime Directive"; and portions of titles: *Twilight Zone*, *Body Snatchers*, and *War of the Worlds*.

As John E. Campbell observes in his socio-political reading of *The X-Files*, "Aliens appear to have invaded the contemporary United States, but not so much with spacecraft and ray guns as with clever advertising, mass marketing, and high primetime ratings" (328), an invasion also reflected in public discourse. While Campbell is primarily concerned with the function of *X-Files* as a politically and socially critical discourse, his assertion that "the alien image, emerging from the margins of popular culture, has developed a powerful iconic presence in the American mainstream" (330–331) supports my examination of mainstream media's absorption of speculative fiction imagery, as references to "alien" cautionary tales take many forms.

Metaphors invoking such emblematic characters as Buffy or Mulder and Scully, for example, provide us with a human entry point into a world of Monsters, Aliens, and "Other" Beings, inviting us to put ourselves, if only briefly, in their shoes as they deal with living in a world where such creatures really exist. Media references to these familiar characters remind us both of the struggles they endure and the strength they embody, while references to the more generic grouping of werewolves play instead on our fear of the hidden monstrous, both within society and within ourselves. Images of these supernaturally strong and resilient creatures bring to mind the power that lies behind the Unknown. Meanwhile, the definitive alien-invasion image of *War of the Worlds* invokes the same nightmare as *Star Trek*'s "resistance is futile": an advanced alien species threatening to destroy our way of life. Discourse using these metaphors relies on a shared cultural experience to convey the fear of losing everything we know and love.

When it comes to Progress nightmares, *The Twilight Zone* is perhaps the epitome of our fear that the world does not work the way it is supposed to, a fear reflected in the many episodes where characters discover that the rules aren't what they thought they were. *Star Trek*'s Prime Directive, on the other hand, provides perhaps the quintessential metaphor for the journey into the Unknown; closer to home, *Invasion of the Body Snatchers*[2] exemplifies the fear that the rules really can change as we sleep. And speaking of sleep, Washington Irving's *Rip Van Winkle*, although usually considered a children's story or fable and not speculative fiction, nevertheless also reflects the Progress nightmare and is often invoked by mainstream media. These images are so culturally pervasive, and persuasive, that even those who have never encountered the original narratives undoubtedly understand references to them. All of these images have become, in modern discourse, part of a cultural shorthand rooted in this genre's reflections of our fears that we will progress ourselves right out of the world we understand.

Media Coverage of Politics, Government, and the Military

As we saw in the other metaphor analysis chapters, much of our public discourse focuses on governmental and political machinations; we thus frequently find speculative fiction images in such discourse. This is especially true in the coverage surrounding the 2004 presidential race. For example, comedian Dennis Miller poked fun at then presidential candidate Howard Dean by claiming, "'The only thing he's done is be the lead guy in a state where his prime directive was to come out of the statehouse once a year, put a nail into a tree, and hang a bucket off it'" (Garvin). More serious coverage of the Democratic primaries also invokes *Star Trek*'s guiding principle as when then front-runner Governor Dean's advisors are reported to believe "the prime directive is to fire up Dean's base so the ground troops of volunteers can turn them out to their neighborhood caucuses" (Fitzgerald). The commentary is more pointed in Elisabeth Bumiller's October 2004 article that quotes Terry McAuliffe, then chairman of the Democratic National Committee, as remarking, "'I think George Bush lives in the twilight zone'" ("Talk").

Both sides of the political-ideological spectrum have also more recently come under attacks that use the imagery of pod people from *Invasion of the Body Snatchers:* Democrats are the target of Jonah Goldberg's critiques while an editorial skewers Republicans for reversing their traditional positions ("Blagg Column"). Even state-level politics attracts speculative fiction references: an article critiquing changes to campaign-finance laws in New Jersey argues that the new rules prohibit all but super-rich candidates from succeeding because "the message to other candidates is clear: Resistance is futile"(Moran). Such metaphors directly connect the process of electing our leaders with our cultural fears that the world will shift right out from under us, thus putting politics into a context, however unconsciously, where the stakes are incredibly high.

The 2003 invasion of Iraq and the ensuing turmoil in many ways provides a real world corollary to our Unknown nightmares and a significant amount of public discourse on this topic has occurred since hostilities began. Many in the media turn to genre images to describe the Unknown conditions both in Iraq and in the United States as we deal with the consequences of the war. A *Vanity Fair* article from July 2003, for example, spotlights the reactions of three famous writers (Norman Mailer, Gore Vidal and Kurt Vonnegut) to the Iraq war, with Vonnegut quoted invoking speculative fiction: "'I feel that our country, for whose Constitution I fought in a just war, might as well have been invaded by Martians and body snatchers'" (Tyrnauer). A year and a half later, the efforts of other opponents to the war are described using the Borg imagery: "As a new year begins that heralds in four more years of the Bush administration — anathema to peaceniks — some might think the protestors feel, more than ever, like their resistance is futile" (Dees). The epic scale of these genre metaphors seem particularly apt when it comes to issues of such monumental public concern.

Coverage of more specific military strategies and tactics in Iraq also employs genre metaphors as we see in a *Los Angeles Times* article's assertion that "the military's sprint to Baghdad initially vindicated Rumsfeld's prime directive to transform the U.S. armed forces into a lighter, more mobile force" (Fineman). Another *Star Trek*-inspired metaphor also appears in connection with military maneuvers in John Diamond and Dave Moniz's article, "No Answer for U.S. Firepower": "The 3rd Infantry Division's devastating armored swing through southwestern Baghdad this weekend was designed to glean information about enemy defenses and convey a message: Resistance is futile." Such metaphors are also used to describe the aftermath of the initial conflict. For example, a *Los Angeles Times* article uses a *Star Trek* image to characterize the plans for rebuilding Iraq — "In recent weeks, the CPA [Coalition Provisional Authority] has assigned two deputies to Bremer who were given one prime directive: Make it work faster" (Hendren) — while life in post-war Iraq is described by Neil MacFarquhar "as a terrifyingly lawless twilight zone." Insurgent attacks are a principal reason for that sense of a world with vastly different rules and T.R Fehrenbach invokes *Star Trek* in his effort to place that aspect of the conflict in historical perspective by examining previous situations where "pacification ... came only after all parties realized that further resistance was futile." By doing so, Fehrenbach reflects the immense stakes by linking the situation in Iraq to a Borg invasion.

Media coverage of the war is itself critiqued using H.G. Wells's imagery in Ron Martz's editorial "War of the Worlds" but such military reporting is not limited to the conflict in Iraq. *The Twilight Zone*, in particular, seems a fitting metaphor for the unsettling conditions that often accompany military involvement anywhere in the world. For example, both a *San*

Francisco Chronicle editorial ("The Gitmo") and a United States Representative, Adam Schiff (see White), compare the prison camp at Guantanamo Bay to the Rod Serling series. The hurricane-ravaged Gulf Coast is the subject of the metaphor in Stephen Hedges's article describing relief efforts headed by Army General Russel Honore. On the other side of the world, the Israeli withdrawal from Gaza in 2005 created a military situation that seems to define the image with the rules literally changing under the feet of residents of towns like "Gush Katif [which] has slipped into a twilight zone, with people grimly going about their business under the pall of approaching upheaval" (Greenberg). Once again, we see metaphors drawn from Unknown nightmares conveying in a few words the tremendous social consequences of political and military decisions.

Public discourse regarding the government, however, does not always involve such monumental issues as war or a presidential election. More routine issues of running the country such as pension reform and public transportation also lead many to rely on speculative fiction imagery to convey a sense of confused bewilderment at navigating such complex waters. For example, in the incredibly complicated yet typically tedious arena of pension regulation, an RJ Reynolds pension administrator testified during a Treasury Department hearing that proposed reforms would create a "legal twilight zone" for many plans (Walsh). On a slightly smaller scope, media coverage of the issue of diversity in government also employs such metaphors as in an Omaha, Nebraska editorial that ran with the headline, "Talent: The Prime Directive; Diversity on the Arena Board is Desirable, but Not as a Mandate." And the battle over legalizing gambling is described by a *Daily News* correspondent with another reference to a Progress nightmare: "Like Rip Van Winkle stirring from a deep sleep, the decades-long quest for casino gambling in the Catskills Mountains is finally awake and kicking" (Pienciak). At an even more local level, the investigation into a Massachusetts police department is declared to be as unknowable as the aliens Mulder and Scully chase ("Here's"), reflecting the immensely complicated nature of the task the authors see ahead for the investigators.

References to *The Twilight Zone* are particularly prevalent in coverage of both the mundane and the vital government functions, leaving virtually no area safe from comparison to a confusing, scary world. In the former category, the headline of a *Baltimore Sun* article on the pains of dealing with impounded cars references the series, "Twilight Zone for Towed Cars" (K. Wilson), while another headline outlines the implications for postal service in Manhattan demonstrating the far-reaching nature of the aftermath of the September 11th attacks: "Twilight Zone for ZIP code at Ground Zero" (Haberman). Substandard subway service is described by Anemona

Hartcollis as "the twilight zone of skip-stop service, a subway phenomenon that is little understood and rarely experienced by most riders." Issues with more critical systems such as Children and Family Services also elicit the use of *Twilight Zone* metaphors as when a "law of unintended consequences and the twilight zone of news" surrounds a change in New York state child welfare regulations (Applebome).

Public discourse regarding the financial aspects of running governments, both national and local, also employs speculative fiction nightmares that reflect our fear of the world changing around us, a world we seldom completely understand. One of the images frequently used in this conversation is one of the originals: Rip Van Winkle. In a similar manner as the Terminator and Frankenstein images from Chapter 4 and the Big Brother references from Chapter 7, though, these metaphors are sometimes used to allay fears rather than agitate them. For example, an article arguing that large federal deficits are not necessarily a catastrophe invokes a "Reagan-era Rip Van Winkle" to connect early twenty-first century politics to those from the 1980s (Nicklaus). In other cases, the references carry a derogatory connotation, such as when a local Massachusetts town commissioner accuses opponents of recently passed changes to the municipal charter of having "'the Rip Van Winkle disease'" for raising concerns more than a year after the formal public debate (Gonsalves). At the broader, state-wide level, an editorial critiquing the failure of tax reform in Kentucky warns those who "wait for state revenues to grow ... [that] they might as well settle in for a Rip Van Winkle nap" ("Editorial"). By turning to this particular image, these reporters employ a metaphor that points to our fears both that the rules will change as we sleep and that we won't be able to understand them, or properly function in the new world, when we wake up.

To the lay person, the criminal justice system seems to be a world of its own, with inexplicable rules and powerful forces locked in battle; public discourse regarding that strange world employs speculative fiction images to reflect that perspective. For example, one of John Allen Muhammad's victims, who was shot and left for dead before the 2002 sniper attacks even began in DC and Maryland, describes his experience of being cross-examined by Muhammad (who was acting as his own lawyer) as being like "'The Twilight Zone ... Defendants aren't supposed to cross-examine you'" (Ruane and Greene). From another perspective, a man exonerated after more than eight years in prison describes the DNA testing that freed him as "the silver bullet to the werewolf of injustice" (Bloodsworth).

Other seemingly unknowable yet powerful aspects of the legal system frequently lead to the use of speculative fiction images, particularly those reflecting the nightmare of aliens and monsters taking over our world. For example, a letter to the *Honolulu Advertiser* condemns a court ruling requiring the Kamehameha Schools to admit non-Hawaiians by comparing it to the Borg's mantra: "'Resistance is futile.' They [the Hawaiian people] shall be absorbed into the collective whole of Western civilization whether they want to or not!" (Wagner). The image is also referenced to explain the physical effects of Taser weapons when a "reporter learns resistance is futile" (Schuknecht). On the other hand, reducing public bewilderment regarding law enforcement is the goal of an article that references the *X-Files*'s main characters: "Forget agents Mulder and Scully investigating the X-Files. One purpose of the [FBI's Citizens] Academy is to demystify the workings of an agency that has inspired Hollywood for years and has taken on a certain mystique in the minds of many" (S. Read). Despite what seems to be the FBI's best efforts, though, public discourse often reflects our sense that elements of the law and order system are as unknowable as aliens and monsters.

Mainstream public discourse often seems wholly engaged with political and civic issues. Within our conversations on elections, military strategy, and other governmental functions, cautionary tales reflecting our fears of the Unknown often provide invaluable images that are then used to invoke the "interpretive frames," to use the Wellcome Trust's term, that connect critical public issues of our time with our fear that what we don't know really can hurt us.

Media Coverage of the Business World

To many Americans, big business also operates in a world of its own, completely separate from their everyday activities, even if they work for the multi-national corporations making headlines. Media coverage of such diverse businesses as global retail outlets and major software companies as well as advertising for local restaurants often mines speculative fiction for effective imagery to reflect this sentiment, as does public discourse surrounding global economics. For example, Paul Krugman describes the US economy as "operating in a twilight zone" and then gives "a brief refresher course on twilight zone Economics 101." Similarly, the chaos that is consumer pricing is portrayed by economist David Resler as a twilight zone (Hilsenrath), a place where the rules do not work the same way they do in real life.

Encounters with the world of finance, whether consumer or international, often leave many of us feeling as if we entered an alien environment, a sentiment the mainstream media reflects with references to cautionary tales that seem as far removed from the reality-based arena of credits and debits as possible. One lawyer, for example, describes the process of clearing up personal credit reports as "'a little day excursion into the twilight zone'" (Whitaker) while those who have not saved for retirement are portrayed as "middle-aged Rip Van Winkles [who] suddenly awake with a jolt to see the financial equivalent of a fully loaded pallet of cinder blocks heading right toward them" (O'Shaughnessy). On the more complex international level, speculative fiction imagery is especially appropriate, such as that employed by a *Futures* magazine reporter who compares the base metal commodity market to werewolves (Simons) and a *US Banker* article that describes Argentina's 2002 recession and banking crisis as "a kind of economic twilight zone reminiscent of the financial and social chaos that characterized the American Great Depression" (Krebsbach). The complexity of the financial world even leads some to find conspiracy theories in the Business section: in 2004, the Cleveland *Plain Dealer* was accused of subliminally endorsing President Bush's Social Security privatization plan because of an article advising readers on how best to invest in the stock market. When the Business section editor addressed the charges of hidden bias, she invoked both *X-Files* and Mulder and Scully by name, leveraging speculative fiction to highlight the absurdity of the theory by comparing it to the show's alien conspiracies (Del Guzzi).

When compared with the seemingly black and white world of finance, we would expect media coverage of giant technology companies to be an even better fit for speculative fiction metaphors. For example, Leslie Walker begins her review of the technology advances in 2002 with just such an image: "Rip Van Winkle could have slept through 2002 and not missed much in tech-land." Similarly, in his analysis of the reasons behind the dominance of America Online, Charles Bermant notes that "the prime directives for MSN 8 ... are to knock off America Online and combine AOL's unctuous user friendliness with real computing power." The same *Star Trek* reference is also invoked in a review, strange as it may seem, of a toddler computer game, *Blue's Clues: Blue Takes You to School*, in which Ann Reeks reports, "Bubbly Blue's prime directive this time [is not] ... teaching kids their ABCs and 1–2–3s."

Star Trek's Borg is another image frequently invoked by the technology media; for example, John Jainschigg's article identifies Instant Messaging as the next great communications revolution, proclaiming "Resistance is futile," and Don Jergler invokes the same image to declare the integration of home and work life via mobile technology to be utterly unavoidable. Not all media coverage of technology, however, is so accepting of the revolution: a business etiquette specialist points out that "two former chief executives ... [argue in their book, *Return of the Body Snatchers*] that while technology can be a great business tool, gadgets have possessed the younger generation" (Pledger). Thus, we see how far the image of pod people permeates our culture, as it extends far beyond its original genesis as social commentary to become part of a cultural vocabulary capable of critiquing technology's ability to remake the world as we know it, perhaps not for the better.

Technology is big business and the stakes of the events reported in the media are often very high. We see this reflected in the Borg-inspired headline of Andrew Leonard's article on the "unholy alliance" between Microsoft and AOL that ended the "browser wars": "Resistance really was futile." The incredibly vast sums involved in the 2005 Google stock price run-up leads one business reporter to describe Wall Street as operating under "a herd mentality ... [with] mutual fund managers ready to declare that resistance is futile: to post the kind of returns that would put them in the upper echelons of performance tables, they need to own shares in Google" (Rivlin). Thus, this intersection of technology and finance is presented as on the same scale as a Borg assimilation. Reflecting a similar sentiment, we find a (perhaps unexpected) reference to *X-Files*[3] when, in the throes of the technology bust, a *Wall Street Journal* article declares, "Scully and Mulder face perhaps their toughest case ever: figuring out why everyone but Bill Gates is croaking" (Swisher). It seems that, when all is not well on Wall Street, the tech business is so alien to the mainstream media that the FBI's two foremost agents are needed to crack the "case," even if they are only fictional characters.

The nation's retailers and other corporations, both international and local, also lead the media to invoke metaphors that imply world-shattering changes; for example, the headline of an article profiling Wal-Mart's[4] new executive vice president of the "people division" (i.e. Human Resources) reads "Resistance is Futile," reflecting the reporter's angle that this executive was fated to work for the world's largest retailer after "having spent years battling Wal-Mart" (Stein). On a much smaller scale, and more humorously, the failure of contemporary copywriters to write clear catalog text is only half-jokingly blamed on an "invasion of the body snatchers, replacing communicators with low-forehead androids" (H. Lewis). The same image is used in a very different way to critique another international chain, Starbucks: "Counting Starbucks is like tallying pods in the old horror flick, *The Invasion of the Body Snatchers*" (Herhold). The images generated by speculative fiction to reflect our fears of the Unknown are so culturally persuasive that the business media seems to find them an invaluable shorthand.

One of the most popular speculative fiction metaphors for corporate marketing is "resistance is futile"; advertisers and reporters seem drawn to this *Star Trek* phrase, trading on the image of the Borg to convince consumers that resistance to particular products or schemes really is futile. A Cadillac commercial that debuted during the Super Bowl on January 26, 2003 featured the line and, oddly enough, mainstream media reports describing food marketing also seem enamored with the reference. Take, for example, a New York *Daily News* article that praises a new steak shop: "Once you smell the fried onions, resistance is futile. You'll be pulled into Carl's Philly Cheesesteaks" (Sax). And the near national obsession with the ninety-year-old fundraiser for the Girl Scouts (those cookies!) also, apparently, calls for the Borg reference: "Girl Scout cookies go on sale today, and, as we have all come to find ... resistance is futile. The tasty treats will pop up around town — and in your office — in the next few weeks" (Alicea). Whether it is the physical aroma of the product or just saturation marketing, *Star Trek* seems to provide the mainstream media with an effective metaphor for describing why we eat what we do.

Media coverage of the corporate world would seem to be the last place we'd expect to find speculative fiction imagery. After all, these articles are usually reporting the "hard facts" of numbers, dollars, and cents; in short, there is little (legitimate) room for the frivolous creativity and imagination usually associated with fiction, let alone *speculative* fiction. And yet, in our public debates, business issues are also some of our most complex concerns that often require highly specialized training to properly comprehend. It has been said that sufficiently advanced technology would appear to be magic; for many of the uninitiated, the intricacies of a global economy, high finance, even balancing a checkbook might as well take place in a magical realm, separate and alien from the real world they inhabit. Media coverage of big business seems to acknowledge this view, employing metaphors like *The Twilight Zone* and "resistance is futile" to invoke that sense of encountering a world that is not like our own, one threatening to take over.

Media Coverage of ... the Media

At times, there is nothing the media likes to talk about more than itself and when that gaze turns inward, the observations are frequently peppered with speculative fiction images. In an article for *Strategy* magazine, for example, Rob Young critiques the proliferation of media "experts" as "a kind of media version of *Invasion of the Body Snatchers*," while Frank Rich's criticism of news reporting is even harsher: "But we've now entered a new twilight zone: in 1972, at least, the press may have been stacked with jokers but not with counterfeit newsmen." The fraud Rich condemns in television news also extends to print journalism, at least according to Armando Acuna, who lamented in May 2005, "The litany of journalistic misdeeds in the last several weeks alone is enough to make you wonder ... whether, like a bad remake of the horror movie *Invasion of the Body Snatchers*, aliens have rewired journalists' circuitry worldwide." Such a seeming loss of journalistic integrity has many in the media turning to images from Unknown cautionary tales to convey their distress.

Also critiquing his own profession, *USA Today* columnist Walter Shapiro relies on still another speculative fiction image to describe his reaction to the all-encompassing media coverage of the Enron scandal not four months after the September 11th attacks: "I felt as baffled as a latter-day Rip Van Winkle." Similar critiques of other out-of-proportion media coverage use genre imagery to take aim at reporting on obesity ("Unless you are Rip Van Winkle just waking from a long nap, you've no doubt seen and heard the word 'obesity' more frequently in the past year or two than in the previous 10 or 20 years") (Conjura), and even the 2005 criminal trial of Michael Jackson: "against firepower like that [Jackson's celebrity connections], resistance is futile" (Robinson). Reality television also comes under media attacks that leverage genre images including the observation that, on the Fox network show *The Swan*, "Resistance is futile. You will be blond" (Bobbin). In addition, Britney Spears's entourage "family" showcased on her reality show, *Britney and Kevin: Chaotic*, is compared to "the family from that *Twilight Zone* episode ["It's A Good Life"[5]] with the evil kid who wishes people he doesn't like into the cornfield" (R. Thomas). Even members of the public, civilians if you will, employ these metaphors to critique the media: A letter to the editor in the *New York Times* accuses National Public Radio of "turn[ing] its back on its prime directive" for opposing community-based radio stations that "serve ignored segments of the population" (Pirodsky). These critiques and condemnations are so varied and complex that analyzing them in any depth would lead us down many diverging (and perhaps disturbing) paths. What they share, however, is a reliance on speculative fiction imagery to convey the sense that encounters with the media often leave us as bewildered as we would be if we confronted an alien or somehow went forward in time.

That bewilderment often leads to calls for Americans to literally tune-out the television and other celebrity-driven media. Ironically, however, such appeals employ images generated by the very media being disparaged, as when an Opinion piece in the *San Gabriel Valley Tribune* (in California) pleads, "So, turn off the tube talk and resign from the celebrity culture club. Or what is our future as a modern race? Forget about invasion of the body snatchers, it is our minds at stake here" ("Mind-Snatchers"). A *New York Times* article, on the other hand, takes the opposite approach, embracing the media and its over-saturation methods, using speculative fiction to do it: "The most-hyped fringe festival in the history of the world returns to take over New York's deadly August theater scene with its usual 200-and-counting shows. Don't even try to ignore it. Resistance is futile" (Zinoman). And media hype shows no sign of abating; rather it is expanding on the wave of mobile technology such as network news streamed to cell phones, and, as Richard Louv claims, the Borg were right once again: "Resistance is futile" when it comes to television on our cell phones. Such technological advances come at a price, however, in addition to the long period of instability as society adapts to Progress. One such conflict finds, for example, free speech on international websites in legal limbo, as reflected in the clash between a group of reporter-activists and several national governments. The *X-Files*'s main characters are invoked by the activists to globally communicate, via the Internet, their resistance to governmental control: they posted altered photographs of Swiss undercover officers at the heart of the controversy, "covering them with photos of the characters Mulder and Scully" (Simon). Thus, we see that not only have traditional and mainstream media outlets absorbed speculative fiction images, but so apparently have their more radical, digital cousins.

Back in the world of more traditional media, we find genre images employed to examine the significant role of the media in the construction of gender relations and, more specifically, in the "market-friendly female role models" Judith Timson examines. Describing *Buffy, the Vampire Slayer* as one option (among others) after whom young women can pattern themselves, Timson leverages our cultural experience with Joss Whedon's adolescent demon fighter to argue that while there is increased variety in role models for the twenty-first century, there is also, unfortunately, a regression to overtly sexualized ones as well. In a similarly reflective article on the current state of feminism, Betty Cuniberti references *Invasion of the Body Snatchers* to contrast the fiction of the women's movement with the fact of the advances women have achieved. Making the opposite argument, however, opinion columnist Cynthia Hall Clements invokes yet another speculative fiction image to declare that, for all intents and purposes, the feminist movement has made little real progress: "These days, though, I am feeling a little more like Rip Van Winkle, waking up from his 20-year nap. Unlike Mr. Van Winkle, who woke from his leisurely slumber — in that self-indulgent, all-else-be-damned way only a man can snooze — to a changed world, American women still face the same workplace challenges that our mothers did a generation ago."

Even coverage of gay and lesbian issues mines speculative fiction for images conveying a world of often unsettling changes. A *USA Today* article on the increasingly positive portrayal of homosexuals in the media quotes Michael Bronski, a researcher into gay-related issues: "'A gay Rip Van Winkle who had fallen asleep in the darkness of the 1950s and woken up in the more enlightened 21st century might well be startled, or completely confused, to discover that two popular shows today were *Queer as Folk* and *Queer Eye for the Straight Guy*'" (C. Wilson).

Some argue that an ironic self-awareness is a defining characteristic of the postmodern world. In that respect, media references to speculative fiction in reflections on its own role in society could be dismissed as merely a near-incestuous manifestation of the self-referential impulse. I would argue, however, that the media's reliance on images pulled from cautionary tales goes beyond this "meaningless" self-reference and instead illustrates the completion of a rhetorical equation: speculative fiction reflects our fears of the Unknown, and consequently, our public discourse regarding such issues as gender relations and media bias reflects back those images the genre created in response to our fears.

There can be no doubt that speculative fiction is ingrained in our cultural shorthand. When members of the media compare the national economy to *The Twilight Zone* or invoke *Star Trek* to explain our inability to resist Girl Scout cookies, this public discourse regarding today's Unknown issues relies on those cautionary tales that reflect our fears in the first place. As our modern culture rushes headlong into the twenty-first century, fears regarding the Unknown become increasingly more pressing: rules change and we are often forced to navigate worlds that seem as alien as Mars, or even Vulcan. Public discourse reflects these uncertainties by invoking images from speculative fiction, demonstrating the power and effectiveness of the genre's cautionary tales in shaping the way we think about and discuss our fears, even if (or when) we don't recognize the source of the metaphors we are using.

The power of the images in this chapter to transcend their original narratives results in a greater variety in the context and tone of media references than we've seen so far. This is perhaps rooted in the fact that these texts have diffused into our cultural consciousness. We see this most especially with the *Star Trek* and *Twilight Zone* references as those original series have gone through so many permutations and been part of popular culture for so long that each generation inherits the images anew. Re-runs of *The Twilight Zone*, for example, can be found in nearly every city in the United States and even for those few who have never seen an episode, the impact of the anthology series is so pervasive that the mere mention of the title still invokes a sense of something creepy and off-balance, even if the details are a bit fuzzy. In a similar way, *Star Trek* series and movies are everywhere and the two phrases that cross over most frequently into public discourse, "resistance is futile" and "Prime Directive," bring their genre connotations with them. It is interesting to note, upon reflection, that the former phrase represents the "bad guys" of the piece (the Borg) while the latter is the guiding principle of the "good guys"; in essence these *Star Trek* metaphors are polar opposites, with the Borg reflecting the nightmare that we could lose our very way of life to an alien invader and the United Federation of Planets representing the effort to avoid causing that nightmare for others, the optimistic reversal, if you will, of Borg assimilation.

While there is, by far, more ambivalence in the way these Unknown images are used in public discourse than we have seen in either of the other two categories, that is perhaps to be expected, given the root of the nightmare in uncertainty. We need to keep in mind, though, that while the Borg imagery, for example, is at times used in playful ways, the power of the phrase "resistance is futile" to reflect our nightmares surrounding war when necessary is not diminished in the least. These images still convey terror when that is what the situation demands. The Unknown cautionary tales reflect an uncertain world that can change overnight, could be upended by the discovery of aliens, or isn't at all what it seems to be. The presence of images from these nightmares in public discourse surrounding the major institutions of society—government, business, and the media—is thus no surprise. Whether the references ask us to metaphorically stand in the shoes of Mulder and Scully or confront an alien pod person with the face of our best friend or repel a Martian invasion, that very variety indicates the intensity with which we have absorbed such reflections of our Unknown fears, and, by extension, all speculative fiction cautionary tales.

Afterword: What Does All This Mean?

Now that we have looked at all seven sub-categories of the Nightmares Model in detail, it's a good time to pull back and focus again on the bigger picture, to reflect on what this analysis might actually mean. In other words, this is where I need to address the (sometimes dreaded) "So what?" question. There are many ways I could answer such a question and many theories I could invoke. Regardless, though, of how I examine the usefulness of the Nightmares Model, the significant rhetorical, political, and cultural impact of the cautionary tales it describes is undeniable. I've decided, then, to end this analysis by focusing on *how* those cautionary tales exert such a powerful influence and on what they add to our understanding of contemporary American society. I will employ a variety of lenses in that discussion, pulling in cultural studies, classical rhetoric, discourse analysis, and even postmodern critique to place the Nightmares Model in a broader context. Finally, I will conclude with both a look back, at the success of cautionary tales so far, and forward, at what nightmares the genre might reflect in the future.

Reflections and Meditations: So What?

While my goal for this book is primarily to link our nightmares with genre texts, there is a related cultural dynamic to consider: Does speculative fiction reflect or create our fears? Would we be afraid of aliens, for example, if H.G. Wells hadn't written *War of the Worlds*? Or, as one of my students recently asked, why are we so afraid robots will try to take over our lives? Is it because that's what speculative fiction tells us? There is no way to know for sure but, as I have argued many times in the preceding chapters, the "fear process" seems to be circular; so the answer to the reflect versus create question would be "yes" to both options. While it is not difficult to argue that the fears reflected in many cautionary tales are not new,[1] speculative fiction manifestations of these stories seem too significantly different from those that came before for the divergence to be a coincidence. The rhetorical symbiosis between our culture and speculative fiction adds a new wrinkle to this question of whether art imitates life or life imitates art, perhaps because of the very nature of the genre as a reflection of progress.

As a result, the potential for speculative fiction to participate in the rhetorical moment at the beginning of the twenty-first century is nearly limitless, perhaps because fantasy seems, as C.S. Lewis describes, to invoke such strong reactions that it must be "a mode of imagination which does something to us at a deep level" (130). As George Slusser and Eric Rabkin identify,

> Imaginary landscapes proliferate in fantasy and science fiction. But only by considering these maps and geographies as mindscapes do we see that this activity—describing and mapping—has been a constant need of Western art and science from the beginnings. ... [and may be] a general human one [x].

The power of these mappings, these narratives of mindscapes, is particularly evident when examined through the lens of Western classical rhetoric, as composition theorist Candace Spigelman does when she draws on Aristotle's *Rhetoric* to examine the "intellectual operation" of narrative argument, which she claims relies on "generalizations emerging from prior assumptions and provided by the audience rather than stated by the rhetor" (73). This operation seems to explain how references to speculative fiction nightmares work in public discourse: if a political commentator condemns the NSA for being "Orwellian," for example, the speaker can count "on the audience's assumptions to supply the logical 'leap' needed to establish a general rule from multiple or extended examples" (73), a leap that occurs when audiences are culturally familiar with the referenced narrative. Aristotle's theory of narrative logic, according to Spigelman, describes the way "examples ... allow the speaker and audience to reason a general rule from particular cases" as this process of "rhetorical induction ... implies that a generalization will be gathered from the presentation of particulars" (72). Such inductive reasoning, from the image out to the generalized fear, explains the second half of the rhetorical symbiosis between the genre's cautionary tales and society's nightmares since "argument by narrative or example features opportunities for interlocutors to generalize a rule that pertains to similar conditions in both the public and private spheres" (74). In this way, life attempts to *avoid* imitating art by employing a cautionary tale to warn about and, hopefully, prevent a nightmare.

Aristotelian rhetoric is also useful in explaining the first half of the rhetorical cycle where the genre reflects our fears; rhetorician Walter R. Fisher, according to Spigelman, uses the "concept of practical reason" to declare narrative to be "so urgent ... to human perspective ... [that we need] a 'narrative paradigm' of communicative rationality" (74). Fisher's "attempts to explain how ordinary people construct arguments necessary for investigating real-world issues or for determining courses of actions" result in his assertion "that narrativity is a dominant form of rationality and that 'human communication should be viewed as historical as well as situational, as stories competing with other stories constituted by good reasons'" (Spigelman 74) Speculative fiction's cautionary tales are key components of these historical and situational narratives that we use as reasons in public discourse. The power of such tales lies in narrative's ability to do what no other form can, an idea reflected in the works of theorists like Mikhail Bakhtin and Frederic Jameson who, according to Spigelman, "have argued for narration as a central mode of human communication and understanding" (75), thus reflecting art's attempts to imitate life.

Speculative fiction narrative holds a particularly effective place in that communication and understanding because, as Nicolas Pethes argues, its "constructions, which are built upon the evaluations of distinctions, circulate among cultural and ethical discourses of a society" (163), providing opportunities where "various discourses coincide or cross ... to reflect on the cultural, social, and anthropological consequences of science" (164). This intersection of multiple discourses is where the genre is most effective, according to Pethes:

> Can we think of an alternative, future-oriented account of the implications of [for example] biotechnology for our conceptions of the human? It must be a discourse that is able to reflect on the discourses of science, ethics, and humanisms of the future. As such, it has to *construct* the distinctions science will use for its operations, the distinctions ethics will use to observe these operations, and the distinctions philosophy will use in order to reshape the conceptions of the human [165].

Thus, by "connect[ing] to all of the discourses, ... [and] contributing to the collective images of technology, ethics, humanity, and society" (165), the genre plays a key role in cultural rhetoric, Pethes argues, when it "reduces the complexity of actual science by the linearity of a narrative"; in public debate, "this reduction of complexity makes it possible to suggest the cultural implications of a specific branch of research" (166). In this way, speculative fiction "examines the possibilities of knowledge and can even serve as a matrix for further scientific discussion" (166) as we saw in Chapter 4 with the use of genre images in genetic engineering discourse.

Whether the speculative fiction images used in public debate and by mainstream media are fair and accurate is, of course, an open question. Michael Mulkay's study of the Frankenstein image suggests they aren't: "We do know, however, that they [the references] were seen from within the scientific community as a characteristically ill-informed attack upon embryo research and upon science more generally" (161). This perceived misuse of genre images seems to point to the tenuous place of science in our culture. On the one hand, it is arguably the basis for Western rational thought and creates so much of what we take for granted: medicines that keep us alive, inventions (such as cell phones and the Internet) that keep us in touch, and the plastics that keep our everyday lives running smoothly. On the other, though, science is often seen as a mysterious, unknowable realm populated by cold, socially-inept yet intellectually brilliant technicians and profit-mad, morally-bankrupt executives looking to make a quick buck.

While I admit these contrasting cultural perceptions are overstated, I believe they do reflect the ways in which the social construction of science complicates any analysis of speculative fiction's role in public discourse; my metaphor analysis is no exception. What it all seems to come down to, however, is that it may not matter whether the public understands science correctly, and thus whether the genre images we invoke are "accurate" from a theoretical perspective. The mere fact that we do invoke them in the first place indicates their power for us. We must recognize and understand this cultural power, regardless of our occupation or inclination, as we negotiate the hard decisions we are bound to face in the coming decades. Cautionary tales are critical elements of the "narrative paradigm," to use Fisher's term, that we will employ in those negotiations.

Returning, though, to the more narrow scope of the Nightmares Model, there is potential in the specific categories themselves to highlight and even generate meaningful knowledge. Chapter 8: Monsters, Aliens, and "Other" Beings, for example, offers a rich pool of material with which to examine what Naeem Inayatullah describes as the "inner other." For example, one speculative fiction concept that comes immediately to mind as potentially fruitful in such an analysis is the Minbari belief, depicted in *Babylon 5*, that the universe is sentient and created all living things by breaking itself into pieces in an effort to better understand itself. Such a conception would bring new complexity to an examination of the "inner other." Other efforts to critique socio-political systems also incorporate speculative fiction nightmares including, as Andrew Ross points out, Donna Haraway's work that advocates using science fiction's technology creations to challenge existing power relations (161). In addition, Pethes points to values often at issue in feminist critiques of essentialism with his assertion that cautionary tales "contrasting the persistence of human values *against* the threat of manipulated mankind [both a Biology and a Progress nightmare] ... demonstrate the anachronism of the idea that these values are self-evident and can be taken for granted" (179).

Further cultural critique is implicated in the Progress nightmare, where, as Richard Swope argues, "Cyberspace works particularly well as a symbol of the kinds of ontological uncertainties that have come to the forefront in the postmodern moment because it has such a clear, metonymic relationship to late capitalism" (235). In many reflections of our nightmare that reality is unstable, the main character, according to Swope, "must come to terms with the fact that his social reality is comprised entirely of images, of a surface lacking depth, leaving him, or the postmodern subject, unable to map his present position within either history or space" (235). Thus, Swope applies the work of Michel Foucault, Frederic Jameson, and Henri Lefebvre to the cautionary tale's examination of the reality question to delve deeper into this nightmare using a postmodern lens: "In this respect, we might view *Dark City* as a surrealist allegory of the postmodern urban space in which the subject struggles to locate his or her position within an overwhelming and increasingly abstract techno-capitalist network" (225). Taking a more pragmatist approach and less of a postmodern one, though, leads us to perhaps the most obvious question when it comes to evaluating such cautionary tales: Do they work? I will attempt to answer that question in the next section.

Success Ratio: How Have We Done So Far?

This question of whether we actually learn anything from speculative fiction warnings is frequently debated within the genre itself. When we try to determine our success ratio, as David Brin points out, we seem to prefer pointing out problems but pay little attention to the successes and avoided mistakes. If we actually look for these successes, Brin argues, we can put together "an impressive roll call of dodged bullets and lucky breaks" ("Self-Preventing"). In an earlier essay, Brin takes a more light-hearted look at the success of speculative fiction cautionary tales:

> Does anyone actually believe a stranded starfarer would be *dissected* in the America of the 1980s? Or a talking ape thrown in a freak show? Naw! All those guilt-tripping movies and books have got us feeling too unworthy. We would probably smother to death any visitor under telegrams from talk-show hosts and ad agencies offering lucrative product promotion deals ["Metaphorical" 75].

George Orwell's *Nineteen Eighty-Four* is perhaps the first cautionary tale that comes to mind when the question of success is raised; W. Russel Gray identifies several ways in which society is better because of the novel, including that we are now

> more aware of the awesome power and responsibility of the media, more alert to the danger of blurring the information and entertainment functions, better able to recognize the ease with which government agencies routinely preempt the propagandist's principles to try to manipulate the media, and more likely to recognize the increasing incursions upon privacy in ostensibly "free" societies as well as the widening parameters of obscurity and misdirection in the language of officialdom [115].

According to Brin, a key difference between American culture in the late 1990s (when he wrote "Self-Preventing Prophecy") and Orwell's nightmare is our openness and accountability: even though the video technology used in the novel is available, Orwell's warnings conditioned us "to ensure that the lenses point both ways." Brin credits such success "to anti–Cassandras like George Orwell whose warnings, heeded, thus never come true." Making a similar point, Gray argues that part of the novel's success is that it "created an instant myth—a construct that made us aware of the deeper implications of otherwise random-seeming events, trends, and language barbarisms in the media" (116). This myth helps us prevent that construct from becoming reality.

But we have not completely avoided falling into Orwell's nightmare, thus ensuring its continued relevance. In his essay (published in 1987), Gray compares the successes mentioned above with some disturbing instances of Orwell's doublethink, including the Roman Catholic Church's recharacterization of Martin Luther from a heretic to a "father of the faith" and the Soviet reglorification of Joseph Stalin after years of treating him as a "nonperson" (116). Gray also describes some examples of what he finds to be chilling invasions of personal privacy that have, as he writes, "an Orwellian ring" including an auto dealer fined for bugging his showroom, a toll-free hotline for citizens to anonymously accuse others of welfare cheating, and the ability to purchase do-it-yourself surveillance equipment at the local Radio Shack (113–14). And more than fifteen years later, after devastating terror attacks and unprecedented governmental response, the urgency has only been heightened, which has not escaped the popular media. Readers, I have no doubt, will certainly have little trouble inserting their own examples of current events with "Orwellian rings," including the controversy over NSA domestic surveillance and the debates over how to protect children from online sexual predators without violating the privacy of the millions who use the Internet every day without breaking any laws.

Despite our slightly mixed results at preventing a Big Brother world, there are several other success stories of avoided nightmares. For example, as A.E. Levin argues, "By painting the horror of nuclear confrontation, SF helped to develop antimilitaristic tendencies" (252); thus it seems the Nuclear War cautionary tales have succeeded, so far. Similarly, the first robot-to-robot transcontinental telephone conversation occurred in 1983 (Cooper) yet, more than twenty years later, we are still far from the robot-assisted future promised in *The Jetsons* and even farther from the more ominous warnings of either complete dependence on artificial intelligences or total destruction at the hands of out-of-control robots. So far, we seem to have dodged that bullet as of the beginning of the twenty-first century, though we may never know exactly how much speculative fiction contributed to that success.

The warnings sounded by speculative fiction's cautionary tales, whether we listen to them or not, can quickly become less speculative and more real, as Stanley Schmidt observed at the 2002 World Science Fiction Convention: "When Dolly was cloned a few years ago, I received calls from several news agencies that asked me what I thought about it. And I said, 'We told you so'" ("Panel 163"). Just what else has the genre already told us and what will it tell us about in the future? I will close my analysis with a few attempts at answering these questions.

Future Nightmares: What's Next?

We may have a fairly solid success ratio of avoiding these nightmares so far, but when it comes to our future success, speculations are even more mixed. On the one hand, Schmidt argues, "At the moment we have the advantage of having thought about a range of possibilities, so that relatively few of them would catch us completely unprepared" ("Who" 7). On the other, even after acknowledging partial success, Connie Willis remarked on a panel at the 2002 World Science Fiction Convention that "the law of unintended consequences" governs human society and, in a reflective way, science fiction: "We are a large, complex, chaotic system that is not linear. We can't take everything into account. We will figure everything out, except...." As an example, Willis pointed out that no one in the 1300s anticipated the Black Death and wondered what was going to be our meteor (like the one that destroyed the dinosaurs). James Van Pelt described speculative fiction as the continual search for the consequences of such chaos: "How many ways can you think that the world might end? How many ways can our future become more dystopic?" ("Request"). No matter how successful cautionary tales are at warning us of the dangers we know we face now, as Van Pelt described, speculative fiction is "the literature of the reality we live in: that nothing will stay the same" (Interview). Something else is always lurking, for as Willis also declared, "We always get one problem figured out, then another one crops up"; in other words, in her estimation, "We always live on the edge of the abyss."

It is almost impossible to predict what nightmares will be generated by the next great discovery. No one knows what surprises we will face as we turn the corner to the future, that's why they are called surprises. But it's a good bet we will have to negotiate our fears of Science and Technology, Power, or the Unknown, as these seem constants across the genre's history; over the next few years, speculative fiction is expected to add new nightmares to its repertoire in addition to tweaking familiar ones. One of the authors leading this new guard is Greg Bear who said, "Personally, in my fiction I'm off to exploring new avenues in the biological sciences, and I think there's a real need for more of that" ("Requested"). It is likely that emerging bio-technology will raise the profile of the nightmares of human cloning, for example, as what had previously been speculative fiction becomes more of a concern for "real" public debate.

In her landmark essay, "A Cyborg Manifesto: Science, Technology, and Socialist-Feminism in the Late Twentieth Century," Haraway applies the trope of the cyborg to socio-political considerations (declaring the cyborg "a creature of social reality as well as a creature of fiction"), arguing that "the boundary between science fiction and social reality is an optical illusion" (149). This illusion, I suggest, may continue to collapse as our science catches up with our fiction. While outside the traditional boundaries of genre criticism, Haraway's work illuminates the social confusion embedded in the Progress nightmare as "the cyborg is a creature in a post-gender world; ... [and] has no origin story in the Western sense" (150). Making a related argument, Gardner Dozois, former editor of *Asimov's*, writes, "I strongly suspect that examination of the idea of posthumanity, with all its complex and sometimes contradictory implications for both good *and* ill, is going to be (in fact, already *is*) one of the major thematic concerns of science fiction in the first part of the twenty-first century" (Preface xi). As we advance into what some describe as the "post-everything" century, there seems to be no limit to the new nightmares that may come from our fear that the rules will change underneath us.

And while the nightmares reflected in such cyberpunk stories as William Gibson's *Neuromancer* and the 1992 movie *The Lawnmower Man* have not yet come to fruition, speculative fiction will continue to reflect our anxiety that information technologies such as the Internet and virtual gaming will blur our sense of identity and reality. Van Pelt identified the dangers of "virtual reality, intrusive or pervasive information technology ... and artificial intelligence" as common themes to expect among speculative fiction in the near future ("Request"). In addition, Brin predicts that potential implications of such technology could include the vast expansion of human cognitive powers and the enhancement of memory via databases that can be accessed by thought alone ("Self-Preventing"). Indeed, the potential exists for technology to become so advanced that not even speculative fiction writers will be able to predict it; Van Pelt warned that "the exponential rise in knowledge seems to be drawing us toward the 'singularity,' the time when human experience can be augmented to such a degree that current humans won't be able to understand it. Fiction on the other side of the singularity is hard to imagine" ("Request"), though that doesn't stop the genre from trying.

In addition, our current fear of terrorism in the United States will also highlight concerns over government intrusions of personal privacy in speculative fiction as well as in public discourse. Crises like the September 11th attacks leave us vulnerable to losing our civil liberties because the fear we have seen exploited by characters in such genre texts as *Star Wars* and *Babylon 5* is now playing out in reality. As Buck Wolf quotes Steven Spielberg:

> "George Orwell's prophecy really comes true, not in the 20th century but in the 21st," Spielberg says. "Big Brother is watching us now and what little privacy we have will completely evaporate in 20 or 30 years, because technology will be able to see through walls, through rooftops, into the very privacy of our personal lives, into the sanctuary of our families."

Underlying these cautionary tales, today and in the future, however, is perhaps one enduring, all-encompassing nightmare: that of our own obsolescence. As Ben Bova writes,

> Life adapts in every way it can, and intelligence—which we regard as the high point of it all—is most likely just another adaptation that has helped our particular species to survive, but may eventually push us into extinction, as our weaponry or heedlessness exceeds our ability to control our passions [45].

And yet, as Ross cautions, we need to be careful about embracing a doom and gloom perspective on technology as fully as readers in the "technophilia" days of the Gernsback era embraced the idea that technology would solve all their problems. Ross argues that both extremes demonstrate a naïveté regarding futurism and that "we can no more afford to see ourselves as unavoidably victims of technological development than as happy beneficiaries of a future that has already been planned and exploited. Such an attitude does not lead to empowerment" (135). Despite the pessimism expressed in many cautionary tales and by many speculative fiction writers, there is reason for hope. That is one of the genre's cornerstones, which Van Pelt described as the sense of wonder that stems from a "state of being for the reader and the writer, not a function of the literature itself. Even dystopic fiction has, at the heart of it, the idea that, when everything is bad, things will change and get better" (Interview).

When all of this is said and done, though, it's clear that only time will tell whether we will heed the warnings of speculative fiction and prevent our nightmares from coming true. Our results so far have been mixed. To this point, we have avoided nuclear holocaust, but many of us also regularly use (abuse?) versions of Bradbury's seashells that keep us constantly "in touch," yet separated from each other.[2] And the advent of quick, nearly effortless Internet communication such as email and Instant Messaging has made it easier to speak regularly with someone from the other side of the world than it is to walk across the lawn to meet the next-door neighbors. But even if we heed the warnings that speculative fiction has sounded so far, there will always be new nightmares for new futures. We will be listening.

Chapter Notes

Introduction

1. While there isn't room here to examine the disrespect with which speculative fiction is often viewed in our culture, most who practice this "trashy" and "slick" genre are painfully aware of how society perceives their chosen field, as we see in the Asimov quote. Mainstream society's disapproval is seen as both a burden and a badge of honor within the speculative fiction community and as such, it is a frequent topic both of casual conversation and formal commentary.
2. I will preserve, though, the term originally used by those whose work I reference. Thus, there are places in the text where science fiction and speculative fiction are used interchangeably.
3. For example, ARGUMENT IS WAR and HAPPY IS UP.
4. Such as Scholes and Rabkin, James Patrick Kelly, Asimov ("Social"), and Van Pelt (Interview).
5. There is much investigation currently going on in globalization theory, including an analysis of the technological roots of globalization. For a review of these efforts, see *Globalization: The Reader*, edited by John Beynon and David Dunkerly, published in 2000 by Routledge.
6. I owe many thanks to Greg Benford for these ideas. Reflecting on his comments led me to add this category to the Nightmares Model.

Part One Introduction

1. Including Greg Bear ("Panel 348"), Gregory Benford ("Panel 348"), and Stanley Schmidt ("Panel 163").

Chapter 1

1. Initially included in 1969's *Opus 100*.
2. Weldes cites two sources for the ideas she attributes to Franklin: 1988's *War Stars: The Superweapon and the American Imagination*, published by Oxford University Press; and "Eternally Safe for Democracy: The Final Solution for American Science Fiction" included in Phillip John Davies's *Science Fiction, Social Conflict, and War* published by Manchester University Press in 1990.
3. See the sections regarding dystopias in Chapter 6 for more discussion of this effect.
4. See the Introduction for a discussion of the modern concept of progress.
5. Greg Bear credits Wells's *World Set Free* with influencing the atomic weapons research of both Leo Szilard and Werner Heisenberg ("Requested").
6. The irony of which, I'm sure, is not lost on readers.
7. Also discussed in Chapter 8.
8. Translated into English in 1925.
9. Also discussed in Chapter 5.
10. At least according to Booker (*Monsters* 88–89).
11. Also described in greater detail in Chapter 9.
12. All three of these books are discussed in greater detail in Chapter 8, and *Dr. Bloodmoney* is also examined in Chapter 5.
13. Also discussed in Chapter 8.
14. This aspect of *Fury* is discussed in Chapter 5.
15. More examples of radiation-created mutants on film and television appear later in the chapter.
16. Of course, perhaps the most famous Japanese anime film is *Akira*. While this movie is set in a post-apocalyptic world, it is not constructed as a cautionary tale and is thus, in a way unfortunately, out of the scope of our discussion.
17. Also discussed in Chapter 3.
18. Also discussed in Chapter 5.
19. This film is also frequently described as a statement on the powerlessness of man in the face of an increasingly mechanized world, a theme that dovetails with the fears in the next chapter.

Chapter 2

1. It was, after all, a speculative fiction work (Karel Capek's play *R.U.R.* in 1923) that first used the word "robot" (Seabury 64), which Cornelia Dean reports is actually the Czech word for "laborer" (F1).
2. See Chapter 1 for a more in-depth discussion of Booker's arguments.
3. This prevalent fear led Daniel H. Wilson to create the spoof *How to Survive a Robot Rising: Tips on Defending Yourself Against the Coming Rebellion* in order to counteract the "'bad rap'" robots get in popular media (C. Dean F4).
4. See Chapter 6 for a more complete discussion of dystopian cautionary tales.
5. Such as Prince Escalus's closing speech from Shakespeare's *Romeo and Juliet* ("For never was there a story of more woe/Than this of Juliet and her Romeo"), which is reduced to one word, "Kids."
6. For a decidedly socio-economic take on this nightmare, see the "Cyberpunk in Boystown" chapter in Ross's *Strange Weather: Culture, Science, and Technology in the Age of Limits*.
7. *Limbo* is also discussed in Chapter 1.
8. Also discussed in Chapter 8.
9. Also discussed in Chapter 9.
10. "Cookie Monster" is also discussed in Chapter 5.
11. For more discussion on this story, see Chapters Three, Five, and Nine.
12. See Chapter 9 for more discussion regarding *The Matrix*.

Chapter 3

1. This issue will be picked up in greater detail in Chapter 9.
2. For more discussion regarding the consequences of immortality, see Chapter 9.
3. Also discussed in Chapter 5.
4. Many of these stories are also discussed in Chapter 8.
5. "Deletion" is also discussed in Chapter 5.
6. *I Am Legend* is also discussed in Chapters One and Eight.
7. I am indebted to Connie Willis for suggesting this novel to me.
8. And one that builds squarely on the potential over-prescription of psychiatric medication to children that is a matter of public debate today.
9. See Chapter 2 for a more detailed discussion of this aspect of the series.
10. Also discussed in Chapter 9.
11. Also discussed in Chapters 5 and 9.
12. See Chapter 9 for a more in-depth analysis of other consequences of living forever.
13. Also discussed in Chapter 1.
14. Also discussed in Chapter 5.
15. Also discussed in more detail in Chapter 6.

Chapter 4

1. Quoted in a fall 2003 book review for the *Los Angeles Times*.
2. By extension, these studies also illuminate the role of such metaphors in the other examples of public discourse we have already examined.
3. Suk's claims were later discredited in late 2005 on reports that he falsified his data.
4. The other being that cloning copies people.

Chapter 5

1. Spencer attributes this quote to Havelock's *The Crucifixion of Intellectual Man* from 1950.
2. The reflection of our nightmares of telepaths and other psychics connects some examples in this chapter with the fear of "homegrown" aliens I describe in more detail in Chapter 8.
3. For a more detailed discussion regarding the distinction between cautionary tales and social commentary that I am working with in this analysis, see the next chapter, Power of the State.
4. For a more detailed examination of the pre–*Frankenstein* roots of the mad scientist, see Goodrich's "The Lineage of the Mad Scientists: Anti-Types of Merlin" where he argues, "The entire cultural history of ideas forms an imaginative continuum out of which popular wizards like Merlin and subsequent wizardly offshoots like science fictional mad scientists emerge" (85).
5. For more discussion of this new reality, see Chapter 1.
6. Or, perhaps, it is more of a return to the previous, early nineteenth-century conception Shelley tapped into, after the technological optimism of the early twentieth-century ran headfirst into the harsh reality of the devastating consequences of that technology.
7. Also discussed in Chapter 1.
8. Both *Dr. Bloodmoney* and *Fury* are also discussed in Chapter 1 while the former is included in Chapter 8 as well.
9. Also discussed in Chapter 3.

10. "Blood Music" was also expanded into a 1985 novel, with mixed critical reception. Some in the genre find the utopian ending of the novel to be out of synch with the more dystopian nature of the story. In addition, there is debate in the genre about whether or not to classify the story as one of the original cyberpunk tales.
11. Also discussed in Chapter 9.
12. Both "The Immortality Plague" and "Deletion" are also discussed in Chapter 3 with "Immortality" included in Chapter 9 as well.
13. Both described in detail in Chapter 2.
14. Also discussed in Chapter 8.
15. For an in-depth discussion of the war games aspect of this novel, see Chapter 8.
16. For a more in-depth discussion of the cyberpunk tradition, see Chapter 2.
17. Perhaps a nod to Bester's character.
18. "Cookie Monster" is also discussed in Chapter 2 while "The Robot Who Came to Dinner" is included in Chapter 3.
19. A consequence also discussed in Chapter 3.
20. While the entire season lays the groundwork for Willow's eventual turn to evil, the final four episodes ("Seeing Red," "Villains," "Two to Go," and "Grave") ratchet up the consequences to the traditionally global, apocalyptic level we came to expect in a *Buffy* season finale.
21. All three of these examples are also discussed in Chapter 3.
22. This subplot of *Babylon 5* is also discussed in Chapter 8.

Chapter 6

1. The other two are "the problem of population explosion" and "the problem of data explosion."
2. From their perspective in the Soviet Union of the late 1980s.
3. Or the past — as in the case of the alternative history sub-genre.
4. Of course, the work of Michel Foucault, particularly in *Discipline and Punish*, speaks directly to the effectiveness of such control. Unfortunately, that sort of in-depth discussion of surveillance and power is beyond the scope of our current discussion.
5. Also described in Chapter 3.

Chapter 7

1. In addition to his Dr. Strangelove moniker mentioned in Chapter 4.

2. While this phrase does have another antecedent, a line from Shakespeare's *The Tempest* (from which Huxley reportedly drew his title), there is enough specificity in the references I discuss that the connection to the speculative fiction novel, and not the play, seems clear.

Part Three Introduction

1. See Chapter 6 for a more detailed discussion of the distinction between the two.

Chapter 8

1. See the discussions in Chapters One and Three, respectively, for the science aspects of these nightmares.
2. For another perspective on this particular nightmare, see Lipschutz's examination of aliens and political economies in Jutta Weldes's collection, *To Seek Out New Worlds*.
3. This suggestion by Benford was very influential in the way I decided to approach this section.
4. Of the Drake Equation Bova's article discusses.
5. For an example of just such a "berserker" depicted in a rather unexpected way, see the discussion of Orson Scott Card's *Ender's Game* later in this chapter.
6. While the scholarship into the cultural work of fairy tales and their literary-social heritage is rich and varied, it is only tangentially related to my analysis here and we just don't have room for the full discussion that would do this topic justice.
7. For more discussion regarding radiation-induced mutations, see Chapter 1.
8. "Cloak of Aesir" is also discussed in Chapter 1 while "Rebellion" is also included in Chapter 2.
9. Based in part on material originally published as a short story of the same name in the August 1977 issue of *Analog*.
10. Both *Nothing Human* and *Childhood's End* are also discussed in Chapter 9.
11. Also discussed in Chapter 2.
12. Also discussed in Chapter 5.
13. *Mutant* and *The Iron Dream* are also discussed in Chapter 1.
14. Also discussed in Chapter 3.
15. Both *I Am Legend* and *Dr. Bloodmoney* are also discussed in Chapter 1; *Legend* is mentioned in Chapter 3 as well, while *Dr. Bloodmoney* is also included in Chapter 5.

16. For a more detailed discussion of Gibson's work, see Chapter 2.
17. See Chapter 1 for an in-depth discussion of what Booker means by this "embattled sense."
18. The Prime Directive will be discussed in more detail in Chapter 9.
19. Discussed in greater detail in Chapter 9.
20. Discussed in greater detail in Chapter 6.
21. Both of these characters are discussed in more detail in Chapter 5.
22. See the Afterword for a more detailed discussion of this idea.

15. "A New Man" and "Persistent Patterns" are discussed in more detail in Chapter 3.
16. Also discussed in Chapter 3.
17. "Choosing Life" is also discussed in Chapter 3.
18. Also discussed in Chapter 2.
19. Also discussed in Chapter 2.
20. Based on Robert R. McCammon's short story.
21. *Invaders from Mars* is also discussed in Chapters 5 and 8.
22. Discussed in detail in Chapter 2.
23. Also discussed in Chapter 8.
24. Also discussed in Chapter 5.

Chapter 9

1. I am indebted to Gregory Benford for the ideas that led to this chapter.
2. Of course, as I will discuss in the Afterword, it shouldn't have been that much of a surprise since, as Schmidt observed, "'We told you so'" ("Panel 163").
3. This nightmare is already alarmingly more real and less speculative as sexual predators troll social networking sites for underage victims, misrepresenting themselves in online profiles.
4. Some of which were discussed in Chapter 3.
5. A mathematical physicist and professor emeritus of physics at the Institute for Advanced Study in Princeton, New Jersey.
6. Both "Green Leopard Plague" and the Sleepless series are also described in Chapter 3.
7. See Chapter 8 for a detailed discussion of the Buggers in *Ender's Game*.
8. "By the Rules" is also discussed in Chapter 8.
9. Simak's story is also the basis for a 1969 episode of the BBC television series *Out of the Unknown*.
10. See Booker (*Monsters* 29–31), who references Frederic Jameson's *Postmodernism, or, the Cultural Logic of Late Capitalism*.
11. Also discussed in Chapter 2.
12. Also discussed in Chapter 5.
13. Both *Nothing Human* and *Childhood's End* are also discussed in Chapter 8.
14. Also discussed in Chapter 5.

Chapter 10

1. As I did in both Chapters 4 and 7.
2. Even though it is frequently analyzed as a postmodern, thinly veiled social commentary regarding the Red Scare.
3. Probably inspired by a riff on Microsoft's X-Box.
4. The target of so much ire with the Godzilla metaphors examined in Chapter 4.
5. Described in Chapter 5.

Afterword

1. For example, the question of what is human carries echoes of the Pinocchio fable and the nature of reality has been up for grabs since, at least, Don Quixote attacked his first windmill.
2. I am almost embarrassed to admit it, but there were plenty of times during this project when I didn't bother to turn off my iPod to talk to someone who came into the room. As I listened to both a real person and the digital music coming out of the earbuds, I sometimes had to rely on guesswork because I couldn't hear everything being said. The irony would hit me then and I couldn't help wondering if I was becoming Millie Montag after all, despite Bradbury's warning.

Works Cited

Acuna, Armando. "The Bee Deserves Answers to Ensure Its Credibility." *Sacramento Bee* 15 May 2005: E3. *America's Newspapers*. News Bank InfoWeb. Fairchild-Martindale Library, Lehigh University, Bethlehem, PA. 9 Sept. 2005 <http://infoweb.newsbank.com>.

Aiex, Patrick K. "Reflections on Science Fiction in Light of Today's Global Concerns." *Viewpoints* 120 (1994). ERIC Document Reproduction Service No. ED364904.

Ain, Stewart. "Untangling Employees' Romantic Liaisons." *New York Times* 15 May 2005, late ed., sec. 14: 6. *America's Newspapers*. News Bank InfoWeb. Fairchild-Martindale Library, Lehigh University, Bethlehem, PA. 13 June 2005 <http://infoweb.newsbank.com>.

Aldiss, Brian W. "Pilgrim Fathers: Lucian and All That." *Billion-Year Spree: The True History of Science Fiction*. By Aldiss. New York: Doubleday, 1973. Rpt. in Knight, *Turning* 73–95.

Alexander, David. "The Human Dress." *Analog Science Fiction and Fact* Mar. 2003: 40–57.

Alicea, Michael. "Which Cookie Will You Choose?" *Palm Beach Post* 16 Jan. 2003, final ed.: 1E. *Academic Universe*. Lexis-Nexis. Campbell Library, Rowan University, Glassboro, NJ. 9 Mar. 2004 <http://web.lexis-nexis.com/universe>.

Amis, Kingsley. *New Maps of Hell*. New York: Ballantine Books, 1960.

"An Khe." *The West Wing*. Writ. John Welles. Dir. Alex Graves. NBC. WCAU, Philadelphia. 18 Feb. 2004.

Applebome, Peter. "Regulating Single Mothers Out of Their Child Care." *New York Times* 12 June 2005, late ed., sec. 1: 41. *America's Newspapers*. News Bank InfoWeb. Fairchild-Martindale Library, Lehigh University, Bethlehem, PA. 23 June 2005 <http://infoweb.newsbank.com>.

Arkell, Harriet. "Now Darth Vader Is the Byword for Evil in New Dictionary." *Evening Standard* 24 Dec. 2002: 14. *Academic Universe*. Lexis-Nexis. Campbell Library, Rowan University, Glassboro, NJ. 6 Nov. 2003 <http://web.lexis-nexis.com/universe>.

Asimov, Isaac. "Science Fiction, an Aid to Science, Foresees the Future." *Smithsonian* May 1970: 41–47.

———. "Social Science Fiction." *Modern Science Fiction, Its Meaning and Its Future*. Ed. Reginald Bretnor. New York: Coward-McCann, 1953. Rpt. in Knight, *Turning* 29–61.

Associated Press. "Poll Shows Public Backs Act 72 Property-Tax Cuts." *Erie Times-News* 9 June 2005: 3. *America's Newspapers*. News Bank InfoWeb. Fairchild-Martindale Library, Lehigh University, Bethlehem, PA. 13 June 2005 <http://infoweb.newsbank.com>.

Atheling, William, Jr. "Cathedrals in Space." *The Issue at Hand*. By Atheling. Chicago: Advent, 1964. Rpt. in Knight, *Turning* 144–62.

Baccolini, Raffaella, and Tom Moylan, eds. *Dark Horizons: Science Fiction and the Dystopian Imagination*. New York: Routledge, 2003.

———. "Introduction: Dystopia and Histories." Baccolini and Moylan, *Dark Horizons* 1–12.

Bainbridge, William Sims. "A Question of Immortality." *Analog Science Fiction and Fact* May 2002: 40–49.
Baldry, Cherith. "The Children's Books." *Terry Pratchett: Guilty of Literature*. Ed. Andrew M. Butler, Edward James, and Farah Mendlesohn. Reading, UK: Science Fiction Foundation, n.d., 20–34.
Bancroft, Colette. "Back to Work." *St. Petersburg Times* 5 Sept. 2005: 1E. *America's Newspapers*. News Bank InfoWeb. Fairchild-Martindale Library, Lehigh University, Bethlehem, PA. 9 Sept. 2005 <http://infoweb.newsbank.com>.
―――. "Lawyers, Guns and Money." *St. Petersburg Times* 25 July 2005: 1E. *America's Newspapers*. News Bank InfoWeb. Fairchild-Martindale Library, Lehigh University, Bethlehem, PA. 28 Nov. 2005 <http://infoweb.newsbank.com>.
Barash, Nanelle, and David P. Barash. "Biology, Culture, and Persistent Literary Dystopias." *Chronicle of Higher Education* 3 Dec. 2004: B10.
Barboza, David. "China's Problems with 'Anti-Pest' Rice." *New York Times* 16 Apr. 2005, late ed.: C1. *America's Newspapers*. News Bank InfoWeb. Fairchild-Martindale Library, Lehigh University, Bethlehem, PA. 23 June 2005 <http://infoweb.newsbank.com>.
Barlow, Rich. "Mother of Inventions; Virtual Cow Fences and Self-Reconfiguring Automatons Are Just Two of MIT Roboticist Daniela Rus's Futuristic Visions." *Boston Globe* 28 Dec. 2003, third ed., Magazine sec.: 12. *America's Newspapers*. News Bank InfoWeb. Campbell Library, Rowan University, Glassboro, NJ. 23 Apr. 2004 <http://infoweb.newsbank.com>.
Barr, Marleen S., ed. *Envisioning the Future: Science Fiction and the Next Millennium*. Middletown, CT: Wesleyan University Press, 2003.
Barron, Arthur S. "Why Do Scientists Read Science Fiction?" *Bulletin of Atomic Scientists* Feb. 1957: 63–65.
Barton, Tom. "Wanted: A Few Good Candidates to Run for School Board Next Year." *Savannah Morning News* 20 Nov. 2005: 19A. *America's Newspapers*. News Bank InfoWeb. Fairchild-Martindale Library, Lehigh University, Bethlehem, PA. 28 Nov. 2005 <http://infoweb.newsbank.com>.
Battlestar Galactica: The Miniseries. Writ. Gary Larson, Ronald D. Moore, and Christopher Eric James. Dir. Michael Rymer. Exec. Prod. David Eick and Ronald D. Moore. Sci-Fi Channel. 8–9 Dec. 2003.
Baxter, Kevin. "Bracing for Old Nemesis." *Miami Herald* 26 Jan. 2004, final ed.: 7D. *America's Newspapers*. News Bank InfoWeb. Campbell Library, Rowan University, Glassboro, NJ. 5 Mar. 2004 <http://infoweb.newsbank.com>.
Bear, Greg. "Greg Bear's Guest of Honor Talk." 59th World Science Fiction Convention. Marriot Hotel, Philadelphia. 31 Aug. 2001.
―――. "Panel 348: Attack of the Killer Bs (Vs even)." 60th World Science Fiction Convention. McEnery Convention Center, San Jose, CA. 31 Aug. 2002.
―――. "Re: Requested Reminder." Email to the author. 31 Oct. 2002.
Benford, Gregory. "The Galactic Center Series." Silverberg 343–45.
―――. "Panel 348: Attack of the Killer Bs (Vs even)." 60th World Science Fiction Convention. McEnery Convention Center, San Jose, CA. 31 Aug. 2002.
―――. "Pascal's Terror." Slusser and Rabkin, *Mindscapes* 271–77.
―――. Personal interview. 1 Sept. 2002.
Bergstein, Brian. "Cyborg Is Not Just for Sci-Fi; Professor Uses Device to Mediate His Reality." *The Press of Atlantic City* 13 Jan. 2004: A4. *America's Newspapers*. News Bank InfoWeb. Campbell Library, Rowan University, Glassboro, NJ. 23 Apr. 2004 <http://infoweb.newsbank.com>.
Bermant, Charles. "AOL Logs Loyal Following with User-Friendly Approach." *Seattle Times* 25 Jan. 2003, Saturday fourth ed.: C5. *Academic Universe*. Lexis-Nexis. Campbell Library, Rowan University, Glassboro, NJ. 6 Nov. 2003 <http://web.lexis-nexis.com/universe>.
Berson, Misha. "Shelley Created a Monster with Enduring Relevance." *Seattle Times*

9 Feb. 2003, final ed.: L5. *Academic Universe.* Lexis-Nexis. Campbell Library, Rowan University, Glassboro, NJ. 31 Mar. 2004 <http://web.lexis-nexis.com/universe>.

Best, Neil. "Sports Watch: Media, Sports Business, and the Fan." *Newsday* 7 Oct. 2005: A83. *America's Newspapers.* News Bank InfoWeb. Fairchild-Martindale Library, Lehigh University, Bethlehem, PA. 28 Nov. 2005 <http://infoweb.newsbank.com>.

Black, Linda. "A Rich Tale of Politics, Public Service, Credit Unions." *Rocky Mountain News* 11 June 2005: 8C. *America's Newspapers.* News Bank InfoWeb. Fairchild-Martindale Library, Lehigh University, Bethlehem, PA. 28 Nov. 2005 <http://infoweb.newsbank.com>.

"Blagg Column: Somebody Made a Switch. Today's GOP Is Acting Anything but GOP." *The Recorder* 28 Mar. 2005. *America's Newspapers.* News Bank InfoWeb. Fairchild-Martindale Library, Lehigh University, Bethlehem, PA. 9 Sept. 2005 <http://infoweb.newsbank.com>.

Bloodsworth, Kirk. Interview. *New York Times* 25 Feb. 2003, late ed.: F5. *ProQuest Newspapers.* ProQuest Information and Learning Company. Campbell Library, Rowan University, Glassboro, NJ. 8 Dec. 2003 <http://proquest.umi.com>.

Bobbin, Jay. "The Learning Channels—Television Can Be a Teacher, If You Know Where to Look." *Times-Picayune* 26 Dec. 2004, sec. TV Focus: 8. *America's Newspapers.* News Bank InfoWeb. Fairchild-Martindale Library, Lehigh University, Bethlehem, PA. 15 Aug. 2005 <http://infoweb.newsbank.com>.

Booker, M. Keith. *The Dystopian Impulse in Modern Literature: Fiction as Social Criticism.* Westport, CT: Greenwood, 1994.

———. *Monsters, Mushroom Clouds, and the Cold War: American Science Fiction and the Roots of Postmodernism, 1946–1964.* Westport, CT: Greenwood, 2001.

Bova, Ben. "Isaac Was Right: N Equals One." *Analog Science Fiction and Fact* Apr. 2003: 40–46.

Bradbury, Ray. "Day After Tomorrow: Why Science Fiction?" *The Nation* 2 May 1953: 364–67.

Braidotti, Rosi. "Cyberteratologies: Female Monsters Negotiate the Other's Participation in Humanity's Far Future." Barr 146–69.

Bratman, Steven. "Deletion." *Analog Science Fiction and Fact* Jan./Feb. 2004: 180–99.

———. "The Immortality Plague." *Analog Science Fiction and Fact* May 2003: 10–35.

"Brave New World." *St. Louis Dispatch* 19 Mar. 2003: B6. *Academic Universe.* Lexis-Nexis. Campbell Library, Rowan University, Glassboro, NJ. 12 Aug. 2003 <http://web.lexis-nexis.com/universe>.

Bray, Hiawatha. "Revving Up the NASCAR Simulations." *Boston Globe* 11 Feb. 2004: D1. *America's Newspapers.* News Bank InfoWeb. Campbell Library, Rowan University, Glassboro, NJ. 5 Mar. 2004 <http://infoweb.newsbank.com>.

Brians, Paul. *Nuclear Holocausts: Atomic War in Fiction, 1895–1984.* Kent, OH: Kent State UP, 1987.

Brin, David. "Metaphorical Drive — Or Why We're Such Good Liars." Slusser and Rabkin, *Mindscapes* 60–77.

———. "The Self-Preventing Prophecy: Or How a Dose of Nightmare Can Help Tame Tomorrow's Perils." *David Brin's Official Website.* 2 Nov. 1999. 30 Sept. 2002 <http://www.davidbrin.com/1984article.html>.

Brooke, James. "Trade Quotas? Ah, the Good Old Days." *New York Times* 9 Apr. 2005, late ed.: C1. *America's Newspapers.* News Bank InfoWeb. Fairchild-Martindale Library, Lehigh University, Bethlehem, PA. 13 June 2005 <http://infoweb.newsbank.com>.

Brown, Harriet. "Just a Rash, and Then It Took Aim at her Heart." *New York Times* 13 July 2004, late ed.: F5. *America's Newspapers.* News Bank InfoWeb. Fairchild-Martindale Library, Lehigh University, Bethlehem, PA. 13 June 2005 <http://infoweb.newsbank.com>.

Brune, Tom. "Senate Showdown: Fil-i-bus-ter n: The Use of Extremem Dilatory Tactics in an Attempt to Delay or

Prevent Action, Especially in a Legislative Assembly." *Newsday* 24 Apr. 2005: A18. *America's Newspapers*. News Bank InfoWeb. Fairchild-Martindale Library, Lehigh University, Bethlehem, PA. 9 Sept. 2005 <http://infoweb.newsbank>.

Bumiller, Elisabeth. "'Cheney in the Morning,' Or Something Like That." *New York Times* 24 Jan. 2005, late ed.: A14. *America's Newspapers*. News Bank InfoWeb. Fairchild-Martindale Library, Lehigh University, Bethlehem, PA. 23 June 2005 <http://infoweb.newsbank.com>.

———. "Talk of Bubble Leads to Battle Over Bulge." *New York Times* 18 Oct. 2004, late ed.: A14. *America's Newspapers*. News Bank InfoWeb. Fairchild-Martindale Library, Lehigh University, Bethlehem, PA. 23 June 2005 <http://infoweb.newsbank.com>.

Burt, Andrew. "Panel 163: The Future of Science Fiction as a Literary Form." 60th World Science Fiction Convention. McEnery Convention Center, San Jose, CA. 30 Aug. 2002.

———. "Panel 441: The Future of the Future." 60th World Science Fiction Convention. McEnery Convention Center, San Jose, CA. 1 Sept. 2002.

Caldera, Pete. "Camping Without a Tent: Matsui Media Frenzy Quiets." *The Record* 28 Feb. 2004: S04. *America's Newspapers*. News Bank InfoWeb. Campbell Library, Rowan University, Glassboro, NJ. 5 Mar. 2004 <http://infoweb.newsbank.com>.

"Camera Shy." Editorial. *New York Times* 8 May 2005, late ed., sec. 14: 17. *America's Newspapers*. News Bank InfoWeb. Fairchild-Martindale Library, Lehigh University, Bethlehem, PA. 13 June 2005 <http://infoweb.newsbank.com>.

Campbell, John E. "Alien(ating) Ideology and the American Media: Apprehending the Alien Image in Television through *The X-Files*." *International Journal of Cultural Studies* 4.3 (2001): 327–47.

Carr, David. "Placing Bets on Miramax the Sequel." *New York Times* 31 Oct. 2005, sec. Business/Financial Desk: 1. *America's Newspapers*. News Bank InfoWeb. Fairchild-Martindale Library, Lehigh University, Bethlehem, PA. 28 Nov. 2005 <http://infoweb.newsbank.com>.

Carter, Paul A. "Extravagant Fiction Today — Cold Fact Tomorrow: A Rationale for the First American Science Fiction Magazines." *Journal of Popular Culture* 5 (1972): 842–857.

Cauvin, Henri E. "D.C. Man Given 24 Years in Activist's Death: Mayor's Aide Was Stabbed at Home in March by a Neighbor High on Crack." *Washington Post* 30 July 2005: B3. *America's Newspapers*. News Bank InfoWeb. Fairchild-Martindale Library, Lehigh University, Bethlehem, PA. 28 Nov. 2005 <http://infoweb.newsbank.com>.

Cheng, Scarlet. "Crash Landing: *Stoked* Charts the Life of Skateboarder Mark Rogowski, Now Serving Time for Murder." *Los Angeles Times* 4 Sept. 2003, home ed., sec. 5: 12. *Academic Universe*. Lexis-Nexis. Campbell Library, Rowan University, Glassboro, NJ. 6 Nov. 2003 <http://web.lexis-nexis.com/universe>.

Chereb, Sandra. "War Games Offer a Dose of Reality." *Los Angeles Times* 14 Sept. 2003, Bulldog ed.: B1. *America's Newspapers*. News Bank InfoWeb. Campbell Library, Rowan University, Glassboro, NJ. 10 Mar. 2004 <http://infoweb.newsbank.com>.

Chestnutt, Charles W. *The Marrow of Tradition*. 1901. Ed. Eric J. Sundquist. New York: Viking Penguin, 1993.

Clareson, Thomas D. ed. "Science Fiction: The New Mythology." *Extrapolation* 10.5 (1969): X69–115.

Clarke, Arthur C. "The Coming 'Cyberclysm.'" *World Press Review* Jan. 1997: 48.

———. "Son of Dr. Strangelove: Or, How I Learned to Stop Worrying and Love Stanley Kubrick." *Report on Planet Three and Other Speculations*. By Clarke. New York: Harper & Row, 1972. Rpt. in Knight, *Turning* 277–284.

Clarke, I. F. *Tales of the Future: From the Beginning to the Present Day*, 3rd ed. London: The Library Association, 1978.

Clements, Cynthia Hall. "Clements: 'Women Writers' Have Opinions, Too." *Lufkin*

Daily News 27 Mar. 2005, sec. News-Opinion. *America's Newspapers*. News Bank InfoWeb. Fairchild-Martindale Library, Lehigh University, Bethlehem, PA. 28 Nov. 2005 <http://infoweb.newsbank.com>.

Coffee, Peter. "Securing for the Future: Sci-fi Can Offer a Useful Window into Corporate Network Security Holes." *PCWeek* 15 Dec. 1997: 95+.

Colliver, Victoria. "Kaiser Has Ambitious Plans: HMO to Spend More Than $10 Billion to Build, Renovate Medical Buildings." *San Francisco Chronicle* 11 Sept. 2005: B1. *America's Newspapers*. News Bank InfoWeb. Fairchild-Martindale Library, Lehigh University, Bethlehem, PA. 28 Nov. 2005 <http://infoweb.newsbank.com>.

Conjura, Ann. "Obesity Weighing Heavily on Americans' Minds, Bodies." *The Herald-Dispatch* 6 Mar. 2005: 7G. *America's Newspapers*. News Bank InfoWeb. Fairchild-Martindale Library, Lehigh University, Bethlehem, PA. 28 Nov. 2005 <http://infoweb.newsbank.com>

Cook, Gareth. "Defending DARPA; The Government's Strangest Research Might Be Its Best." *Boston Globe* 3 Aug. 2003, third ed.: E1. *America's Newspapers*. News Bank InfoWeb. Campbell Library, Rowan University, Glassboro, NJ. 23 Apr. 2004 <http://infoweb.newsbank.com>.

Cooper, Brenda. "Panel 441: The Future of the Future." 60th World Science Fiction Convention. McEnery Convention Center, San Jose, CA. 1 Sept. 2002.

Cooper, Thomas W. "Fictional *1984* and Factual 1984: Ethical Questions Regarding the Control of Consciousness by Mass Media." *The Orwellian Moment: Hindsight and Foresight in the Post-1984 World*. Ed. Robert L. Savage, James Combs, and Dan Nimmo. Fayetteville, AK: University of Arkansas Press, 1989. 83–107.

Crawford, Neta C. "Feminist Futures: Science Fiction, Utopia, and the Art of Possibilities in World Politics." Weldes, *Seek* 195–220.

Csicsery-Ronay, Istvan, Jr. "Science Fiction and Empire." *Science Fiction Studies* 30 (2003): 231–45.

Cuniberti, Betty. "From Marrying Up to Dumbing Down, Women Win Across the Board Nowadays." *St. Louis Post-Dispatch* 8 Sept. 2002: E1. *Academic Universe*. Lexis-Nexis. Campbell Library, Rowan University, Glassboro, NJ. 6 Nov. 2003 <http://web.lexis-nexis.com/universe>.

Curry, Jack. "Martinez Is Filling That Expensive Void at First in the Bronx." *New York Times* 12 May 2005, late ed.: D1. *America's Newspapers*. News Bank InfoWeb. Fairchild-Martindale Library, Lehigh University, Bethlehem, PA. 23 June 2005 <http://infoweb.newsbank.com>.

D'Ammassa, Don. "A Good Offense." *Analog Science Fiction and Fact* May 2003: 80–88.

D'Avolio, Lauren. "Plano Biology Instructor Named State Teacher of the Year: Hats Off to Her." *Dallas Morning News* 13 Oct. 2005: 1B. *America's Newspapers*. News Bank InfoWeb. Fairchild-Martindale Library, Lehigh University, Bethlehem, PA. 28 Nov. 2005 <http://infoweb.newsbank.com>.

Dalkin, Gary S. "Keep Watching the Skies: The Legacy of *The War of the Worlds*." *Vector* Nov. 1998: 12–18.

de Borchgrave, Arnaud. "What Did Musharraf Know?" *Washington Times* 3 Mar. 2004, final ed.: A17. *Academic Universe*. Lexis-Nexis. Campbell Library, Rowan University, Glassboro, NJ. 9 Mar. 2004 <http://web.lexis-nexis.com/universe>.

Dean, Cornelia. "If Robots Ever Get Too Smart, He'll Know How to Stop Them." *New York Times* 14 Feb. 2006: F1+.

Dean, John W. "Liberties Disappearing Before Our Eyes." Rev. of *Why Societies Need Dissent*, by Cass R. Sunstein; *Freedom and the Court: Civil Rights and Liberties in the United States*, by Henry J. Abraham and Barbara A. Perry; *The Soft Cage: Surveillance in America From Slavery to the War on Terror*, by Christian Parenti; *Lost Liberties: Ashcroft and the Assault on Personal Freedom*, ed. Cynthia Brown; *Enemy Aliens: Double Stan-*

dards and Constitutional Freedoms in the War on Terrorism, by David Cole; The War on Our Freedoms: Civil Rights in the Age of Terrorism, ed. Richard C. Leone and Greg Anrig, Jr.; and The War on the Bill of Rights — and the Gathering Resistance, by Nat Hentoff. Los Angeles Times 21 Sept. 2003, home ed.: R3. America's Newspapers. News Bank InfoWeb. Campbell Library, Rowan University, Glassboro, NJ. 5 Mar. 2004 <http://infoweb.newsbank.com>.

Dees, Matt. "Vigils Enter Yet Another Year." Chapel Hill News 5 Jan. 2005: A1. America's Newspapers. News Bank InfoWeb. Fairchild-Martindale Library, Lehigh University, Bethlehem, PA. 15 Aug. 2005 <http://infoweb.newsbank.com>.

Del Guzzi, Kristen. "The Secret is Out! Investing Section Plot Revealed." The Plain-Dealer 14 Nov. 2004: G2. America's Newspapers. News Bank InfoWeb. Fairchild-Martindale Library, Lehigh University, Bethlehem, PA. 15 Aug. 2005 <http://infoweb.newsbank.com>.

"Design." Law & Order: Special Victims Unit. Writ. Lisa Marie Peterson. Dir. David Platt. NBC. WCAU, Philadelphia. 27 Sept. 2005.

Dexter, Charlie. "Sadly, SAD Can Be One Reason Behind Crummy Customer Service." Fairbanks Daily News-Miner 9 Oct. 2005, sec. Past News. America's Newspapers. News Bank InfoWeb. Fairchild-Martindale Library, Lehigh University, Bethlehem, PA. 28 Nov. 2005 <http://infoweb.newsbank.com>.

Diamond, John, and Dave Moniz. "No Answer for U.S. Firepower." USA Today 7 Apr. 2003, final ed.: 4A. Academic Universe. Lexis-Nexis. Campbell Library, Rowan University, Glassboro, NJ. 9 Mar. 2004 <http://web.lexis-nexis.com/universe>.

"Dr. Strangedeal; Nuclear Proliferation." The Economist 11 Mar. 2006: 9. ProQuest Newspapers. ProQuest Information and Learning Company. Fairchild-Martindale Library, Lehigh University, Bethlehem, PA. 3 Apr. 2006 <http://proquest.umi.com>.

Dowd, Maureen. "Out of Africa." Editorial. New York Times 18 July 2004, late ed., sec. 4: 13. America's Newspapers. News Bank InfoWeb. Fairchild-Martindale Library, Lehigh University, Bethlehem, PA. 23 June 2005 <http://infoweb.newsbank.com>.

_____. "Uncle Dick and Papa." Editorial. New York Times 23 Apr. 2005, late ed.: A13. America's Newspapers. News Bank InfoWeb. Fairchild-Martindale Library, Lehigh University, Bethlehem, PA. 23 June 2005 <http://infoweb.newsbank.com>.

Doyle, Jim. "California Ka-Ching! No Big Winner Yet in the Multimillion-Dollar Battle over Indian Gambling." San Francisco Chronicle 1 June 2003, final ed.: D1. Academic Universe. Lexis-Nexis. Campbell Library, Rowan University, Glassboro, NJ. 12 Aug. 2003 <http://web.lexis-nexis.com/universe>.

Dozois, Gardner. Preface. Supermen: Tales of the Posthuman Future. Ed. Dozois. New York: St. Martin's Press, 2002. ix-xiii.

_____. "Panel 137: Disposable Skiffy?: Does SF Have a Sell-by Date?" 60th World Science Fiction Convention. McEnery Convention Center, San Jose, CA. 30 Aug. 2002.

Dunn, Thomas P., and Richard D. Erlich. "A Vision of Dystopia: Beehives and Mechanization." Journal of Higher Education 33.1 (1981): 45–57.

Easton, Tom. "Reference Library." Analog Science Fiction and Fact Jan. 2003: 128–133.

_____. "Reference Library." Analog Science Fiction and Fact Apr. 2003: 132–137.

_____. "Reference Library." Analog Science Fiction and Fact Jan./Feb. 2004: 230–235.

Egan, Timothy. "A Mayor's Secret Life Jolts a Northwest City." New York Times 8 May 2005, late ed., sec. 1: 24. America's Newspapers. News Bank InfoWeb. Fairchild-Martindale Library, Lehigh University, Bethlehem, PA. 13 June 2005 <http://infoweb.newsbank.com>.

Egoff, Sheila. "Science Fiction." Only Connect: Readings on Children's Literature. Ed. Sheila Egoff, G. T. Stubbs, and L. F.

Ashley. Toronto: Oxford UP, 1969. 384–398.

Eisenberg, Anne. "Seeking Answers in Computer Analyses of Brushwork and Other Details." *New York Times* 23 Dec. 2004, late ed.: E1. *America's Newspapers*. News Bank InfoWeb. Fairchild-Martindale Library, Lehigh University, Bethlehem, PA. 23 June 2005 <http://infoweb.newsbank.com>.

Elliott, Christopher. "If HAL the Computer Audited Your Expenses." *New York Times* 12 Oct. 2004, late ed.: C11. *America's Newspapers*. News Bank InfoWeb. Fairchild-Martindale Library, Lehigh University, Bethlehem, PA. 23 June 2005 <http://infoweb.newsbank.com>.

"Enemy." *Law & Order*. Writ. Alfredo Barrios, Jr. Dir. Richard Dobbs. NBC. WCAU, Philadelphia. 1 Dec. 2004.

Erlanger, Steven. "Israel Trades One Nightmare for Another." *New York Times* 10 Oct. 2004, late ed., sec. 4: 3. *America's Newspapers*. News Bank InfoWeb. Fairchild-Martindale Library, Lehigh University, Bethlehem, PA. 23 June 2005 <http://infoweb.newsbank.com>.

Fahim, Kareem. "Fire Response Lags in the City, Exposing a Rift." *New York Times* 27 May 2005, late ed.: A1. *America's Newspapers*. News Bank InfoWeb. Fairchild-Martindale Library, Lehigh University, Bethlehem, PA. 13 June 2005 <http://infoweb.newsbank.com>.

Faiola, Anthony. "Dr. Clone: Creating Life or Trying to Save It?" *Washington Post* 29 Feb. 2004, F ed.: A1. *America's Newspapers*. News Bank InfoWeb. Campbell Library, Rowan University, Glassboro, NJ. 10 Mar. 2004 <http://infoweb.newsbank.com>.

Farmer, John. "Bush the Conservative Is Really a Radical." Editorial. *The Star-Ledger* 10 Mar. 2003, final ed.: 15. *America's Newspapers*. News Bank InfoWeb. Campbell Library, Rowan University, Glassboro, NJ. 5 Mar. 2004 <http://infoweb.newsbank.com>.

Fehrenbach, T.R. "Are Insurgents Barbaric? Well, That Depends." Editorial. *San Antonio Express-News* 12 Dec. 2004: 3H.

America's Newspapers. News Bank InfoWeb. Fairchild-Martindale Library, Lehigh University, Bethlehem, PA. 15 Aug. 2005 <http://infoweb.newsbank.com>.

Filmer, Kath. "Dreaming Each Other: The Discourse of Fantasy in Contemporary News Media." *Twentieth-Century Fantasists: Essays on Culture, Society and Belief in Twentieth-Century Mythopoeic Literature*. Ed. Kath Filmer. New York: St. Martin's Press, 1992. 193–206.

Fineman, Mark, Robin Wright, and Doyle McManus. "Preparing for War, Stumbling to Peace." *Los Angeles Times* 18 July 2003, home ed.: A1. *America's Newspapers*. News Bank InfoWeb. Campbell Library, Rowan University, Glassboro, NJ. 10 Mar. 2004 <http://infoweb.newsbank.com>.

Fisch, Michael. "Nation, War, and Japan's Future in the Science Fiction Anime Film *Patlabor II*." *Science Fiction Studies* 27 (2000): 49–68.

Fitzgerald, Thomas. "Front-Runner Dean Talks Like an Underdog." *The Record* 13 Jan. 2004: A01. *America's Newspapers*. News Bank InfoWeb. Campbell Library, Rowan University, Glassboro, NJ. 10 Mar. 2004 <http://infoweb.newsbank.com>.

Foote, Bud. "Verne's *Paris in the Twentieth Century*: The First Science Fiction Dystopia?" *New York Review of Science Fiction* Dec. 1995: 8–10.

Franklin, H. Bruce. "Science Fiction Before Gernsback." *Future Perfect: American Science Fiction of the Nineteenth Century*. Ed. H. Bruce Franklin. New York: Oxford UP, 1966. Rpt. in Knight, *Turning* 96–99.

Frascella, Lawrence. Rev. of *Far Away*, dir. Caryl Churchill. *Entertainment Weekly* 13 Dec. 2002: 92.

Gaiman, Neil. "The Wolfe & Gaiman Show." *Locus: The Newspaper of the Science Fiction Field* Sep. 2002: 6+.

Galtseva, Renata, and Irina Rodnyanskaya. "The Obstacle: The Human Being, or the Twentieth-Century in the Mirror of Dystopia." *South Atlantic Quarterly* 90.2 (1991): 293–322.

Garvin, Glenn. "CNBC's Newest 'Newsman': People Shouldn't Trust Me." *Miami Herald* 16 Jan. 2004, state ed.: 4A. *America's Newspapers*. News Bank InfoWeb. Campbell Library, Rowan University, Glassboro, NJ. 10 Mar. 2004 <http://infoweb.newsbank.com>.

"The Gitmo Twilight Zone." Editorial. *San Francisco Chronicle* 12 June 2005: C4. *America's Newspapers*. News Bank InfoWeb. Fairchild-Martindale Library, Lehigh University, Bethlehem, PA. 9 Sept. 2005 <http://infoweb.newsbank.com>.

Glassman, Mark. "When Grace Flees Under Fire." *New York Times* 25 July 2004, late ed., sec. 4: 7. *America's Newspapers*. News Bank InfoWeb. Fairchild-Martindale Library, Lehigh University, Bethlehem, PA. 23 June 2005 <http://infoweb.newsbank.com>.

Goldberg, Jonah. "'Invasion of American Snatchers.'" *Kansas City Star* 19 May 2005: B7. *America's Newspapers*. News Bank InfoWeb. Fairchild-Martindale Library, Lehigh University, Bethlehem, PA. 9 Sept. 2005 <http://infoweb.newsbank.com>.

Goldstein, David. "Democratic Rivalry Deepens; Onetime Friends, Dean and Gephardt Are Caught in an Intensifying Battle." *Milwaukee Journal Sentinel* 11 Oct. 2003: 7A. *Academic Universe*. LexisNexis. Campbell Library, Rowan University, Glassboro, NJ. 6 Nov. 2003 <http://web.lexis-nexis.com/universe>.

Gonsalves, Sean. "Mashpee Charter Scrutinized." *Cape Cod Times* 15 Apr. 2005. *America's Newspapers*. News Bank InfoWeb. Fairchild-Martindale Library, Lehigh University, Bethlehem, PA. 15 Aug. 2005 <http://infoweb.newsbank.com>.

Goodman, Ellen. "Wives Caught in the Crossfire." Editorial. *Boston Globe* 29 Jan. 2004, third ed.: A15. *America's Newspapers*. News Bank InfoWeb. Campbell Library, Rowan University, Glassboro, NJ. 5 Mar. 2004 <http://infoweb.newsbank.com>.

Goodrich, Peter H. "The Lineage of Mad Scientists: Anti-Types of Merlin." *Extrapolation* 27.2 (1986). Rpt. in *Dionysus In Literature: Essays on Literary Madness*. Ed. Branimir M. Rieger. Bowling Green, OH: Bowling Green UP, 1994. 71–85.

Gray, W. Russel. "*Nineteen Eighty-Four* and the Massaging of the Media." *George Orwell*. Eds. Courtney T. Wemyss and Alexej Ugrinsky. New York: Greenwood Press, 1987. 111–17.

"The Great Race." *New York Times* 14 Aug. 2005, sec. Westchester Weekly Desk: 11. *America's Newspapers*. News Bank InfoWeb. Fairchild-Martindale Library, Lehigh University, Bethlehem, PA. 9 Sept. 2005 <http://infoweb.newsbank.com>.

Green, Michelle Erica. "There Goes the Neighborhood: Octavia Butler's Demand for Diversity in Utopias." *Utopian and Science Fiction by Women: Worlds of Difference*. Ed. Jane L. Donawerth and Carol A. Kolmerton. Syracuse, NY: Syracuse UP, 1994. 166–89. *Literature Resource Center*. Gale Group. Campbell Library, Rowan University, Glassboro, NJ. 28 Sept. 2001 <http://infotrac.galegroup.com/menu>.

Greenberg, Joel. "Hope Dries Up for Gaza Settlers: As Withdrawal Date Nears, Expectations of the Evacuation Order Being Reversed Shrivel in Jewish Enclaves." *Chicago Tribune* 2 Aug. 2005, sec. News: 3. *America's Newspapers*. News Bank InfoWeb. Fairchild-Martindale Library, Lehigh University, Bethlehem, PA. 9 Sept. 2005 <http://infoweb.newsbank.com>.

Greenland, Colin. "Images of *Nineteen Eighty-Four*: Fiction and Prediction." Slusser, Greenland, and Rabkin 124–134.

Gunn, James. "The End-of-the-World-Ball." 1989. Barr 29–48.

Haberman, Clyde. "Protecting New Yorkers from Opinions." *New York Times* 22 Apr. 2005, late ed.: B1. *America's Newspapers*. News Bank InfoWeb. Fairchild-Martindale Library, Lehigh University, Bethlehem, PA. 23 June 2005 <http://infoweb.newsbank.com>.

_____. "Twilight Zone for ZIP code at Ground Zero." *New York Times* 14 Nov.

2003, late ed.: B1. *ProQuest Newspapers*. ProQuest Information and Learning Company. Campbell Library, Rowan University, Glassboro, NJ. 10 Dec. 2003 <http://proquest.umi.com>.

Haraway, Donna J. "A Cyborg Manifesto: Science, Technology, and Socialist-Feminism in the Late Twentieth Century." *Simians, Cyborgs, and Women: The Reinvention of Nature*. New York: Routledge, 1991. 149–182.

Harris, Mason. "Psychology of Power in Tolkein's *Lord of the Rings*, Orwell's *Nineteen Eighty-Four*, and LeGuin's *A Wizard of Earthsea*." *Mythlore* 15.1 (1988): 46–56.

Harrison, Harry. Introduction. *The Demolished Man*. By Alfred Bester. 1951. New York: Vintage Books (Random House), 1996. vii–x.

Hartocollis, Anemona. "Freedom Riders on the No. 9." *New York Times* 16 Jan. 2005, late ed., sec. 14: 1. *America's Newspapers*. News Bank InfoWeb. Fairchild-Martindale Library, Lehigh University, Bethlehem, PA. 23 June 2005 <http://infoweb.newsbank.com>.

Hatch, Daniel. "Seed of Destiny." *Analog Science Fiction and Fact* Jan. 2003: 8–41.

Hedges, Stephen J. "'We're Trying to Fix Things': The Situation in New Orleans Was Nightmarish, and the Rescue and Relief Effort Was Halting at Best." *Chicago Tribune* 9 Sept. 2005, sec. News: 5. *America's Newspapers*. News Bank InfoWeb. Fairchild-Martindale Library, Lehigh University, Bethlehem, PA. 9 Sept. 2005 <http://infoweb.newsbank.com>.

Heinlein, Robert A. "Pandora's Box." *The Worlds of Robert A. Heinlein*. By Heinlein. New York: Ace, 1966. Rpt. in Knight, *Turning* 238–258.

——. "Science Fiction: Its Nature, Faults and Virtues." *The Science Fiction Novel*. By Heinlein. Chicago: Advent, 1959. Rpt. in Knight, *Turning* 3–28.

Hendren, John. "Financing the Future of Iraq." *Los Angeles Times* 20 Dec. 2003, home ed.: A11. *America's Newspapers*. News Bank InfoWeb. Campbell Library, Rowan University, Glassboro, NJ. 10 Mar. 2004 <http://infoweb.newsbank.com>.

Henry, Amanda. "Prone to Clone." *Tampa Tribune* 11 Sept. 2005: 16. *America's Newspapers*. News Bank InfoWeb. Fairchild-Martindale Library, Lehigh University, Bethlehem, PA. 28 Nov. 2005 <http://infoweb.newsbank.com>.

"Here's Our List We Checked It Twice." *The Sun* 19 Dec. 2004, sec. Local. *America's Newspapers*. News Bank InfoWeb. Fairchild-Martindale Library, Lehigh University, Bethlehem, PA. 15 Aug. 2005 <http://infoweb.newsbank.com>.

Herhold, Scott. "Help! We're Surrounded by Starbucks." *San Jose Mercury News* 5 June 2005: 1B. *America's Newspapers*. News Bank InfoWeb. Fairchild-Martindale Library, Lehigh University, Bethlehem, PA. 9 Sept. 2005 <http://infoweb.newsbank.com>.

Hillegas, Mark. "Dystopian Science Fiction: New Index to the Human Situation." *New Mexico Quarterly* 31 (1961): 238–249.

——. "Science Fiction and the Idea of Progress." *Extrapolation* 1.5 (1960): 25–28.

Hilsenrath, Jon. E. "The Economy: CPI Reflects Big Split in Economy." *Wall Street Journal* 17 Jan. 2003, eastern ed.: A2. *ProQuest Newspapers*. ProQuest Information and Learning Company. Campbell Library, Rowan University, Glassboro, NJ. 10 Dec. 2003 <http://proquest.umi.com>.

Hintz, Carrie. "Monica Hughes, Lois Lowry, and Young Adult Dystopias." *The Lion and the Unicorn* 26 (2002): 254–64.

——, and Elaine Ostry. "Introduction." Hintz and Ostry, *Utopian* 1–20.

—— and ——, eds. *Utopian and Dystopian Writing for Children and Young Adults*. New York: Routledge, 2003.

Hintz, Carrie, Elaine Ostry, Kay Sambell, and Rebecca Carol Noël Totaro. "Annotated Bibliography of Utopian and Dystopian Writing for Children and Young Adults." Hintz and Ostry, *Utopian* 200–31.

Holden, Stephen. "Party On! It's a Civic Duty." Rev. of *The Girl from Monday*, dir. Hal Hartley. *New York Times* 4 May 2005, late ed.: E5. *America's Newspapers*. News Bank InfoWeb. Fairchild-Martindale Library, Lehigh University, Bethlehem, PA. 13 June 2005 <http://infoweb.newsbank.com>.

Hougham, Aaron. "Theologian Probes Stem Cells, Cloning at Oregon State U. Lectures." *University Wire* 23 Oct. 2003. *Academic Universe*. Lexis-Nexis. Campbell Library, Rowan University, Glassboro, NJ. 31 Mar. 2004 <http://web.lexis-nexis.com/universe>.

Hozic, Aida A. "Forbidden Places, Tempting Spaces, and the Politics of Desire: On *Stalker* and Beyond." Weldes, *Seek* 123–40.

Hughes, Monica. "The Struggle between Utopia and Dystopia in Writing for Children and Young Adults." Hintz and Ostry, *Utopian* 156–60.

Hughes, Zondra, and Joy Bennett Kinnon. "The Truth about One-Night Stands." *Ebony* Aug. 2003: 84+. *Academic Universe*. Lexis-Nexis. Campbell Library, Rowan University, Glassboro, NJ. 12 Aug. 2003 <http://web.lexis-nexis.com/universe>.

Huxley, Aldous. "Chemical Persuasion." *Brave New World Revisited*. By Huxley. New York: Harper & Row, 1958. Knight, *Turning* 231–37.

"In Cloning, Don't Think Big." *Los Angeles Times* 4 Apr. 2005: B-8. *America's Newspapers*. News Bank InfoWeb. Fairchild-Martindale Library, Lehigh University, Bethlehem, PA. 9 Sept. 2005 <http://infoweb.newsbank.com>.

Inayatullah, Naeem. "Bumpy Space: Imperialism and Resistance in *Star Trek: The Next Generation*." Weldes, *Seek* 53–75.

"Into the Fire." *Babylon 5*. Writ. J. Michael Straczynski. Dir. Kevin Dobson. Exec. Prod. Straczynski and Douglass Netter. Syndicated Series. 3 Feb. 1997.

Jackson, Patrick Thaddeus, and Daniel H. Nexon. "Representation is Futile? American Anti-Collectivism and the Borg." Weldes, *Seek* 143–67.

Jainschigg, John. "What's Really Going to Happen to IM?—Answer: It's Going to Embrace Everything. Resistance Is Futile." *Communications Convergence* 1 Mar. 2003: 4. *Academic Universe*. Lexis-Nexis. Campbell Library, Rowan University, Glassboro, NJ. 9 Mar. 2004 <http://web.lexis-nexis.com/universe>.

Jergler, Don. "Get Back to Work—Companies Gear Up, Mentally and Physically, As End of Summer Hits." *Long Beach Press-Telegram* 5 Sept. 2005: A19. *America's Newspapers*. News Bank InfoWeb. Fairchild-Martindale Library, Lehigh University, Bethlehem, PA. 9 Sept. 2005 <http://infoweb.newsbank.com>.

Johnson, Kenneth. DVD director's commentary. *V: The Original Miniseries*. Writ./Dir. Johnson. Warner Bros. Video, 2001.

Johnson, Kirk. "When E-Mail Points the Way Down the Rabbit Hole." *New York Times* 2 Sept. 2004, late ed.: G8. *America's Newspapers*. News Bank InfoWeb. Fairchild-Martindale Library, Lehigh University, Bethlehem, PA. 23 June 2005 <http://infoweb.newsbank.com>.

Johnson, Reed. "Rooting for the Robot: In the Battle between Man and Machine, Which Has More Soul? Science Fiction Has Disturbing Answers." *Los Angeles Times* 25 May 2003: E-1. *America's Newspapers*. News Bank InfoWeb. Campbell Library, Rowan University, Glassboro, NJ. 7 Apr. 2004 <http://infoweb.newsbank.com>.

Kahn, Joseph. "Missing Persons; Machines Can Take on Human Tasks, but They Can't Replace Human Touch." *Boston Globe* 13 Dec. 2003, third ed.: E1. *America's Newspapers*. News Bank InfoWeb. Campbell Library, Rowan University, Glassboro, NJ. 7 Apr. 2004 <http://infoweb.newsbank.com>.

Kehl, D.G., and Howard Livingston. "Doublespeak Detection for the English Classroom." *The English Journal* 88.6 (1999): 77–82.

Kelly, James Patrick. "Panel 481: Visions of the Singularity." 60th World Science Fiction Convention. McEnery Convention Center, San Jose, CA. 1 Sept. 2002.

Kepner, Tyler. "Matsui Is Still Playing, Despite His Struggles." *New York Times* 30 May 2005, late ed.: D4. *America's Newspapers*. News Bank InfoWeb. Fairchild-Martindale Library, Lehigh University, Bethlehem, PA. 23 June 2005 <http://infoweb.newsbank.com>.

Kern, Gary. "The Revolutionary Mindscape." Slusser and Rabkin, *Mindscapes* 278–84.

Kifner, John. "What Traffic? A Portrait of a City Nowhere Close to Crisis." *New York Times* 28 July 2004, late ed.: P4. *America's Newspapers*. News Bank InfoWeb. Fairchild-Martindale Library, Lehigh University, Bethlehem, PA. 23 June 2005 <http://infoweb.newsbank.com>.

Kirkland, Kyle. "Artificial Chromosomes for Gene Therapy and Designer Babies." *Analog Science Fiction and Fact* Mar. 2004: 50–58.

Knight, Damon, ed. *Turning Points: Essays on the Art of Science Fiction*. New York: Harper & Row Publishers, 1977.

———. "What Is Science Fiction?" Knight, *Turning* 62–69.

———. "Writing and Selling Science Fiction." Knight, *Turning* 218–28.

Kokoski, Paul. Letter. *New York Times* 7 June 2005, late ed.: F4. *America's Newspapers*. News Bank InfoWeb. Fairchild-Martindale Library, Lehigh University, Bethlehem, PA. 23 June 2005 <http://infoweb.newsbank.com>.

Krebsbach, Karen. "Crying for Argentina." *US Banker* Oct. 2002: 66–70. *ABI/INFORM Global*. ProQuest Information and Learning Company. Campbell Library, Rowan University, Glassboro, NJ. 10 Dec. 2003 <http://proquest.umi.com>.

Kress, Nancy. "Sleeping Dogs." Silverberg 262–93.

———. "The Sleepless." Silverberg 259–61.

Krugman, Paul. "Twilight Zone Economics." Editorial. *New York Times* 15 Apr. 2003, late ed.: A29. *ProQuest Newspapers*. ProQuest Information and Learning Company. Campbell Library, Rowan University, Glassboro, NJ. 10 Dec. 2003 <http://proquest.umi.com>.

"Lady Heather's Box." *CSI: Crime Scene Investigation*. Writ. Carol Mendelsohn, Andrew Lipsitz, Naren Shankar, and Eli Talbert. Dir. Richard J. Lewis. CBS. KYW, Philadelphia. 13 Feb. 2003.

Lakoff, George, and Mark Johnson. *Metaphors We Live By*. Chicago: University of Chicago Press, 1980.

Lee, Jennifer 8. "Private Cameras Transform Police Work." *New York Times* 22 May 2005, late ed., sec. 1: 33. *America's Newspapers*. News Bank InfoWeb. Fairchild-Martindale Library, Lehigh University, Bethlehem, PA. 13 June 2005 <http://infoweb.newsbank.com>.

LeGuin, Ursula K. *The Language of the Night: Essays on Fantasy and Science Fiction*. Ed. Susan Wood. New York: Perigee Books (G.P. Putnam's Sons), 1979.

Leibovich, Mark. "For Alan Colmes, Nothing but Left-Handed Praise; Talk Show Liberal Takes Heat From His Own Kind." *Washington Post* 29 Nov. 2003, F ed.: C1. *America's Newspapers*. News Bank InfoWeb. Campbell Library, Rowan University, Glassboro, NJ. 5 Mar. 2004 <http://infoweb.newsbank.com>.

Leonard, Andrew. "Resistance Really Was Futile." *Salon.com* 2 June 2003. *Academic Universe*. Lexis-Nexis. Campbell Library, Rowan University, Glassboro, NJ. 9 Mar. 2004 <http://web.lexis-nexis.com/universe>.

Lerner, Edward M. "By the Rules." *Analog Science Fiction and Fact* Jun. 2003: 100–113.

Levin, A.E. "English Language SF as a Socio-Cultural Phenomenon." *Science Fiction Studies* 4 (1977): 246–56.

Lewis, C. S. "On Science Fiction." *Of Other Worlds: Essays and Stories*. By Lewis. Ed. Walter Hooper. New York: Harcourt, Brace, & World, Inc., 1967. 59–74. Rpt. in Knight, *Turning* 119–31.

Lewis, Herschell Gordon. "It Ain't Supposed to Be a Challenge." *Catalog Age* 1 Oct. 2003: 11. *Academic Universe*. Lexis-Nexis. Campbell Library, Rowan University, Glassboro, NJ. 6 Nov. 2003 <http://web.lexis-nexis.com/universe>.

Lipschutz, Ronnie D. "Aliens, Alien Nations, and Alienation in American Political Economy and Popular Culture." Weldes, *Seek* 79–98.

Locke, Michelle. "Strap-on Legs Could Produce Super Troopers." *Miami Herald* 14 Mar. 2004, final ed.: 16A. *America's Newspapers*. News Bank InfoWeb. Campbell Library, Rowan University, Glassboro, NJ. 23 Apr. 2004 <http://infoweb.newsbank.com>.

Lomax, William. "Landscape and the Romantic Dilemma: Myth and Metaphor in Science-Fiction Narrative." Slusser and Rabkin, *Mindscapes* 242–56.

"Lord John Marbury." *The West Wing*. Writ. Aaron Sorkin, and Patrick Caddell. Dir. Kevin Rodney Sullivan. 5 Jan. 2000. NBC. WCAU, Philadelphia. 18 Feb. 2004.

"Lost City, Part I." *Stargate SG-1*. Writ. Brad Wright and Robert G. Cooper. Dir. Martin Wood. Exec. Prod. Michael Greenberg, Wright, Jonathan Glassner, and Richard Dean Anderson. Sci-Fi Channel. 11 Mar. 2004.

Louv, Richard. "A 24-Hour Connection to 'Fear TV.'" *San Diego Union-Tribune* 17 May 2005: B7. *America's Newspapers*. News Bank InfoWeb. Fairchild-Martindale Library, Lehigh University, Bethlehem, PA. 15 Aug. 2005 <http://infoweb.newsbank.com>.

Lyall, Sarah. "In Decorous Mayfair These Days, the U.S. Is Out of Place." *New York Times* 17 Sept. 2004, late ed.: A4. *America's Newspapers*. News Bank InfoWeb. Fairchild-Martindale Library, Lehigh University, Bethlehem, PA. 23 June 2005 <http://infoweb.newsbank.com>.

MacFarquhar, Neil. "Open War Over, Iraqis Focus on Crime and Hunt for Jobs." *New York Times* 16 Sept. 2003, late ed.: A1. *ProQuest Newspapers*. ProQuest Information and Learning Company. Campbell Library, Rowan University, Glassboro, NJ. 10 Dec. 2003 <http://proquest.umi.com>.

Magnier, Mark. "War with Iraq/In the South; British Try a Softer Approach with Civilians." *Los Angeles Times* 3 Apr. 2003, home ed.: A18. *America's Newspapers*. News Bank InfoWeb. Campbell Library, Rowan University, Glassboro, NJ. 23 Apr. 2004 <http://infoweb.newsbank.com>.

Maney, Kevin. "For Future Nano Info, Nano-philes Are Keeping Their Eye on Nanosys." *USA Today* 17 Mar. 2004: 4B. *America's Newspapers*. News Bank InfoWeb. Campbell Library, Rowan University, Glassboro, NJ. 23 Apr. 2004 <http://infoweb.newsbank.com>.

Mann, George, ed. *The Mammoth Encyclopedia of Science Fiction*. New York: Carroll and Graf Publishers, 2001.

Marsa, Linda. "At DNA's Ends, the Clues Begin." *Los Angeles Times* 23 June 2003, home ed., sec. 6: 3. *Academic Universe*. Lexis-Nexis. Campbell Library, Rowan University, Glassboro, NJ. 6 Nov. 2003 <http://web.lexis-nexis.com/universe>.

Martz, Ron. "War of the Worlds." *Editor and Publisher* 12 May 2003: 30. *ProQuest Newspapers*. ProQuest Information and Learning Company. Campbell Library, Rowan University, Glassboro, NJ. 8 Dec. 2003 <http://proquest.umi.com>.

Mason, Marilynne S. "Today's Problems Tomorrow: Television's Growing Fleet of Science-Fiction Dramas Paint a Brighter—or Darker—Future." *Christian Science Monitor* 2 Mar. 1993: 12.

"Maternal Mirrors." *Strong Medicine*. Writ. Ethlie Ann Vare. Dir: Jerry London. Lifetime: Television for Women. 14 Sept. 2003.

May, Rollo. "Psychotherapy and the Daimonic." *Myths, Dreams, and Religion: Eleven Visions of Connection*. Ed. Joseph Campbell. New York: MJF Books (Penguin Putnam), 1970. 196–210.

McKee, Bradford. "In This Ring, a Designer Slugfest." *New York Times* 4 Nov. 2004, late ed.: F13. *America's Newspapers*. News Bank InfoWeb. Fairchild-Martindale Library, Lehigh University, Bethlehem, PA. 23 June 2005 <http://infoweb.newsbank.com>.

McNally, Joel. "Media Stands on Sidelines Behind Cloak of Fairness." *Capital Times* 22 Oct. 2005: 10A. *America's Newspapers*. News Bank InfoWeb. Fairchild-Martindale Library, Lehigh University, Bethlehem, PA. 28 Nov. 2005 <http://infoweb.newsbank.com>.

McNurlin, Kathleen W. "A Question of Ethics: Themes in the Science Fiction Genre." *Interdisciplinary Humanities* 12.3 (1995): 9–22.

———. "A Question of Ethics: Themes in the Science Fiction Genre, Part II." *Interdisciplinary Humanities* 12.4 (1995): 19–36.

"Melissa Scott: Of Masks & Metaphors." *Locus: The Newspaper of the Science Fiction Field* Jan. 1999: 6+.

Meyer, David S. "Star Wars, Star Wars, and American Popular Culture." *Journal of Popular Culture* 26.2 (1992): 99–115.

Michaelson, L.W. "Social Criticism in Science Fiction." *Antioch Review* Dec. 1954: 502–508.

Miller, Laura. "On Writers and Writing: It's Philip Dick's World, We Only Live in It." *New York Times* 24 Nov. 2002, late ed., sec. 7: 39. *Academic Universe*. Lexis-Nexis. Campbell Library, Rowan University, Glassboro, NJ. 3 Dec. 2003 <http://web.lexis-nexis.com/universe>.

"'Mind-Snatchers' Isn't a Movie." *San Gabriel Valley Tribune* 26 June 2005, sec. Opinion. *America's Newspapers*. News Bank InfoWeb. Fairchild-Martindale Library, Lehigh University, Bethlehem, PA. 9 Sept. 2005 <http://infoweb.newsbank.com>.

Moran, Tom. "New Rules Bankrupt All but the Rich Candidates." *Star-Ledger* 19 Nov. 2004, sec. New Jersey: 29. *America's Newspapers*. News Bank InfoWeb. Fairchild-Martindale Library, Lehigh University, Bethlehem, PA. 15 Aug. 2005 <http://infoweb.newsbank.com>.

Mouawad, Jad. "Oil Briefly Rises Above $55 and Seems Likely to Stay High." *New York Times* 4 Mar. 2005, late ed.: C6. *America's Newspapers*. News Bank InfoWeb. Fairchild-Martindale Library, Lehigh University, Bethlehem, PA. 13 June 2005 <http://infoweb.newsbank.com>.

Moylan, Tom. "'The Moment is Here...and It's Important': State, Agency, and Dystopia in Kim Stanley Robinson's *Antarctica* and Ursula K. LeGuin's *The Telling*." Baccolini and Moylan, *Dark Horizons* 135–53.

Mulkay, Michael. "Frankenstein and the Debate Over Embryo Research." *Science, Technology, & Human Values* 21.2 (1996): 157–76. *J-Stor*. Campbell Library, Rowan University, Glassboro, NJ. 23 Jan. 2004 <http://www.jstor.org>.

Mulshine, Paul. "Both Sides Distort Stem Cell Issue." *Star-Ledger* 24 May 2005, sec. Editorial: 15. *America's Newspapers*. News Bank InfoWeb. Fairchild-Martindale Library, Lehigh University, Bethlehem, PA. 9 Sept. 2005 <http://infoweb.newsbank.com>.

Murphy, Kim. "In Russia, Defanged B-52 Is Da Bomb." *Los Angeles Times* 21 Aug. 2003, home ed., sec. 1: 3. *Academic Universe*. Lexis-Nexis. Campbell Library, Rowan University, Glassboro, NJ. 6 Nov. 2003 <http://web.lexis-nexis.com/universe>.

Nerlich, Brigitte, David D. Clarke, and Robert Dingwall. "Fictions, Fantasies, and Fears: The Literary Foundations of the Cloning Debate." *Journal of Literary Semantics* 30 (2001): 37–52. *Academic Search Premier*. EBSCOhost. Campbell Library, Rowan University, Glassboro, NJ. 21 July 2003 <http://search.epnet.com>.

Neumann, Iver B. "'To know him was to love him. Not to know him was to love him from afar': Diplomacy in *Star Trek*." Weldes, *Seek* 31–52.

"New Nuclear-Weapons Push Invites a Dangerous Backlash." Editorial. *USA Today* 13 Aug. 2003: 10A. *America's Newspapers*. News Bank InfoWeb. Campbell Library, Rowan University, Glassboro, NJ. 5 Mar. 2004 <http://infoweb.newsbank.com>.

Newman, John, and Michael Unsworth. *Future War Novels: An Annotated Bibliography of Works in English Published Since 1946*. London: Oryx Press, 1984.

Nicklaus, David. "Do Large Deficits Really Matter That Much Anymore?" *St. Louis Post-Dispatch* 9 Feb. 2005: C1. *America's Newspapers*. News Bank InfoWeb. Fairchild-Martindale Library, Lehigh University, Bethlehem, PA. 15 Aug. 2005 <http://infoweb.newsbank.com>.

"Nullification." *Law & Order*. Writ. David

Black. Dir. Constantine Makris. NBC. WCAU, Philadelphia. 5 Nov. 1997.

O'Donnell, Maureen. "Teacher Convicted of Battery in Wedding Brawl." *Chicago Sun-Times* 13 May 2003: 3. *Academic Universe.* Lexis-Nexis. Campbell Library, Rowan University, Glassboro, NJ. 6 Nov. 2003 <http://web.lexis-nexis.com/universe>.

O'Hehir, Andrew. Rev. of *X-Men*, dir. Brian Singer. *Salon.com* 14 Jul. 2000. 9 Feb. 2003 <http://dir.salon.com/ent/movies/review/2000/7/14/x_men/index.html?CP=IMD&DN=110>.

Olian, Judy. "Brave New World of Employment Screening." *Scripps Howard News Service*: 21 Feb. 2003. *Academic Universe.* Lexis-Nexis. Campbell Library, Rowan University, Glassboro, NJ. 12 Aug. 2003 <http://web.lexis-nexis.com/universe>.

O'Shaughnessy, Lynn. "Retirement? Sock It Away Early and Be a Millionaire." *San Diego Union-Tribune* 15 May 2005: H-1. *America's Newspapers.* News Bank InfoWeb. Fairchild-Martindale Library, Lehigh University, Bethlehem, PA. 15 Aug. 2005 <http://infoweb.newsbank.com>.

"Overreaction to Cloning Claim Poses Other Risks." *USA Today* 3 Jan. 2003, final ed.: 8A. *Academic Universe.* Lexis-Nexis. Campbell Library, Rowan University, Glassboro, NJ. 31 Mar. 2004 <http://web.lexis-nexis.com/universe>.

Paddock, Richard C. "Outbreak in Asia." *Los Angeles Times* 8 May 2003, home ed.: 1. *Academic Universe.* Lexis-Nexis. Campbell Library, Rowan University, Glassboro, NJ. 12 Aug. 2003 <http://web.lexis-nexis.com/universe>.

Pallay, Jessica. "A Brave New World—Bloomberg Sees Biometrics as the Key to Preventing Unauthorized Access to Its Terminals, but Will End Users View the New Technology as Too Intrusive?" *Wall Street & Technology* 1 Aug. 2003: 31. *Academic Universe.* Lexis-Nexis. Campbell Library, Rowan University, Glassboro, NJ. 12 Aug. 2003 <http://web.lexis-nexis.com/universe>.

Parent, Richard. "Double Vision: Robert Sawyer's Utopian Dystopia." *New York Review of Science Fiction* June 2004: 19–22.

Parriot, James D. Letter. *Los Angeles Times* 19 Oct. 2003, home ed.: M4. *America's Newspapers.* News Bank InfoWeb. Campbell Library, Rowan University, Glassboro, NJ. 5 Mar. 2004 <http://infoweb.newsbank.com>.

Pennavaria, Katherine. "Representations of Books and Libraries in Depictions of the Future." *Libraries and Culture* 37.3 (2002): 229–248.

Pethes, Nicolas. "Terminal Men: Biotechnological Experimentation and the Reshaping of 'the Human' in Medical Thrillers." *New Literary History* 36 (2005): 161–85.

Pienciak, Richard T. "Catskill Casino Plan—It's War." *Daily News* 6 July 2003, sports final ed.: 4. *Academic Universe.* Lexis-Nexis. Campbell Library, Rowan University, Glassboro, NJ. 6 Nov. 2003 <http://web.lexis-nexis.com/universe>.

Piercy, Marge. "Love and Sex in the Year 3000." Barr 131–145.

Pirodsky, Richard. Letter. *New York Times* 25 Nov. 2001, late ed., sec. 2: 4. *Academic Universe.* Lexis-Nexis. Campbell Library, Rowan University, Glassboro, NJ. 6 Nov. 2003 <http://web.lexis-nexis.com/universe>.

Pledger, Marcia. "A Budget Request Via E-mail?" *The Plain-Dealer* 18 July 2005: E3. *America's Newspapers.* News Bank InfoWeb. Fairchild-Martindale Library, Lehigh University, Bethlehem, PA. 9 Sept. 2005 <http://infoweb.newsbank.com>.

Pohl, Frederick. "Coming Up on 1984." Slusser, Greenland, and Rabkin 97–113.

———. "The Politics of Prophecy." *Extrapolation* 34.3 (1993): 199–208.

Postman, Neil. "Building a Bridge to the Eighteenth-Century." Barr 19–28.

Prieto-Pablos, Juan. "The Ambivalent Hero of Contemporary Fantasy and Science Fiction." *Extrapolation* 32.1 (1991): 64–80.

"Public Applause for Gov. Rendell." Editorial. *Erie Times-News* 11 June 2005: 2. *America's Newspapers.* News Bank InfoWeb. Fairchild-Martindale Library, Lehigh University, Bethlehem, PA. 13

June 2005 <http://infoweb.newsbank.com>.

"Reactionaries and Cloning." Editorial. *Capital Times* 3 Mar. 2003: 6A. *Academic Universe*. Lexis-Nexis. Campbell Library, Rowan University, Glassboro, NJ. 31 Mar. 2004 <http://web.lexis-nexis.com/universe>.

Read, Simon. "Even in Midst of Gunfire, FBI Agents Give Public an Insiders View." *Oakland Tribune* 23 Apr. 2005, sec. Tri-Valley. *America's Newspapers*. News Bank InfoWeb. Fairchild-Martindale Library, Lehigh University, Bethlehem, PA. 15 Aug. 2005 <http://infoweb.newsbank.com>.

Read, Wolf. "Between Singularities." *Analog Science Fiction and Fact* Feb. 2003: 102–109.

Reeks, Anne. "Blue the TV Pup Clues in Kids About the Fun of Starting School." *Houston Chronicle* 14 Aug. 2003: 10. *Academic Universe*. Lexis-Nexis. Campbell Library, Rowan University, Glassboro, NJ. 6 Nov. 2003 <http://web.lexis-nexis.com/universe>.

Rich, Frank. "Gonzo Gone, Rather Going, Watergate Still Here." *New York Times* 6 Mar. 2005, late ed., sec. 2: 1. *America's Newspapers*. News Bank InfoWeb. Fairchild-Martindale Library, Lehigh University, Bethlehem, PA. 23 June 2005 <http://infoweb.newsbank.com>.

Rivenburg, Ron. "Awash in a World of Deja Voodoo." *Los Angeles Times* 23 Jan. 2004, home ed.: E22. *America's Newspapers*. News Bank InfoWeb. Campbell Library, Rowan University, Glassboro, NJ. 5 Mar. 2004 <http://infoweb.newsbank.com>.

Rivlin, Gary. "At $300 a Share, Google Looks Pricey and Still Irresistible." *New York Times* 28 June 2005, sec. Business/Financial Desk: 1. *America's Newspapers*. News Bank InfoWeb. Fairchild-Martindale Library, Lehigh University, Bethlehem, PA. 9 Sept. 2005 <http://infoweb.newsbank.com>.

Robertson, Campbell. "T. Rex Find Proves Irresistible (to Some)." *New York Times* 26 Mar. 2005, late ed.: B3. *America's Newspapers*. News Bank InfoWeb. Fairchild-Martindale Library, Lehigh University, Bethlehem, PA. 23 June 2005 <http://infoweb.newsbank.com>.

Robinson, Eugene. "Trial of the Century: 'Got to be There.'" Editorial. *Washington Post* 29 Mar. 2005: A15. *America's Newspapers*. News Bank InfoWeb. Fairchild-Martindale Library, Lehigh University, Bethlehem, PA. 15 Aug. 2005 <http://infoweb.newsbank.com>.

Ross, Andrew. *Strange Weather: Culture, Science, and Technology in the Age of Limits*. New York: Verso, 1991.

Ruane, Michael E., and Marcia Slacum Greene. "Witnesses Face the Surreal — and Muhammad." *Washington Post* 22 Oct. 2003, final ed.: A20. *Academic Universe*. Lexis-Nexis. Campbell Library, Rowan University, Glassboro, NJ. 10 Dec. 2003 <http://web.lexis-nexis.com/universe>.

Russ, Joanna. "Alien Monsters." Knight, *Turning* 132–43.

Russell, Sabin. "Mother Believed to be Schizophrenic, Off Drugs." *San Francisco Chronicle* 21 Oct. 2005: A16. *America's Newspapers*. News Bank InfoWeb. Fairchild-Martindale Library, Lehigh University, Bethlehem, PA. 28 Nov. 2005 <http://infoweb.newsbank.com>.

Rybacki, Karyn Charles, and Donald Jay Rybacki. *Visions of the Apocalypse: A Rhetorical Analysis of* The Day After. Presented at the Annual Meeting of the International Communication Association, 24–28 May 1984, San Francisco, CA. ERIC Document Reproduction Service, No. ED246516.

Saltzman, Jonathan. "Some School Lunch Lines Are Going High-Tech; Natick Considers Fingerprint ID." *Boston Globe* 17 July 2003, third ed.: 1. *Academic Universe*. Lexis-Nexis. Campbell Library, Rowan University, Glassboro, NJ. 12 Aug. 2003 <http://web.lexis-nexis.com/universe>.

Sambell, Kay. "Presenting the Case for Social Change: The Creative Dilemma of Dystopian Writing for Children." Hintz and Ostry, *Utopian* 163–78.

Sargent, Pamela. "Utmost Bones." Barr 116–30.

Sawyer, Kathy. "Scientists Prepare to Fix Ailing Rover; Attention Is Split as a Second Craft Readies for Descent." *Washington Post* 24 Jan. 2004, F ed.: A12. *America's Newspapers*. News Bank InfoWeb. Campbell Library, Rowan University, Glassboro, NJ. 7 Apr. 2004 <http://infoweb.newsbank.com>.

Sax, Irene. "Check Out This Philly." *Daily News* 18 Oct. 2003, final ed.: 24. *Academic Universe*. Lexis-Nexis. Campbell Library, Rowan University, Glassboro, NJ. 9 Mar. 2004 <http://web.lexis-nexis.com/universe>.

Schlobin, Roger C. "Dark Shadows and Bright Lights: Generators and Maintainers of Utopias and Dystopias." *The Utopian Fantastic: Selected Essays from the Twentieth International Conference on the Fantastic in the Arts*. Ed. Martha Bartter. Westport, CT: Praeger, 2004. 11–16.

Schmidt, Stanley. "Design Flaw." Editorial. *Analog Science Fiction and Fact* Dec. 2002: 4–6.

———. "Fear Pollution." Editorial. *Analog Science Fiction and Fact* Mid-Dec. 1989. Rpt. in Schmidt, *Which Way* 137–42.

———. "The Fermi Plague." Editorial. *Analog Science Fiction and Fact* Oct. 1998. Rpt. in Schmidt, *Which Way* 45–49.

———. "Haste Makes Haste." Editorial. *Analog Science Fiction and Fact* Jan. 1999. Rpt. in Schmidt, *Which Way* 185–90.

———. "King of the Hill (No Matter What)." Editorial. *Analog Science Fiction and Fact* Aug. 1998. Rpt. in Schmidt, *Which Way* 17–23.

———. "Musing from the Bio-Ethical Frontier." Editorial. *Analog Science Fiction and Fact* Mar. 2002: 4–8.

———. "On Being Human." Editorial. *Analog Science Fiction and Fact* Feb. 1990. Rpt. in Schmidt, *Which Way* 39–43.

———. "Panel 163: The Future of Science Fiction as a Literary Form." 60th World Science Fiction Convention. McEnery Convention Center, San Jose, CA. 30 Aug. 2002.

———. "The Old Timer Effect." Editorial. *Analog Science Fiction and Fact* Feb. 1990. Rpt. in Schmidt, *Which Way* 123–27.

———. "The Return of the Mad Scientist." Editorial. *Analog Science Fiction and Fact* May 2003: 4–6.

———. "Scarce Skills and Scattered Substitutes." Editorial. *Analog Science Fiction and Fact* Oct. 2003: 4–7.

———. "Still Guessing, After All These Years." Editorial. *Analog Science Fiction and Fact* Apr. 2003: 4–7.

———. "Tilting with Straw Men." Editorial. *Analog Science Fiction and Fact* July 1992. Rpt. in Schmidt, *Which Way* 53–57.

———. "Time Unbinding." Editorial. *Analog Science Fiction and Fact* Feb. 1999. Rpt. in Schmidt, *Which Way* 25–29.

———, ed. *Which Way to the Future? Selected Essays from* Analog. New York: Tor Books, 2001.

———. "Who Needs Company?" Editorial. *Analog Science Fiction and Fact*, Jun. 2004: 4–7.

Scholes, Robert, and Eric S. Rabkin. *Science Fiction: History, Science, Vision*. London: Oxford University Press, 1977.

Schuknecht, Bruce. "Reporter Learns Resistance Is Futile." *Journal Advocate* 24 Aug. 2004, sec. Top Story. *America's Newspapers*. News Bank InfoWeb. Fairchild-Martindale Library, Lehigh University, Bethlehem, PA. 15 Aug. 2005 <http://infoweb.newsbank.com>.

Schulte, Bret. "Asimo: Honda's New Compact Comes in Peace; It's Not Man's Best Friend, But It's No Terminator Either." *Washington Post* 3 Aug. 2002, F ed.: C1. *America's Newspapers*. News Bank InfoWeb. Campbell Library, Rowan University, Glassboro, NJ. 23 Apr. 2004 <http://infoweb.newsbank.com>.

Schulte, Brigid. "Old Ties Put Buhl in a Bind; In Past, Michigan Agency at Odds with Environmentalists." *Washington Post* 5 Mar. 2003, final ed.: A10. *Academic Universe*. Lexis-Nexis. Campbell Library, Rowan University, Glassboro, NJ. 6 Nov. 2003 <http://web.lexis-nexis.com/universe>.

Seabury, Marcia Bundy. "Images of a Networked Society: E.M. Forster's 'The Machine Stops.'" *Studies in Short Fiction* 34.1 (1997): 61–72.

Shaffer, Catherine H. "You Can Change Your Genes." *Analog Science Fiction and Fact* Sept. 2003: 46–53.

Shales, Tom. "Dull Paean; Showtime's *DC 9/11* is a Shameless Bush Booster." Rev. of *DC 9/11*. *Washington Post* 6 Sept. 2003, F ed.: C1. *America's Newspapers*. News Bank InfoWeb. Campbell Library, Rowan University, Glassboro, NJ. 5 Mar. 2004 <http://infoweb.newsbank.com>.

Shapiro, Walter. "Enron Shows Us Much Hasn't Changed." *USA Today* 18 Jan. 2002, final ed.: 10A. *Academic Universe*. Lexis-Nexis. Campbell Library, Rowan University, Glassboro, NJ. 6 Nov. 2003 <http://web.lexis-nexis.com/universe>.

Shelton, Deborah L. "Computer Aids His Independent Life; Don Holbert, Paralyzed Below the Waist, Relies on Ralph, a Home-Automation System." *Philadelphia Inquirer* 7 Aug. 2003, city ed.: C08. *America's Newspapers*. News Bank InfoWeb. Campbell Library, Rowan University, Glassboro, NJ. 7 Apr. 2004 <http://infoweb.newsbank.com>.

Shepard, Lucius. "Film: Attack of the Clooneys." Rev. of *Solaris*, dir. Stephen Soderbergh. *Magazine of Fantasy & Science Fiction* Apr. 2003: 94–98.

Siegel, Harry. "Back to the Future for Mayoral Hopefuls." *New York Observer* 18 July 2005, sec. Politics: 5. *America's Newspapers*. News Bank InfoWeb. Fairchild-Martindale Library, Lehigh University, Bethlehem, PA. 9 Sept. 2005 <http://infoweb.newsbank.com>.

Siemaszko, Corky. "Now, Cloning around with DNA Tests." *Daily News* 3 Jan. 2003, final ed.: 9. *Academic Universe*. Lexis-Nexis. Campbell Library, Rowan University, Glassboro, NJ. 31 Mar. 2004 <http://web.lexis-nexis.com/universe>.

Silverberg, Robert, ed. *Far Horizons: All New Tales from the Greatest Worlds of Science Fiction*. New York: Avon Eos, 1999.

Silverman, Elissa. "Reining in Risk Turns into Big Business; Sarbanes-Oxley Creates Winners." *Washington Post* 13 June 2005, final ed.: D1. *Academic Universe*. Lexis-Nexis. Fairchild-Martindale Library, Lehigh University, Bethlehem, PA. 13 June 2005 <http://web.lexis-nexis.com/universe>.

Simmons, Dan. "The Hyperion Cantos." Silverberg 207–210.

Simon, Ellen. "Web Server Shutdown Called Speech Threat." *Sun-Herald* 27 Oct. 2004: B8. *America's Newspapers*. News Bank InfoWeb. Fairchild-Martindale Library, Lehigh University, Bethlehem, PA. 15 Aug. 2005 <http://infoweb.newsbank.com>.

Simons, Howard L. "Base Metal Werewolves in London." *Futures* Oct. 2003: 38. *ProQuest Newspapers*. ProQuest Information and Learning Company. Campbell Library, Rowan University, Glassboro, NJ. 8 Dec. 2003 <http://proquest.umi.com>.

Simpson, Ian J. "The Music of the Spheres—Part One: The Influence of Science Fiction on Modern Popular Music." *Vector* Jan./Feb. 1999: 12–15.

Slusser, George E., and Eric S. Rabkin, eds. *Mindscapes: The Geographies of Imagined Worlds*. Carbondale and Edwardsville: Southern Illinois University Press, 1989.

Slusser, George E., Colin Greenland, and Eric S. Rabkin, eds. *Storm Warnings: Science Fiction Confronts the Future*. Carbondale: Southern Illinois UP, 1987.

Sommer, Mark. "Big Brother at the Library: FBI's Right to Data Raises Privacy Issues." *Buffalo News* 11 Nov. 2002, final ed.: A1. *Academic Universe*. Lexis-Nexis. Campbell Library, Rowan University, Glassboro, NJ. 10 Dec. 2003 <http://web.lexis-nexis.com/universe>.

———. "Frankenstein Dissected; Exhibit on 19th-Century Monster Transcends Horror Genre to Reinforce Cautionary Tales of Unbridled Medical and Scientific Power—Issues That Are Haunting as Ever." *Buffalo News* 9 Feb. 2004, final ed.: B1. *Academic Universe*. Lexis-Nexis. Campbell Library, Rowan University, Glassboro, NJ. 31 Mar. 2004 <http://web.lexis-nexis.com/universe>.

Spielman, Fran, and Frank Main. "City

Deploys High-Tech Cameras to Fight Crime." *Chicago Sun-Times* 11 July 2003, News special ed.: 1. *Academic Universe*. Lexis-Nexis. Campbell Library, Rowan University, Glassboro, NJ. 12 Aug. 2003 <http://web.lexis-nexis.com/universe>.

Spencer, Susan. "The Post-Apocalyptic Library: Oral and Literate Culture in *Fahrenheit 451* and *A Canticle for Leibowitz*" (excerpt). *Extrapolation* 32.4 (1991): 331–42. *Literature Resource Center*. Gale Group. Campbell Library, Rowan University, Glassboro, NJ. 28 Sept. 2001 <http:// infotrac.galegroup.com/menu>.

Spigelman, Candace. "Argument and Evidence in the Case of the Personal." *College English* 64 (2001): 63–87.

Star Wars: Episode I: The Phantom Menace. Screenplay, Dir., and Exec. Prod. George Lucas. Exec. Prod. Rick McCallum. Lucasfilm Limited, 1999.

Star Wars: Episode VI: Return of the Jedi. Story by George Lucas. Screenplay by Lucas and Lawrence Kasdan. Dir. Richard Marquand. Lucasfilm Limited, 1983.

Stein, Mark A. "Resistance Is Futile." *New York Times* 17 Oct. 2004, late ed., sec. 3: 2. *America's Newspapers*. News Bank InfoWeb. Fairchild-Martindale Library, Lehigh University, Bethlehem, PA. 23 June 2005 <http://infoweb.newsbank.com>.

Stern, Seth. "From Paper to the Battlefield." *Christian Science Monitor* 20 Mar. 2003: 15. *America's Newspapers*. News Bank InfoWeb. Campbell Library, Rowan University, Glassboro, NJ. 5 Mar. 2004 <http://infoweb.newsbank.com>.

Stevenson, Sharon. "The Nature of 'Outsider Dystopias': Atwood, Starhawk, and Abbey." *The Utopian Fantastic: Selected Essays from the Twentieth International Conference on the Fantastic in the Arts.* Ed. Martha Bartter. Westport, CT: Praeger, 2004. 129–36.

Stewart, Gene. "Science Fiction Writers Face a Tough Jury." *Writer* Dec. 2000: 17–18. *Academic Search Premier*. EBSCOhost. Campbell Library, Rowan University, Glassboro, NJ. 28 Sept. 2001 <http://search.epnet.com>.

Stiglitz, Joseph E. "Global Playing Field: More Level, but It Still Has Bumps." Rev. of *The World is Flat: A Brief History of the 21st Century* by Thomas L. Friedman. *New York Times* 30 Apr. 2005, late ed.: B18. *America's Newspapers*. News Bank InfoWeb. Fairchild-Martindale Library, Lehigh University, Bethlehem, PA. 13 June 2005 <http://infoweb.newsbank.com>.

Stingl, Jim. "Jim Stingl: In My Opinion: What Film Doesn't Say — At a Bargain." *Milwaukee Journal Sentinel* 16 Nov. 2005, sec. B News: 1. *America's Newspapers*. News Bank InfoWeb. Fairchild-Martindale Library, Lehigh University, Bethlehem, PA. 28 Nov. 2005 <http://infoweb.newsbank.com>.

Stolberg, Sheryl Gay. "House Votes to Ban All Human Cloning." *New York Times* 28 Feb. 2003, late ed.: A22. *Academic Universe*. Lexis-Nexis. Campbell Library, Rowan University, Glassboro, NJ. 31 Mar. 2004 <http://web.lexis-nexis.com/universe>.

Sugiura, Ken. "Red-Light Runners Try Loopholes; Plate Blockers: Some Use Spray, Plastic Hoping to Hide License from Surveillance Cameras." *Atlanta Journal-Constitution* 13 June 2005, home ed.: 1JJ. *Academic Universe*. Lexis-Nexis. Fairchild-Martindale Library, Lehigh University, Bethlehem, PA. 13 June 2005 <http://web.lexis-nexis.com/universe>.

Summar, Polly. "The Hard Questions about Anger." *Albuquerque Journal* 1 May 2005, sec. Sage: 8. *America's Newspapers*. News Bank InfoWeb. Fairchild-Martindale Library, Lehigh University, Bethlehem, PA. 28 Nov. 2005 <http://infoweb.newsbank.com>.

Swirski, Peter. "Dystopia or Dischtopia? The Science-Fiction Paradigms of Thomas M. Disch." *Science Fiction Studies* 18 (1991): 161–79.

Swisher, Kara. "Boom Town: Stay Tuned for the Next Episode of the Tech Show — Will Everybody Love or Hate Carly? Will the Cast Be Survivors or Six Feet Under?" *Wall Street Journal* 10 Sept. 2001, eastern ed.: B1. *ProQuest Newspapers*. ProQuest Information and Learning Company. Campbell Library, Rowan University, Glassboro, NJ. 8 Dec. 2003 <http://proquest.umi.com>.

Swope, Richard. "Science Fiction Cinema and the Crime of Social-Spatial Reality." *Science Fiction Studies* 29 (2002): 221–45.

"Talent: The Prime Directive." *Omaha World Herald* 31 July 2003, sunrise ed.: 6B. *Academic Universe*. Lexis-Nexis. Campbell Library, Rowan University, Glassboro, NJ. 6 Nov. 2003 <http://web.lexis-nexis.com/universe>.

"Tax Dodderization." Editorial. *Courier-Journal* 8 Mar. 2005: 6A. *America's Newspapers*. News Bank InfoWeb. Fairchild-Martindale Library, Lehigh University, Bethlehem, PA. 15 Aug. 2005 <http://infoweb.newsbank.com>.

Tedeschi, Michael. Rev. of Adobe Acrobat 6.0. *Washington Post* 22 June 2003, F. ed.: F8. *America's Newspapers*. News Bank InfoWeb. Campbell Library, Rowan University, Glassboro, NJ. 7 Apr. 2004 <http://infoweb.newsbank.com>.

Thomas, Landon, Jr. "Depression, a Frequent Visitor to Wall St." *New York Times* 12 Sept. 2004, late ed., sec. 3: 1. *America's Newspapers*. News Bank InfoWeb. Fairchild-Martindale Library, Lehigh University, Bethlehem, PA. 13 June 2005 <http://infoweb.newsbank.com>.

Thomas, Rob. "Spears, Spouse Utterly Appalling." *The Capital Times* 31 May 2005: 1C. *America's Newspapers*. News Bank InfoWeb. Fairchild-Martindale Library, Lehigh University, Bethlehem, PA. 9 Sept. 2005 <http://infoweb.newsbank.com>.

Thomasson, William. "Panel 441: The Future of the Future." 60th World Science Fiction Convention. McEnery Convention Center, San Jose, CA. 1 Sept. 2002.

Throop, Kelvin. "Do Unto Others." *Analog Science Fiction and Fact* June 2004: 82–83.

Timmons, Mark. *Moral Theory: An Introduction*. Lanham, MD: Rowman & Littlefield Publishers, 2002.

Timson, Judith. "What's a Girl to Do?" *Maclean's* 3 Sept. 2001: 44+. *ABI/INFORM Global*. ProQuest Information and Learning Company. Campbell Library, Rowan University, Glassboro, NJ. 8 Dec. 2003 <http://proquest.umi.com>.

Tommasini, Anthony. "Maazel Offers a Salute to Orwell's Vision." Rev. of *1984*, comp. Lorin Maazel. *New York Times* 5 May 2005, late ed.: E1. *America's Newspapers*. News Bank InfoWeb. Fairchild-Martindale Library, Lehigh University, Bethlehem, PA. 13 June 2005 <http://infoweb.newsbank.com>.

Turan, Kenneth. "When We Last Saw Our Heroes..." Rev. of *Star Wars: Episode II: Attack of the Clones*, dir. George Lucas. *Los Angeles Times Online* 13 May 2002. 9 Feb. 2003 <http://www.calendarlive.com/movies/reviews/cl-movie0000 33752may13.story>.

Turner, Allan. "Human Cloning Spurs Ethical Worries." *Houston Chronicle* 28 Dec. 2002, star ed.: A29. *Academic Universe*. Lexis-Nexis. Campbell Library, Rowan University, Glassboro, NJ. 31 Mar. 2004 <http://web.lexis-nexis.com/universe>.

Twersky, David. "Dr. Strangelove, I Presume?" Editorial. *New York Sun* 28 Aug. 2003: 8. *Academic Universe*. Lexis-Nexis. Campbell Library, Rowan University, Glassboro, NJ. 9 Mar. 2004 <http://web.lexis-nexis.com/universe>.

"Two Cents: What Should Israel Do about Yassar Arafat?" *San Francisco Chronicle* 21 Sept. 2003, final ed.: D2. *Academic Universe*. Lexis-Nexis. Campbell Library, Rowan University, Glassboro, NJ. 6 Nov. 2003 <http://web.lexis-nexis.com/universe>.

Tyrnauer, Matt. "America's Writing Forces." *Vanity Fair* July 2003: 126. *Academic Universe*. Lexis-Nexis. Campbell Library, Rowan University, Glassboro, NJ. 6 Nov. 2003 <http://web.lexis-nexis.com/universe>.

V: The Original Miniseries. Writ./Dir. Kenneth Johnson. Prods. Johnson, Chuck Bowman, and Patrick Boyriven. Warner Bros. Video, 2001.

Van Gelder, Gordon. "Re: Follow-up on Research Request." Email to the author. 25 Oct. 2002.

Van Pelt, James. Personal interview. 1 Sept. 2002.

———. "Re: Request for Research Assistance at Con Jose." Email to the author. 26 Oct. 2002.

Varricchio, Mario. "Power of Images/Images of Power in *Brave New World* and *Nineteen Eighty-Four*." *Utopian Studies* 10.1 (1999): 98–114.

Varsam, Maria. "Concrete Dystopia: Slavery and Its Others." Baccolini and Moylan, *Dark Horizons* 203–24.

Vecsey, Laura. "This Godzilla Is Monstrous at the Plate, Across Japan." *Baltimore Sun* 20 Oct. 2003, final ed.: 1D. *Academic Universe*. Lexis-Nexis. Campbell Library, Rowan University, Glassboro, NJ. 9 Mar. 2004 <http://web.lexis-nexis.com/universe>.

Vennochi, Joan. "A New Reality for Democrats." Editorial. *Boston Globe* 8 Jan. 2004, third ed.: A11. *America's Newspapers*. News Bank InfoWeb. Campbell Library, Rowan University, Glassboro, NJ. 5 Mar. 2004 <http://infoweb.newsbank.com>.

Vinge, Vernor. "Panel 481: Visions of the Singularity." 60th World Science Fiction Convention. McEnery Convention Center, San Jose, CA. 1 Sept. 2002.

Vos Post, Jonathan, and Kirk L. Kroeker. "Writing the Future: Computers in Science Fiction." *Computer* Jan. 2000: 29–37.

Wagner, Ed. Letter. *Honolulu Advertiser* 14 Aug. 2005: 2B. *America's Newspapers*. News Bank InfoWeb. Fairchild-Martindale Library, Lehigh University, Bethlehem, PA. 9 Sept. 2005 <http://infoweb.newsbank.com>.

Walker, Leslie. "A Yawn of a Year in Tech." *Washington Post* 26 Dec. 2002, final ed.: E01. *Academic Universe*. Lexis-Nexis. Campbell Library, Rowan University, Glassboro, NJ. 6 Nov. 2003 <http://web.lexis-nexis.com/universe>.

Walsh, Mary Williams. "Proposal on Pension Conversion Attacked." *New York Times* 10 Apr. 2003, late ed.: C2. *ProQuest Newspapers*. ProQuest Information and Learning Company. Campbell Library, Rowan University, Glassboro, NJ. 10 Dec. 2003 <http://proquest.umi.com>.

Weldes, Jutta. "Popular Culture, Science Fiction, and World Politics: Exploring Intertextual Relations." Weldes, *Seek* 1–27.

———, ed. *To Seek Out New Worlds: Exploring the Links between Science Fiction and World Politics*. New York: Palgrave Macmillian, 2003.

Wellcome Trust Medicine in Society Programme. *Public Perspectives on Human Cloning: A Social Research Study*. London: Wellcome Trust, 1998. 23 Apr. 2004 <www.wellcome.ac.uk/en/images/cloning_report_slimversion_2816.pdf>.

Westfahl, Gary. "Islands in the Sky: Space Stations in the Universe of Science Fiction." Slusser and Rabkin, *Mindscapes* 211–225.

Whitaker, Barbara. "How to Mend a Credit Report That's Not Really Broken." *New York Times* 1 Aug. 2004, late ed., sec. 3: 5. *America's Newspapers*. News Bank InfoWeb. Fairchild-Martindale Library, Lehigh University, Bethlehem, PA. 23 June 2005 <http://infoweb.newsbank.com>.

White, Josh. "Military Trials for Detainees to Resume: Four Cases to Be Heard Immediately." *Washington Post* 19 July 2005: A13. *America's Newspapers*. News Bank InfoWeb. Fairchild-Martindale Library, Lehigh University, Bethlehem, PA. 9 Sept. 2005 <http://infoweb.newsbank.com>.

Wickham, James. "'I Want to Be a Cyborg'; Roboprof Fills Body with Chips." *Daily Star* 9 Feb. 2003: 31. *Academic Universe*. Lexis-Nexis. Campbell Library, Rowan University, Glassboro, NJ. 31 Mar. 2004 <http://web.lexis-nexis.com/universe>.

Wilcox, Clyde. "Guest Editor's Pad." *Extrapolation* 34.3 (1993): 195–97.

Williams, Walter Jon. "The Green Leopard Plague." *Asimov's Science Fiction* Oct./Nov. 2003: 10–58.

Willis, Connie. "Panel 441: The Future of the Future." 60th World Science Fiction Convention. McEnery Convention Center, San Jose, CA. 1 Sept. 2002.

Wilson, Craig. "There's Little Queer about

the Word Anymore." *USA Today* 5 Aug. 2003, final ed.: 2D. *Academic Universe.* Lexis-Nexis. Campbell Library, Rowan University, Glassboro, NJ. 6 Nov. 2003 <http://web.lexis-nexis.com/universe>.

Wilson, Kimberly A.C. "Twilight Zone for Towed Cars." *Baltimore Sun* 9 Nov. 2003, final ed., sec. Telegraph: 1A. *Academic Universe.* Lexis-Nexis. Campbell Library, Rowan University, Glassboro, NJ. 10 Dec. 2003 <http://web.lexis-nexis.com/universe>.

Wolf, Buck. "Why Spielberg's Scared: 'Big Brother' Is Watching Us Now — and It Will Get Worse, Director Says." *ABC-News.com* 20 June 2002. 20 June 2002 <http://abcnews.go.com/sections/entertainment/DailyNews/minorityreport020619.html>.

Wolfe, Gary K. "Locus Looks at Books: Reviews by Gary K. Wolfe." *Locus: The Newspaper of the Science Fiction Field* Feb. 2003: 15+.

Young, Rob. "The Amateurs Are among Us." *Strategy* 10 Feb. 2003: 9. *Academic Universe.* Lexis-Nexis. Campbell Library, Rowan University, Glassboro, NJ. 6 Nov. 2003 <http://web.lexis-nexis.com/universe>.

Zakaria, Fareed. "Bush Administration Takes Jekyll-and-Hyde Approach to Muslims." *Charleston Gazette* 6 June 2005: P4A. *America's Newspapers.* News Bank InfoWeb. Fairchild-Martindale Library, Lehigh University, Bethlehem, PA. 9 Sept. 2005 <http://infoweb.newsbank.com>.

Zinoman, Jason. "Shakespeare Here, Shakespeare There." *New York Times* 1 May 2005, late ed., sec. Arts and Leisure Desk: 27. *America's Newspapers.* News Bank InfoWeb. Fairchild-Martindale Library, Lehigh University, Bethlehem, PA. 15 Aug. 2005 <http://infoweb.newsbank.com>.

Index

Abbey, Edward 123
Across the Sea of Suns see Galactic Center series
Acuna, Armando 202
Adams, Richard 122–123
addiction 52, 67, 72
Aiex, Patrick K. 21–22, 97, 120
Ain, Stewart 140
Akira 217n
Alas, Babylon 30
Aldiss, Brian 25, 112, 179
Alexander, David 47
Alicea, Michael 201
Alien 150
aliens 146–147, 149–153, 156–160, 162–166, 177–178, 189, 193, 198, 202, 205, 210, 219n; first contact 49, 101, 145, 150, 153, 156–158, 163–165, 177–178, 186; interference 158–160, 163, 165–166, 178, 180–181, 185–186, 188; invasion 28, 47, 146–147, 149–153, 156–157, 162–163, 168, 180, 182, 187, 193
All Flesh Is Grass 159
All Hallows Eve 98
"All Stood Still" see Ultravox
Althusser, Louis 113
The Amazing Colossal Man 36
The Amazing Spiderman 33
Amis, Kingsley 8, 113, 169
And the Angel with Television Eyes 158
Anderson, Poul 31, 33, 158, 176
androids 41, 47, 48, 53–54, 161–162, 189, 200
Andromeda Strain (1969) 72
Andromeda Strain (1971) 72
Angel 106, 128
"Answer" 47
Anvil, Christopher 67, 156
apocalyptic change 31–32, 35, 37, 145–146, 178–179, 193, 195, 198–200, 202–203, 205
Applebome, Peter 197
Arachne 48
Argonaut 156
Ariss, Bruce 31
Aristotelian rhetoric 207–208
Arkell, Harriet 6
Arnold, Jack 36, 104

Arnold, Matthew 39, 42
"The Artificer's Tale" 99
Artificial Intelligence (AI) 22, 40–41, 46, 47–50, 52–53, 55, 64, 66, 80–82, 125, 158, 212, 214
Ashes, Ashes 29
ASIMO 40–41, 80
Asimov, Isaac 6, 10, 13, 24, 26–27, 40–41, 46–49, 52, 55, 151, 156, 171, 217n
Atheling, William, Jr. 171–172
"The Atom Smasher" 29
Attack of the Crab Monsters 36
Attack of the Giant Leeches 36
Attack of the Puppet People 104
Atwood, Margaret 113, 117, 123, 130
"Autofac" 48
The Awakening Water 121
"Aye, and Gomorrah" 176

Babylon 5 73–74, 93, 106–108, 127–128, 130, 165–166, 209, 214; "Confessions and Lamentations" 73; "Deathwalker" 73; "Infection" 73; "Into the Fire" 190
Baccolini, Raffaella 90–91, 112, 115–116, 129
"Background Noise" 50, 180
Bainbridge, William Sims 63–64, 68, 175
Baird, Thomas 122
Bakhtin, Mikhail 208
Baldry, Cherith 123, 151–152
Bancroft, Colette 78–79
Banks, Pendelton 31
Barash, David P. 117, 123
Barash, Nanelle 117, 123
Barboza, David 82
Barjavel, Rene 29
"Bar-Lev, a Traveler's Tales of Twenty Words" 48
Barlow, Rich 80
Barnes, John 51, 68, 100
Barron, Arthur S. 26
Barton, Tom 135
Battlestar Galactica (1978) 53
Battlestar Galactica (2003) 53, 55
Baxter, Kevin 79
Beacon Project 152–153, 159–160

Bear, Greg 7, 9, 11, 64–65, 69, 99, 146, 152–153, 161, 177, 213, 217n
"The Bear's Baby" 158
The Beast from 20,000 Fathoms 36, 72
Becker, Ernest 150
Beggars and Choosers see Sleepless series
Beggars in Spain see Sleepless series
Beggars Ride see Sleepless series
Beginning of the End 36
Being John Malkovich 192
Beirut 126
Benford, Gregory 17, 49, 150–152, 154, 159, 170, 177, 217n, 219–220n
Bergstein, Brian 81
Bermant, Charles 199
Bernds, Edward 35
Berson, Misha 83
Best, Neil 78
Bester, Alfred 101–102, 122, 160, 166
"Between Singularities" 49, 184
Bierce, Ambrose 41, 47
Big Brother see *Nineteen Eighty-Four*
"Big Brother" see Bowie, David
bio-ethics 22, 57–62, 65, 67–68, 71, 87, 208
bio-technology 22, 50, 60, 63, 66, 69, 71, 73–74, 122, 124, 208, 213
bio-terrorism 22, 57, 63, 65, 92
Black, Linda 78
Blade Runner 53, 83, 189
The Blair Witch Project 167
Blake's 7 126
Blish, James 154, 176–177
"Blood Music" 99, 219n
Blood Music 219n
Bloodsworth, Kirk 197
Blue's Clues: Blue Takes You to School 199
Bobbin, Jay 202
"The Bodyguard" 31
Bohnhoff, Maya Kaathryn 159
Booker, M. Keith 27, 29–30, 32–35, 37–38, 40–41, 45, 66, 71, 98, 105, 112, 119, 155, 162, 165, 170–171, 187, 217–218n, 220n
Borges, Jorge Luis 150
Bova, Ben 151–154, 214, 219n
Bowie, David 138
A Boy and His Dog 35
The Boys from Brazil (1976) 64
The Boys from Brazil (1978) 64
Bradbury, Ray 9–10, 15, 30–31, 41, 43, 45, 89, 118–119, 121, 215
Braidotti, Ray 150, 154
The Brain That Wouldn't Die 71
brainwashing 116, 120, 122, 124–25
Bratman, Steven 50–51, 65, 70, 99–100
Brave New World 16–17, 20–21, 42, 61, 64, 72, 91, 97, 111, 115, 117, 119, 120, 124–125, 132, 141–143
Bray, Hiawatha 78
Brazil 125
Brians, Paul 25–29, 31–33, 47, 156, 158, 160

"A Brief History of the Human and Post-Human Species" 46
Brin, David 6, 10, 21, 32, 112, 183, 210–211, 214
Bronski, Michael 204
Brooke, James 142
Brown, Eric 50
Brown, Frederic 32, 47
Brown, Harriet 136
Brown, Maurice 29
Browne, Alan 126
Brune, Tom 135
Buffy the Vampire Slayer 70, 89, 93, 103, 108, 128, 193, 203, 219n; "Beauty and the Beasts" 99; "Dead Things" 105; "Gingerbread" 166; "Grave" 219n; "I Robot, You Jane" 54; "Phases" 167; "Seeing Red" 219n; "Some Assembly Required" 71, 104; "Two to Go" 219n; "Villians" 219n
Bug-Eyed Monsters (BEM) 146, 150
Bug Jack Barron 101
Bumiller, Elisabeth 77, 194
Burgess, Anthony 124
Burns, Stephen L. 65
Burstein, Michael A. 51, 159, 160
Burt, Andrew 170, 175
Bush, Kate 127
Butler, Octavia 111
"By the Rules" 158, 178, 220n

Cadigan, Pat 50, 180
"Caged" 67
Caldera, Pete 79
Camp Concentration 122
Campbell, John E. 193
Campbell, John W. 25–26, 28, 47, 156, 162, 174
Candle see "Meme War" series
A Canticle for Leibowitz 21, 30–31
Capek, Karel 29, 48, 218
Card, Orson Scott 48, 101, 157, 177, 219n
The Carpet People 152
Carr, David 78
Carrie 154
Carroll, Lewis 179
Carter, Chris 186
Carter, Paul A. 24
Cartmill, Cleve 25, 28–29
"A Case of Conscience" 176–177
cautionary tale: definition of 8–11, 206–207; success of 210–213; versus social commentary 29, 110–111, 147, 154–155, 170–171
Cauvin, Henri E. 136
"The Chapter Ends" 176
Charmed 105; "All Hell Breaks Loose" 167; "Charmed Again, Parts I and II" 167; "Chris-Crossed" 105; "It's a Bad, Bad, Bad World, Parts I and II" 105; "Witch Way Now" 167
Chase, Robert 161

Chasm City 180
Cheng, Scarlet 136
Chereb, Sandra 134
Chesterton, G.K. 119
Chestnutt, Charles W. 135
Chiang, Doug 48
Child, Lincoln 48
Childhood's End 158, 181
The China Syndrome 36
"Choosing Life" 68–69, 183
Chronicles of Thomas Covenant [*Lord Foul's Bane*; *The Illearth War*; *The Power That Preserves*; *The Wounded Land*; *The One Tree*; *White Gold Wielder*] 105
The Chrysalids 32, 160–161
Churchill, Caryl 64, 124
The City and the Stars 47
"The City of the Living Dead" 50
Clareson, Thomas D. 118
Clarke, Arthur C. 31, 34, 39, 41, 47, 52, 65, 68, 158, 160, 181
Clarke, David D. 64, 76, 83–84
Clarke, I.F. 16, 109, 112, 120, 124
Clarkson, Helen 30
The Clash 127
The Clash of Civilizations 149
Clay see *Robot Stories*
Clements, Cynthia Hall 203
"Cloak of Aesir" 28, 156
A Clockwork Orange (1962) 124–125
A Clockwork Orange (1971) 124–125
Cloned Lives 63
cloning 57–60, 63–64, 68, 71, 82–87, 145, 149, 172–173, 212–213, 218n
The Cloning of Joanna May 64
Close Encounters of the Third Kind 150, 164
"Cloudbusting" *see* Bush, Kate
Coffee, Peter 43–44, 81, 96
Cold War 24, 26, 30, 34, 37–38, 41, 79, 171, 185
Colliver, Victoria 78
"The Color of Pain" 157
comic books 11, 24, 33, 48, 71, 123, 150, 161, 167–168
"Coming of Age" 181
communication technology 42, 44, 46, 50, 215
The Computer Connection 122
"The Computer That Went on Strike" 46
computers 21–22, 39–56, 80–81, 122, 125, 172; and communication 42, 46, 56, 142, 215; and dependence 22, 40, 43–48, 50–53, 55, 181; and privacy 39, 42, 81, 211, 214; and social isolation 39, 44, 54–55, 220n
"Computers Don't Argue" 51
Conjura, Ann 202
conspiracies 47, 64–65, 70, 99, 101, 106, 127–128, 179–180, 186, 196, 199, 203
Contact (1985) 186
Contact (1997) 186

control over books 115–116, 119, 124
control over information 114–116, 122, 126–127, 178, 211
control over language 115–116, 211
Cook, Gareth 81
"Cookie Monster" 50, 102
Cooper, Brenda 68–69, 174–175, 183, 212
Cooper, Edmund 30
Cooper, Louise 98
Cooper, Thomas W. 89, 119–120, 139
Cope, Julian 165–166, 185
Corman, Roger 34, 36
corporate power 50, 69, 94–95, 101–103, 107–108, 123, 125
Count Zero see Sprawl series
Counterfeit World see Simulacron 3
Coyote 123
The Crack of Doom 25, 28
Crawford, Neta C. 132–133
Crawlers 159
The Creature from the Black Lagoon 104
The Creature Walks Among Us 104
Crichton, Michael 41, 53, 63, 66, 68, 72–73, 182
Crick, Bernard 120
crime prevention 42, 51, 67–69, 71, 73, 118–119, 124–125, 182, 211, 220n
Cromie, Robert 25, 28
Cronenberg, David 104
Crosby, Sills & Nash 37
CSI: Crime Scene Investigation: "Lady Heather's Box" 141
Csicsery-Ronay, Istvan, Jr. 8
"Cult of the I" 67
cults 32, 67, 177
cultural vocabulary/rhetoric 5–7, 10–11, 19–20, 75–87, 130–143, 150, 192–205, 207–209
Cuniberti, Betty 203
The Cure 121
Curry, Jack 79
cyberpunk 42, 45, 49–50, 54, 69, 80–81, 102, 154, 162, 213–214, 218n, 219n
Cyberpunk see Idol, Billy
Cyberpunk: The Roleplaying Game of the Dark Future 69
cyberspace 22, 40, 42–43, 48–50, 54, 56, 80, 158, 183–184, 213–214
cyborgs 48, 69–70, 73–74, 81, 162, 164, 213

Dalkin, Gary S. 156, 164
Damiano trilogy [*Damiano*; *Damiano's Lute*; *Raphael*] 98
D'Ammassa, Don 46, 178
"Dancing with Tears in My Eyes" *see* Ultravox
Dark City 165, 188, 210
Darnton, John 64
Darwin, Charles 155
Darwin's Children 65, 161
Darwin's Radio 64

David Brin's Out of Time: Yanked! 182
D'Avolio, Lauren 87
Dawn 111
The Day After 11, 14–15, 21, 35, 37
The Day the Earth Caught Fire 35
The Day the Earth Stood Still 150, 164
The Day the World Ended 34
Daybreak 126
The Daymaker see Transformations Trilogy
The Dead Zone 17, 168
"Deadline" 25, 28
Dean, Cornelia 218n
Dean, John W. 77
Death Match 48
De Borchgrave, Arnaud 77
"Decisions" 159–160
"deck.halls@boughs/holly" 46
Dees, Matt 195
Degeneration 155
dehumanization 17, 39, 42, 52, 69, 73–74, 81–82, 103, 105, 109, 112–117, 120, 125, 182, 217n
Delaney, Samuel R. 176
"Deletion" 65, 100
DelGuzzi, Kristen 199
del Ray, Lester 29–30, 33, 68
The Demolished Man 101–102, 160, 166, 168
Demolition Man 51, 55
demons 70, 93–94, 106, 166
"The Denial of Death" 150
Devil on My Back 122
Dexter, Charlie 136
Diamond, John 195
Diamond Dogs see Bowie, David
Dick, Philip K. 32, 40–42, 47–48, 53, 55, 98, 119, 161–162, 180, 185, 189, 192
Dickson, Gordon 51
dictatorship 90, 97, 100–101, 103, 106, 109, 127
Dingwall, Robert 64, 76, 83–84
Disch, Thomas 122
Discipline and Punish 219n
"Distance" 159
Do Androids Dream of Electric Sheep? 53, 162, 189
Do or Die 107
"Do Unto Others" 70
Dr. Bloodmoney, or: How We Got Along after the Bomb 32, 98, 161
Dr. Strangelove, or: How I Learned to Stop Worrying and Love the Bomb 34, 37–38, 76–77, 79–80, 86–87, 219n
Don Quixote 147, 220n
Donaldson, Stephen 101
Donovan's Brain 105
Dowd, Maureen 133
Doyle, Jim 141–142
Dozois, Gardner 154, 157, 160, 176, 213
"Draft Dodger's Rag" 182
Drake, Frank 176, 220

Drake Equation 151–54, 219n
Dune/Dune Chronicles 80, 90, 100–101, 108
Dunn, Thomas P. 113–114, 116, 120, 122
Dyson, Freeman 176, 220n
dystopias 10, 27, 43, 49, 81, 90–91, 106, 110–17, 119–30, 147, 150, 212, 215, 217n, 218n

"E for Effort" 179
E.T.: The Extra-Terrestrial 146, 150, 153, 162, 164
Earth Abides 66
Earth vs. the Flying Saucers 164–165
Easton, Tom 49, 51, 122, 177
economics 94–95, 108, 124, 142, 156, 159, 184
Egan, Greg 100, 135
Egan, Timothy 135
Egoff, Sheila 63
Eisenberg, Anne 82
Eldridge, Roger 122
Elliott, Christopher 82
Ellison, Harlan 41, 47
"The-End-of-the-World Ball" 46
Ender series [*Ender's Game; Ender's War; Speaker for the Dead; Xenocide; Children of the Mind*] 101, 157, 168, 177, 219n
Endymion see Hyperion cantos
Enron 89, 95, 202
environmental damage 62, 66–67, 123, 158, 180–181
Eon series [*Eon; Eternity; Legacy*] 177
"Equalization" 121, 129
Equilibrium 72, 124
Erlanger, Steven 76
Erlich, Richard D. 113–114, 116, 120, 122
Eternity see Eon series
evolution/de-evolution 46, 59–61, 66, 117, 155, 157–158, 161, 176–177, 179, 181, 184, 214
The Experiment 64
The Eyewitness 122

Fahim, Kareem 139
Fahrenheit 451 10, 15, 43, 45, 111, 115, 117–119
Fail Safe 34
"The Faithful" 29
The Fall of Hyperion see Hyperion cantos
family 58, 64–65, 73, 100, 117, 121, 172, 175–176
Faoila, Anthony 85
Far Away 124
"Far from the Emerald Isle" 66
Farmer, John 77
"The Feeling of Power" 47
Fehrenbach, T.R. 195
Filmer, Kath 20, 138–139
The Final Cut see Pink Floyd
Fineman, Mark 195
Firefly 136–137
"The Fireman" 118
"First Contact National Monument" 177–178

"The First Lesson" 181
Fisch, Michael 34
Fisher, Walter R. 208–209
Fitzgerald, Thomas 194
Five 33
The Fly (1958) 104
The Fly (1986) 104
Fools 180
Foote, Bud 111, 119, 120
Forbidden Planet 81
The Forever War 177
"Forgetfulness" 28
Forster, E.M. 44, 46, 55
Foucault, Michel 210, 219n
"Four Short Novels" 181
Four-Sided Triangle 63
"The Fox and the Forest" 31
Foxtrot see Genesis
Frank, Pat 30
Frankenstein 14, 17, 20, 57, 63, 68, 70–71, 82–86, 95, 97, 103–104, 132, 136–137, 140, 197, 209
Franklin, H. Bruce 26
Frascella, Lawrence 134
Friday 183
Friedman, Thomas 142
Full Circle 31
Furious Gulf see Galactic Center series
Fury 33, 98–99

Gaiman, Neil 10
Galactic Center series [*In the Ocean of Night*; *Across the Sea of Suns*; *Great Sky River*; *Tides of Light*; *Furious Gulf*; *Sailing Bright Eternity*] 49, 159, 177
Galouye, Daniel F. 188
Galtseva, Renata 109, 113–117, 137
gaming 50, 55, 69, 78, 214
Garvin, Glenn 194
Gather Darkness! 122
Gathering Blue 121
Gattaca 72, 84, 124
gender 111, 126, 174, 176, 184, 203–04, 209
Genesis 72, 167
genetics 18, 22, 32–33, 57–60, 64–66, 69, 70, 72, 82–87, 117, 137, 161, 170, 174, 213; gene therapy 22, 60–61, 72, 104, 190; genetic engineering 51, 59–60, 64–66, 70, 72, 99–100, 104, 124, 147, 176, 180–181, 183; genetic screening 61, 65, 67, 126; genetically-modified food 69, 82–83, 103
"The Gentle Vultures" 156
George, Peter 34
George Orwell: A Life 120
Gernsback, Hugo 95, 156, 214
"Get 'em out by Friday" *see Genesis*
Gibson, William 42, 49–50, 60, 80, 96, 102, 162, 213
Giles, Gordon A. 29
Gilliam, Terry 125

The Girl from Monday 125
The Giver 121
Glass, James C. 157
Glasser, Vernon W. 31
Glassman, Mark 134
globalization 13, 142, 217n
Globalization: The Reader 217n
Godfrey, Hollis 28
Godsend 71
Godzilla 21, 36, 38, 76, 78–79, 82, 86–87, 140, 143
Goldberg, Jonah 194
Goldstein, David 133
Gonsalves, Sean 197
Good News 123
"A Good Offense" 178
Goodman, Ellen 77
Goodrich, Peter H. 93, 95, 108, 218n
Gordon, Burt I. 36, 104–105
The Gospel According to the Meninblack see The Stranglers
Goulart, Ron 69, 103
government 16–17, 29–30, 32, 34, 47, 51, 64–65, 70, 89, 91, 100–101, 109–130, 132, 164, 166, 172, 179, 211, 214
graphic novels *see* "comic books"
The Grateful Dead 37
Gray, W. Russel 120, 211
"Greater Fleas Have Lesser Fleas" 159
Green, Michelle Erica 111
"The Green Leopard Plague" 176, 182, 220n
Greenberg, Joel 196
Greene, Marcia Slacum 197
Greener Than You Think 66
Greenland, Colin 110, 138
Greybeard 179
"Groovy Times" *see* The Clash
Guest, Val 35
Gulliver's Travels 111
Gunn, James 46

Haberman, Clyde 78, 196
hackers 43, 50–51, 81, 95–96, 99–100
HAL 40, 52, 81–82
Halam, Ann 122
Haldeman, Joe 67, 177, 181
Halperin, James 176
Hamm, Nick 71
The Handmaid's Tale 113, 117, 123
Haraway, Donna 209, 213
Hardware 53
Harris, Mason 16, 89–90, 109, 115–116
Harrison, Harry 101–102
"Harrison Bergeron" 121
Hartocollis, Anemona 196–197
Hatch, Daniel 59, 64
Havelock, Eric A. 93, 95, 218n
Hecht, Jeff 182
Hedges, Stephen J. 196
Heinlein, Robert A. 14, 28, 109, 158, 177, 183

Heir Apparent 50
Heisenberg, Werner 217n
"'Hello,' Said the Stick" 33
Henderson, Zenna 65
Hendren, John 195
Henry, Amanda 58, 64
Henry IV 113
Herbert, Frank 90, 100–101
Herhold, Scott 200
"The Hero as Werewolf" 176
Highlander see Queen
"The Highway" 30
Hillegas, Mark 14, 169
Hilsenrath, Jon E. 198
Hintz, Carrie 90–91, 109, 117, 121–122
Hiroshima 24–27, 37, 160
Hitler, Adolf 89–90, 97, 109, 112
Hoban, Russell 31–32
Holden, Stephen 125
Hollow Man 104
holograms 50–51, 180
Home 122
"Homo Sapiens Declared Extinct" 184
Horowitz, Anthony 64, 99
Hougham, Aaron 86
How to Survive a Robot Uprising: Tips on Defending Yourself Against the Coming Rebellion 218n
Hoyt, Daniel M. 50, 180
Hozic, Aida A. 185
Hughes, Monica 122
Hughes, Zondra 142
human, definition of 18, 55–56, 58, 69, 73–74, 145, 152, 154, 170, 172, 174–176, 180–184, 189–191, 220n
"The Human Dress" 47
Huxley, Aldous 16, 21, 42, 61, 64, 72, 91, 97, 114, 119–121, 127, 130, 141–143, 219n
hybrids 66, 70, 72, 104, 159
Hyperion cantos [*Hyperion*; *The Fall of Hyperion*; *Endymion*; *The Rise of Endymion*] 181

I Am Legend 33, 66, 161
"I Have No Mouth and I Must Scream" 47
I, Robot 52
Icarus 11, 93, 95, 99
identity 43, 49, 54, 58–60, 71, 116, 123, 154, 171, 175, 180, 182–183, 192
Idol, Billy 54
"If I Forget Thee, Oh Earth" 31
The Illearth War see Chronicles of Thomas Covenant
immortality 49, 60, 62–63, 68–69, 73, 107, 175–176, 181, 183, 189–190
"The Immortality Plague" 50–51, 70, 99–100
Imperial March see Williams, John
"In Her Image" 51
Inayatullah, Naeem 153, 164, 186, 209
The Incredible Shrinking Man 36

Independence Day 146, 150, 162, 168
individuality, loss of 39, 49, 54, 58, 60, 71, 114, 116, 121, 145, 164, 171, 177
Industrial Revolution 13–14, 39, 171, 174
Infinite Jest 192
infinity, concept of 150–51, 154
information security 43, 50–51, 81, 96
information theory 42–43, 45, 94, 219n
The Initiate see Time Master series
intellect, fear of 15, 93–95, 101, 105, 218n
Invaders from Mars 104, 163, 187, 191
Invasion of the Body Snatchers (1956) 170, 185, 190, 193–194, 200–203, 205
Invisible Man (1897) 90, 103–104, 181
Invisible Man (2000–2002) 104
The Iron Dream 33, 161
Irving, Washington 193
Ishiguro, Kazuo 64
The Island 71
The Island of Dr. Moreau 99
Islands in the Net 50
It Came from Beneath the Sea 36
It Came from Outer Space 165
It Can't Happen Here 119

Jackson, Patrick Thaddeus 164
Jainschigg, John 199
Jameson, Frederic 208, 210, 220n
"The Jameson Satellite" 68
Janifer, Laurence M. 68
Jehovahkill 165–166, 185
Jekyll and Hyde see *The Strange Case of Dr. Jekyll and Mr. Hyde*
Jeremiah 71
Jergler, Don 199
The Jetsons 40, 212
Johnny and the Dead 123
Johnson, Kenneth 128
Johnson, Kirk 82
Johnson, Mark 6, 11–12, 19–20, 75, 169
Johnson, Reed 39–40, 42, 173–174
Jones, L.Q. 35
Jones, Neil R. 68
Judge Dredd 71, 125
Jurassic Park series 63, 83, 86–87

Kafka 124
Kahn, Joseph 82
Kaleidoscope Century see "Meme War" series
Kehl, D.G. 138
Kelly, James Patrick 217n
Kepner, Tyler 79
Kern, Gary 120
Kesteven, G.R. 121
Kidnapped 51
Kifner, John 133
Kiln People 183
King, Stephen 17, 66, 127, 154, 168
Kinnon, Joy Bennett 142
Kirkland, Kyle 60–61, 67

Index

Knight, Damon 7, 12–13
Kokoski, Paul 85
Kornbluth, C.M. 30
Krakatit: An Atomic Fantasy 29
Krebsbach, Karen 199
Kress, Nancy 65, 158, 176, 178, 180–182
Kroeker, Kirk L. 15–16, 19, 21, 47
Krugman, Paul 198
Kubrick, Stanley 34, 76, 124
Kuttner, Henry 32, 98–99, 160; with C.L. Moore 33

Lakoff, George 6, 11–12, 19–20, 75, 169
The Lamb Lies Down on Broadway see Genesis
Landis, Geoffrey A. 46
Lang, Fritz 124
Last and First Man 31, 184
The Last Day 30
The Last Man 66
The Last Man on Earth 33
The Lathe of Heaven 99, 180, 187
"Lavender in Love" 183
Law & Order: "Enemy" 139; "Nullification" 139
Law & Order: Special Victims Unit: "Design" 85
The Lawnmower Man 213
Lebbon, Tim 178
Lee, Jennifer 8, 140
Lee, Mary Soon 181
Lefebvre, Henri 210
The Left Hand of Darkness 111
Legacy see Eon series
legal system 58–59, 65, 68, 71, 106, 139–140, 146–147, 161, 166, 172, 182–183
LeGuin, Ursula K. 7, 97–99, 111, 180, 187
Leiber, Fritz 122
Leibovich, Mark 78
Leinster, Murray 30
Lem, Stanislaw 189
Leonard, Andrew 200
Lerner, Edward M. 158, 178
"Letter to a Phoenix" 32
Level 7 47–48
Levin, A.E. 15, 42, 48, 212
Levinson, Paul 122
Levitin, Sonia 121
Lewis, C.S. 8, 207
Lewis, Herschell Gordon 200
Lewis, Sinclair 119
Limbo 32, 48, 218n
Lipschutz, Ronnie D. 53, 149, 154, 164, 172–173, 186, 189, 219n
Livingston, Howard 138
Locke, Michelle 81
Logan's Run (1967) 179
Logan's Run (1976) 125, 179
Lomax, William 66, 178–179
Lombrosco, Cesare 155
"Loophole" 160

Lord Acton 16, 92
Lord Foul's Bane see *Chronicles of Thomas Covenant*
Lord of Light 99
The Lord of the Rings 8, 17, 92–94, 97, 103
Lost Continent 35
Louv, Richard 203
Lovett, Richard A. 51, 121
Lowry, Lois 121
Lucas, George 6, 103, 125, 132–134
Lyall, Sarah 133

MacAvoy, Roberta Anna 98
Macdonald, Caroline 122
MacFarquhar, Neil 195
"The Machine Stops" 46, 55
mad scientists 17, 63, 93, 95, 97, 99–100, 104–105, 107–108, 137, 218n
magic 94, 97–98, 103, 105–106, 108, 122, 128, 146, 166–167, 219n
Magnier, Mark 81
Main, Frank 141
mainstream media use of SF images: business 78–79, 140, 142, 198–201; government 76–77, 84–85, 131–132, 135, 138–141, 194, 196–198; media 78, 201–204; medicine 61, 81–87, 132, 135–136; military/police 76–77, 81, 133–134, 194–196, 198; politics 76–78, 84–86, 131–133, 135, 138–142, 194; sports 79, 132–133; technology 80–87, 132, 139–140, 142, 199–200
mainstream television use of SF images 76, 83, 85, 133, 139, 141, 204
Mamoru, Oshii 34
Man Plus 68
The Man Who Ended War 28
Maney, Kevin 81
Manhattan Project 25
Manifesto see Roxy Music
Manison, Pete D. 179
Mann, George 49–50, 63, 68, 72–73, 122, 124–125, 180
Manning, Laurence 50
The Marrow of Tradition 135
Marsa, Linda 135
Martz, Ron 195
Marusek, David 49, 180
Mason, Lisa 48, 54
Mason, Marilynne S. 54
Matheson, Richard 33, 36, 66, 161
The Matrix trilogy [*The Matrix*; *The Matrix Reloaded*; *The Matrix Revolutions*] 39, 52, 55, 80–82, 173–174, 187–188, 192
Maurai series ["Sky People"; "Progress"; *Orion Shall Rise*] 31
Max Headroom 125–126; "The Blanks" 126
Maximum Light 65
May, Rollo 92–93
McAuley, Paul 66
McCammon, Robert R. 220n

McCarthy, Joseph 89, 118–19, 129
McKee, Bradford 84
McManus, Doyle 195
McNally, Joel 78
McNurlin, Kathleen W. 28, 36, 66–67, 121
mechanization 39, 42, 52–53, 55, 114–115, 217n
medical implants 22, 60, 67–69, 73–74, 81, 122–123, 182
medicine 22, 60–63, 65, 67–69, 72–73, 83, 107, 124, 132, 135–136, 141, 161, 175
"Meme War" series [*Candle*; *The Sky So Big and Black*; *Kaleidoscope Century*] 51, 68, 100
Memento 192
memory 68, 81, 115, 179–180, 182–183, 185, 192, 214
Men in Black 146, 167
Men in Black II 146
mental illness 22, 61–62, 67–69, 98, 103–104, 135–136, 166, 180, 182, 187
Merril, Judith 30, 33, 98
metaphor analysis 6–7, 10–11, 19–20, 75–87, 131–143, 169, 192–205, 217n, 218n
Metaphors We Live By 6, 11, 75
Metropolis 16, 124
Meyer, David S. 133–134
Michaelson, L.W. 26, 118
"Microcosmic God" 50
Miller, Dennis 194
Miller, Laura 192
Miller, Walter 21, 30–31
mind control 33, 67–69, 93–94, 105–106, 158, 187
Ming, Marie 67
"The Minority Report" (1956) 42, 192
Minority Report (2002) 42, 119, 125, 192
Minsky, Marvin 40
Modern Times 39
Moffett, Julie 158
Molvray, Mia 158–159
Mona Lisa Overdrive see Sprawl series
Moniz, Dave 195
Monsters, Mushroom Clouds, and the Cold War: American Science Fiction and the Roots of Postmodernism, 1946–1964 27, 29–30, 32–35, 40–41, 45, 66, 71, 98, 105, 155, 162, 165, 170–171, 187, 217n, 220n
Moore, Alan 117, 123, 130
Moore, Ward 66
Moran, Tom 194
More Than Human 65
"Morning Dew" *see* The Grateful Dead
Morressy, John 99
"Mortimer Gray's History of Death" 157
Mouawad, Jad 142
"Moxon's Master" 47
Moylan, Tom 90–91, 112, 113, 115–116, 129
Mulkay, Michael 137, 209
Muller, Edward 181
Mulshine, Paul 86
Murphy, Kim 133

Mutant 32, 160–161
Mutant X 72, 104; "Crossroads of the Soul" 189; "The Meaning of Death" 190
mutants 25, 29, 32–33, 35, 65, 72, 104, 147, 149, 154, 158, 161, 167–168, 190
Mysterious Island 98

nanotechnology 69, 80, 156, 174
The Napoleon of Notting Hill 119
narrative theory 207–208
nature versus technology 113–115, 120–121
Nazis 29, 61, 97, 123, 128
Nerlich, Brigitte 64, 76, 83–84
Nerves 33
Neumann, Iver 163
Neuromancer see Sprawl series
Never Let Me Go 64
"A New Man" 68, 182
New Maps of Hell 8
New York Nights 50
Newfield, Sam 35
Newman, John 28, 37
Newmann, Kurt 104
Nexon, Daniel H. 164
Niccol, Andrew 72, 84, 124
Nicklaus, David 197
Nicols, Robert 29
Nicolson, Harold 29
"Nightfall" 183
Nightmares Model 11–19
Nineteen Eighty-Four 10, 16–17, 91, 111–112, 115–116, 119–120, 124, 129, 131–132, 137–141, 211; Big Brother 5, 11, 132, 137–140, 143, 197, 212, 214
The Ninth Gate 106
Niven, Larry 68–69, 183
"No Truce with Kings" 158
"None So Blind" 67
Nordau, Max 155
Not This August 30
Nothing Human 158, 180–181
nuclear war 9, 21, 24–38, 76–79, 98, 112, 119, 156, 158–160, 212, 215, 217n; fallout 30–31, 34–35, 37; monsters 35–36, 66, 72, 161; mutations 25, 29, 32–33, 35, 104, 149, 155, 161, 217n; politics 26, 28–29, 32, 34, 76–77, 123; power generation 33, 36, 77; survivor tales 25, 30–35, 37; testing 35–36, 104
Numan, Gary 54
A Number 64
Nyby, Christian 162

Oboler, Arch 33
Odd John 101, 160
O'Donnell, Maureen 136
O'Hehir, Andrew 167–168
Olian, Judy 142
The Omega Expedition 177
Omega Man 33
On the Beach 34

The One Tree see *Chronicles of Thomas Covenant*
Only You Can Save Mankind 123
Operation Mindcrime see Queensryche
optimism in SF 10, 32, 91, 110, 129, 151, 214–215
"Oracles" 178
Orion Shall Rise see *Maurai* series
Orwell, George 6, 10, 16–17, 91, 112, 114–116, 119–121, 127, 130, 132, 137–141, 143, 207, 211, 214
O'Shaughnessy, Lynn 199
Ostry, Elaine 90–91, 117, 121–122
"The Other Side of the Sky" 68
Out of the Unknown 220n
The Outcast see *Time Master* series
Outer Limits: "Afterlife" 189
"Overdrawn at the Memory Banks" 50
overpopulation 62, 70, 125, 219n

Paddock, Richard C. 141
Padgett, Lewis *see* Kuttner, Henry
Pak, Grey 189–190
Pallay, Jessica 141
"Pandora's Planet" 156
"The Paradise Crater" 29
Parent, Richard 110
Parriot, James D. 77
Patlabor II 34
"Paycheck" (1953) 185
Paycheck (2003) 185
Pennavaria, Katherine 115, 118
"Persistent Patterns" 67–68, 182
Pethes, Nicolas 57, 59–60, 67–68, 182, 208–210
"Pets" *see* Porno for Pyros
Pienciak, Richard T. 196
Piercy, Marge 175–176
Pink Floyd 37, 127, 167
Pirodsky, Richard 202
The Pixel Eye 122
plagues 33, 51, 66, 71–73, 99, 126, 185
Planet of the Apes 178
Plante, Brian 183
Platt, Charles 183
Player Piano 46, 55
"Playing God," implications of 41, 48, 57–60, 63–64, 66, 70–71, 82–83, 86, 137
Pledger, Marcia 200
Pohl, Frederick 34, 50, 68, 118, 138, 141
Point Blank 64, 99
political use of SF images 77–78, 84–86, 131–133, 135, 138–140, 141, 194, 196
politicians 17, 29, 34, 47, 64, 68, 89–90, 101–103, 123, 127–128, 159, 161, 179, 185–186
popular music 36–37, 54, 72, 99, 106, 127, 163, 165–167, 185
Porno for Pyros 163
Positronic Robot series [*I, Robot*; *The Caves of Steel*; *The Naked Sun*; *The Complete Robot*; *The Robots of Dawn*; *Robots and Empire*] 48, 52
post-humanity 65, 68–69, 147, 154, 160–161, 176, 184, 213
"The Postman" (1982) 32
The Postman (1985) 32
The Postman (1997) 32
Postman, Neil 39–40, 42, 58–59
Postmodernism 41, 102, 106, 148, 150, 171, 173, 180, 189, 204, 208, 210, 213, 220n
Postmodernism, or, the Cultural Logic of Late Capitalism 220
The Power That Preserves see *Chronicles of Thomas Covenant*
Pratchett, Terry 123, 151–152
Pratt, Fletcher 50
"Praying to the Aliens" *see* Numan, Gary
Prieto-Pablos, Juan 92, 96, 100–101
The Prisoner 126–127
privacy 39, 42, 81, 93, 116, 139–140, 143, 160, 166, 168, 171, 211, 214
"Private Eyes" 67
Probability series [*Probability Sun*; *Probability Moon*; *Probability Space*] 178
"Progress" see *Maurai* series
"Promises, Promises" 158–159
Proyas, Alex 165, 188
psychiatry 61–62, 67, 218n
psychopharmaceuticals 61–62, 67, 72, 120–121, 124, 126
public discourse 6–7, 10–11, 19–20, 61, 75–87, 131–143, 192–205, 207–209
Public Faces 29
public perception of science 14–16, 61–63, 83–87, 137, 209
"Punctuated Equilibrium" 179
The Puppet Masters 158
The Purple Cloud 98

Queen 106, 190
Queensryche 106
Queer as Folk 204
Queer Eye for the Straight Guy 204

Rabkin, Eric S. 8, 11–12, 24, 94, 98–99, 101, 111–112, 207, 217n
Radio K.A.O.S. see Waters, Roger
Randall, Robert 178
Raphael *see Damiano* trilogy
The Raven see *The Stranglers*
Read, Simon 198
Read, Wolf 49, 184
Reagan, Ronald 5, 133, 197
reality, nature of 99, 115, 147–148, 172–174, 179–180, 186–189, 190–192, 194–199, 220n
Reaves, Michael 98
"Rebellion" 47, 156
Re-birth see *The Chrysalids*
Red Alert 34
Red Planet Mars 164

Reed, Robert 178
Reeks, Anne 199
religion 31, 72, 100, 123, 125, 145, 172–173, 177
reproductive control 117, 122–123, 125, 158, 160, 176
resurrection from the dead 63–64, 71, 104
Revenge of the Creature 104
Reynolds, Alastair 180
Rich, Frank 201–202
Riddley Walker 31–32, 179
Ring Around the Sun 158
Rip Van Winkle 171, 177, 190, 193, 196–197, 199, 202–204
The Rise of Endymion see *Hyperion* cantos
Rivenburg, Ron 77
Rivlin, Gary 200
Robertson, Campbell 86
Robinson, Eugene 202
RoboCop 73, 80–81
Robot Stories (Clay) 189–190
"The Robot Who Came to Dinner" 69, 103
Robota 48
robots 18, 40–41, 47–49, 52–55, 80–82, 183, 187, 191, 212, 218n
Rocketship X-M 35
Roddenberry, Gene 6
Rodnyanskaya, Irina 109, 113–117, 137
Rollins, Grey 67, 159
Roshwald, Mordecai 47–48
Ross, Andrew 27, 43, 49–50, 60, 69, 95, 102, 162, 214, 218n
Roswell 165; "The White Room" 165
Roxy Music 99
Ruane, Michael E. 197
Rucker, Rudy 49
ruins 165, 178–179
The Running Man (1982) 127
The Running Man (1987) 127
R.U.R. 48, 218n
Rusnak, Josef 188
Russ, Joanna 16
Russell, Sagin 136
Rybacki, Donald Jay 15, 27
Rybacki, Karyn Charles 15, 27

Sagan, Carl 152, 186
Saltzman, Jonathan 142
Sambell, Kay 90, 121–122
Sargent, Pamela 63, 69, 183–184
Sawyer, Kathy 82
Sawyer, Robert J. 182–183
Sax, Irene 201
Schild's Ladder 100
Schismatrix 69
Schlee, Ann 121
Schmidt, Stanley 5, 44–45, 57, 59, 61–62, 70, 92, 95, 151, 153, 155–156, 170, 173–175, 212, 217n, 220n
Scholbin, Roger C. 116

Scholes, Robert 8, 11–12, 24, 94, 98–99, 101, 111–112, 217n
Schuknecht, Bruce 198
Schulte, Bret 80
Schulte, Brigid 133
Scott, Melissa 80
Scott, Ridley 189
Seabury, Marcia Bundy 48
Seaquest DSV: "Playtime" 55
"Seed of Destiny" 59, 64
Seed of Light 30
"Seed of Reason" 64
"The Sentinel" 52
Serenity 126
Serling, Rod 6, 106, 163, 187, 196
"Seven Seas of Rhye" *see* Queen
Shadow of the Gloom-World 122
Shadow on the Hearth 30, 98
Shaffer, Catherine H. 61
Shakespeare, William 113, 218n, 219n
Shales, Tom 77
Shapiro, Walter 202
"Shed Skin" 182–183
Shelley, Rick 177–178
Shelley, Mary 14, 21, 63, 66, 71, 83, 95, 218n
Shelton, Deborah L. 82
Shepard, Lucius 173
Sherred, Thomas 179
Shiel, M.P. 98
Shiner, Lewis 49
Shiras, Wilmar 65
Shirley, John 49, 158–159
The Shrinking Man 36
The Shrouded Planet 178
Shute, Nevil 34
Shyamalon, M. Night 6
Siege Perilous 68
Siegel, Harry 135
Siemaszko, Corky 86
The Silicone Man 183
Silverman, Elissa 140
Simak, Clifford 156, 158–159, 179, 220n
Simmons, Dan 181
Simon, Ellen 203
Simons, Howard L. 199
Simpson, Ian J. 37, 54, 72, 99, 106, 127, 163, 165, 167, 185
simulacra 47, 51, 184, 192
The Simulacra 47
Simulacron 3 188
simulated worlds 22, 50, 160, 173–174, 180, 187–188
Singularity Sky 49
Singularity, Technological 49, 56, 184, 214
Sirens of Titan 121–122
Sirius 66
The 6th Day 71
"Sky People" *see Maurai* series
The Sky So Big and Black see "Meme War" series

The Skybreaker see Transformations Trilogy
"Sleeping Dogs" 176
Sleepless series [*Beggars in Spain*; *Beggars and Choosers*; *Beggars Ride*] 65, 176
Sliders: "California Reich" 126; "Just Say Yes" 72; "My Brother's Keeper" 71; "Net Worth" 54–55; "State of the Art" 53; "This Slide of Paradise" 72, 104
"Slow Life" 157–158
Slusser, George E. 207
Smart House 53
Smart Rats 122
social change: adaptation to 9–10, 13–14, 17–19, 21, 145, 147, 155, 169–172, 176–179, 200; resistance to 17–19, 145, 170–172, 177–179, 185–186, 188, 190, 193–194, 196, 202–205
Solaris (1972) 189
Solaris (2002) 189
"Solution Unsatisfactory" 28
Sommer, Mark 82, 139
space exploration 49, 66, 68, 72, 99, 106, 123, 147, 152–153, 156–160, 163–164, 172, 176–177
Space Platform 30
space stations 30, 68
speculative fiction, definition 7–8, 13–14, 217n
Speilberg, Steven 42, 46, 86, 119, 164, 214
Speilman, Fran 141
Spencer, Susan 93, 95, 218n
Spigelman, Candace 207–208
Spinrad, Norman 33, 101, 161
Sprawl series [*Neuromancer*; *Count Zero*; *Mona Lisa Overdrive*; and "Johnny Mnemonic," "New Rose Hotel," and "Burning Chrome"] 42, 49, 50, 80, 96, 102, 162, 213
Stableford, Brian 31, 157, 177
Stalin 89, 109, 112, 211
Stalker 185
The Stand 66
Stapledon, Olaf 65–66, 101, 160, 184
Star Trek 7–8, 54, 80–81, 152–153, 164, 168, 204–205; Prime Directive 11, 163, 185, 193–194, 196, 199, 205; *Enterprise* 164
Star Trek: Deep Space Nine 107
Star Trek: The Next Generation 54, 107, 164, 166, 189, 195; "11001001" 52; "Datalore" 164; "Deja Q" 107; "The Drumhead" 106; "First Contact" 186; "Home Soil" 163; "The Outcast" 126; Resistance Is Futile 195, 198–205; "The Schizoid Man" 104, 189; "Silicon Avatar" 164; "The Survivors" 107; "Transfigurations" 186; "Up the Long Ladder" 71; "Violations" 166; "Where Silence Has Lease" 63; "Who Watches the Watchers?" 186
Star Trek Voyager 107
Star Wars 5, 7–8, 11, 74, 89, 92, 103, 130–135, 137, 214; Darth Vader 6, 11, 74, 103, 108, 114, 133–135, 137, 140, 143; *Episode I: The Phantom Menace* 103, 127; *Episode II: Attack of the Clones* 127, 134; *Episode III: Revenge of the Sith* 74, 127; *Episode VI: Return of the Jedi* 74, 129; The Force 8, 108; Jedi 103, 127, 134
Stargate SG-1: "Lost City, Pt. I" 185; "Momento" 186
The Stars My Destination 102
Steele, Allen 123
Stein, Mark A. 200
Step to the Stars 30
Sterling, Bruce 49–50, 69, 184
Stern, Seth 77
Stevenson, Robert Louis 16, 51, 94, 99, 135
Stevenson, Sharon 111, 113, 123
Stewart, Gene 9
Stewart, George R. 66
Stiglitz, Joseph E. 142
Stingl, Jim 78
Stoked: The Rise and Fall of Gator 136
Stolberg, Sheryl Gay 84–85
Stone, Oliver 54
The Strange Case of Dr. Jekyll and Mr. Hyde 16, 99, 132, 135–137; Jekyll and Hyde 5, 94, 103–104, 135–137, 140, 143; *Jekyll and Hyde, the Musical* 99
Strange Weather: Culture, Science, and Technology in the Age of Limits 27, 43, 49–50, 60, 69, 95, 102, 162, 218, 218n
A Stranger in a Strange Land 177
The Stranglers 166
Strategic Defense Initiative 5, 133
Strong Medicine: "Maternal Mirrors" 83
Stross, Charles 49, 183
"Student Body" 157
Sturgeon, Theodore 50, 64–65
Sugiura, Ken 139
Summar, Polly 136
Superman 11
superweapons 26, 217n
surveillance 39, 42, 114–115, 118–119, 122–123, 126, 128, 139–141, 143, 211, 214
The Survivors 71–72
Swanwick, Michael 33, 157–158
"Swings" 107
Swirski, Peter 122
Swisher, Kara 200
Swope, Richard 173, 188, 189, 210
Synners 50
Szilard, Leo 217

Tarantula 36, 104
"Target Generation" 179
Target: Terra 68
Tarkovsky, Andrey 185
technology dependence 22, 40, 43–49, 51–52, 55, 114, 181, 212
technophilia versus technophobia 14–16, 21, 39, 42–43, 53, 82, 214–215, 218n

Tedeschi, Michael 82
Tek War 52
telepathy 32–33, 35, 93–94, 101, 105–108, 147, 149, 154, 160–162, 166–168
Temple, William F. 63
The Terminal Man (1972) 73, 182
The Terminal Man (1974) 67
Terminator 52, 63, 80–82, 85, 197
Terminator 2 12, 80
Terrahawks 53
Terry, Megan 122
"That Only a Mother" 33
Them 36
"There Will Come Soft Rains" 30
They Walked Like Men 156
The Thing 162
The Thing from Another World 162–163
The Thirteenth Floor 188
Thomas, Landon, Jr. 136
Thomas, Rob 202
Thomasson, William 175
"334" 122
Throop, Kelvin 70
Through the Looking Glass 179
THX-1138 125
Tiger! Tiger! see *The Stars My Destination*
Time Master series [*The Initiate*; *The Outcast*; *The Time Master*] 98
Time Out of Joint 180
time travel 31, 49, 182, 185
Timmons, Mark 176
Timson, Judith 203
To Live Forever 68
"To the Future" see "The Fox and the Forest"
Tolkien, J.R.R. 6, 17, 90, 97–98, 103
Tommasini, Anthony 124
torture 104, 116, 165
Total Recall 180, 190
totalitarianism 17, 89–91, 109–110, 112, 113–117, 119–130, 137–141
Totaro, Rebecca Carol Noël 121–122
Toumey, Christopher 137
Tourtellotte, Shane 67–68, 182
"The Tower" see Cope, Julian
Transformations Trilogy [*The Daymaker*; *Transformations*; *The Skybreaker*] 122
Tron 191
Trouble with Lichen 69
Truback, L.L. 68
"True Names" 50, 96, 100
The Truman Show 192
The Truth Machine 176
Tudor, Andrew 137
"Tunnel Under the World" 50
Turan, Kenneth 134
Turner, Allan 85
"Turning Point" 31
28 Days Later 8, 71
Twenty-Thousand Leagues Under the Sea 98
Twersky, David 77

Twilight World 33
The Twilight Zone 20, 34–35, 186, 191, 193, 195–199, 201–202, 204; "Appointment on Route 17" 72; "The Brain Center at Whipple's" 52; "Chameleon" 163; "Dreams for Sale" 189; "Father and Son Game" 73; "Five Characters in Search of an Exit" 187; "From Agnes with Love" 52; "In His Image" 53, 187; "It's a Good Life" 105–106, 202; "It's Still a Good Life" 105–106; "The Lateness of the Hour" 186–187; "The Little People" 105; "Memories" 185; "The Mind and the Matter" 187; "The Monsters Are Due on Maple Street" 163; "Mute" 166; "Nightcrawlers" 187; "Number Twelve Looks Just Like You" 72–73, "The Old Man in the Cave" 34; "On Thursday We Leave for Home" 106; "One More Pallbearer" 34; "Our Sylena Is Dying" 73; "Person or Persons Unknown" 187; "The Shelter" 163; "Shelter Skelter" 35; "Something in the Walls" 166; "Stopover in a Quiet Town" 165; "A Thing About Machines" 53; "Time Enough at Last" 34; "The Trade-Ins" 190; "Will the Real Martians Please Stand Up" 163; "A World of Difference" 187; "A World of His Own" 187
"Two Suns in the Sunset" see Pink Floyd
2001: A Space Odyssey 34, 40, 52, 80–82
Tyrnauer, Matt 195

Ultravox 37
"Uncalculated Risk" 67
"Uncertainty" 156
Underworld 107
universe as ecosystem 146–147, 152–153, 159
"Unseen" 161
Unsworth, Michael 28, 37
uploaded consciousness 50, 69, 103–104, 183–184, 189–190
"Upwards at 45 Degrees" see Cope, Julian
"Utmost Bones" 69, 183–184
utopias 27, 90–91, 110–113, 129, 147, 150, 188

V: The Final Battle 129
V: The Original Miniseries 117, 128, 130, 165
V for Vendetta (1989) 117, 123, 129
V for Vendetta (2005) 123, 129
vampires 33, 66, 107, 149, 161
Van Gelder, Gordon 8–10, 145
Van Pelt, James 10, 13, 42, 49, 66, 169–170, 212–215, 217
Van Vogt, A.E. 65, 180
Vance, Jack 68
The Vandal 121
Varley, John 50
Varricchio, Mario 114, 116
Varsam, Maria 113
Vault of the Ages 31
Vecsey, Laura 79

Velde, Vivian Vande 50
Vennochi, Joan 79
Verne, Jules 89, 98
Vickers, Jay *see* Simak, Clifford
The View from Hell 159
Vinge, Vernor 17, 50, 96, 100, 102
virtual reality 22, 50, 52, 54–55, 173–174, 180, 187–189, 214
viruses: biological 33, 66, 71–73, 99–100, 166, 180; computer 43, 50–51, 68, 96
visual media, impact of 37, 55–56, 74, 108, 129, 168, 190–191
Vitals 69
Vonnegut, Kurt 46, 55, 69, 112, 121, 122, 195
Voodoo Child 98
Vos Post, Jonathan 15–16, 19, 21, 47

Wachowski Brothers 39, 52, 55, 80–82, 173–174, 187, 192
Wagner, Ed 197
"The Wait" 65
Walker, Leslie 199
The Wall see Pink Floyd
Wallace, David Foster 192
Wallace, F.L. 157
Walsh, Mary Williams 196
The War of the Worlds (1895) 8, 146, 156–157, 168, 193, 206
The War of the Worlds (2005) 164
Waters, Roger 167
Watership Down 122–123
We 112, 116, 119–120, 124
"We Can Remember It for You Wholesale" 180
"Weapons of Mass Distraction" 51
"The Wedding Album" 180
"Welcome to Monkey House" 69
Welcome Trust Medicine in Society Programme 83, 85, 198
Weldes, Jutta 26, 34, 102, 131–133, 217
Weldon, Fay 64
Wells, H.G. 6, 14, 25–26, 28, 90, 99, 103–104, 111–112, 129, 156, 181, 195, 206
werewolves 107, 147, 149, 167, 193, 197, 199
The West Wing: "An Khe" 133; "Lord John Marbury" 76
Westfahl, Gary 12, 30, 68
Westworld 53
Whedon, Joss 126, 167, 203
When You Care, When You Love 64
Whitaker, Barbara 199
White 178
White, Josh 196
White Devils 66
White Gold Wielder see Chronicles of Thomas Covenant

"Who Goes There?" 162
"Who Wants to Live Forever" *see* Queen
Wickham, James 81
Wilcox, Clyde 153
Wild Palms 54
Williams, Charles 98
Williams, John 132–133
Williams, Walter Jon 69, 176, 182
Willis, Connie 9, 12, 22, 25, 44, 46, 212, 218n
Wilson, Craig 204
Wilson, Daniel H. 218n
Wilson, Kimberly A.C. 196
Wings over Europe: A Dramatic Extravaganza on a Pressing Theme 29
witchcraft 94, 103, 105, 146–147, 149, 154, 166–167, 219n
"With Flaming Swords" 29
A Wizard of Earthsea 97–98
wizards 94, 97–98, 146, 154, 218n
Wolf, Buck 42, 46, 119, 214
Wolfe, Bernard 32, 48
Wolfe, Gene 10, 176
Wolfe, Gary K. 65, 145–146, 161, 169
"Wooden Ships" *see* Crosby, Stills & Nash
"The Word Mill" 46, 55
The World Is Flat: A Brief History of the 21st Century 142
The World Jones Made 32
The World of Null-A 180
World Peace 9, 100, 128, 158, 181–82
World Science Fiction Convention: 2001 (Philadelphia) 7–9; 2002 (San Jose) 5, 7, 9, 17, 22, 25, 146–147, 152, 157, 170, 174–175, 212, 213
The World Set Free 25, 28, 217n
World Without End 35
The Wounded Land see Chronicles of Thomas Covenant
Wright, Robin 195
Wylie, Philip 29
Wyndham, John 32, 65, 69, 160–161

X-Files 52, 186, 193, 198–200, 203, 205; "Eve" 72; "Young at Heart" 72
X-Men (1963) 154, 161, 167
X-Men (2000) 150, 167–168

Young, Rob 201
Youngstein, Max 34

Zakaria, Fareed 135
Zamyatin, Yevgeny 112, 119–121, 124–125, 127
Zelazny, Roger 99
Zinoman, Jason 203

www.ingramcontent.com/pod-product-compliance
Ingram Content Group UK Ltd.
Pitfield, Milton Keynes, MK11 3LW, UK
UKHW041935140426
5217IPUK00014B/485

9 780786 429165